I0753206

# HISTORIC PHOTOS OF
# WINSTON-SALEM

TEXT AND CAPTIONS BY WADE G. DUDLEY

TURNER
PUBLISHING COMPANY

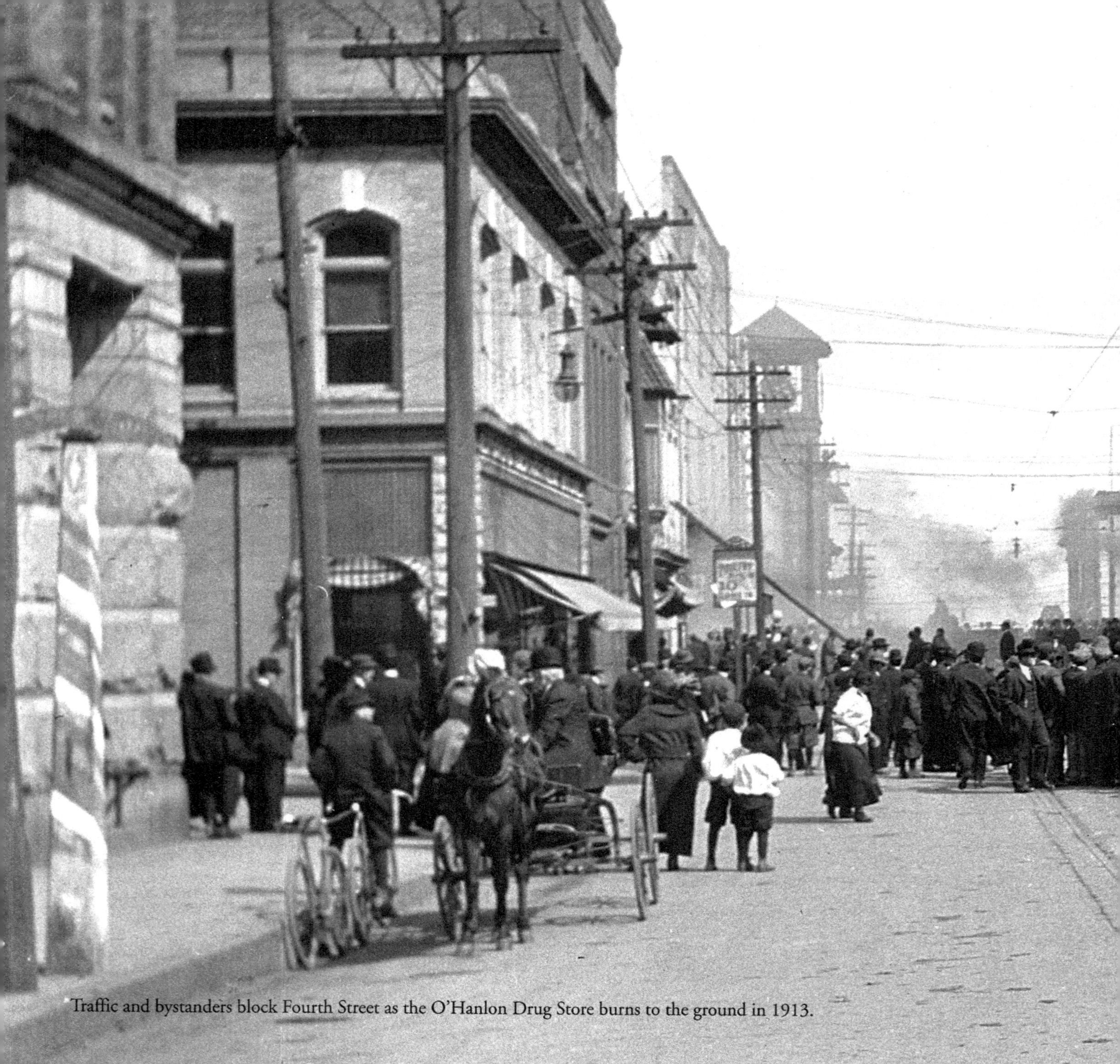

Traffic and bystanders block Fourth Street as the O'Hanlon Drug Store burns to the ground in 1913.

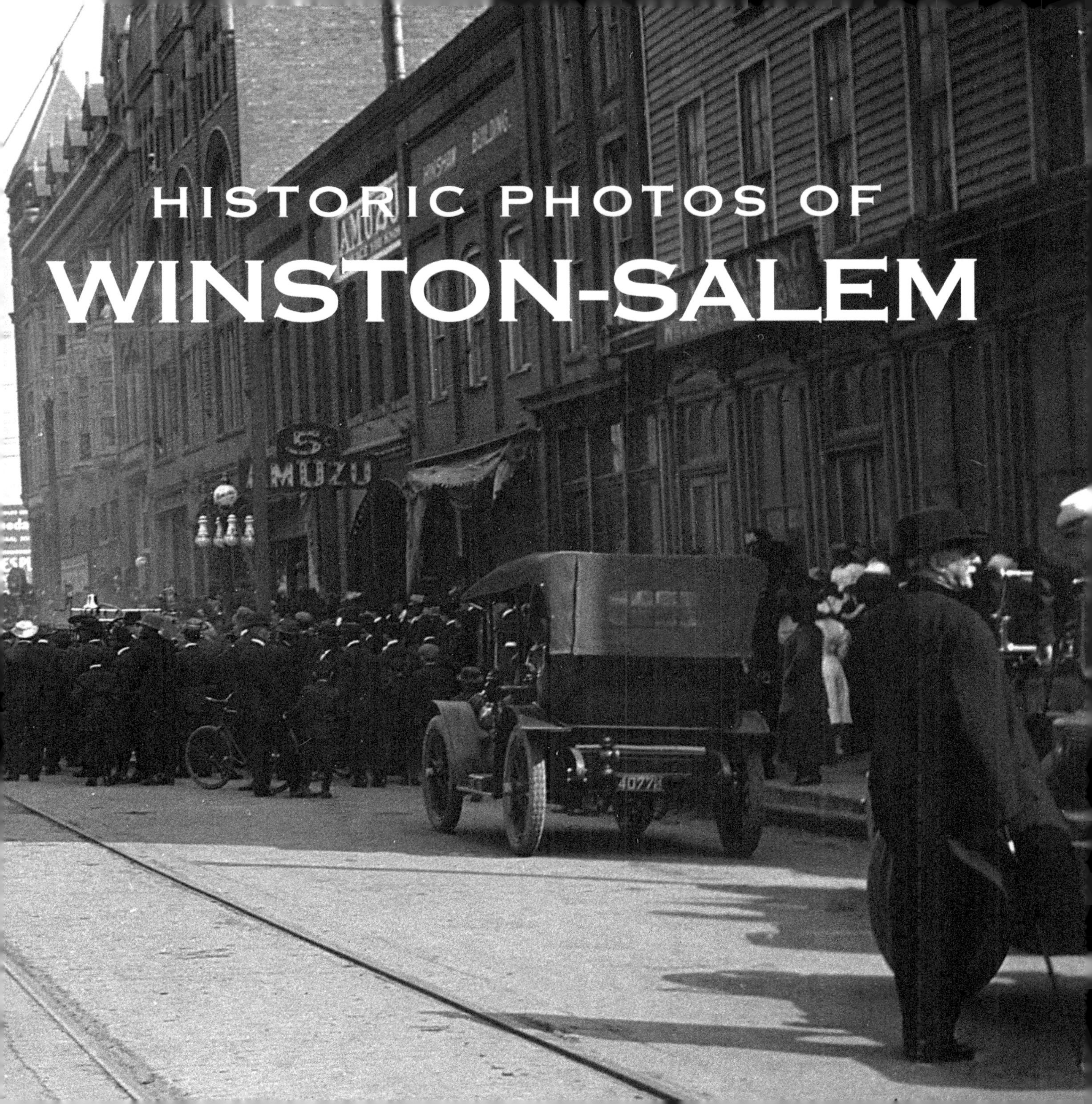


# HISTORIC PHOTOS OF WINSTON-SALEM

Turner Publishing Company
4507 Charlotte Avenue • Suite 100
Nashville, Tennessee 37209
(615) 255-2665

www.turnerpublishing.com

*Historic Photos of Winston-Salem*

Copyright © 2008 Turner Publishing Company

All rights reserved.
This book or any part thereof may not be reproduced or transmitted in any form or by any means, electronic or mechanical, including photocopying, recording, or by any information storage and retrieval system, without permission in writing from the publisher.

Library of Congress Control Number: 2007937032

ISBN-13: 978-1-59652-421-7

ISBN-13: 978-1-68336-997-4 (hc)

Printed in the United States of America

08 09 10 11 12 13 14 15—0 9 8 7 6 5 4 3 2 1

# CONTENTS

Pharmacist Edward W. O'Hanlon opted to replace his old building on the corner of Fourth and Liberty streets with a nine-story brick building, completed in 1915 and generally recognized as Winston-Salem's first skyscraper.

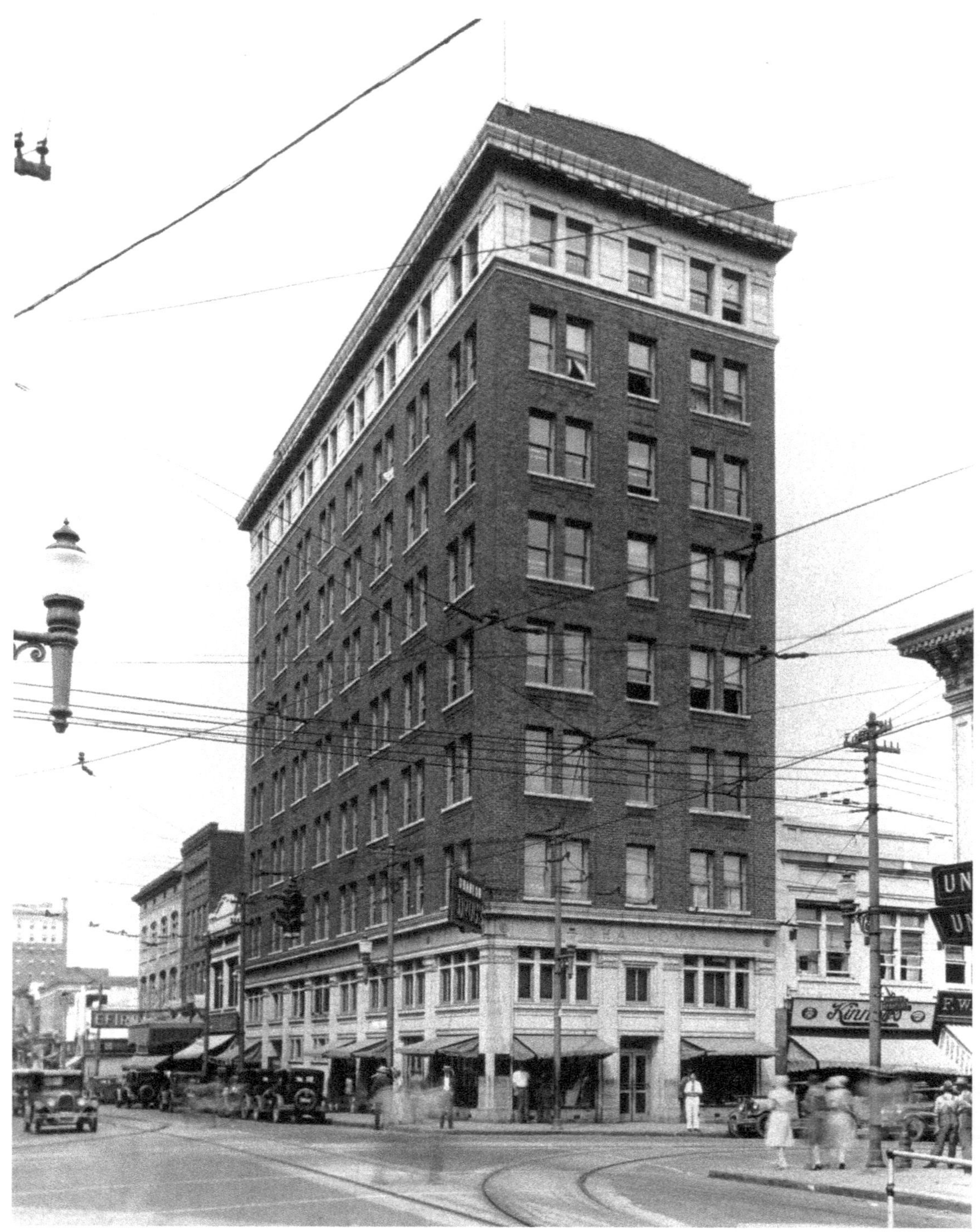

# Acknowledgments

With the exception of cropping images where needed and touching up imperfections that have accrued over time, no other changes have been made to the photographs in this volume. The caliber and clarity of many photographs are limited by the technology of the day and the ability of the photographer at the time they were made.

This volume, *Historic Photos of Winston-Salem,* is the result of the cooperation and efforts of many individuals, organizations, and corporations. It is with great thanks that we acknowledge the valuable contribution of the following for their generous support:

Forsyth County Public Library
Library of Congress
North Carolina State Archives

Thanks to the always helpful staff of the Verona Joyner Langford North Carolina Collection at East Carolina University.

# PREFACE

In 1753, fifteen weary Moravian men reached the Crown colony of North Carolina. The first of many Moravians to walk the Old Wagon Road from Pennsylvania or face the hardships of travel upriver, then to cross trackless Carolina wilderness, they settled on 100,000 acres of land purchased from the last of Carolina's Lord Proprietors: John Carteret, Earl of Granville. By 1766, settlers began building a new Moravian town: Salem. Governed under the edicts of the church, Salem prospered, its citizens thriving as farmers, merchants, and manufacturers. Other North Carolinians came to know the people of Salem as people with good hearts, always willing to help others in need.

In 1849, Salem granted land to the state for a new village a mile or so up the road. It would be the seat of a new county, Forsyth County. The town fathers of Salem felt that a "worldly" courthouse, and the people attending court sessions therein, would be disruptive of the Moravian way of life. A little later, this sleepy hamlet received the name of Winston, and over the next decades some of its inhabitants became industrialists with overflowing purses.

Built on profits from bright leaf tobacco and textiles, Winston prospered from 1880 to 1900. It embraced the modern age of electricity: utility poles lined its streets and electric trolleys carried its workers to their jobs by 1890. Most of Salem's citizens felt a kinship with the good people of Winston, especially as expansion brushed away previous boundaries. By 1900, both groups called themselves, unofficially, the Twin City.

In 1913, Winston-Salem incorporated. Already the major economic power in North Carolina, the city kept expanding, especially after the automobile arrived. By then, a very wealthy upper class had been granted de facto control of Winston-Salem. They frequently used their money for the good of the city, especially to improve the city's image. By 1929, skyscrapers created an impressive skyline—and then, the sky fell.

The Depression years, followed by the war, seemed to leech the life from Winston-Salem. The economy stayed relatively strong, one of the ten strongest in the United States, but to maintain its pace during the Great Depression and to increase that pace during World War II meant corners had to be cut. By 1950, a dirty, shabby city with a broken infrastructure needed strong leadership to revitalize its streets, buildings, and people.

Despite challenges, Winston-Salem rose to the occasion, becoming a model city by 1959. Politicians visited, businesses boomed, and a major college relocated to Winston-Salem. The 1960s brought cold war, integration, and business worries to the fore, but again, its citizens rose to the occasion.

This book is the story of two dynamic communities that joined forces to build a single city where mere villages once stood. The period covered stretches from 1880 to almost 1980. It is a history, of sorts, but a history told primarily with photographs: seconds in time captured by the flash of a camera. Words can be twisted, but these images offer a very solid reality of their own. This is, of course, a study of change; but in the end, one may just discover that the most important things have not changed at all.

—*Wade G. Dudley*

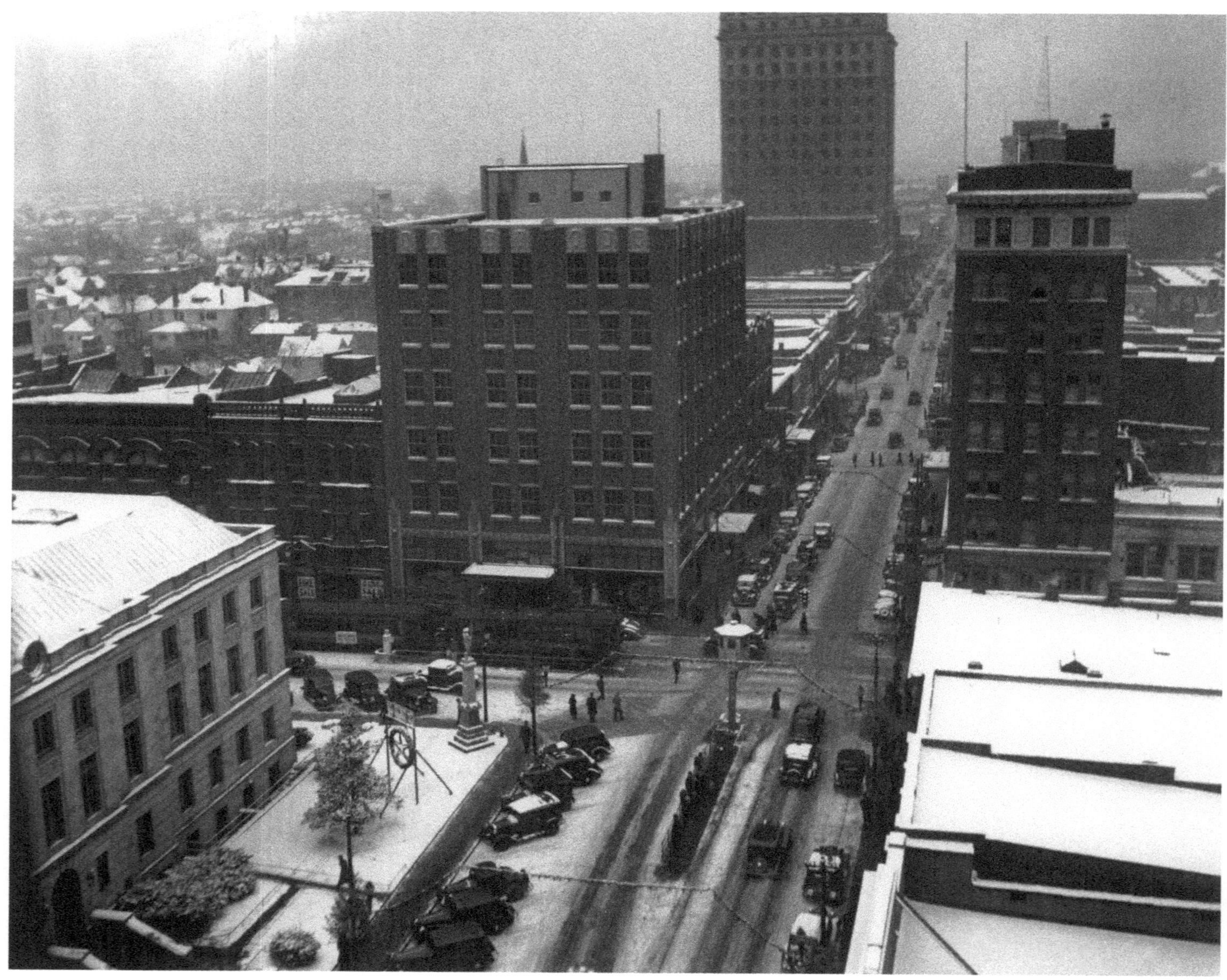

The distinctive, white-faced top floor of the O'Hanlon Building stands out in this view across the roofs at the intersection of West Fourth and Liberty streets around 1935. Directly opposite stands the Pepper Building, and the Forsyth County Courthouse is in the left foreground. It had replaced the lovely but outdated Romanesque courthouse in 1926.

# Winston and Salem

## (1880–1899)

By 1860, the newly created Winston had seen little growth, unlike the older and more prosperous Salem. But industry, coupled with cultural attitudes in the South, created divisiveness and destroyed the long-standing Moravian control of the local economy. In 1837, Salem Manufacturing Company had opened its doors. A textile mill, it drew most of its workers from surrounding counties. The mill's rapidly growing work force included men, women, and children who neither worshipped as Moravians nor wished their few precious hours outside work to be constrained by the tight control of Moravian elders. Three years later, industrialist Francis Fries built a woolen mill operated by slave labor—a practice forbidden by the Moravian Church. Forbidden or not, other businessmen soon emulated Fries. In 1847, the Church abandoned its rules forbidding slavery within Salem. As businesses boomed, Moravian elders found it increasingly difficult to monitor economic enterprises, and in 1856, the Church abandoned any semblance of economic control. This opened the door to industrial expansion in Salem and Winston.

War intervened. Though Forsyth County escaped the physical ravages of the Civil War, the drain of men and supplies to feed the Southern war effort resulted in a severely depressed economy. Then several events happened over a short period of time. Caswell County native Thomas J. Brown opened a successful tobacco-auction warehouse in 1872 in Winston. In 1873, a railroad line from Greensboro finally reached that town. Drawn by good raw material, cheap labor, and reliable transportation, the P. H. Hanes family opened a tobacco factory in Winston that same year. Then, in 1874, a most remarkable Virginian moved to the small town and began a dynasty based on bright leaf tobacco. His name was Richard Joshua "R. J." Reynolds.

Local businesses prospered, from wagon works to grocery stores, as new industry followed new industry, and thousands of workers poured into the area. Entrepreneurs pumped profits from tobacco into textiles, electric power generation, and other enterprises. As population increased from a few hundred souls to almost 14,000 residents by 1900, captains of industry became city leaders, and they decided to have the finest city in the state. By the same year, most local residents agreed that though North Carolina listed their towns as Winston and Salem, the two were really one city, the Twin City: Winston-Salem.

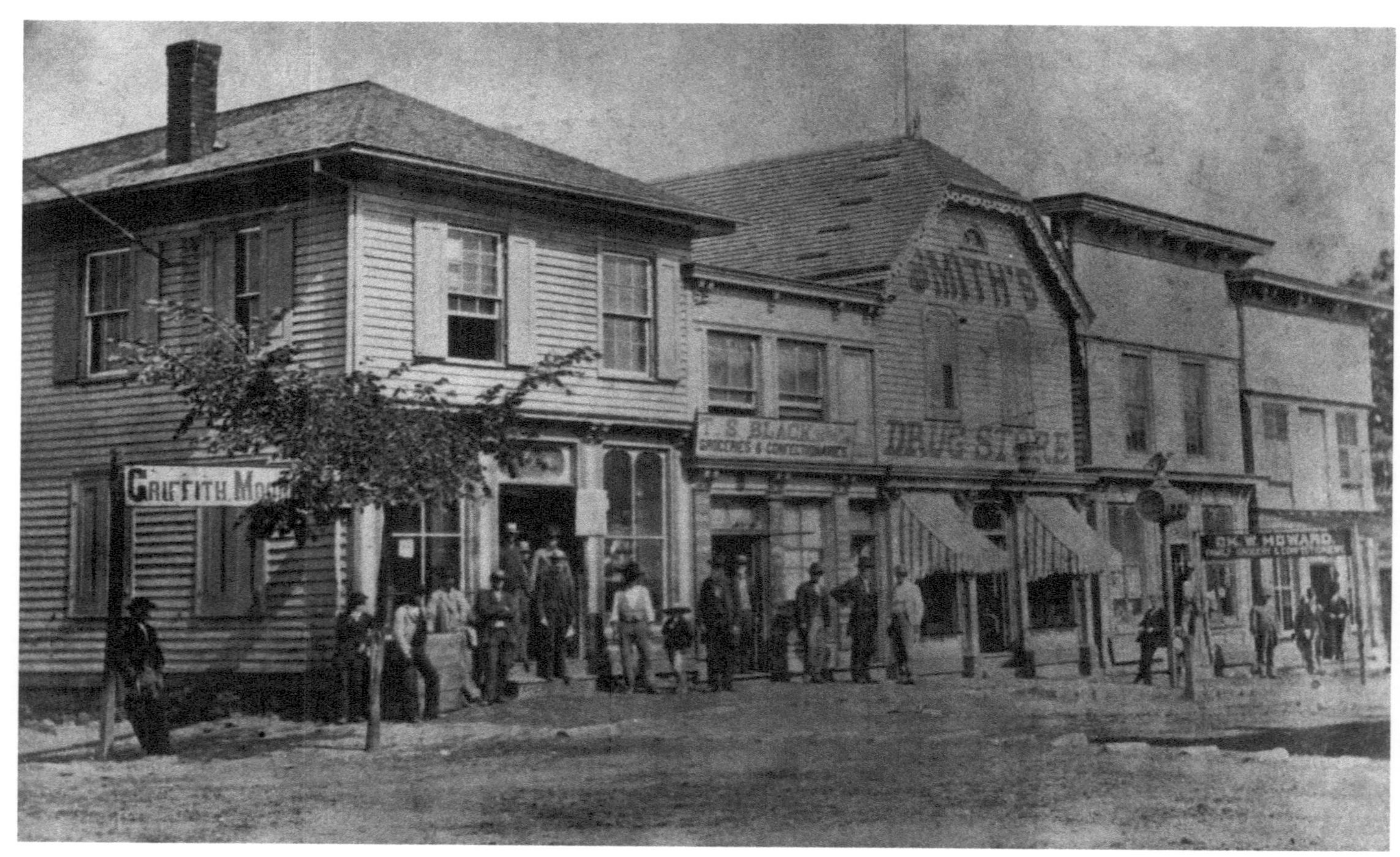


By 1880, Winston had grown beyond its eight stores and a few houses of 1865, though this section of the 400 block of North Liberty Street is reminiscent of any number of small, sleepy southern towns where old men gathered in front of stores to lament the lost cause of two decades past.

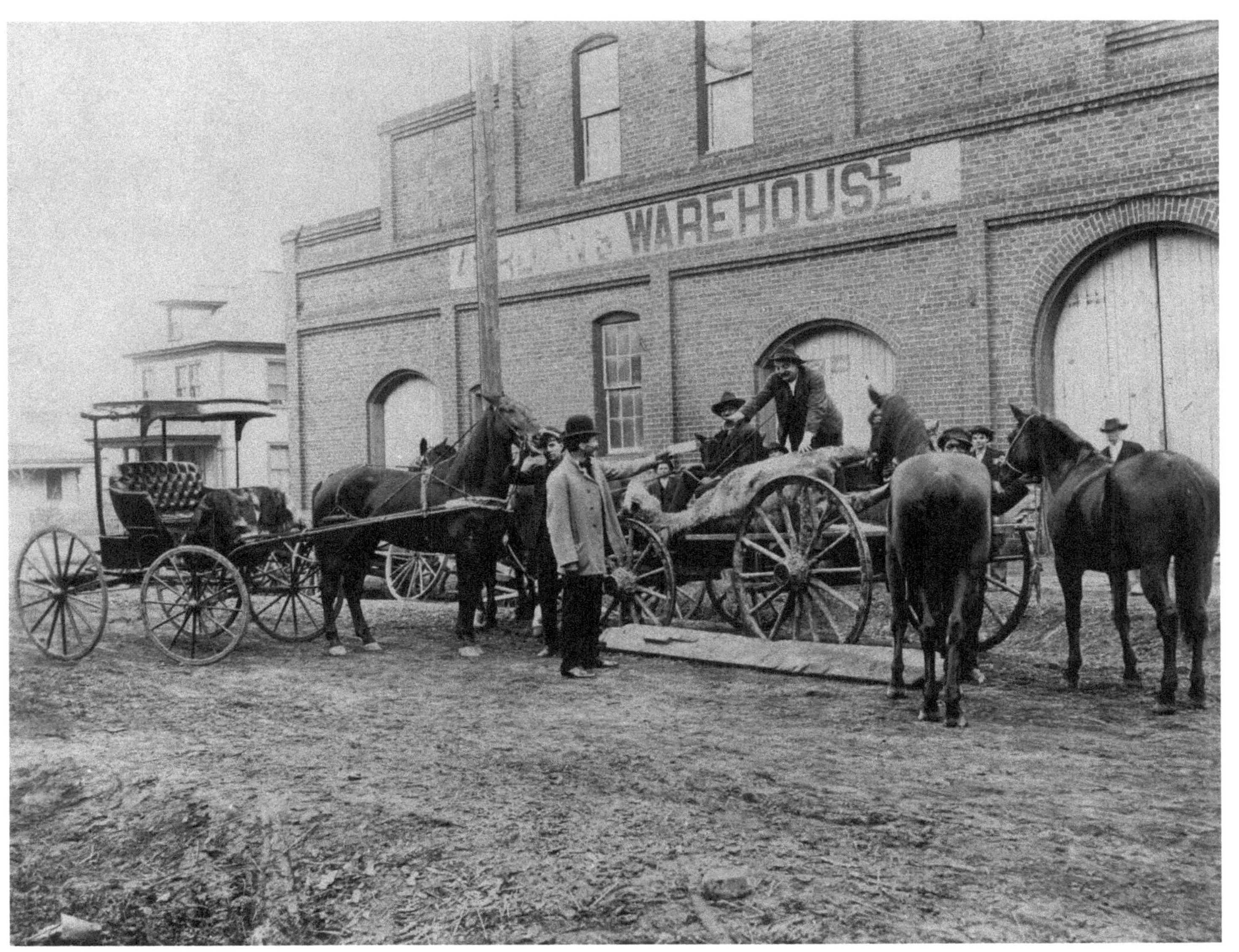


In 1872, Thomas J. Brown opened Winston's first permanent tobacco-auction warehouse in a wooden building on the corner of Church and Third streets to exploit the growing bright-leaf tobacco production in the county. Success followed, and Brown opened an 18,000-square-foot warehouse in 1884 on Main Street. This photo from around 1885 illustrates that business never stopped, even during the off-season.

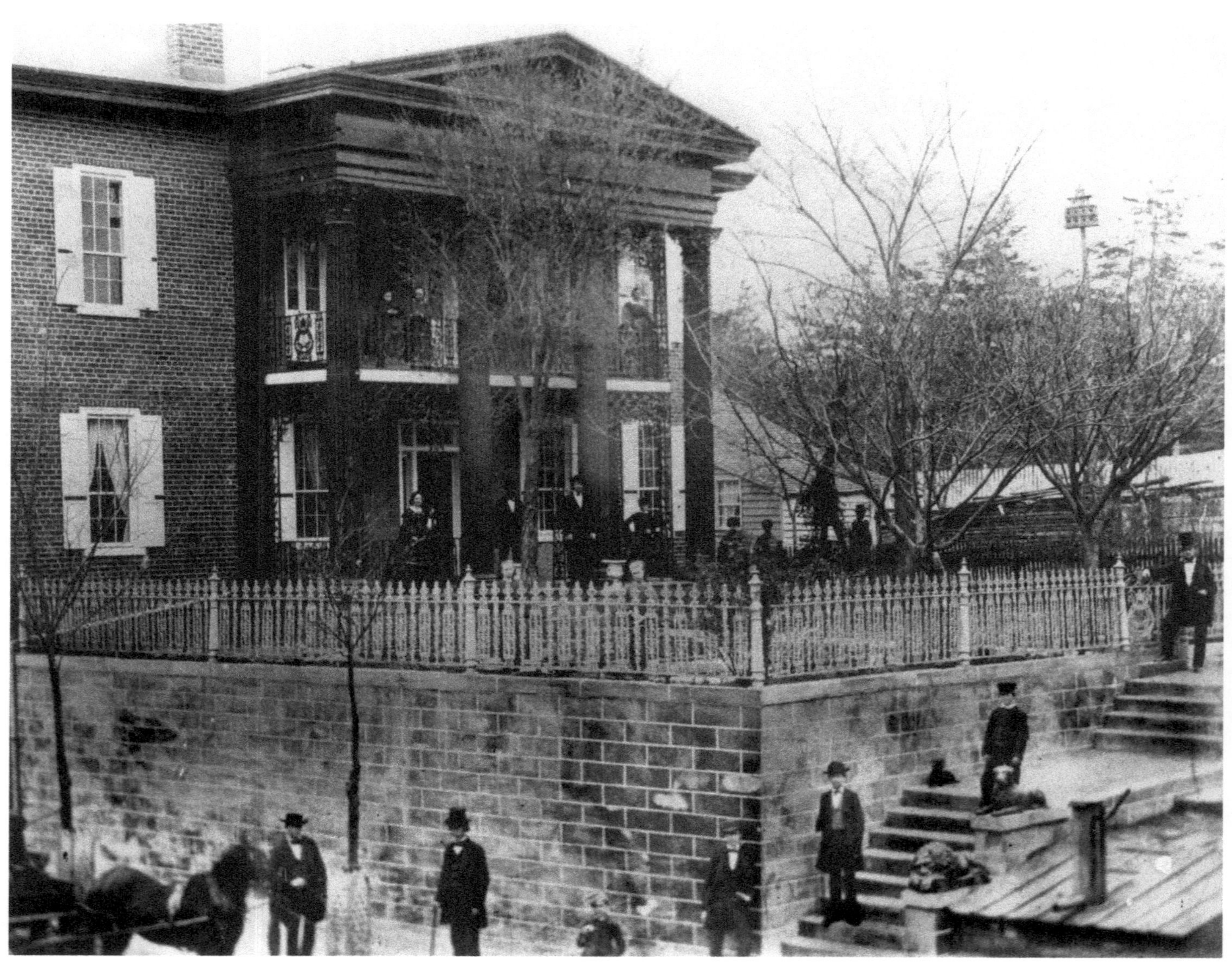

Edward Belo, a leading merchant of Salem, built a mansion on Salem's Main Street in 1860. Both the mansion and the family business, a department store on the first floor of the building, survived the Civil War, and Edward served as vice-president of Wachovia National Bank when it formed in 1879. This view from around 1890 of the side entrance appears to have been taken at a society gala.

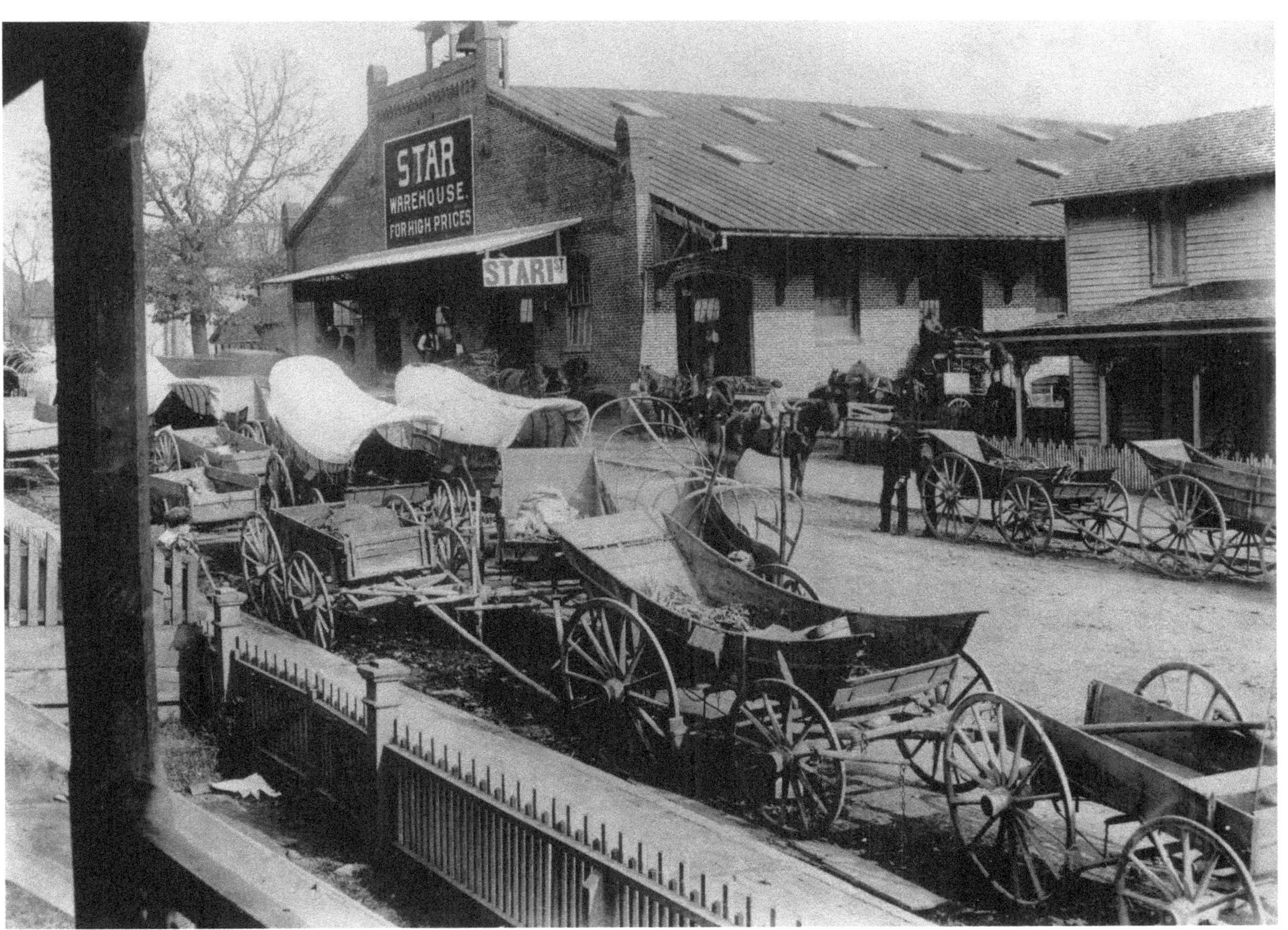


By 1890, numerous warehouses supported some thirty-five tobacco factories in Winston and Salem. These empty wagons outside Star Warehouse on North Main Street mark the last days of another successful season, and serve to illustrate that tobacco supported more than just warehouses and chewing-tobacco factories. These were probably built at the Nissen Wagon Works or at Spach Brothers Wagon Works, business competitors since the 1830s enriched by the need to haul the bright leaves.

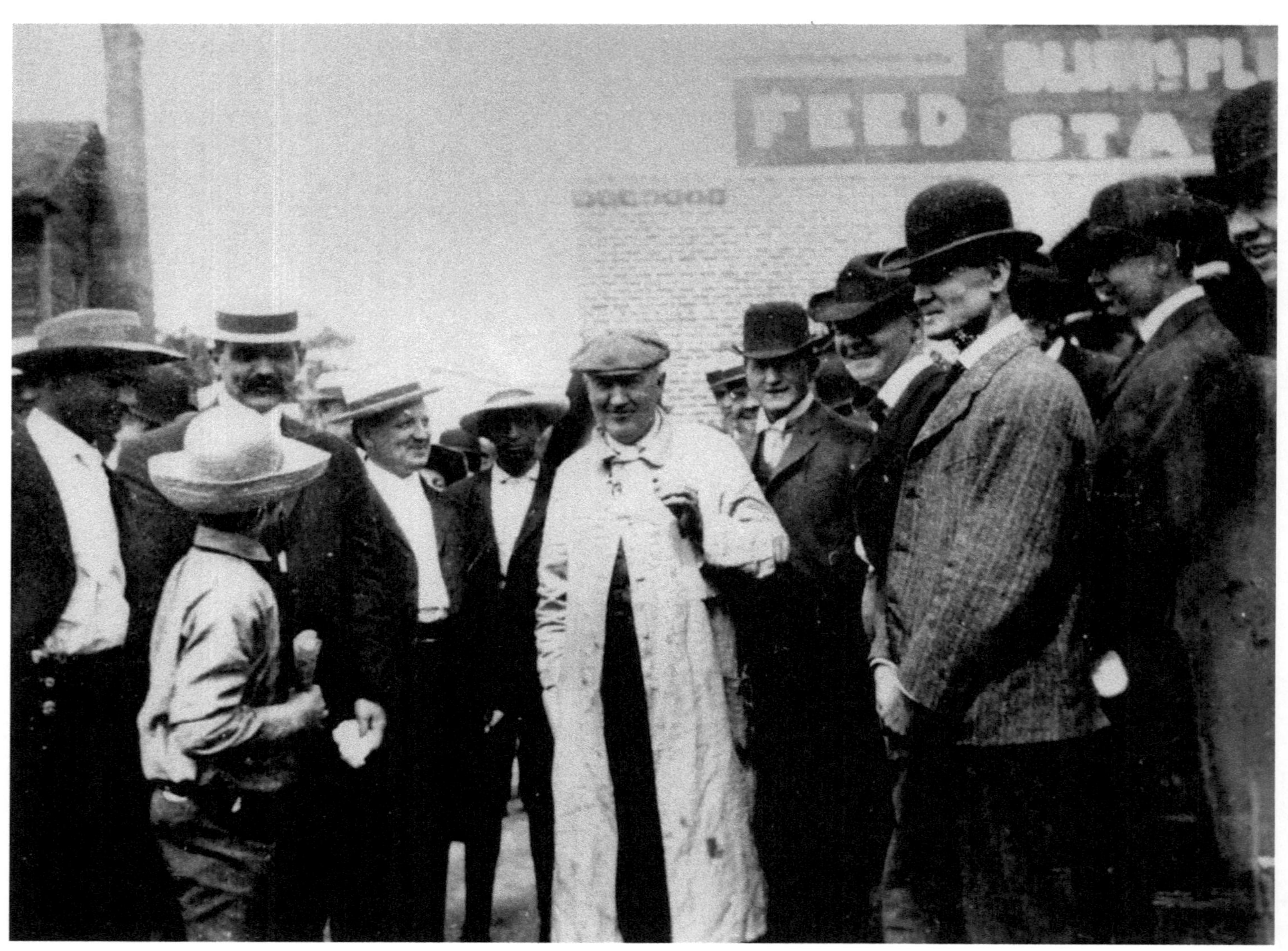


No less a person than Thomas A. Edison visited the twin towns in 1890 to inaugurate the new streetcar service.

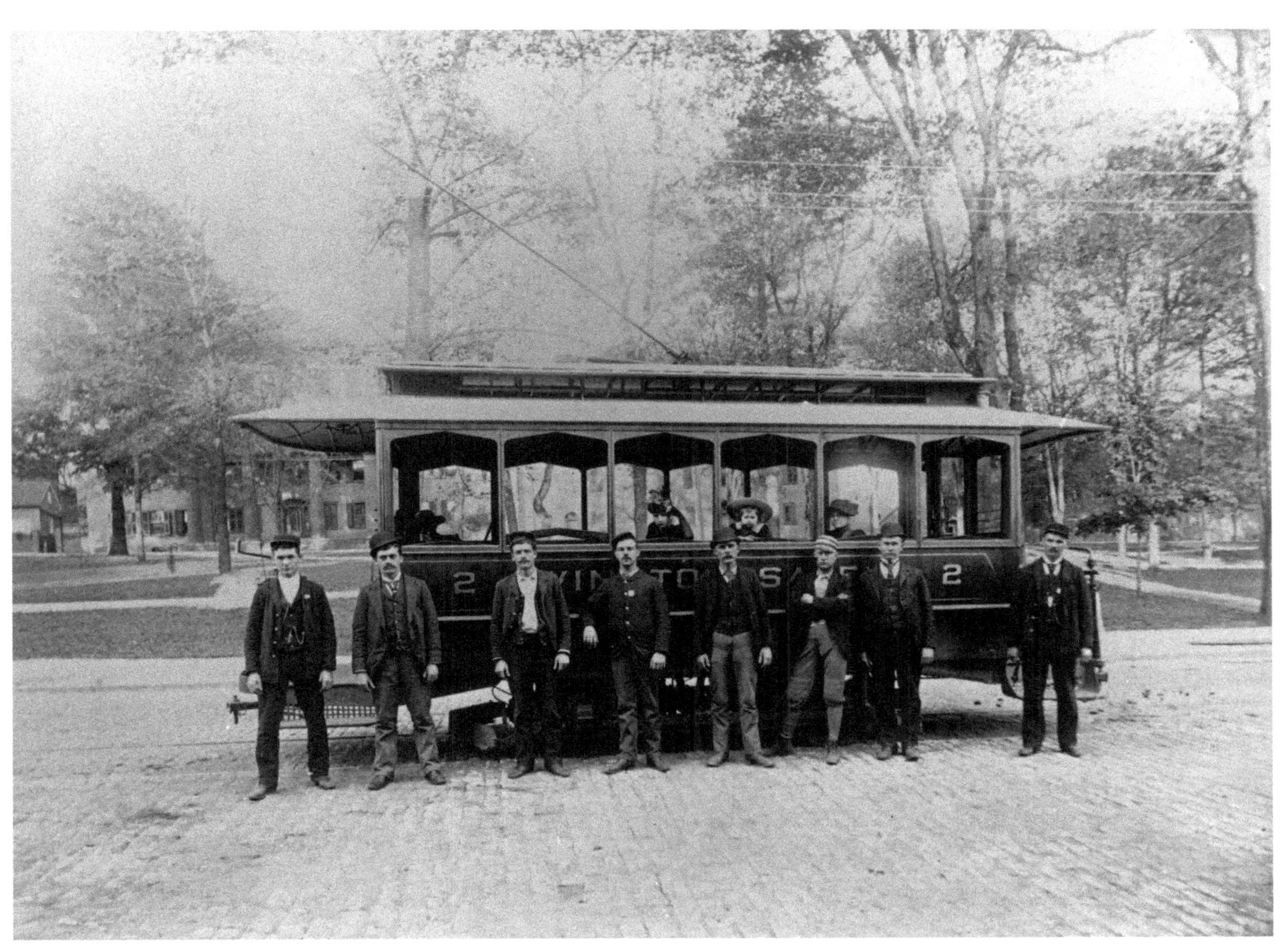

Winston and Salem entered the electric age in 1890 with the introduction of telephone service and electric streetcars. In this photograph, conductors pose near one of their charges in Courthouse Square.

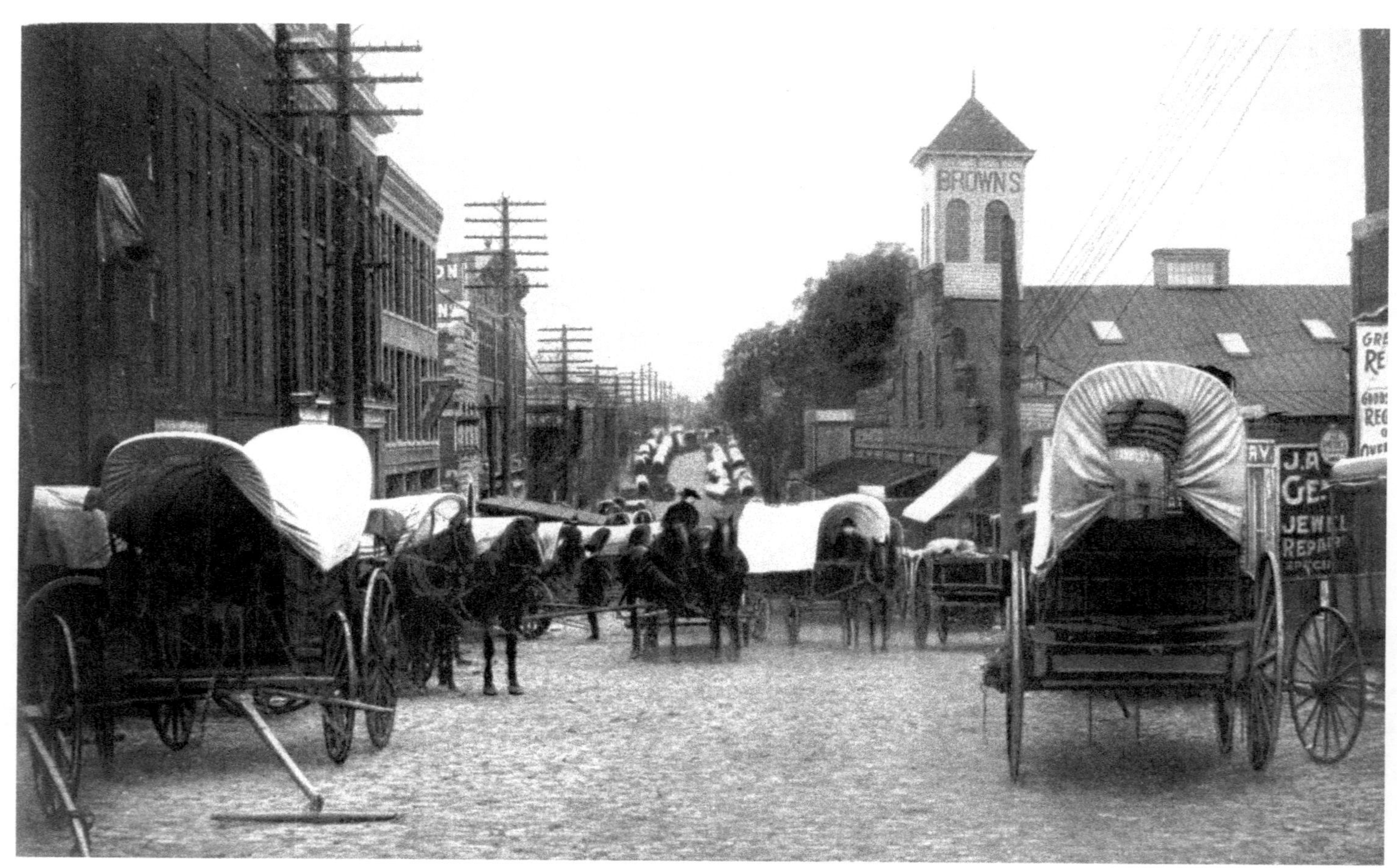


With tobacco season in full swing, wagons crowd Main Street near Brown's Warehouse in the waning years of the 1890s. Their appearance contrasts sharply with utility poles supporting newfangled electrical and telephone wires.

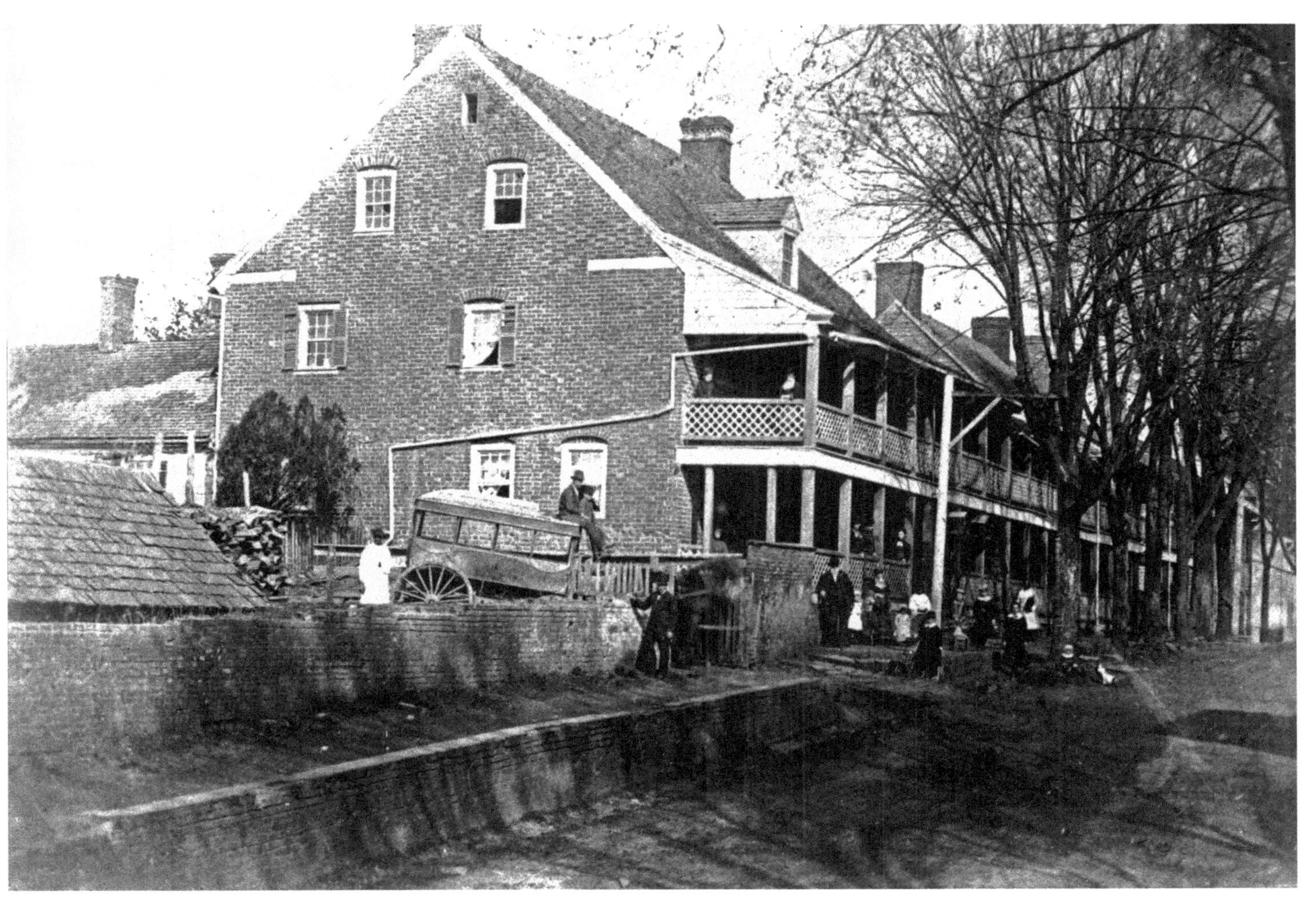

The wealthy families of Winston and Salem were a decided minority. In this photo from the mid-1890s, working families crowd houses on an unnamed street, typical of those souls who operated the machinery of American industry and would one day become the American middle class.

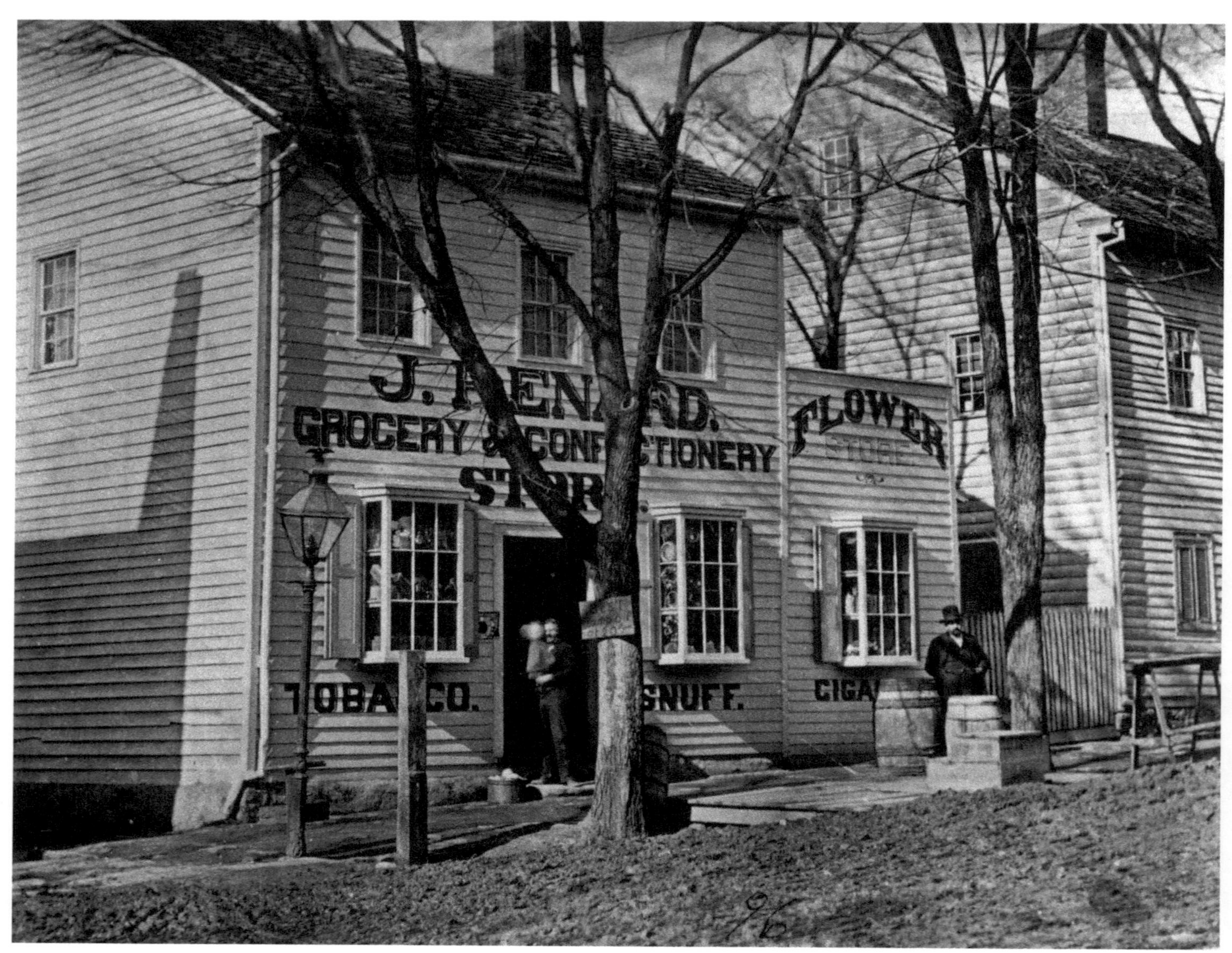


The corner grocery, almost lost to modern times, flourished in the 1890s. Joseph Renard's enterprise sought to profit by sustaining both body and soul of its customers, combining a grocery store with a florist shop.

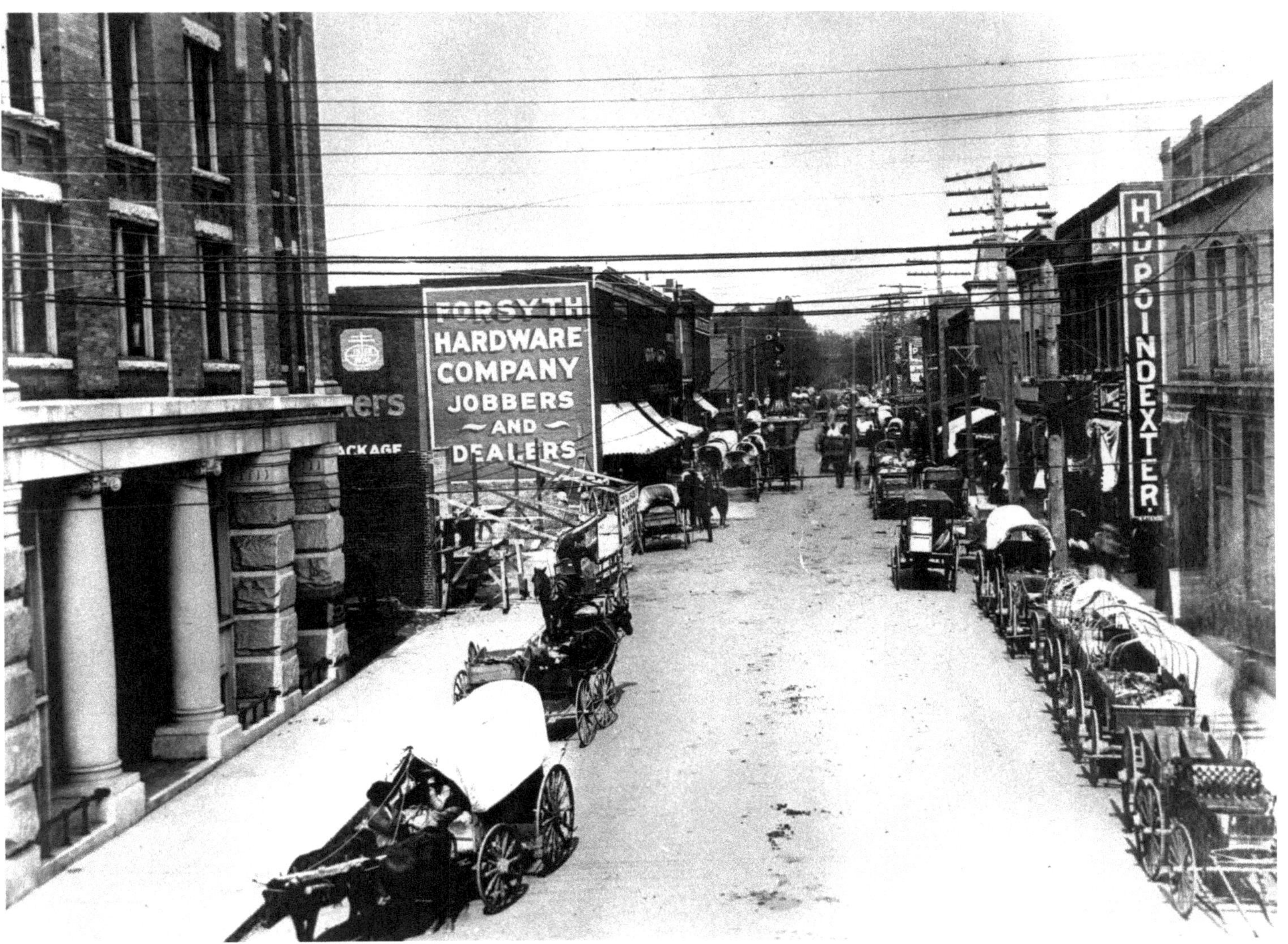


This is a Saturday street scene in the early 1890s, as local farming families visit town. The husband may be at Forsyth Hardware, or a general store similar to it (though he may sneak down a side street for a quick sip at one of the many saloons in downtown Winston). His wife and kids are probably shopping at H. D. Poindexter's dry goods emporium for clothes, flour, and perhaps a sweet treat or two.

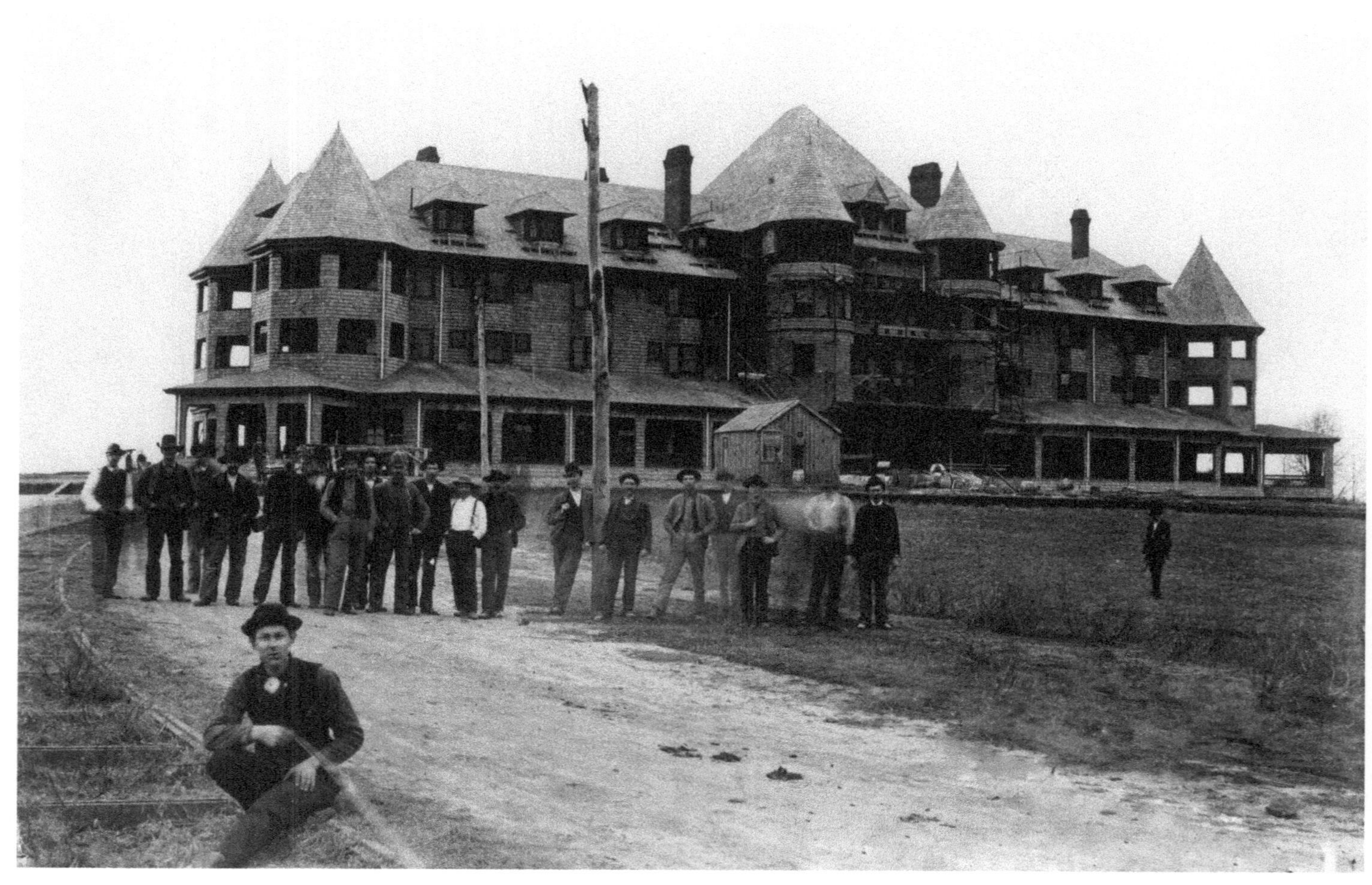

In the 1880s, several wealthy members of Winston society formed the West End Hotel and Land Company. They built a magnificent structure, Hotel Zinzendorf, on the west side of Winston. Completed in May 1891, the hotel featured steam-heated rooms, bathrooms on every floor, and top-notch service. The first tourist magnet in the area seemed well on its way to success.

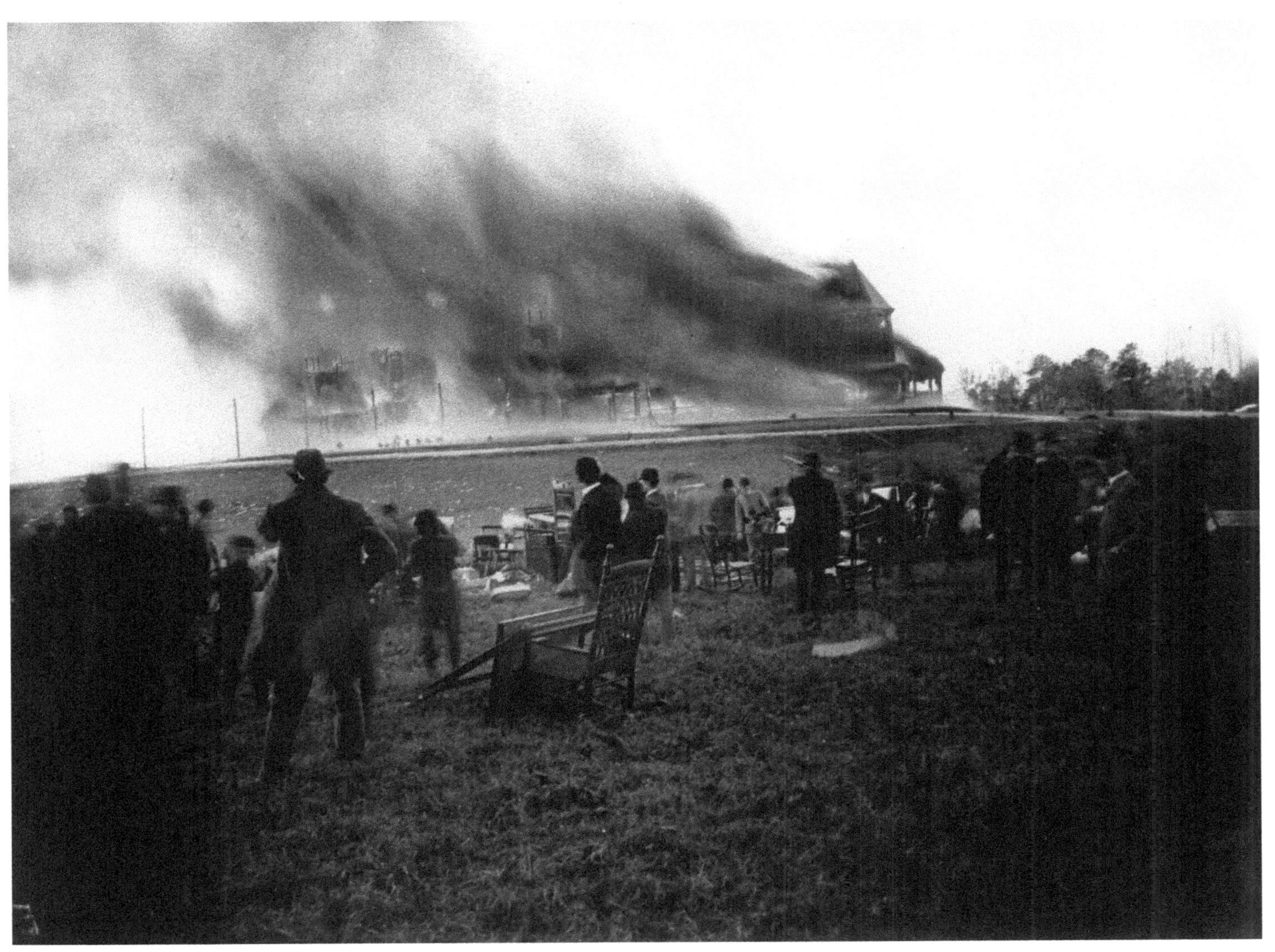

At 11:00 A.M. on Thanksgiving Day of 1892, guests at Hotel Zinzendorf heard someone scream "Fire!" By the time fire companies from Winston and Salem arrived, flames had spread from the laundry room to engulf the structure. By the next morning, only brick chimneys and ashes remained of Winston's first experiment with tourism.

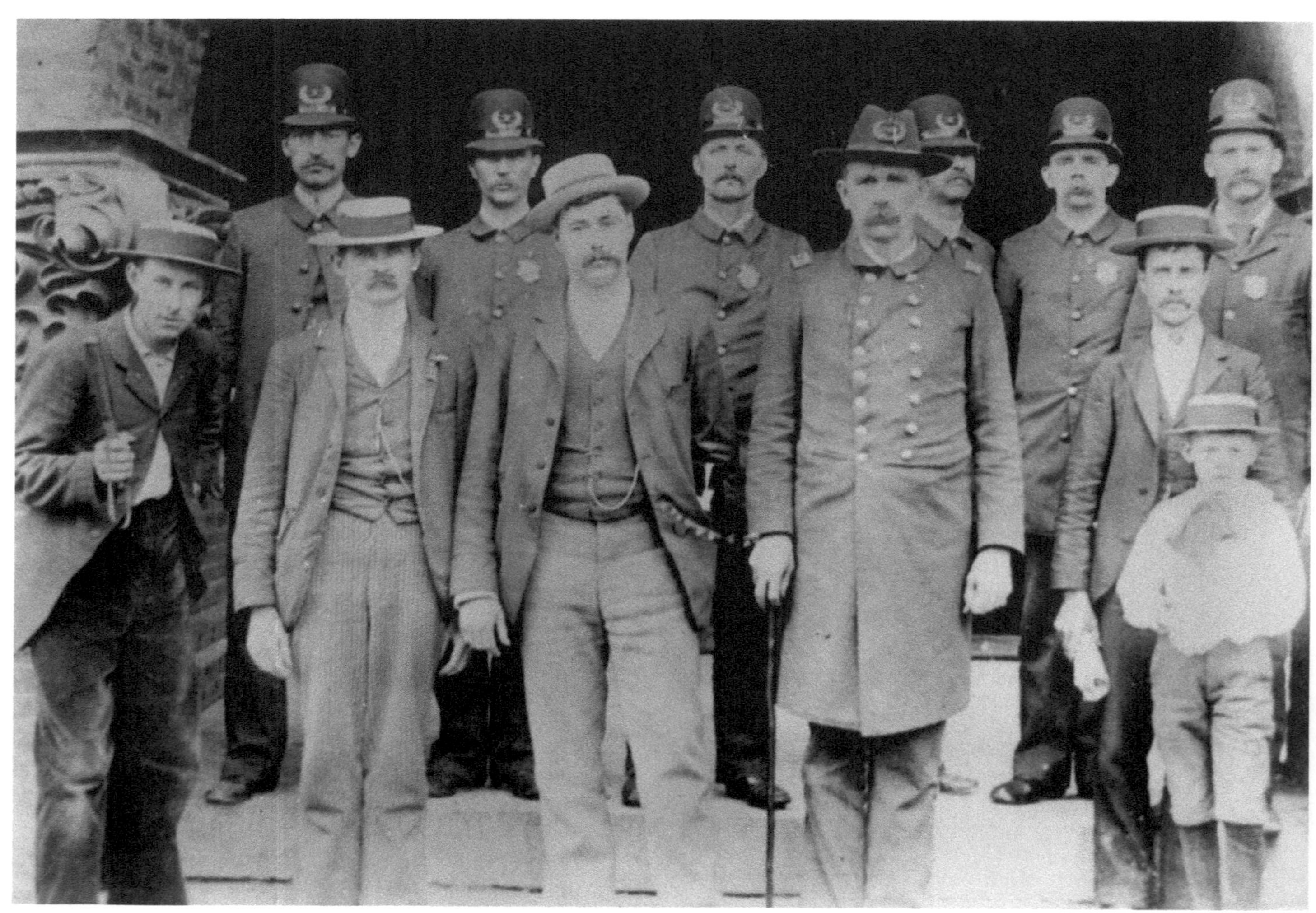

Winston police officers pose in 1894 in front of City Hall. As the fastest-growing city in North Carolina, events frequently strained local law enforcement. One year after this photograph, the shooting death of a police officer sparked a race riot in which local militia fired into a crowd of several hundred African Americans, killing and injuring an unknown number of people.

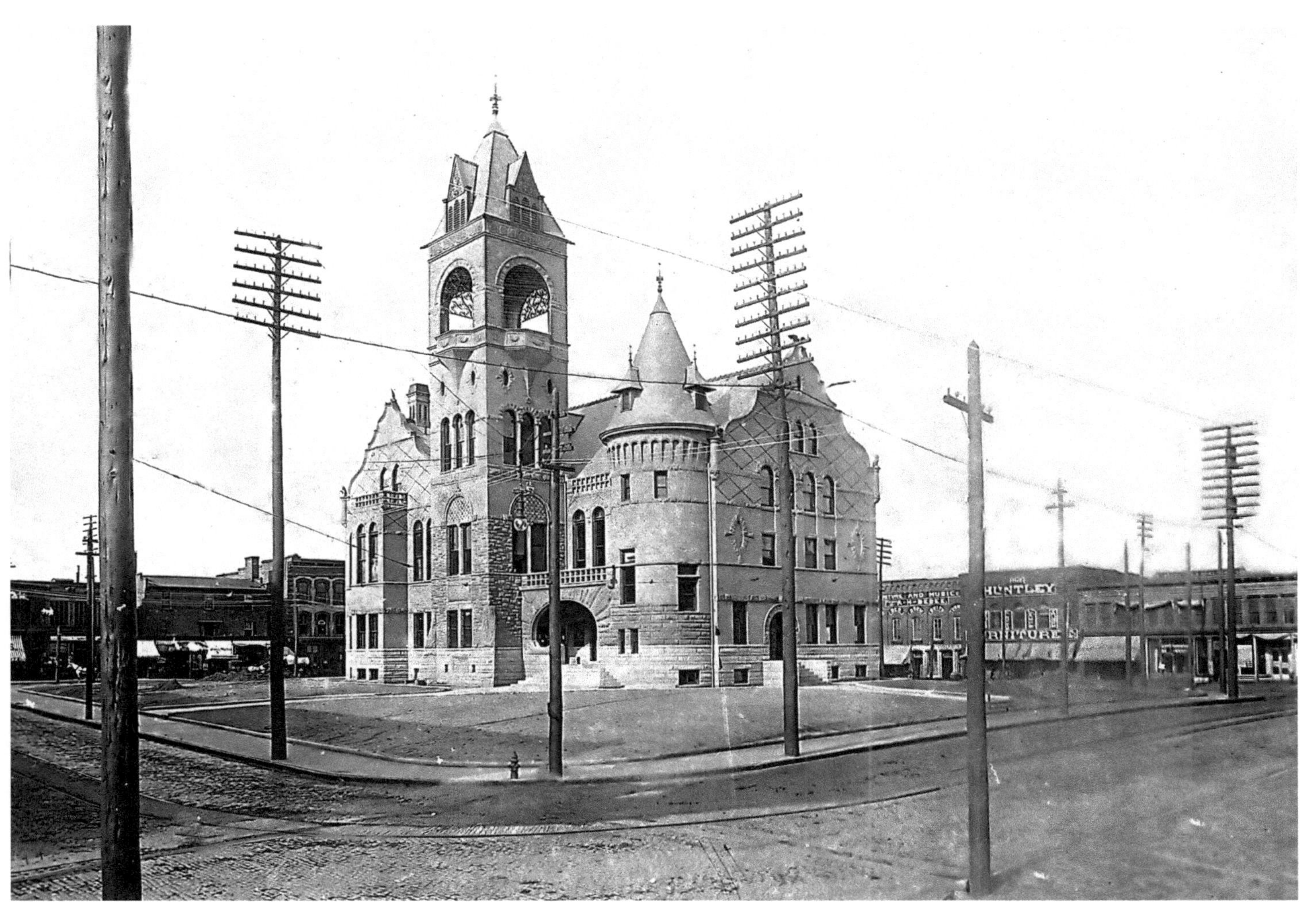


Architect Frank R. Milburn designed the replacement for Forsyth County's old courthouse. Built of granite, brick, and brownstone, the new courthouse with its Romanesque design impressed all who viewed it. Dedicated in 1897, it embodied the growth and economic power of Winston, Salem, and Forsyth County.

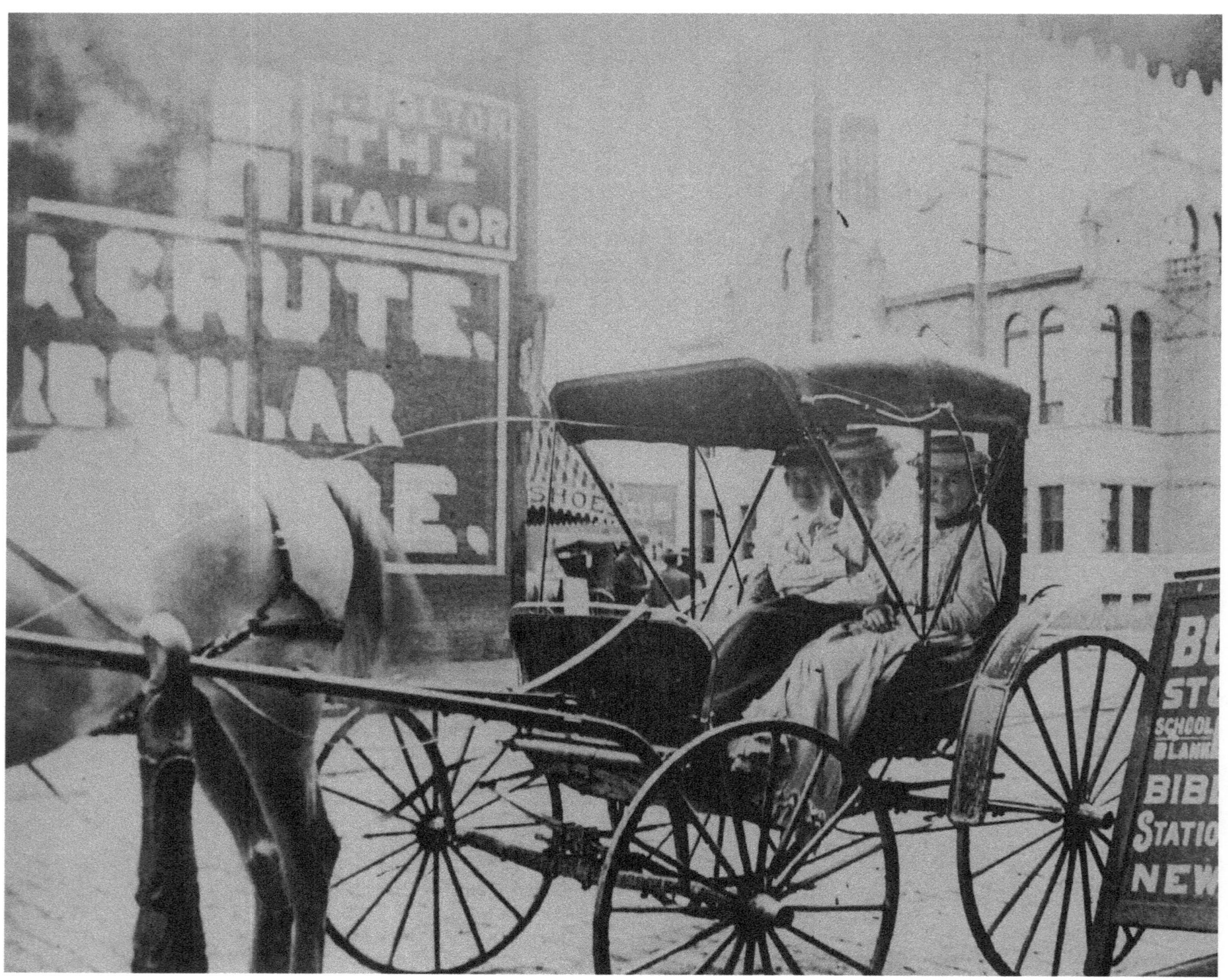


Many women of the late 1890s, such as these ladies driving their own carriage on Liberty Street near the new courthouse, found a degree of liberation in the growth and fast pace of life in Winston. The proliferation of bookstores, such as the one in front of which they have stopped, marked a rise in literacy in North Carolina in the decades after the Civil War.

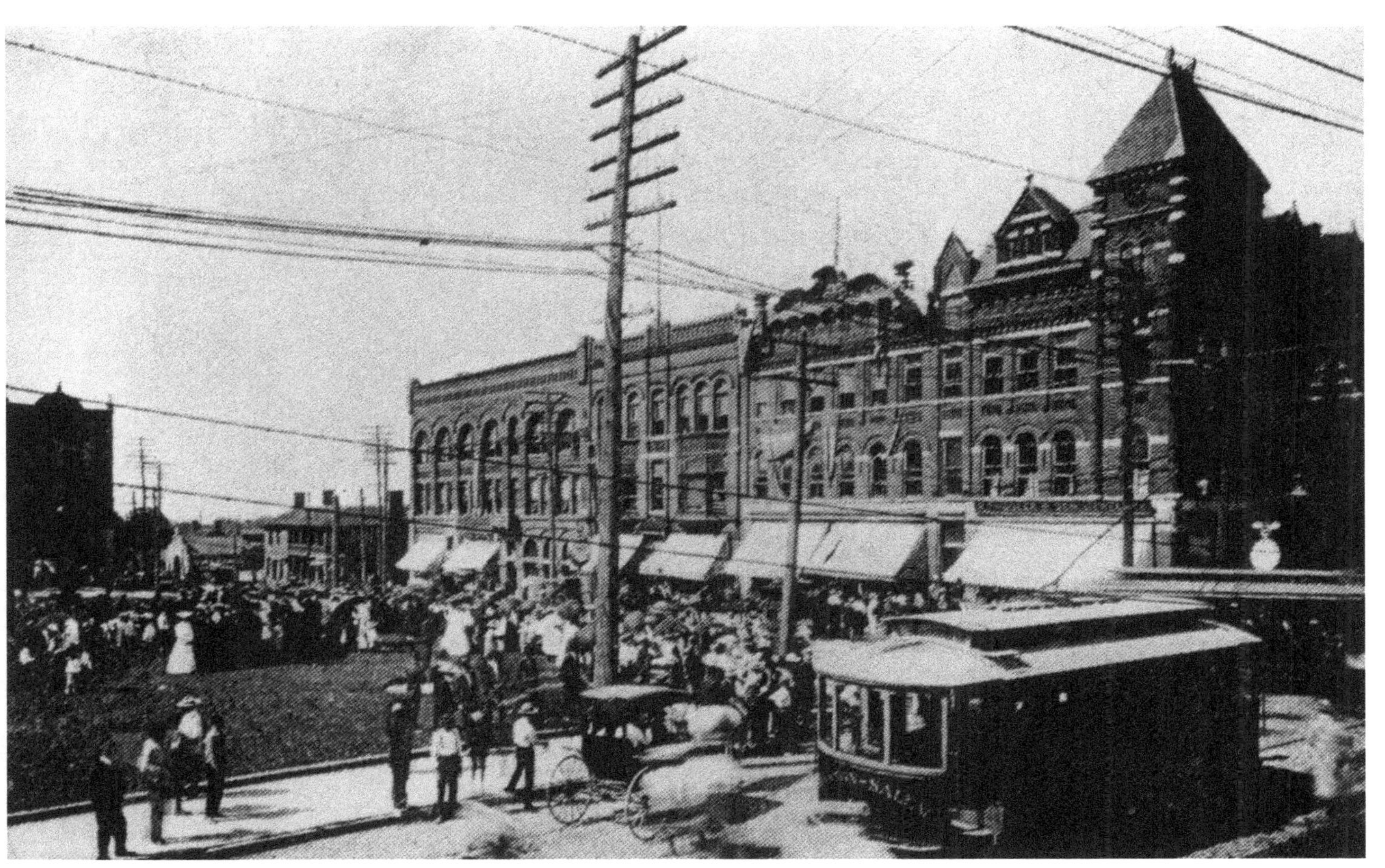

This view, looking towards Liberty Street from Fourth Street in the late 1890s, captures the effort placed on modernization in Winston.

In 1893, Winston opened the doors of its new City Hall. Housing the fire and police services as well as the town's public officials on its upper levels, the building offered rentable market stalls along part of the lower floor. Located on the corner of Main and Fourth streets, City Hall featured a four-story clock tower.

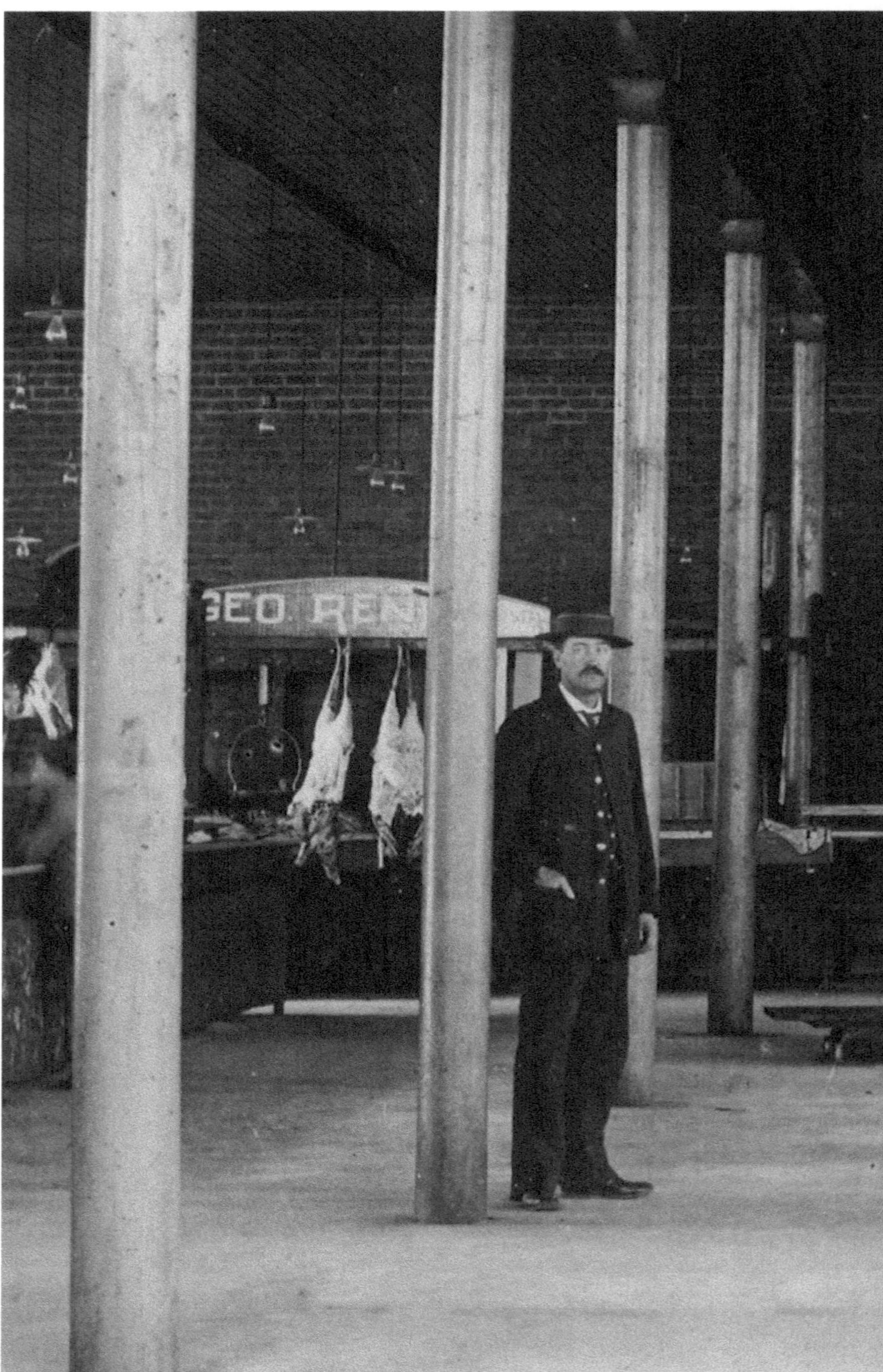

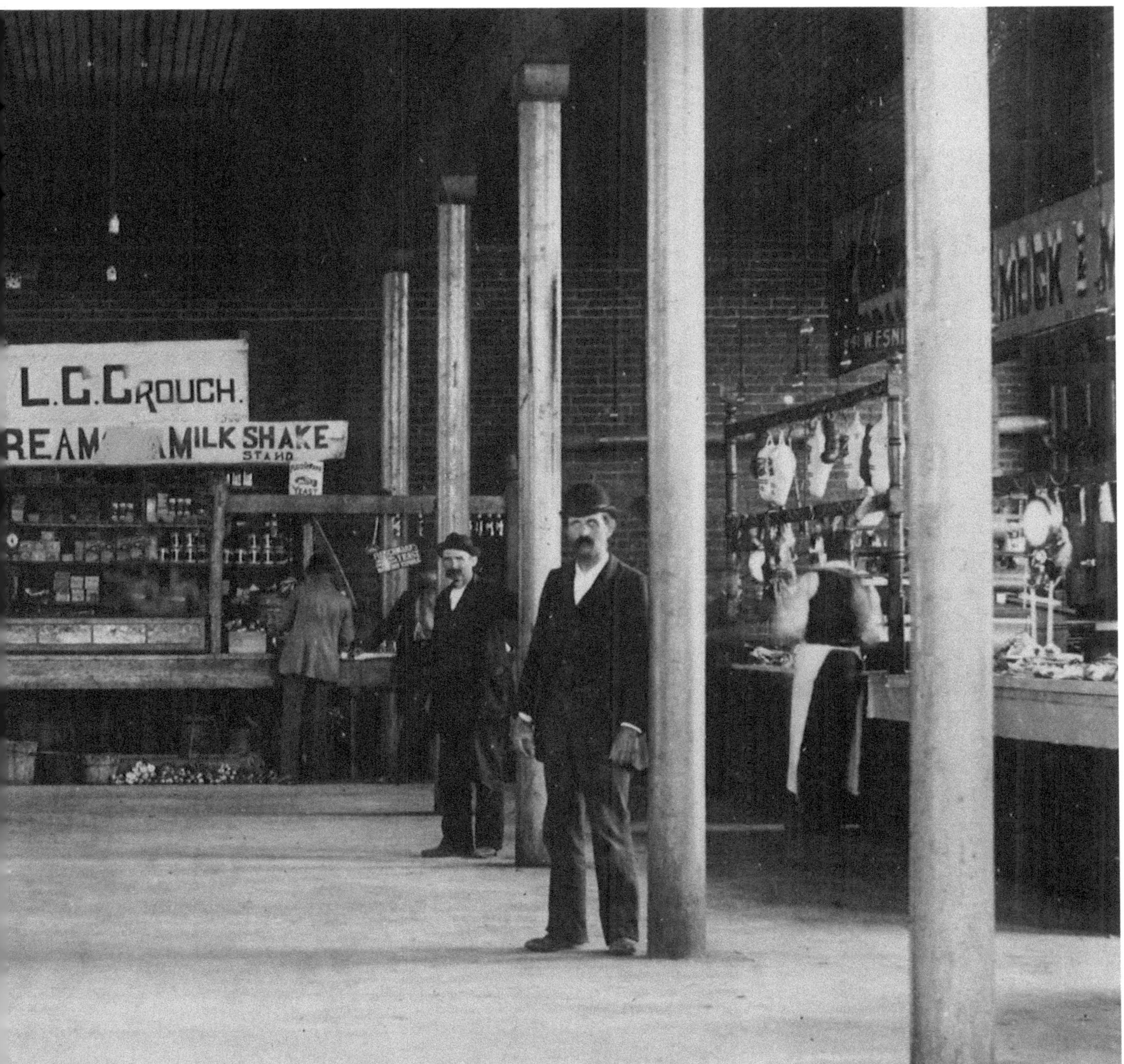
L. C. CROUCH.
REAM MILK SHAKE
STAND
MOCK & M
W. F. SNI

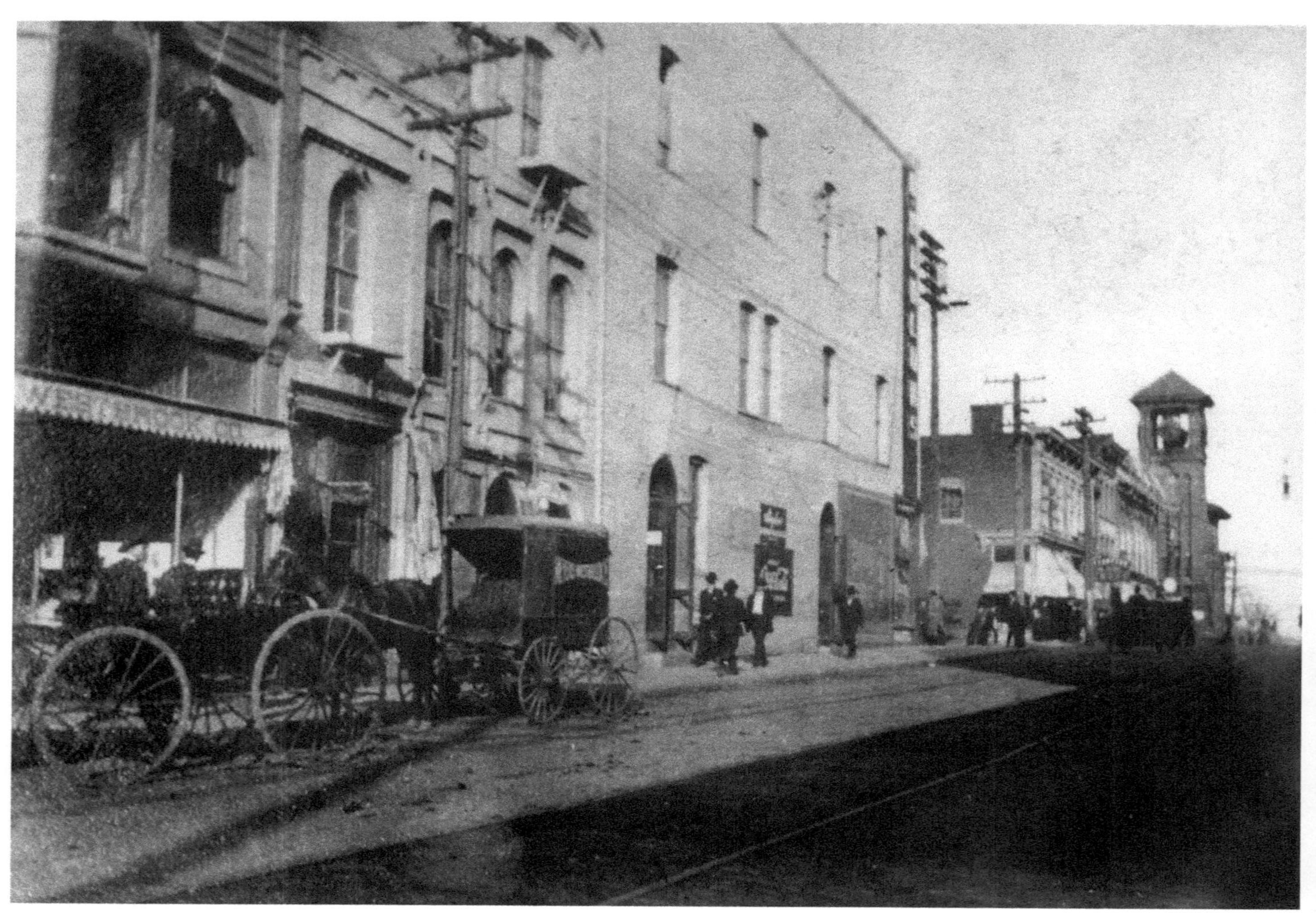

This post-1893 photograph looks east along West Fourth Street. Note the clock tower of City Hall on the far right.

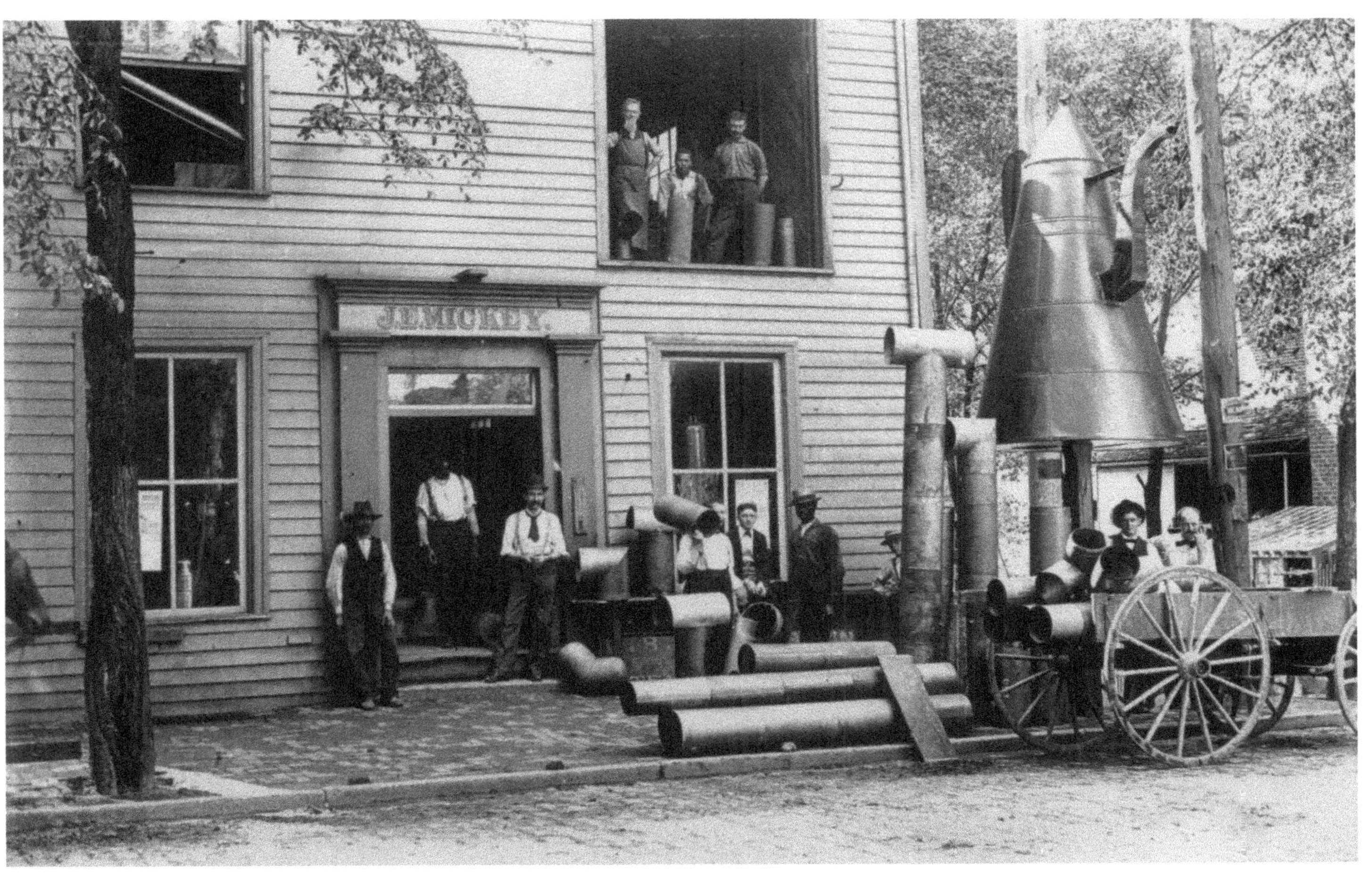


In 1858, Julius E. and Samuel Mickey opened a tinsmith shop. To advertise, they placed a giant, tin coffee pot outside the shop. Photographed so frequently—as in this shot from the 1890s—that it became the unofficial symbol of Winston-Salem, the pot remained a fixture in front of the old J. E. Mickey Shop until 1959, when the city relocated it elsewhere on Main Street.

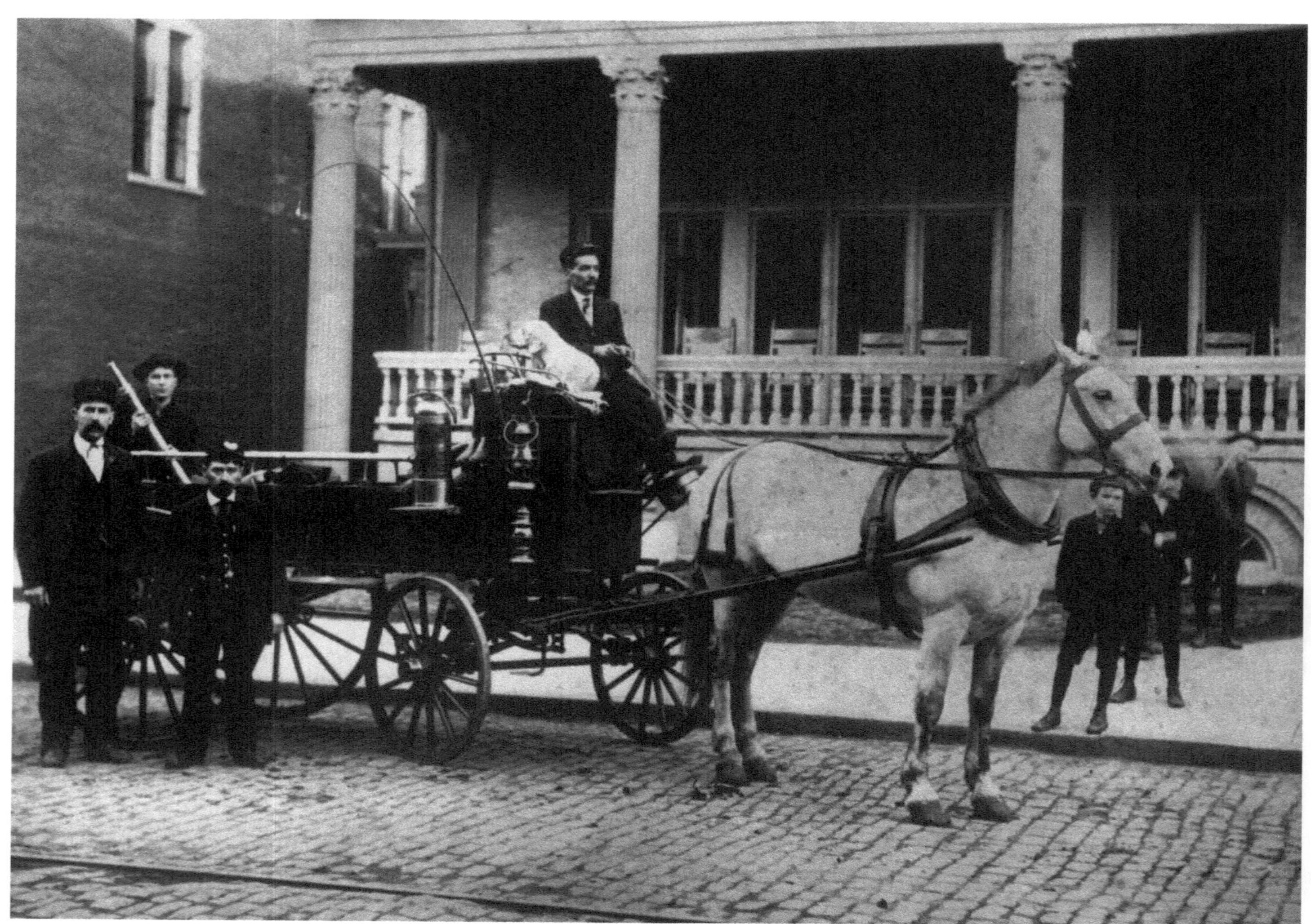

Winston's ladder truck and crew, photographed around 1898, proved their worth time and again as fire ravaged the wooden buildings that housed much of the city's industry and most of its citizens.

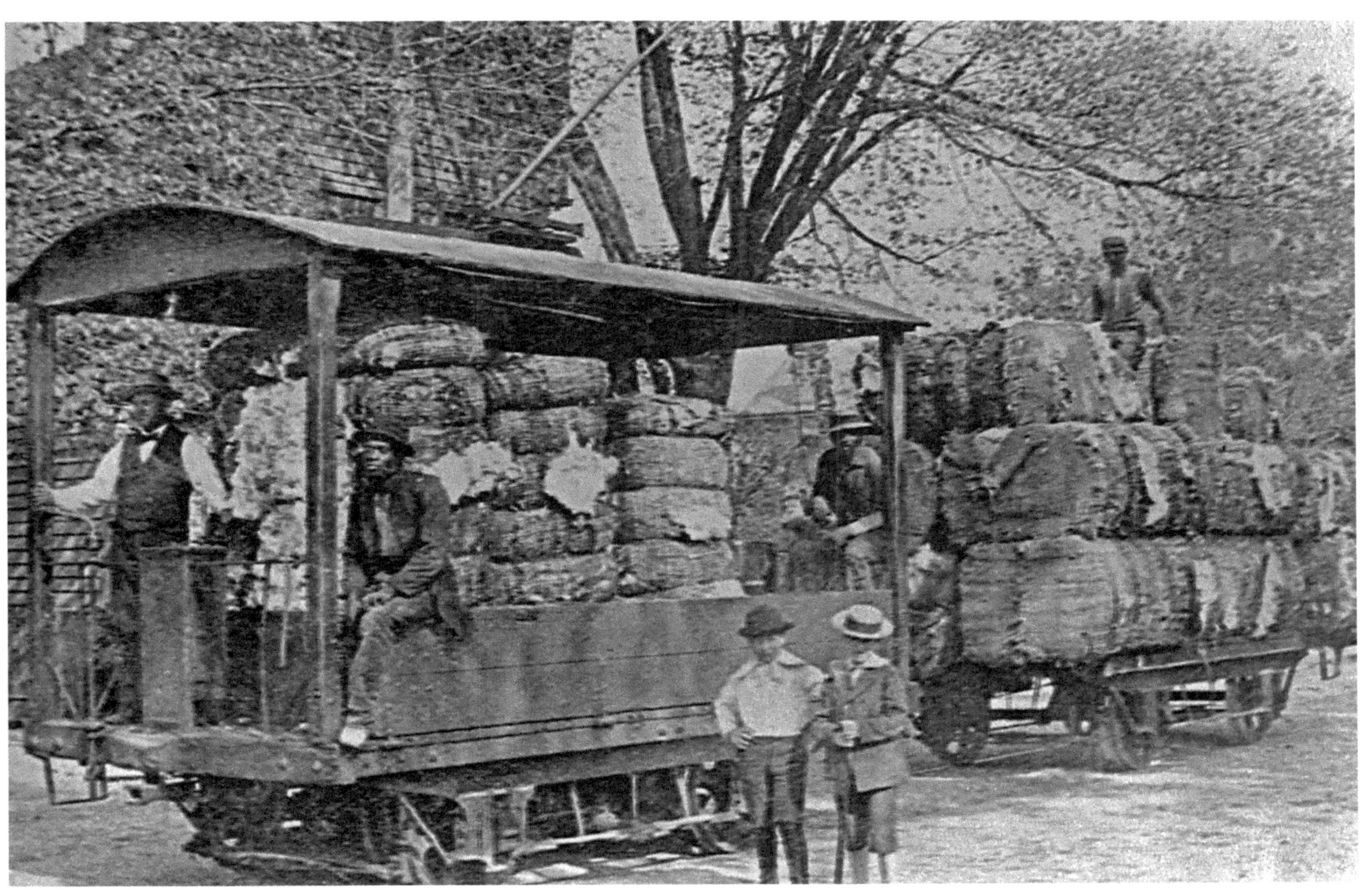

F. & H. Fries Company processed cotton in Salem from 1846 through much of the twentieth century. Though cotton production declined in favor of bright leaf tobacco after the Civil War, production continued and contributed to the growth of Winston and Salem. Here, cotton bales await ginning at the Fries Cotton Mill in Salem in the late 1890s.

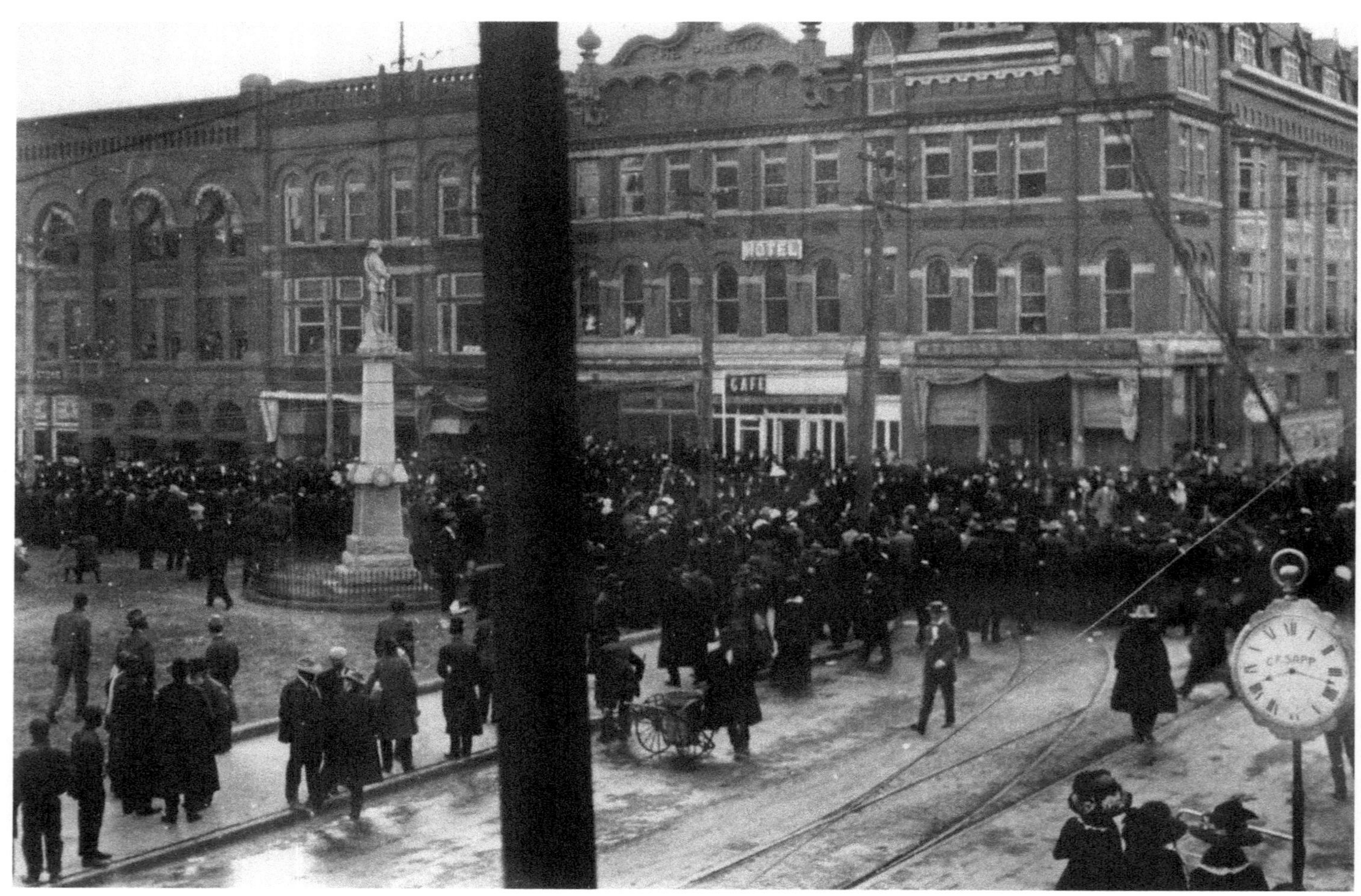


In 1894, Winston's first public school for whites, West End Graded School, opened its doors. The first public school for blacks, Depot Street School, opened in 1897. These schools marked a commitment to literacy in Winston, especially by the city's wealthy elite. This photograph of a school parade in Winston probably dates to 1895 or 1896.

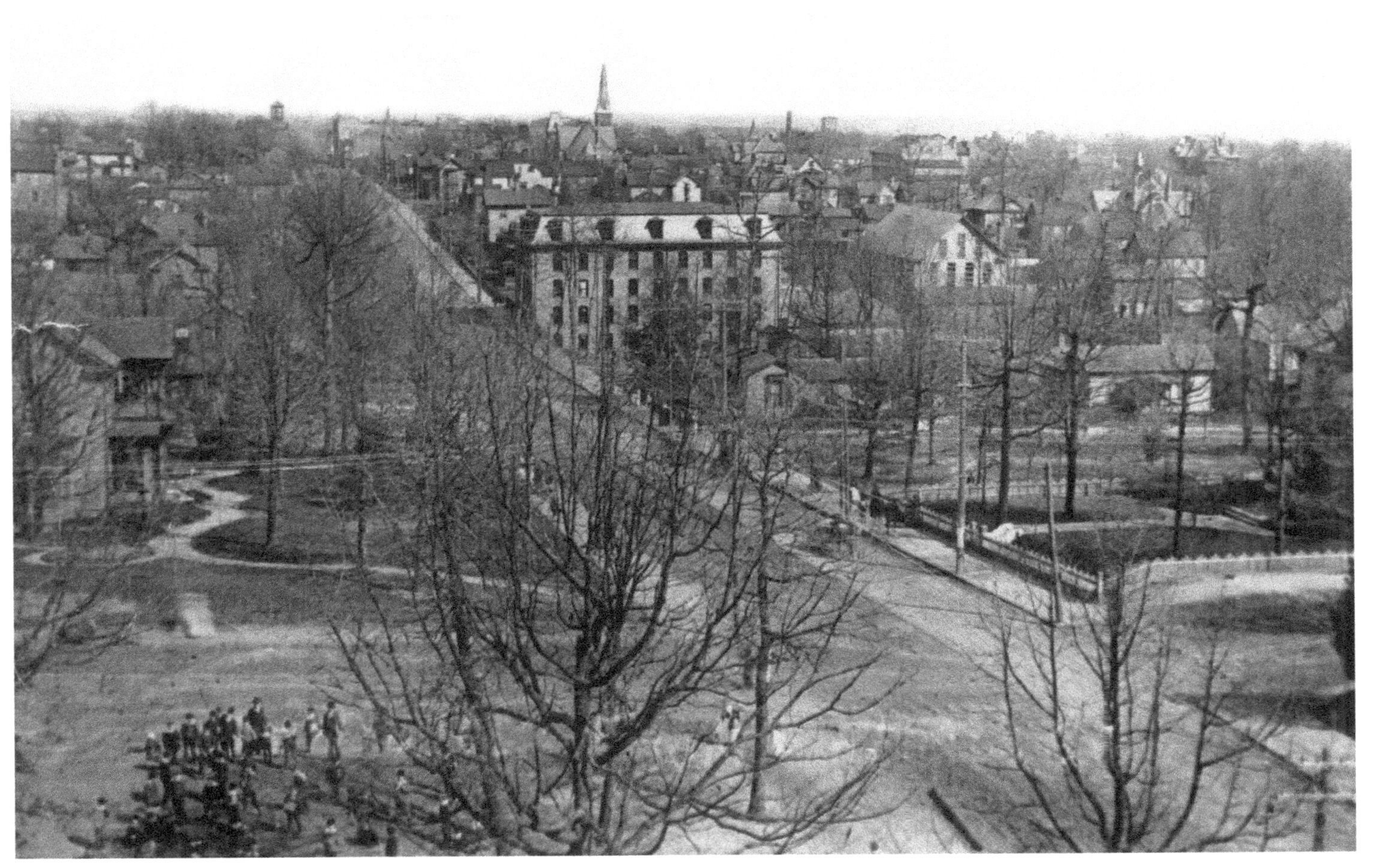

This is a winter view of West Fourth Street from Broad Street taken sometime in the 1890s.

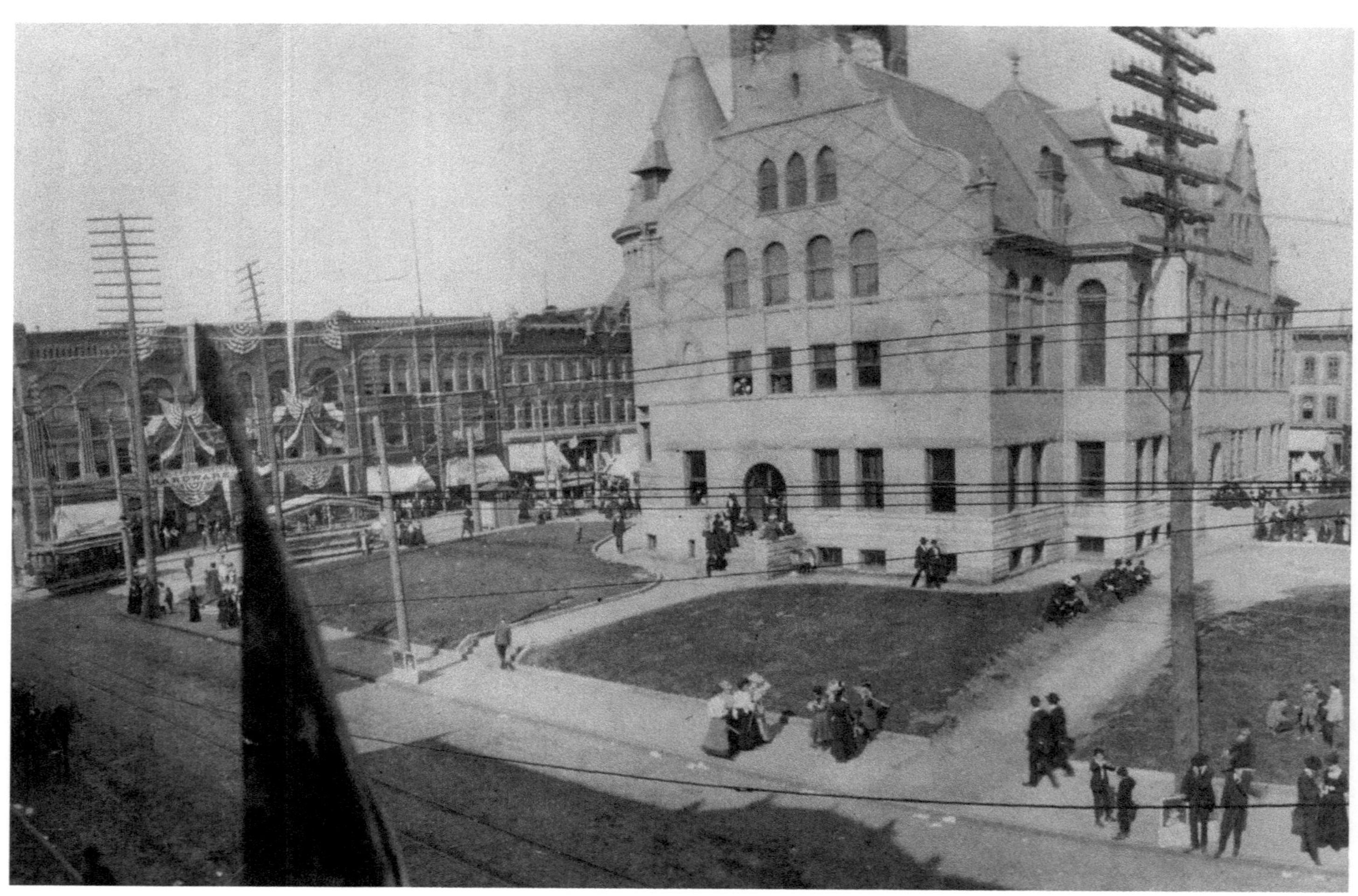

Court is in session at the Forsyth County Courthouse in the late 1890s.

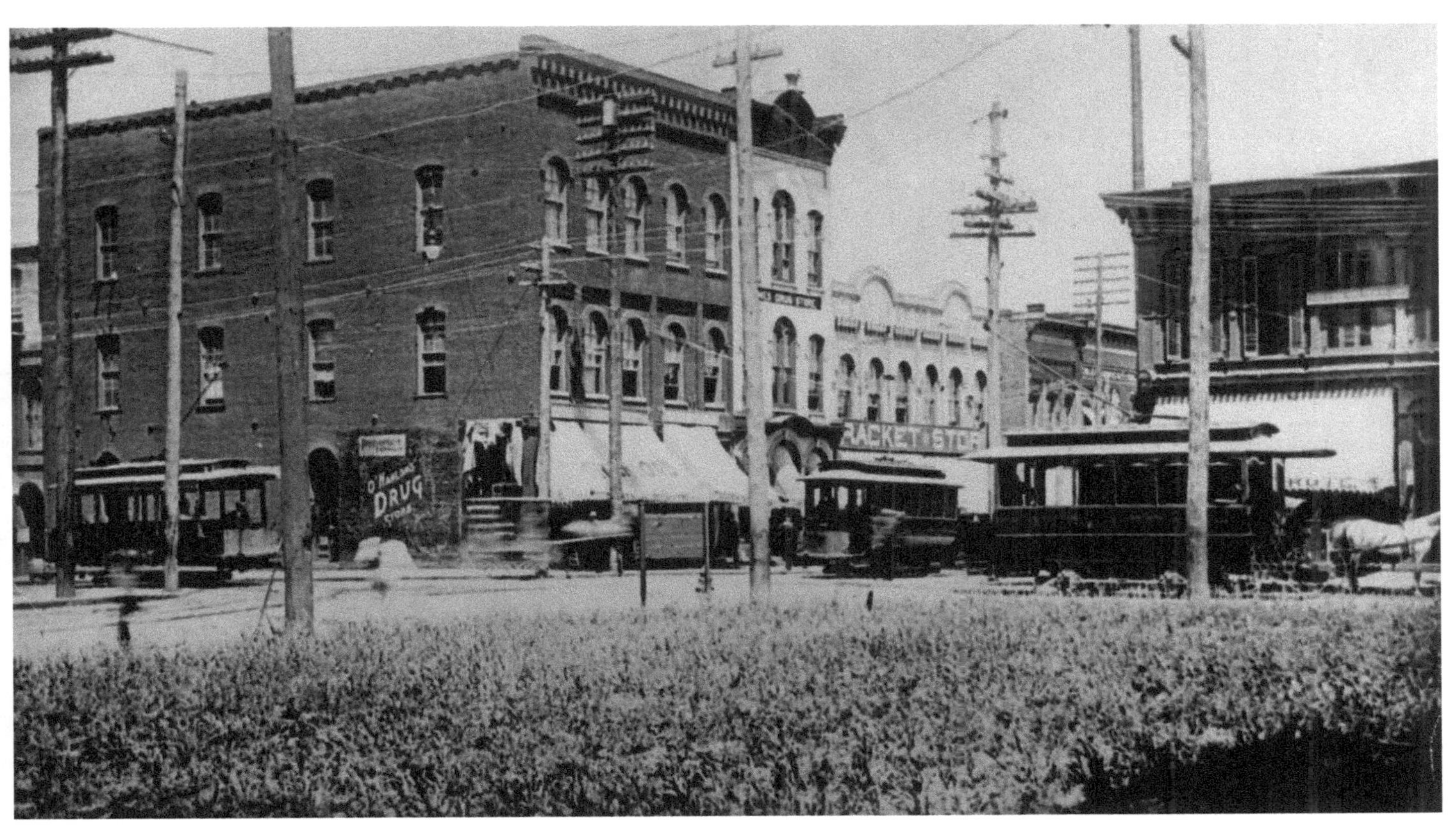


Trolley lines converge here at the intersection of West Fourth Street and Liberty Street in the late 1890s.

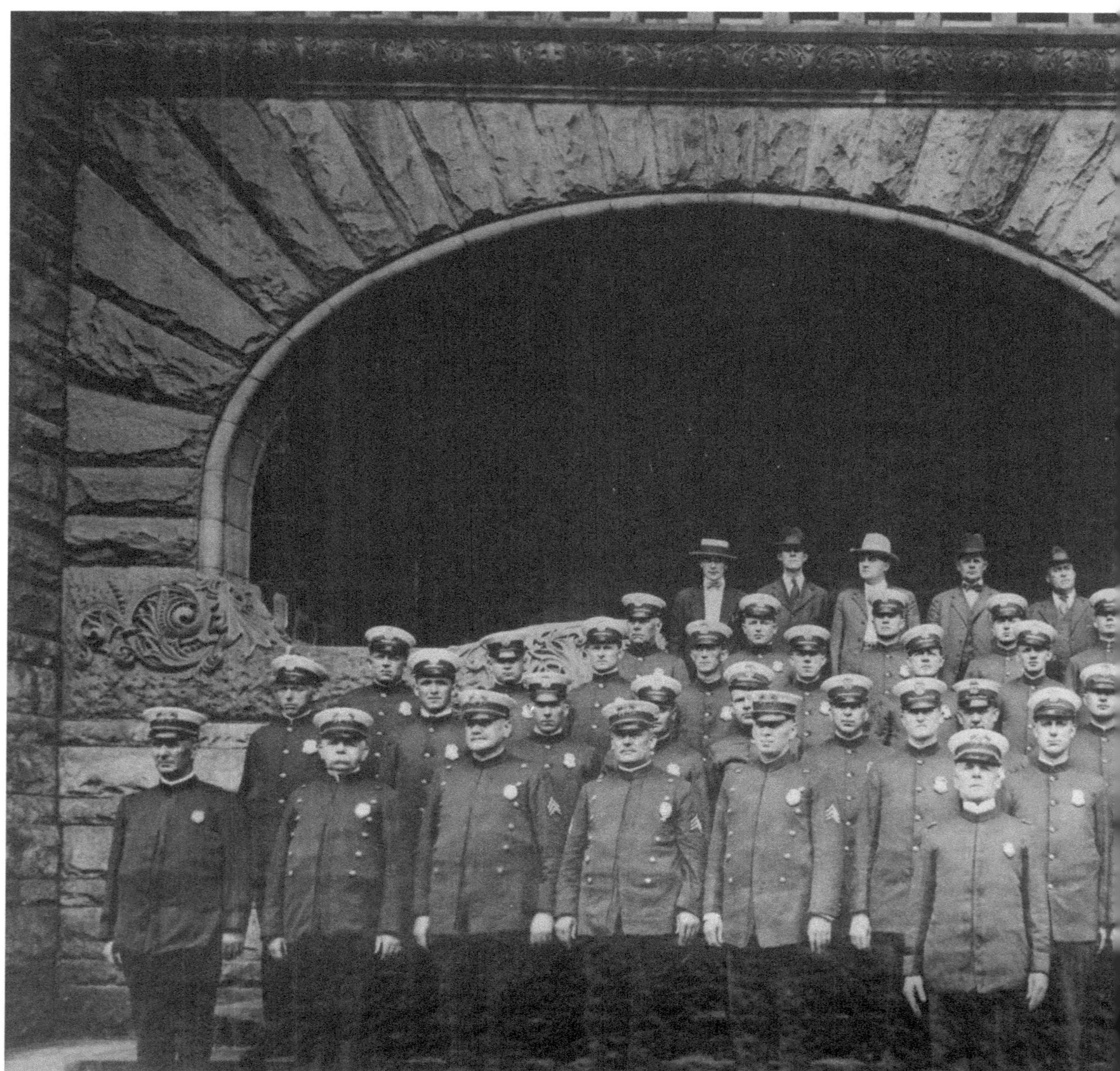

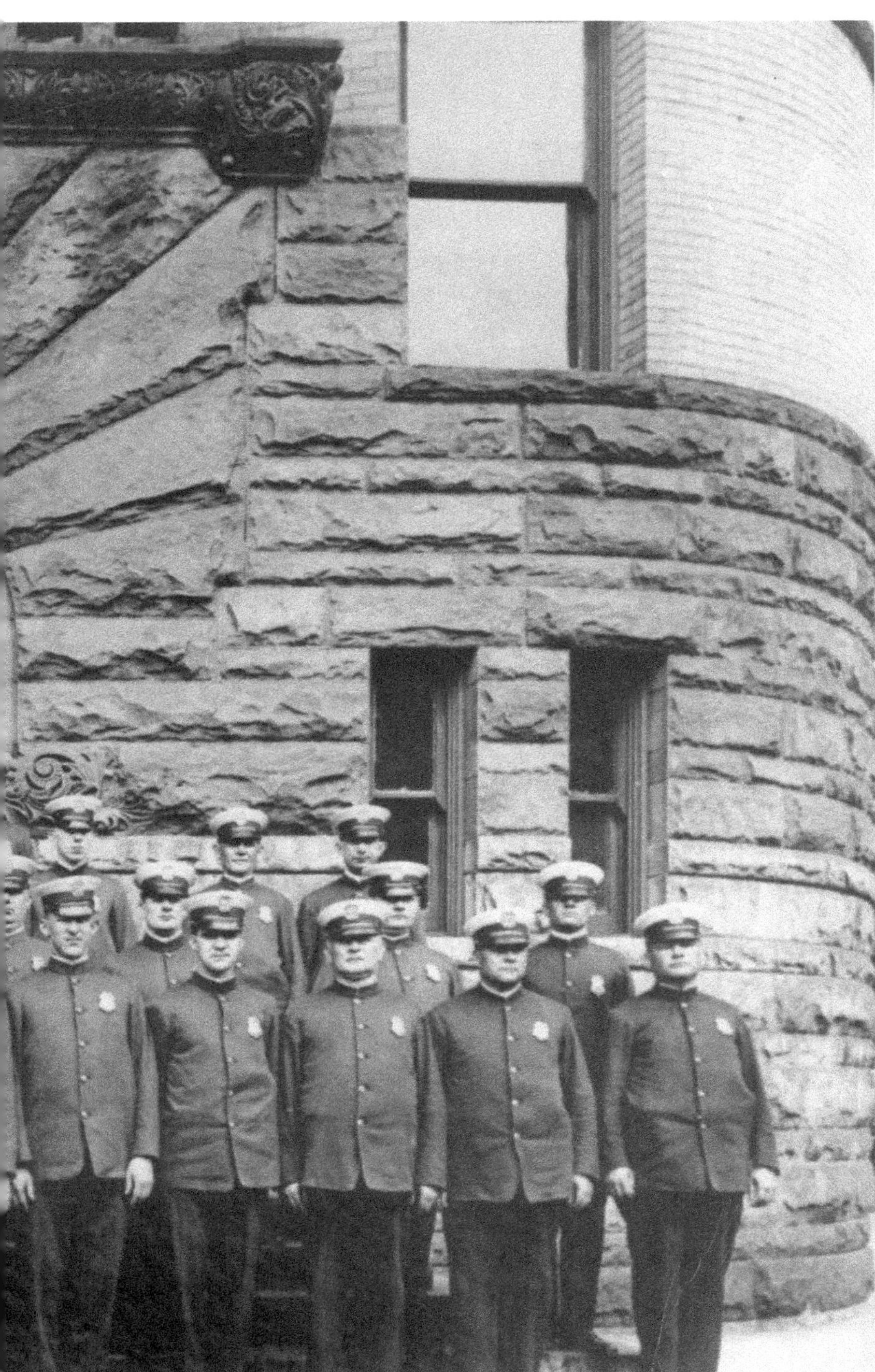

By 1898, the Winston-Salem Police Force, standing here in front of the new Forsyth County Courthouse, was as professional as any such force in the South—and snappy dressers as well!

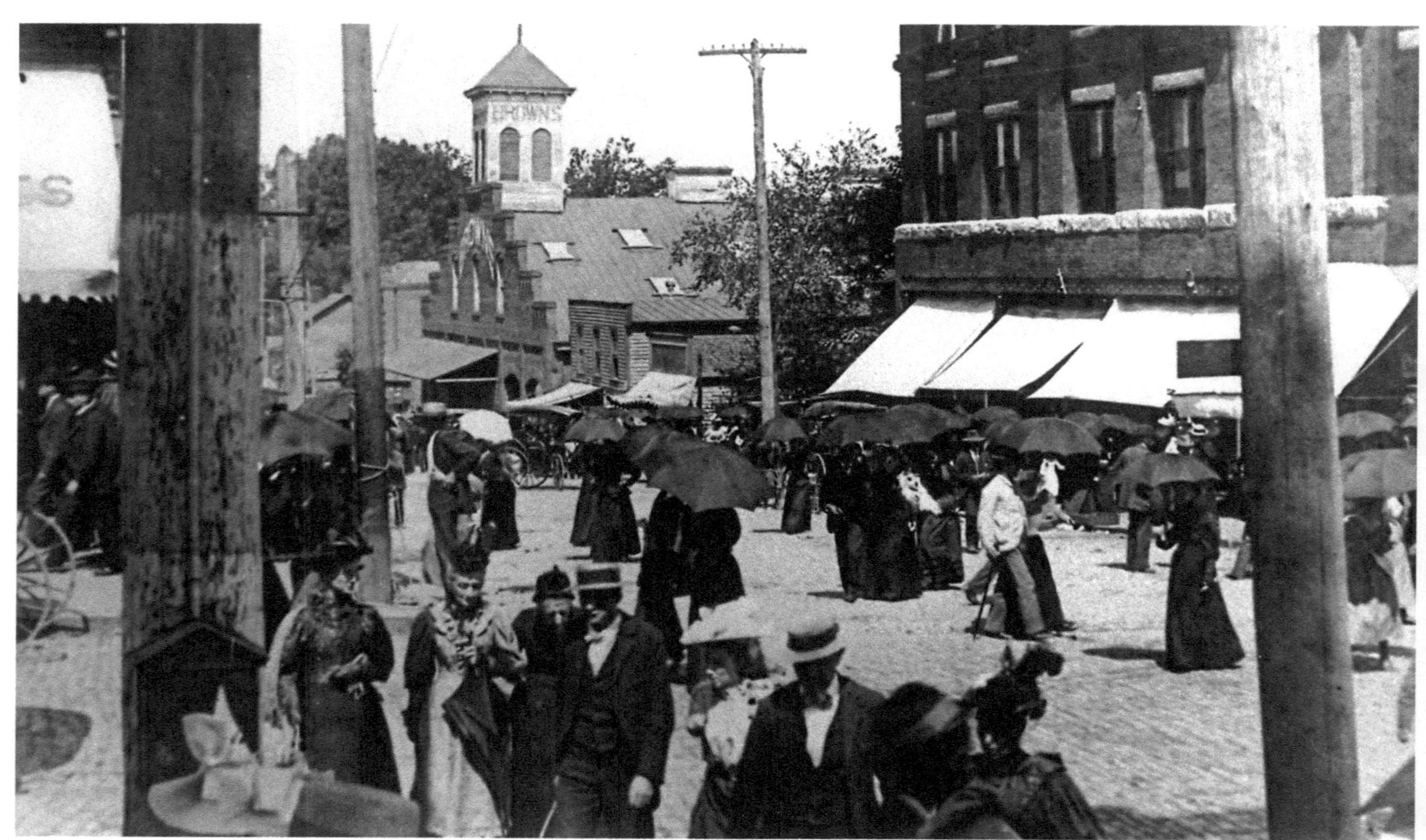

Prosperous shoppers throng the intersection of Main and Fourth streets in this 1896 photograph. They reflect the amazing growth of Winston, and the hope that marked the Gay Nineties in America.

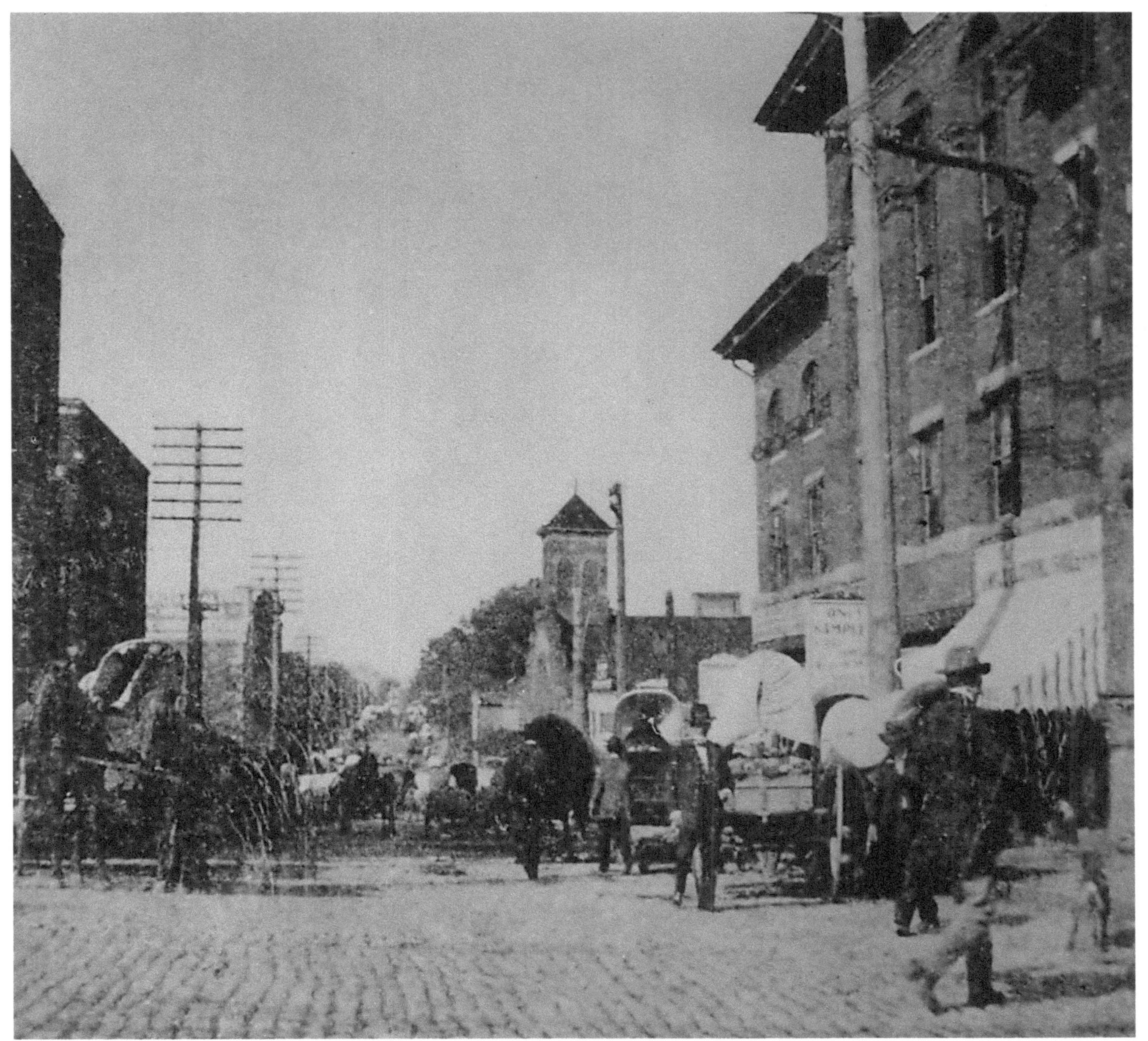

North Main Street in the late 1890s; the clock tower of City Hall rises in the center of the photograph.

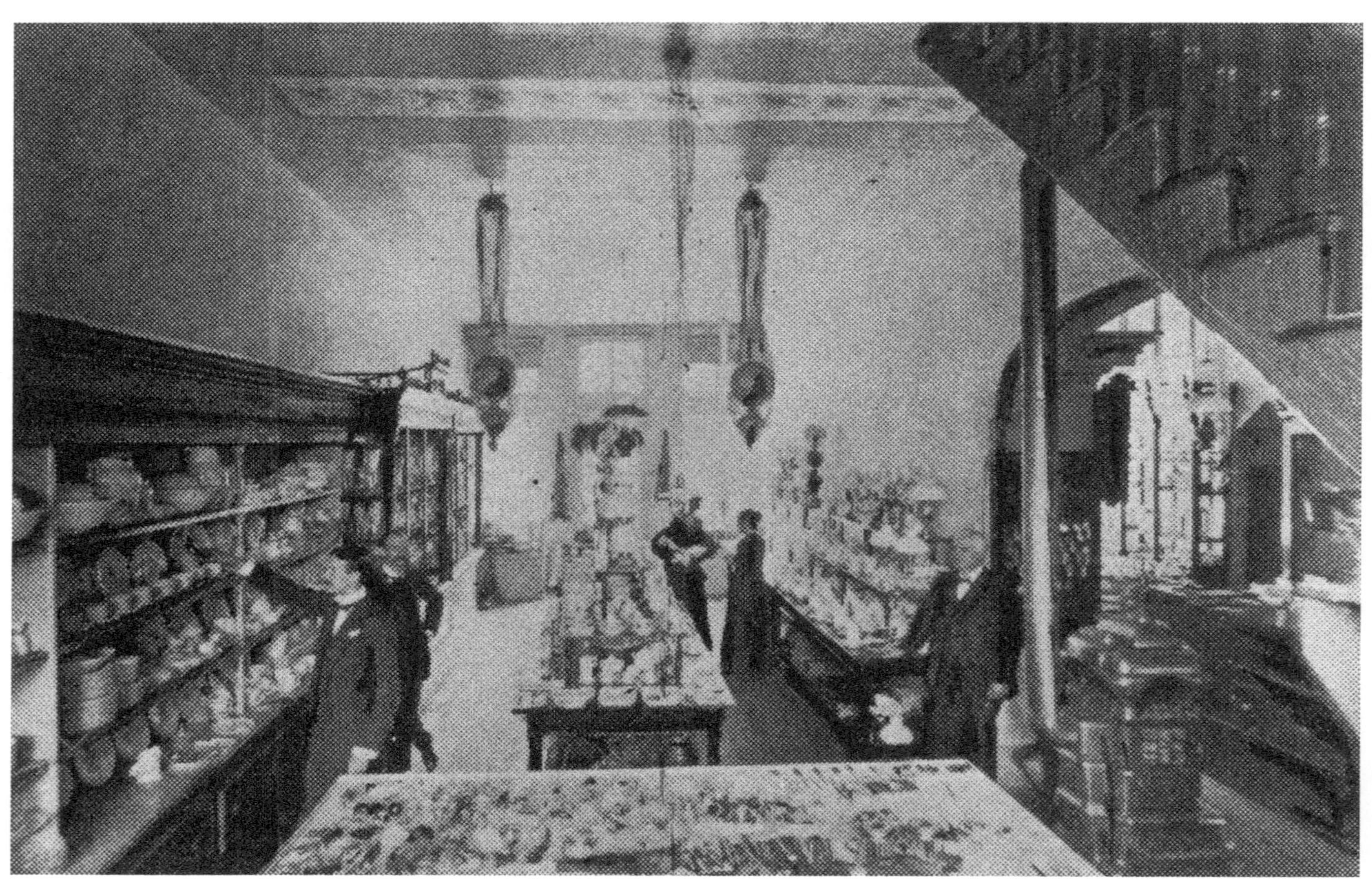

W. T. Vogler & Sons Jewelry Store, pictured here in 1899, reflects the affluence of the upper class of Winston, such as those who lived on "Millionaire's Row," a stretch of West Fifth Street extending from Pine Street to Broad Street. It would not have been unusual to see members of the Reynolds, Hanes, or Brown families in such a shop—at the expensive cases.

# The Good Times

## (1900–1929)

The Twin City prospered through the early 1900s, officially becoming Winston-Salem in 1913. In 1906, Winston featured more industrial investments than any other six cities in the state combined. That same year, mergers made Wachovia Bank & Trust the largest bank in the state, and one of the most successful such institutions in the nation. Between 1900 and 1920, the Reynolds family managed to acquire most of the tobacco businesses in the city, leading to increased efficiency and increased profitability. In 1913, Reynolds Tobacco entered the pre-rolled cigarette business with its Camel line (three other Reynolds brands failed to survive long-term). Only 1.1 million Camels made it to the streets that first year, but Reynolds produced 30 billion cigarettes in 1929.

The Hanes family sold their tobacco business to Reynolds, investing the resulting capital in textiles. Shamrock Mills, manufacturing socks in 1900, became Hanes Hosiery in 1914. Hanes Knitting Company organized in 1901. In 1913, it began production of Hanes underwear. Nine years later, the Hanes Dye and Finishing Company joined the lineup. Hanes even had its own company town, appropriately known as Hane, on the outskirts of the city.

Unlike well-planned Salem, Winston developed haphazardly—a factory here, houses there, and trolleys and utilities added as afterthoughts. But the rising industrialist elite wanted a showcase city with an appearance reflective of their wealth and status. Paved streets accommodated new automobiles by 1908, and a sewer system replaced open gutters. The first nine-story skyscraper appeared in 1915, to be followed by others, creating an impressive city skyline by 1929. Carnegie Public Library, opened in 1906, and new schools brought education to at least some of the masses. In 1919, the opening of a municipal airport, Maynard Field (replaced by Miller Airport in 1927), began a process that would eventually make Winston-Salem a transportation hub.

Yet, in a sense, the Twin City remained two cities in one with its strict segregation laws. In 1912, the city council deemed entire blocks to be for either black or white residency. An African American city emerged within Winston-Salem with its own upper-middle-class professionals, its own education system, its own bus system, and an absolute knowledge that all living therein were regarded second-class citizens in the town that their hard labor, as much as the capital of the leading families, had built.

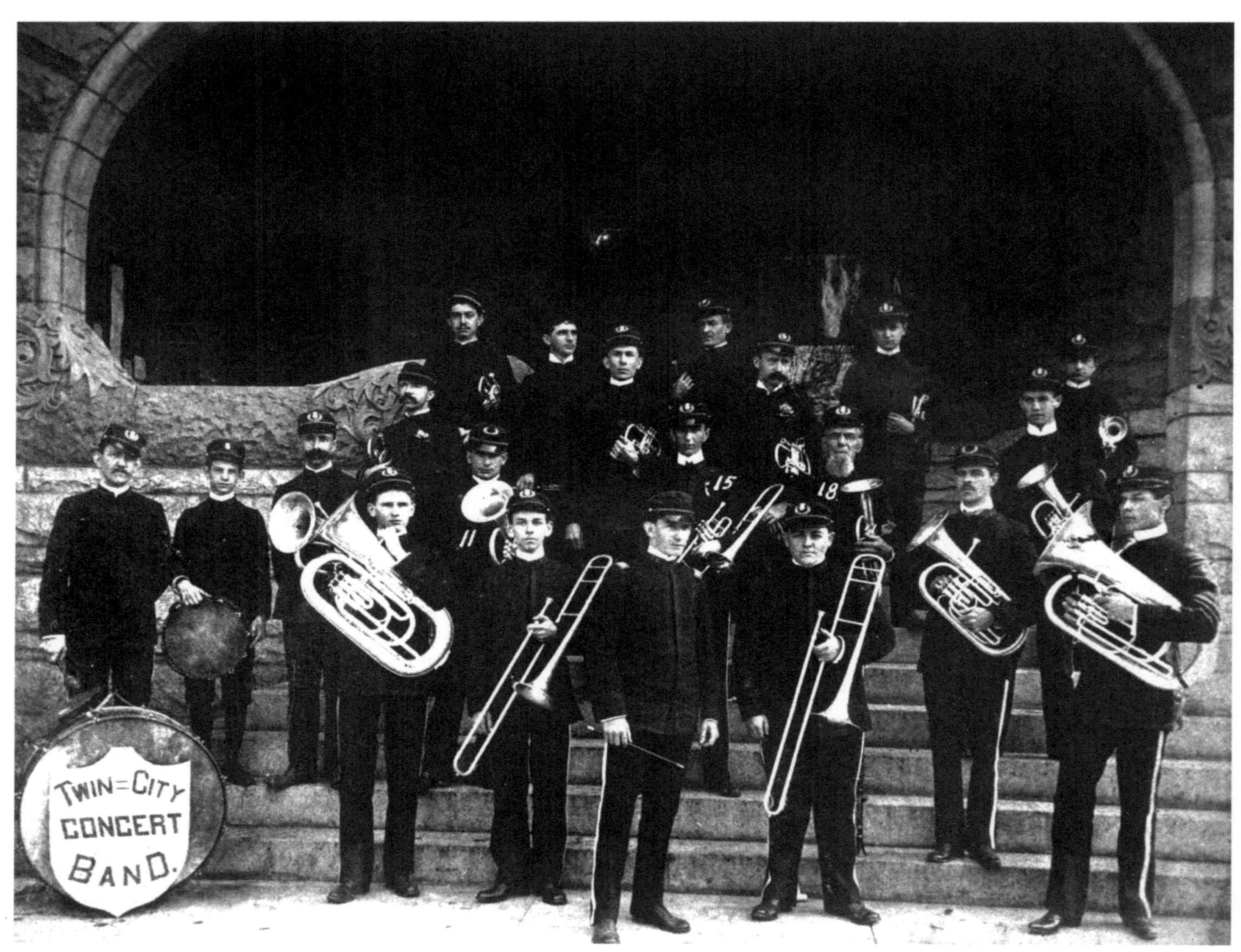


As Winston and Salem ushered in a new century, their citizens increasingly thought of them as one municipality. Thus the Twin-City Concert Band, pictured here in 1900, exemplified not just a desire for culture or entertainment but the very real desire for a merger of Winston and Salem.

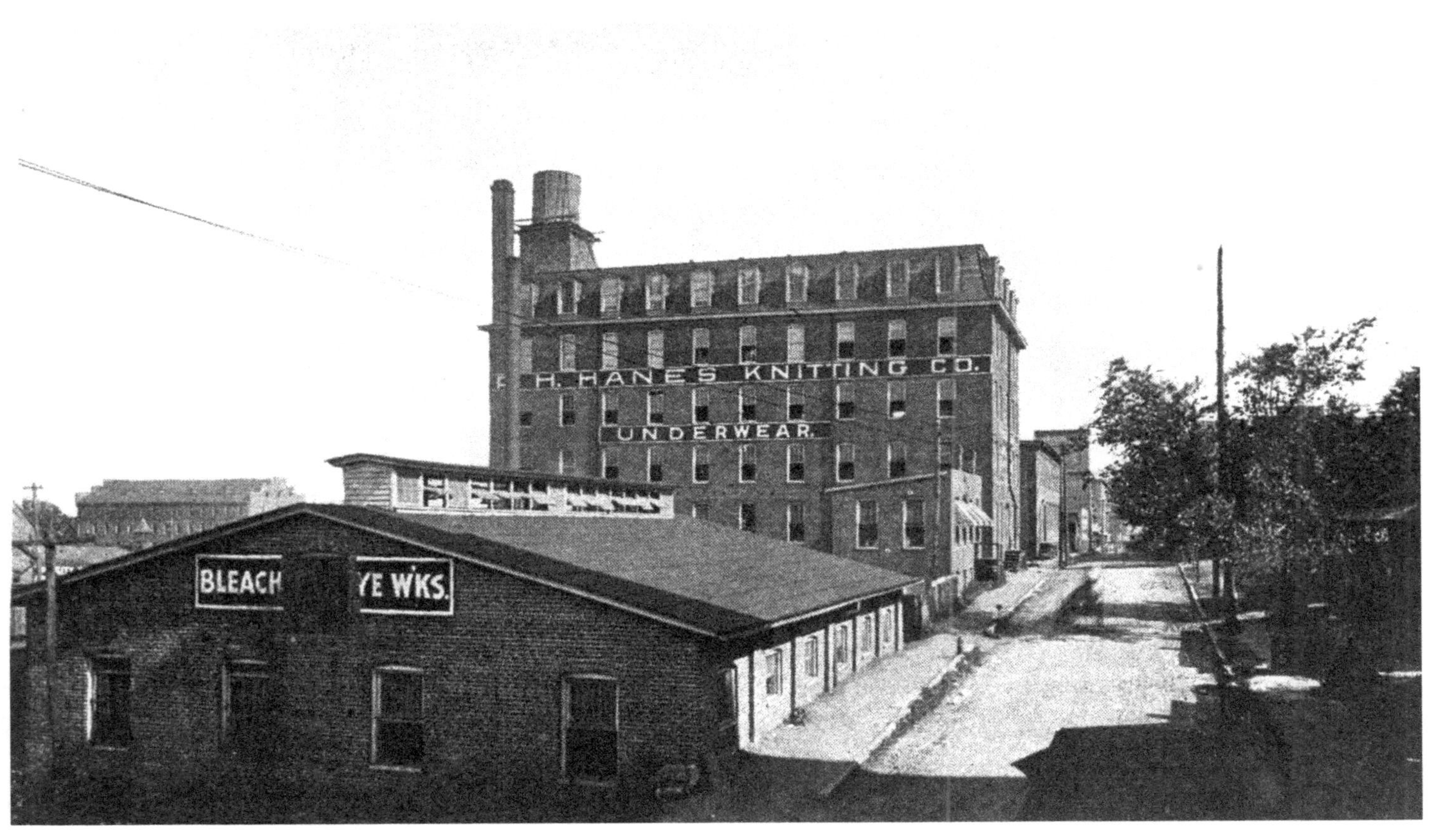


In 1873, the Hanes family opened a tobacco factory in Winston that eventually employed over 600 people and processed more than 3,000,000 pounds of tobacco per year, making it the largest such factory in the United States at that time. The Haneses sold their business to R. J. Reynolds in 1900 and began construction of P. H. Hanes Knitting Company at Sixth and Church streets. Success in the tobacco industry allowed such diversification in Winston-Salem again and again.

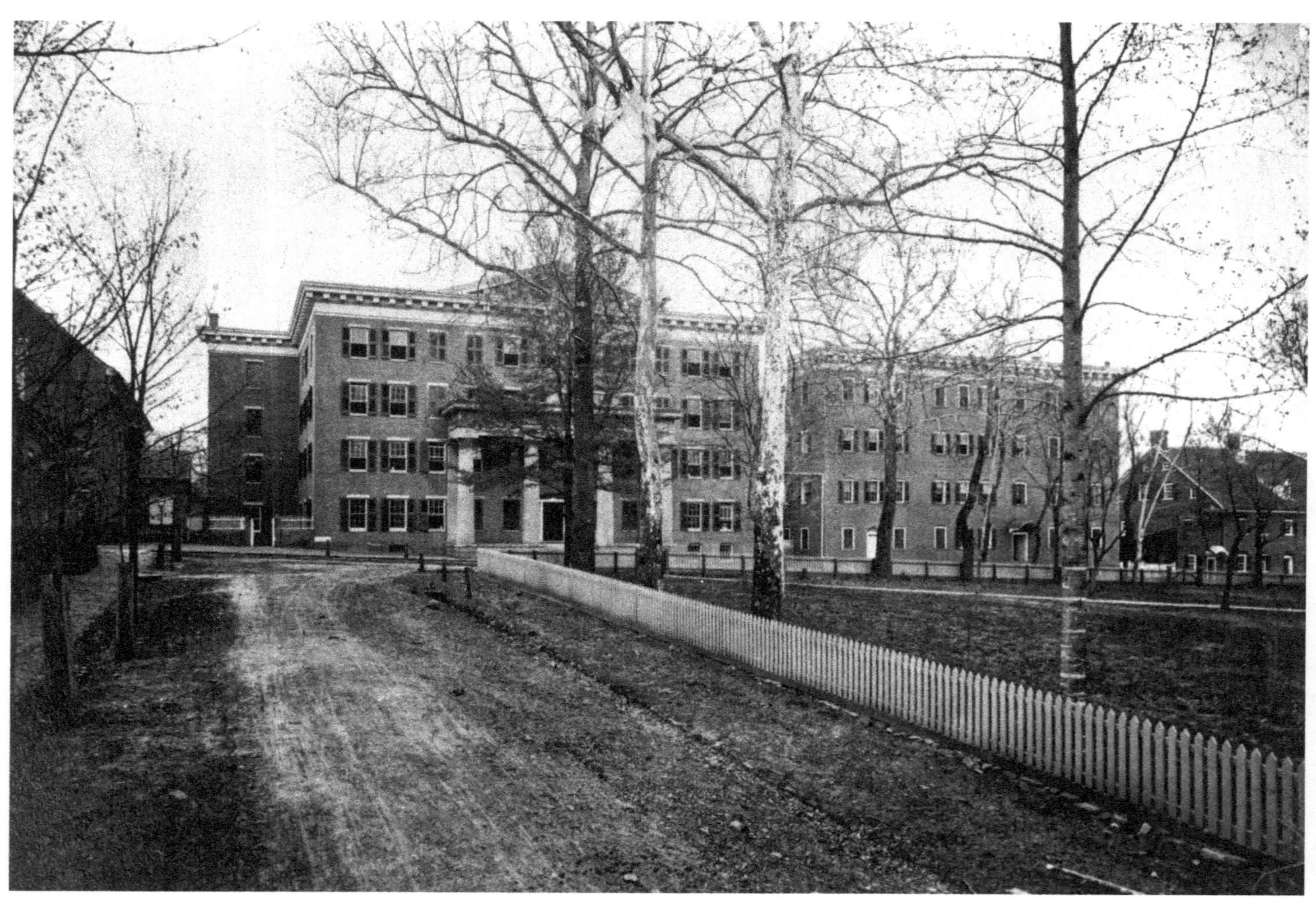

Salem College traces its roots to a Moravian school for girls, the Gemein Haus, of 1772. This makes it the oldest educational institution in North Carolina. When this photograph of its campus was taken, around 1900, Salem Academy and College included a preparatory school for young ladies.

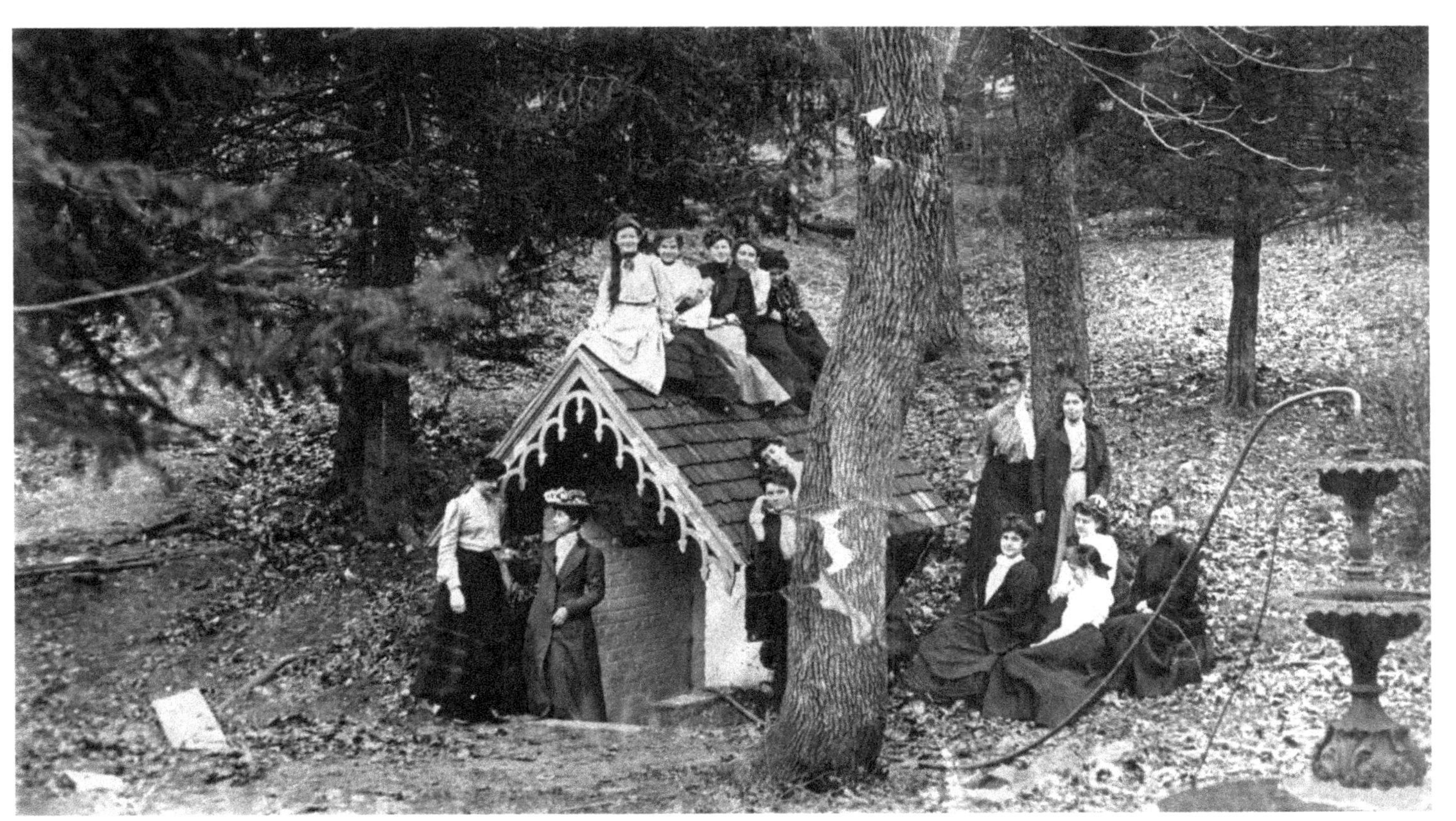

In 1903, as today, college meant socializing as well as study. Here, students relax at the Salem College Spring House.

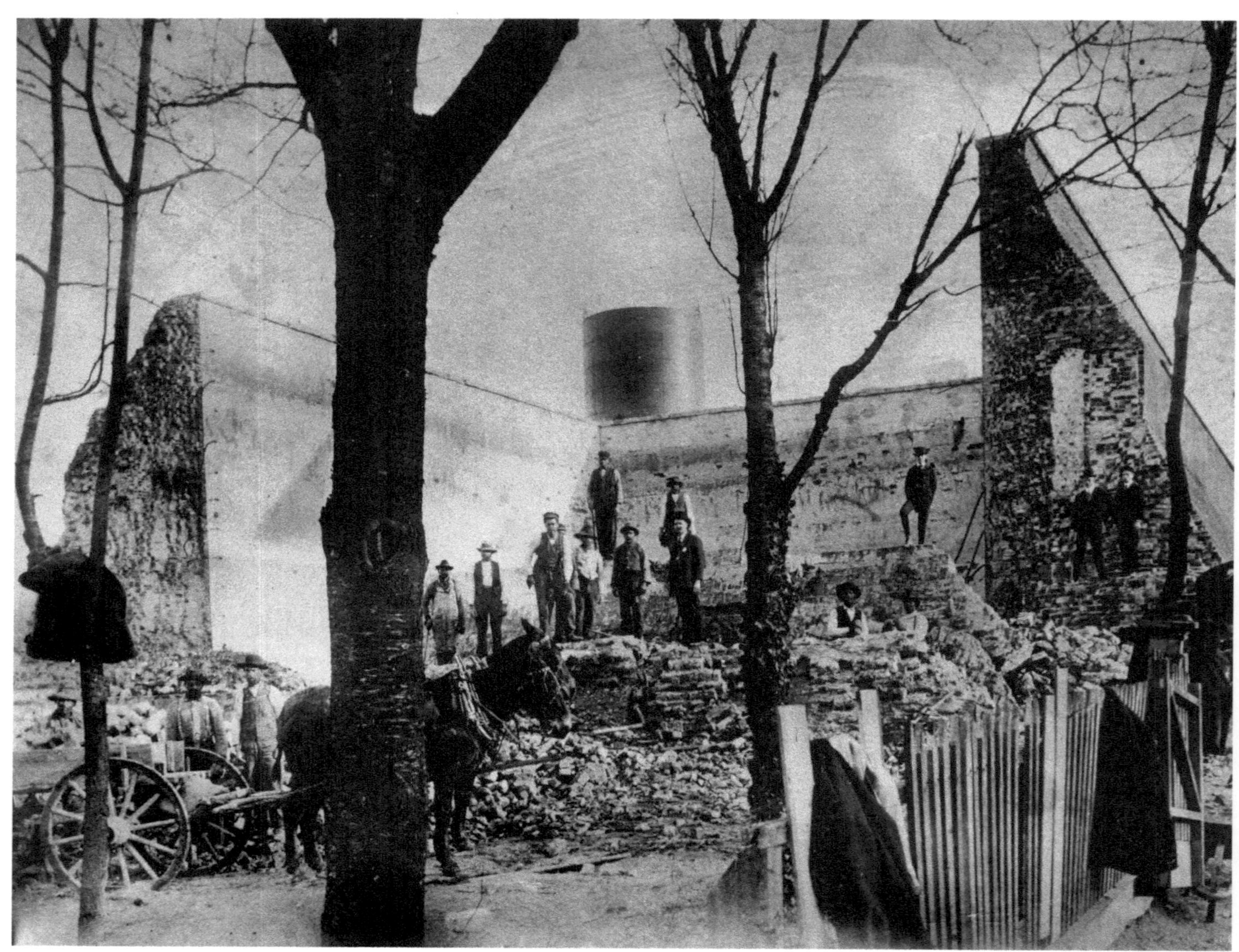

In 1882, Winston built a brick-and-cement reservoir on a hill near Trade and Eighth streets to provide potable water to its citizens. On November 2, 1904, one end of the structure collapsed, and a million gallons of water swept down the hill, destroying everything in its path.

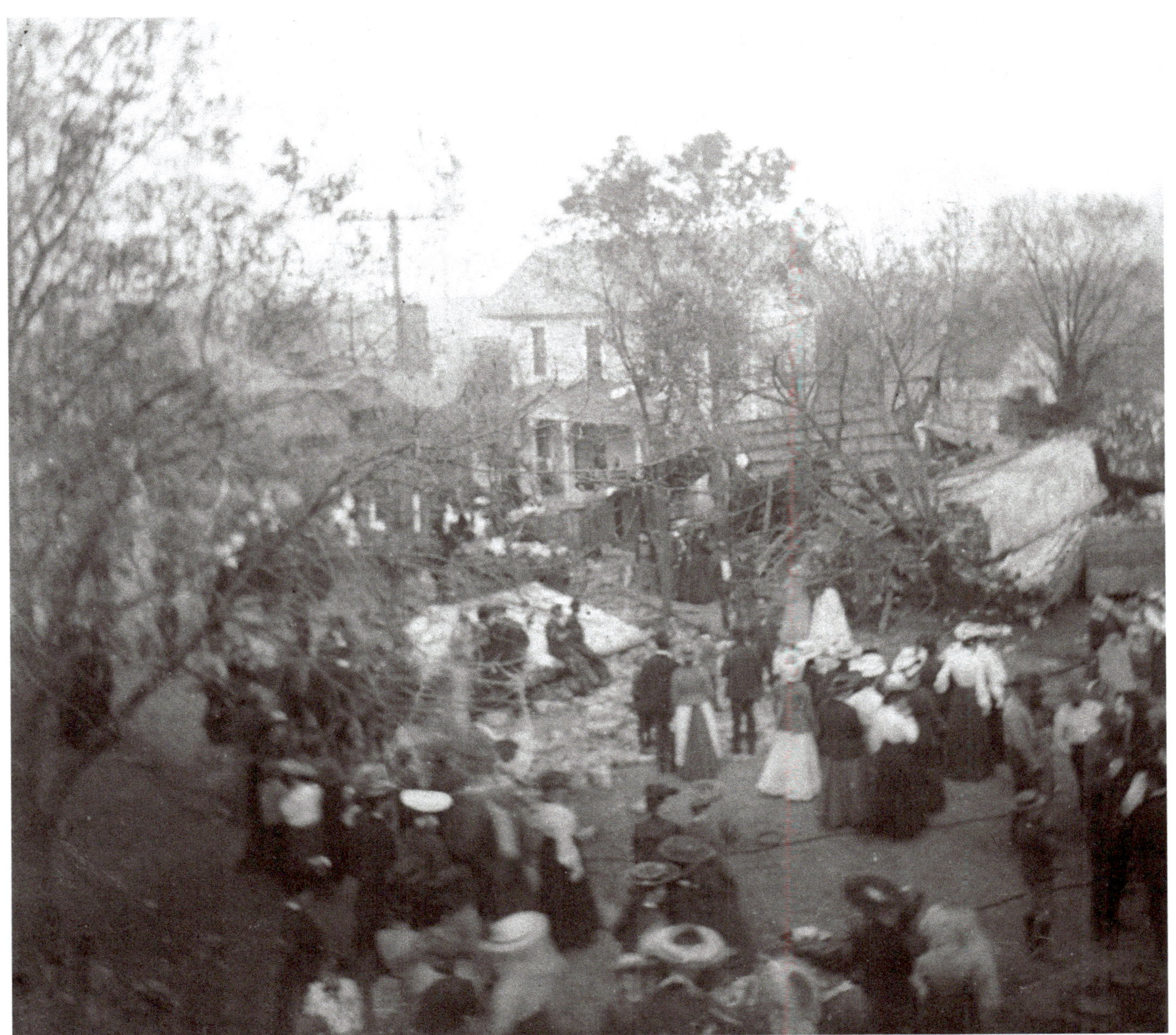

Nine people died and eight suffered serious injuries in the 1904 reservoir collapse as the wall of water swept away eight houses, all rented by black families. Searchers discovered bodies as much as a mile away from the homes. Many people rushed to help, but as this scene shows, even more hurried to gawk at the catastrophe.

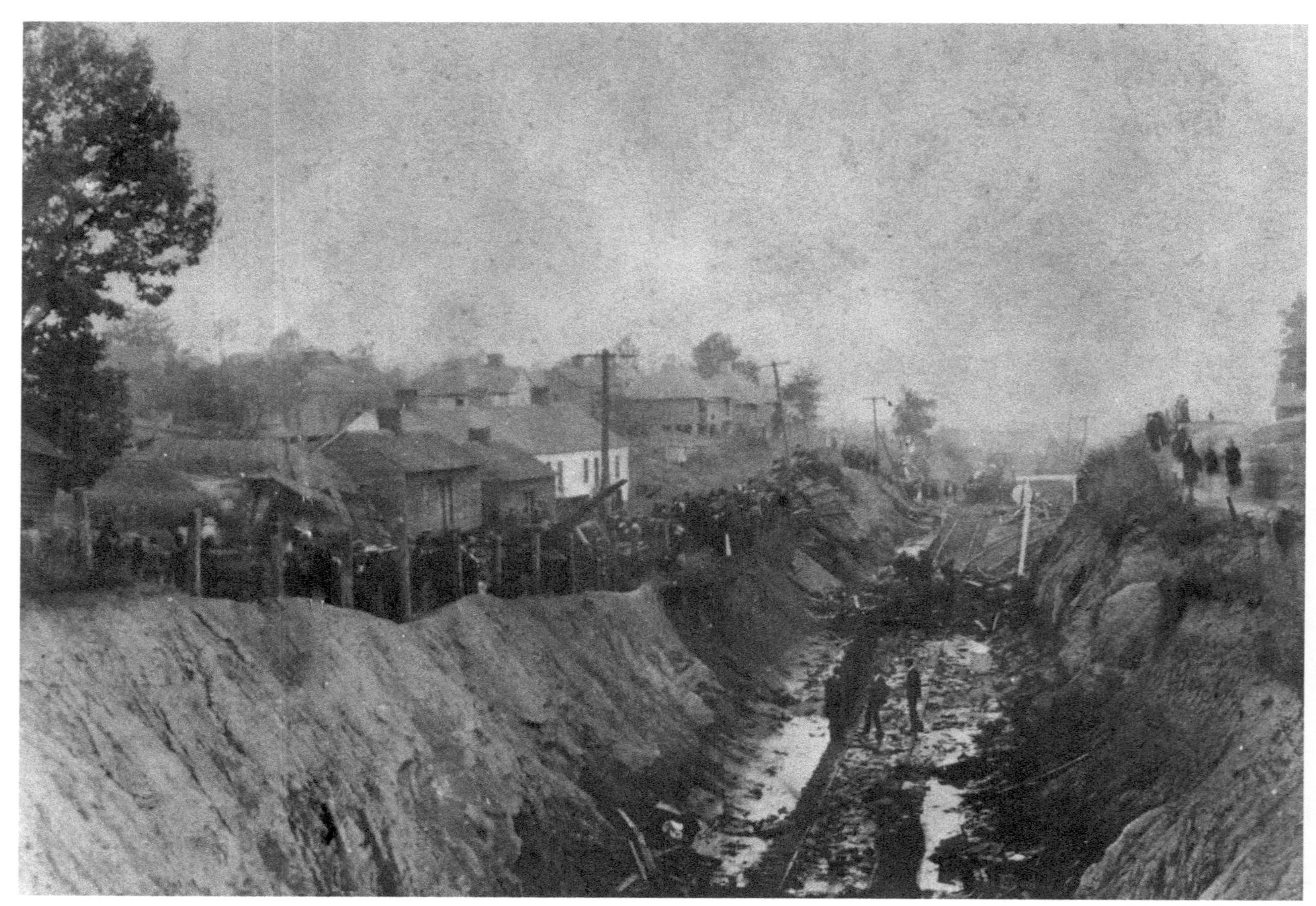

Floodwater made its way to low-lying areas, such as this railroad cut, where it disrupted commerce for days until city crews repaired streets and railroads. Surely, as the *Union Republican* recorded, November 2, 1904, marked the "Saddest Chapter in Our History."

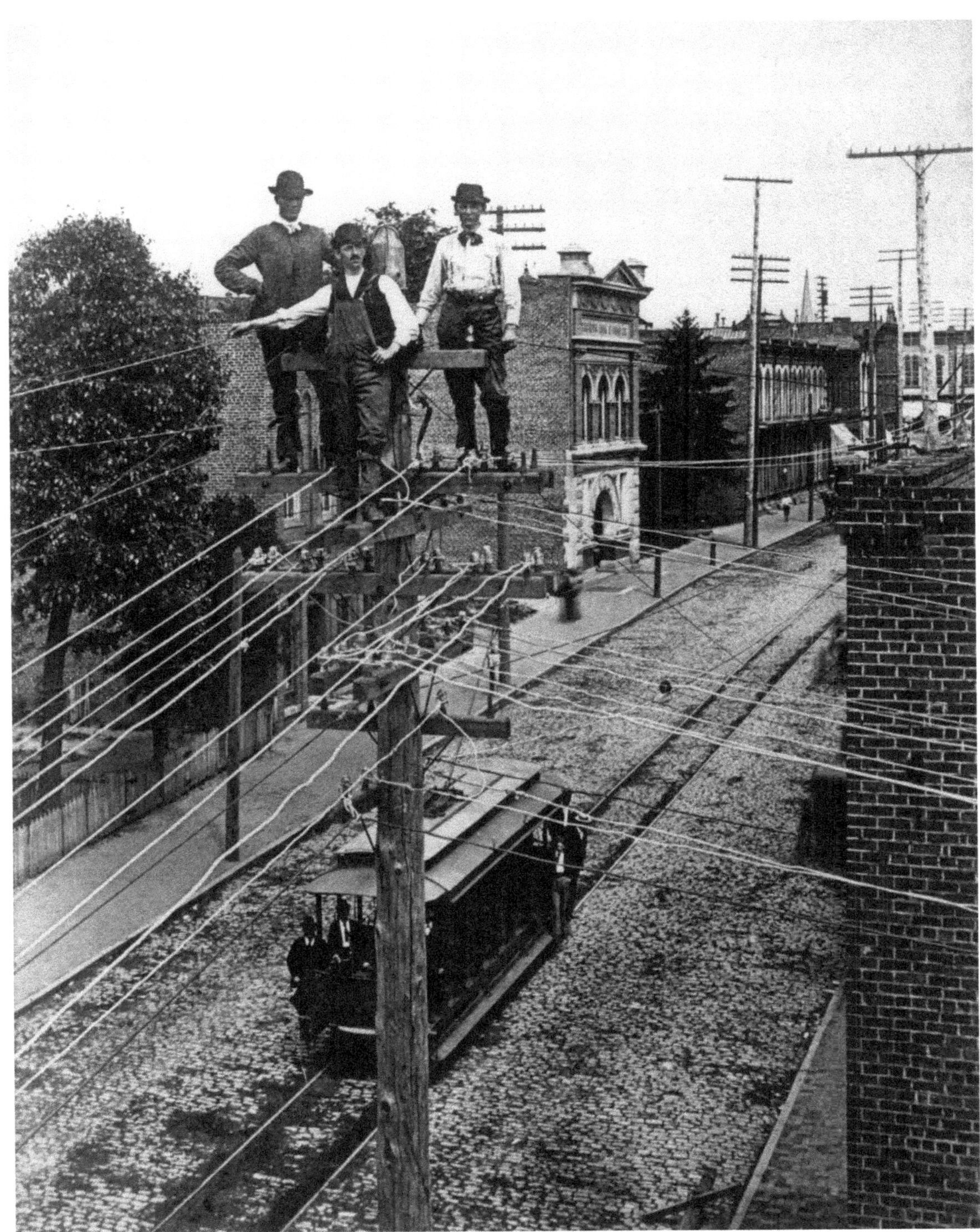

The growth of Winston and Salem can be attributed to industry, but the growth of infrastructure that industry brought to the Twin City created new specializations outside the factories. These city linemen, photographed atop their charges around 1904, kept electricity flowing to customers. Note the trolley tracks below the linemen in the photo. By 1904, such tracks lined the center of most thoroughfares throughout Winston and Salem.

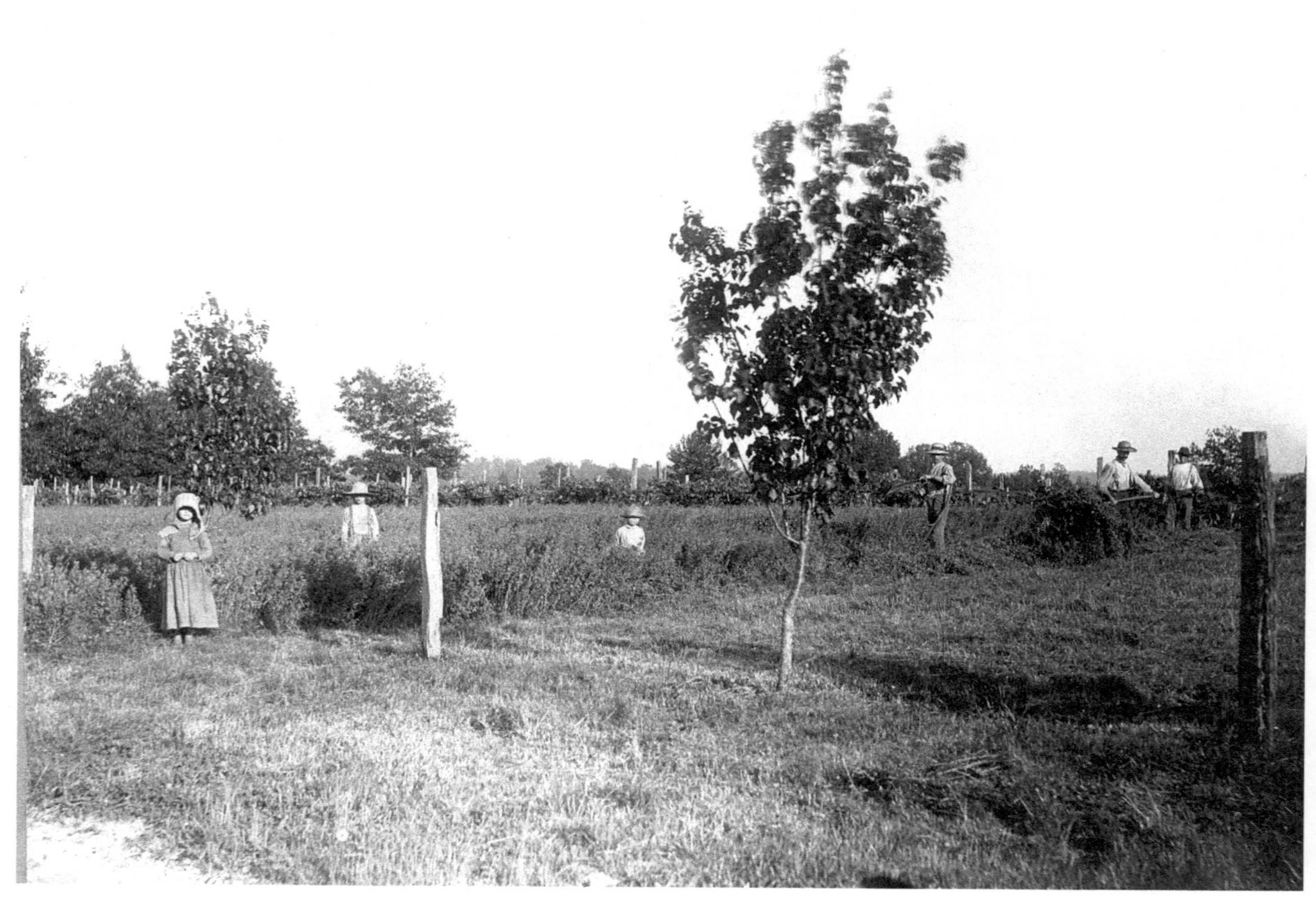

The electricity that brought light to the city flowed less readily into the surrounding countryside. There, family farms predominated and family members labored to pull crops from the soil. Though the yearly tobacco market dominated attention, many farms had truck gardens that provided fresh vegetables to the markets of Winston and Salem from April through November. In this photograph, from around 1904, young and old worked the fields together, perhaps daydreaming of a Saturday trip to town.

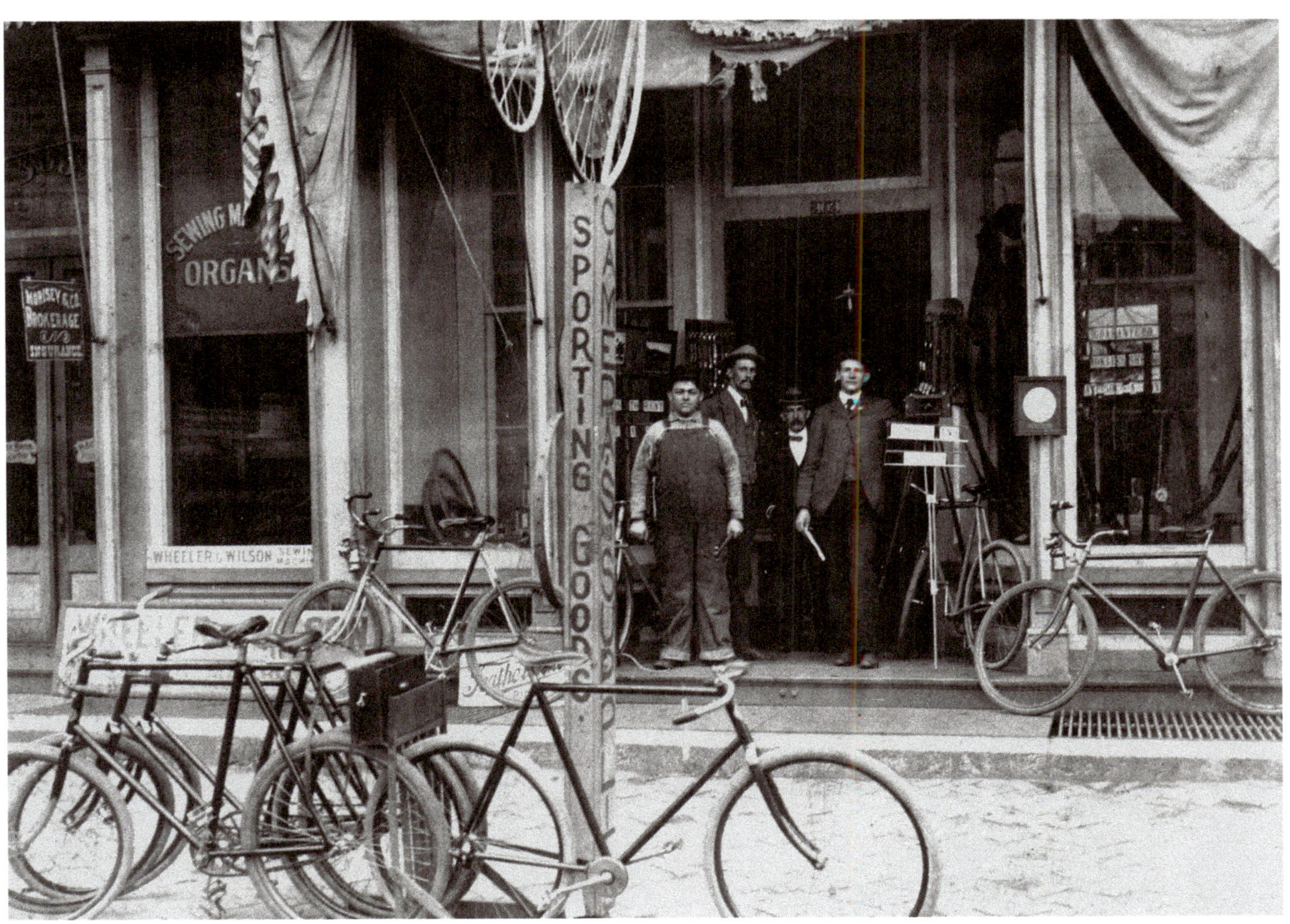


As leisuretime and wages increased for Americans across the first decades of the 1900s, businessmen sought to exploit a new market. Winston's first Golf Club organized in 1898, and Hege Sporting Goods found good profit in golf and bicycling. Though golf remained a sport of the wealthy elite for many years, bicycling became ever more practical as Winston continued to expand its thoroughfares to accommodate a booming population.

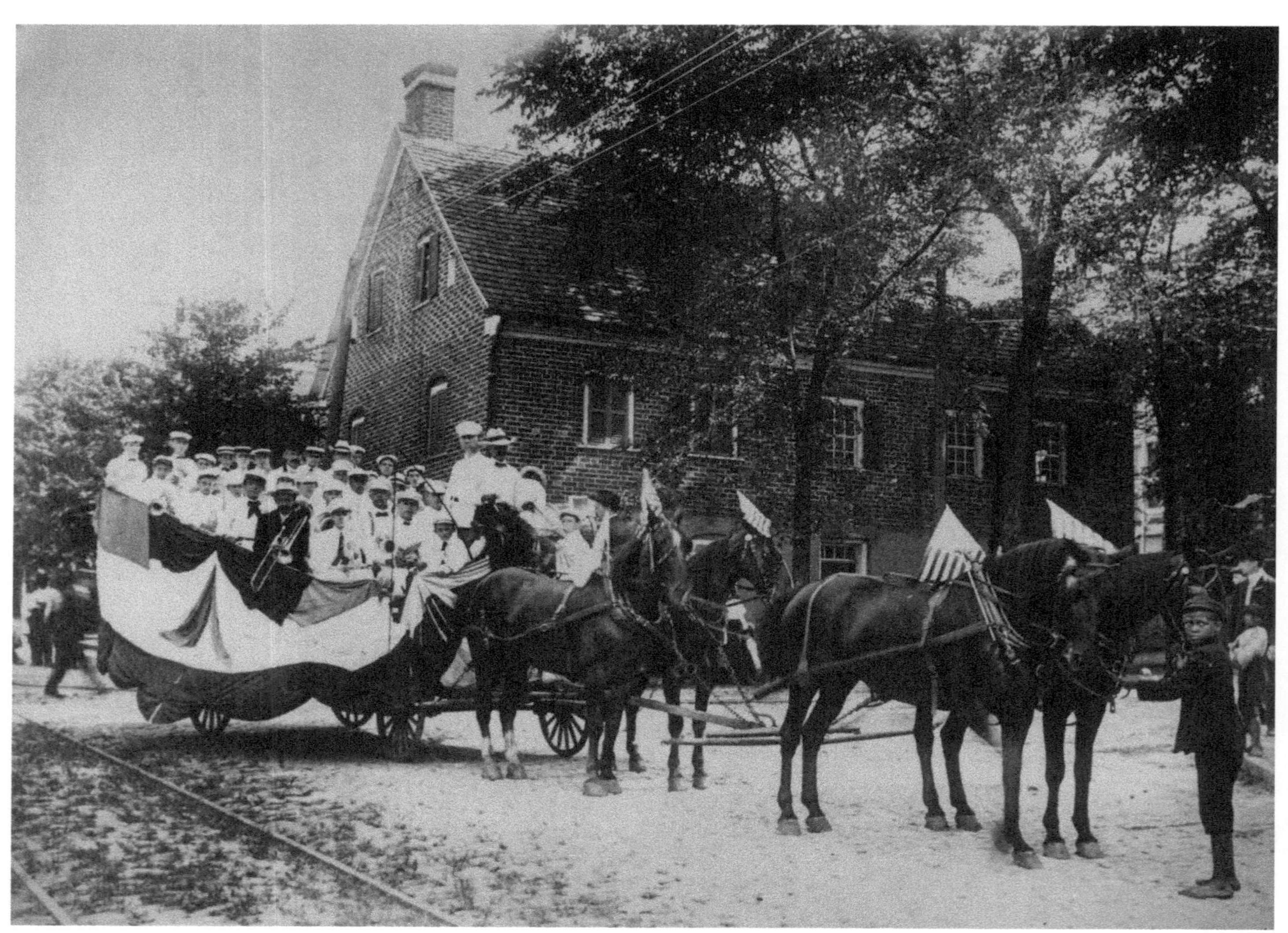

Though many citizens pushed for a merger of Winston and Salem, each town retained its unique identity through the first decade of the 1900s. Here, the Salem Bandwagon participates in a parade around 1905, possibly on Independence Day.

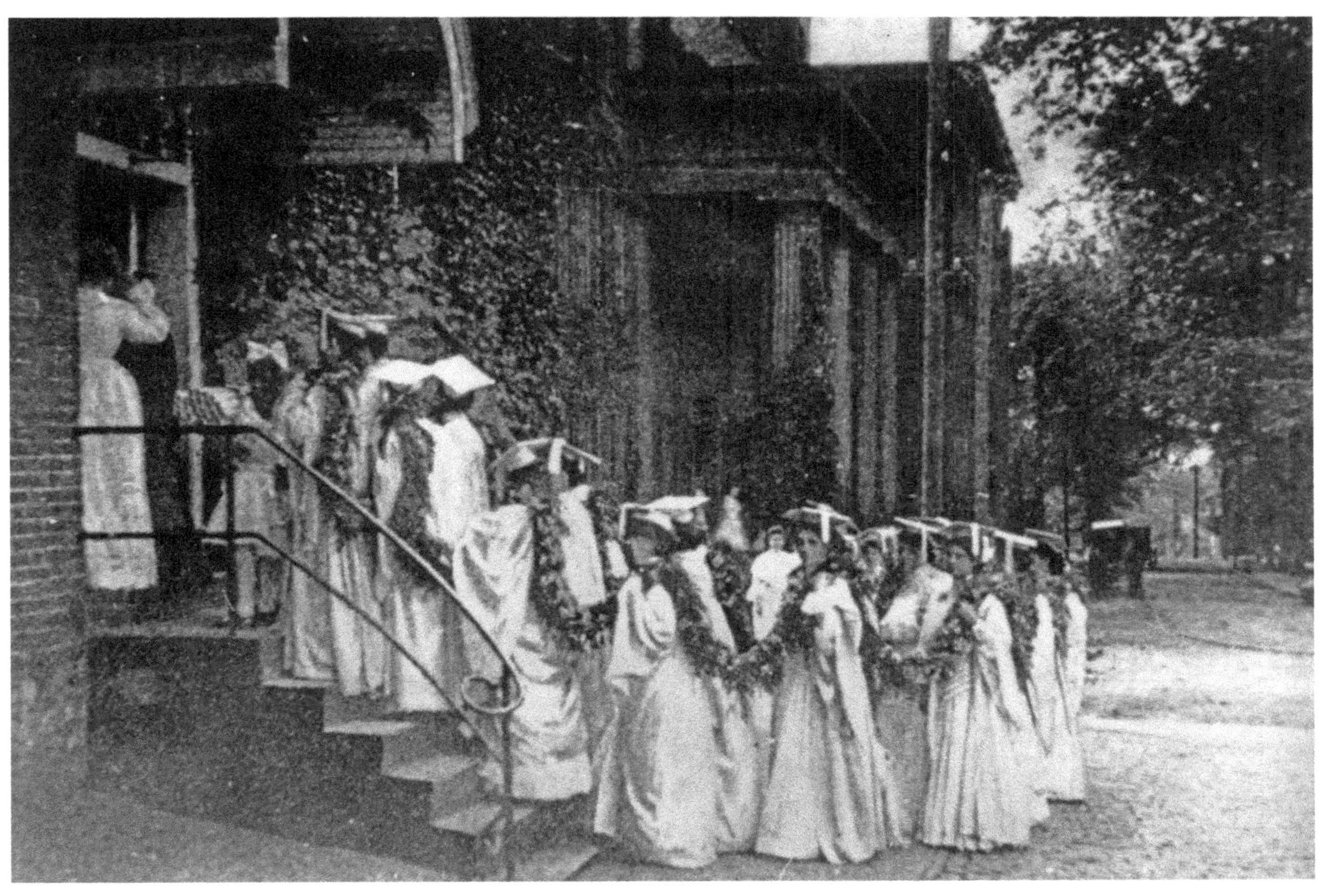

Another class of students prepare to take their place in the world in this photograph of a graduation exercise at Salem College. Dress and buildings date the photo to apparently the first decade of the twentieth century.

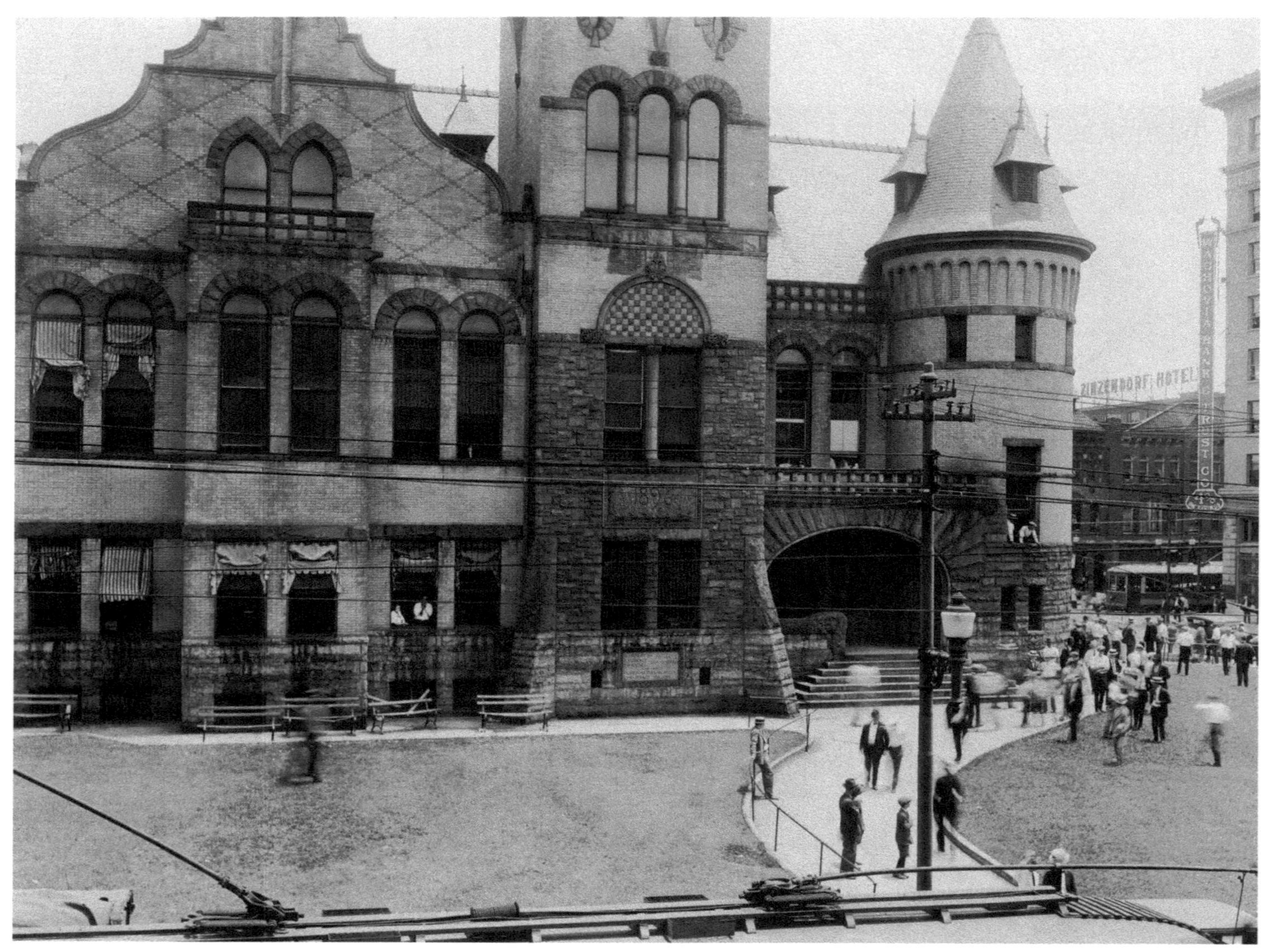


Whatever the decade, business at the Forsyth County Courthouse continued as usual, as depicted in this photograph from around 1907.

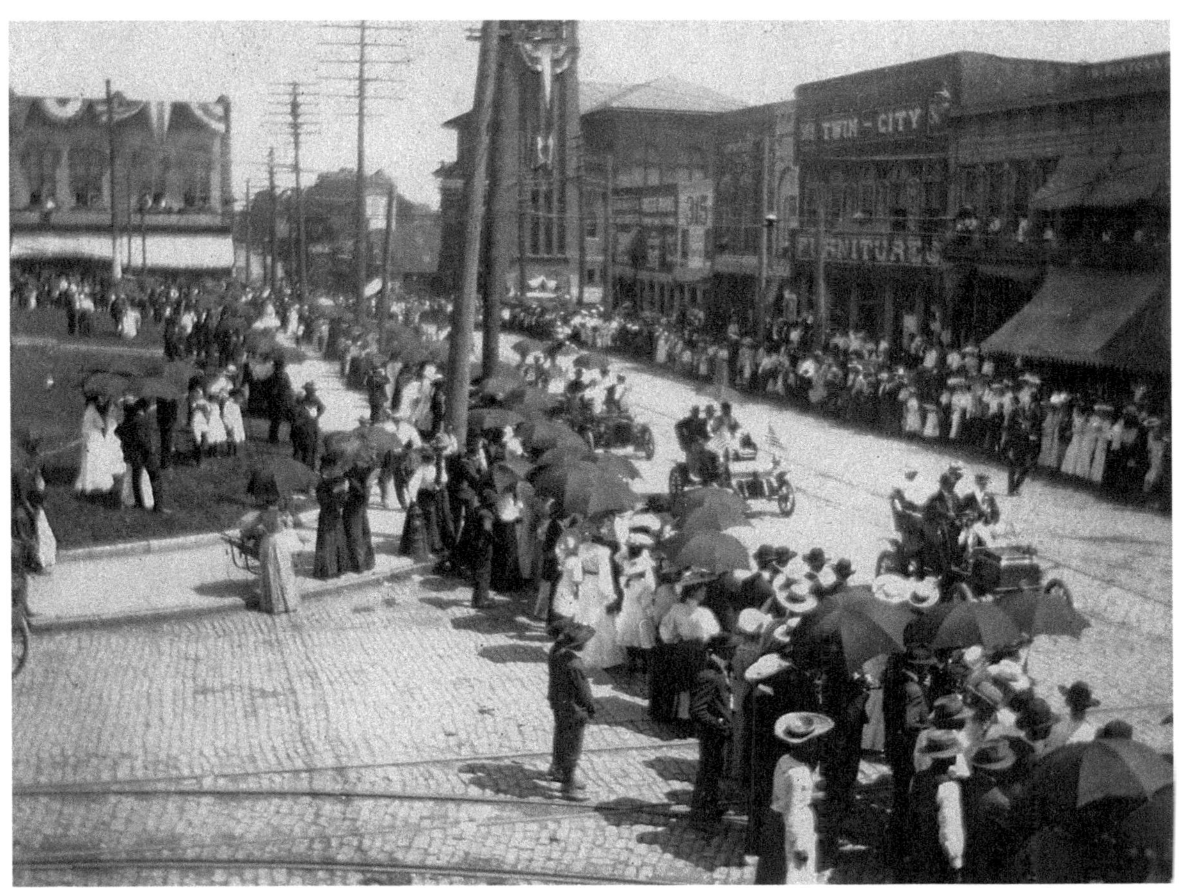


This Winston parade scene at Main and Third streets dates to 1908 or later. Gasoline-powered automobiles, beginning to appear on city streets in numbers in 1908, marked the beginning of a new phase in Winston-Salem's history, though they shared the streets with horses—and horse apples—for years to come.

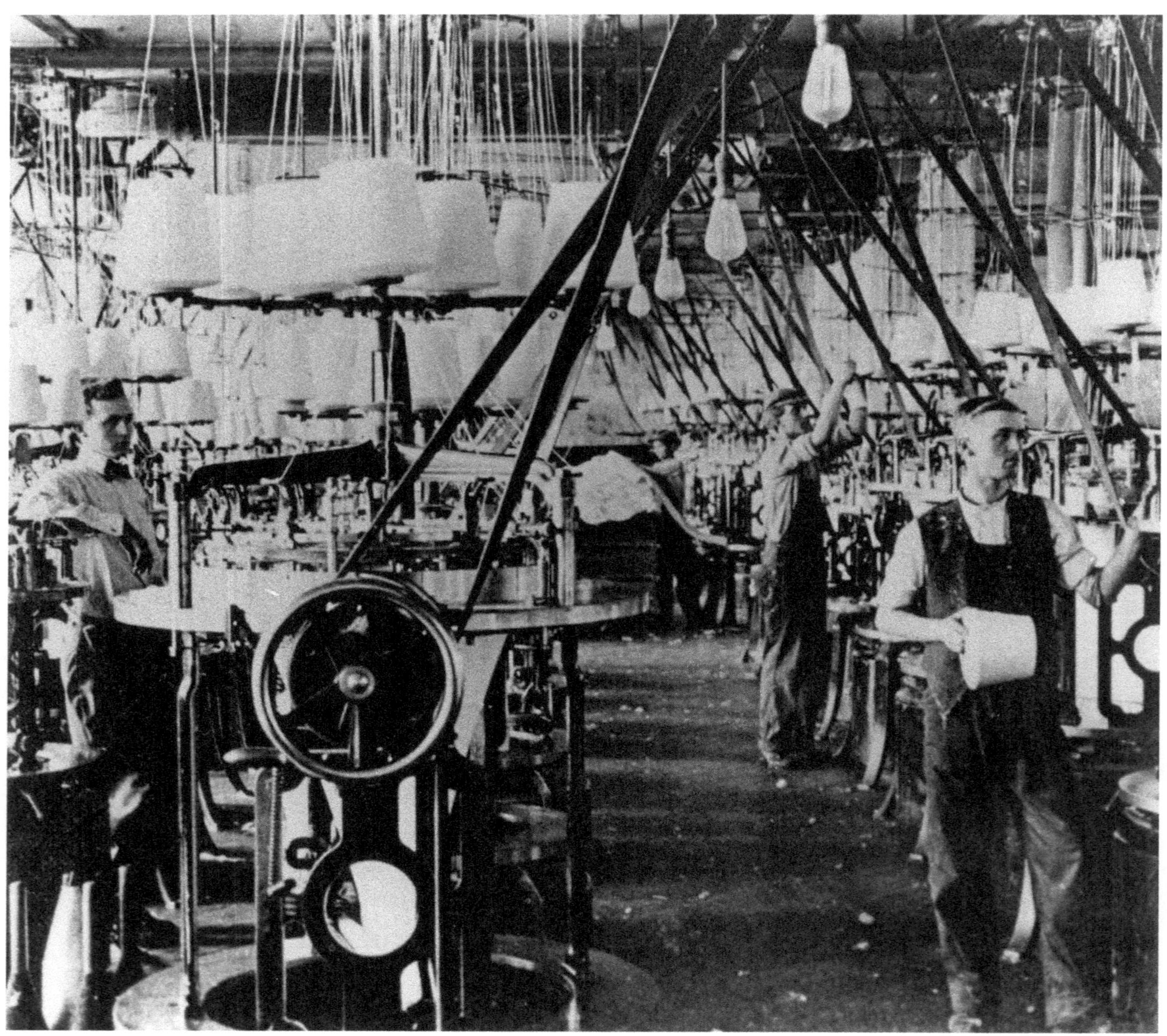

For the average factory worker in the early 1900s, the hours were long, the labor repetitive, the conditions frequently unsafe and unsanitary, and the pay meager. Many lived in company housing, when not laboring at the company's mills, and ended life in debt to a company store. Here, men operate machinery at Hanes Knitting Company, around 1905.

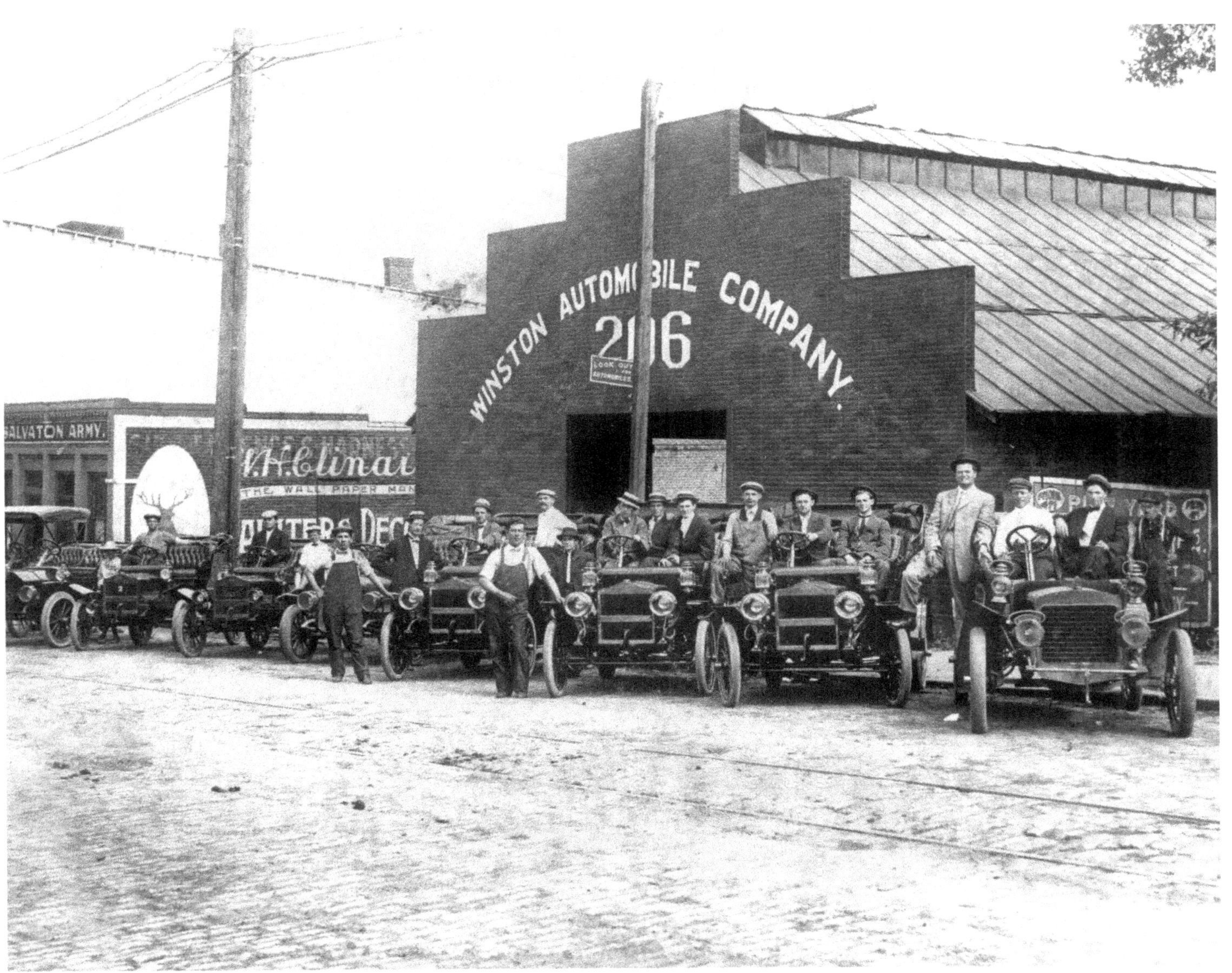


In 1908, cars began to appear in numbers on the streets of the Twin City, thanks to dealers such as the Winston Automobile Company, possibly a sales outlet for the Winston Automobile Company manufacturing firm based in Cleveland, Ohio. Over the next decade, a focus on developing and improving roads required the investment of a substantial portion of Winston-Salem's tax revenue—with near disastrous results in the 1930s.

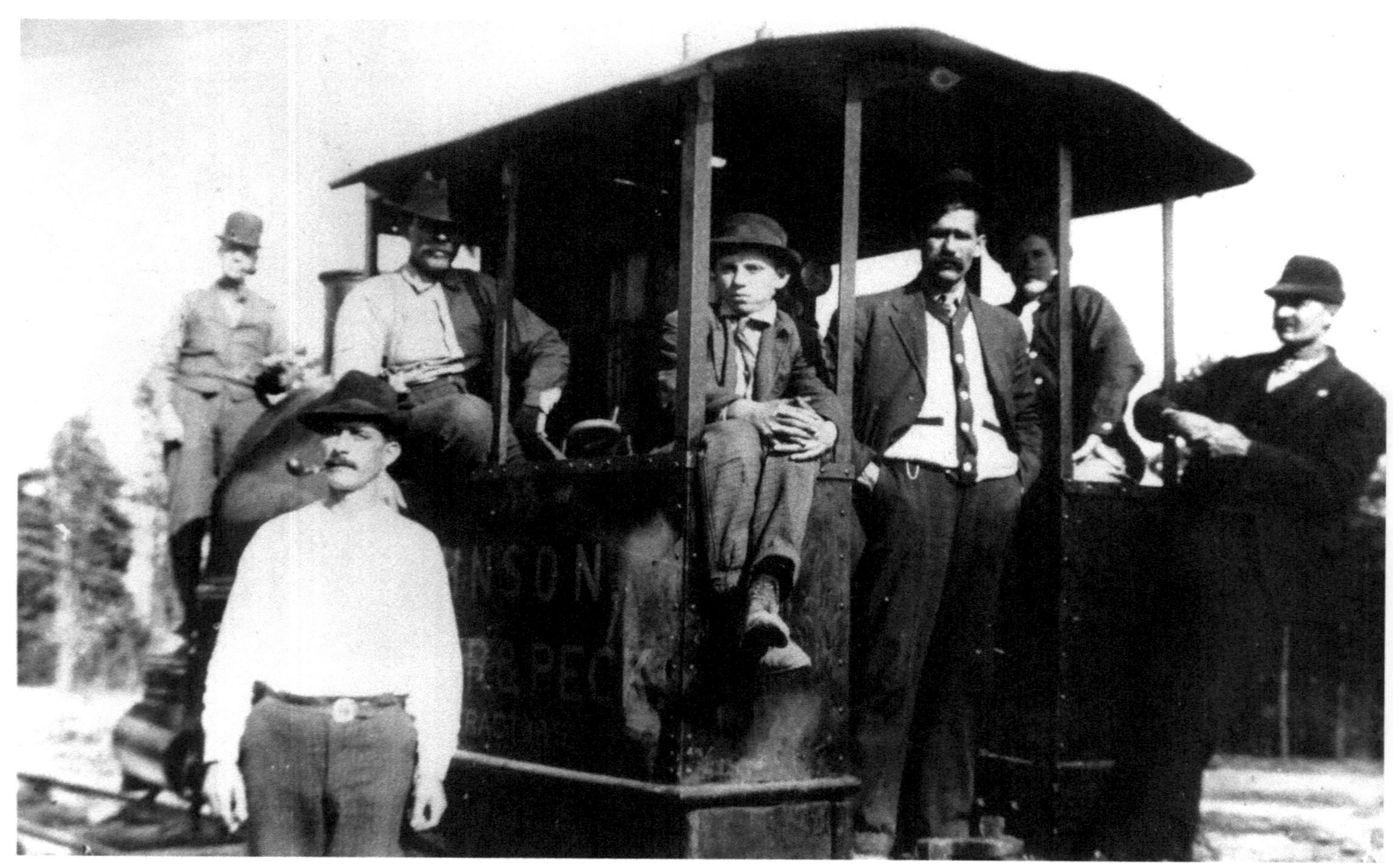

As industry thrived in the Twin City, its population boomed, and construction became a continual process, whether of factories, housing, or the infrastructure to support the city. Numerous contractors, such as Proctor & Peck, the team pictured here in 1909, found wealth in the growth experienced by Forsyth County.

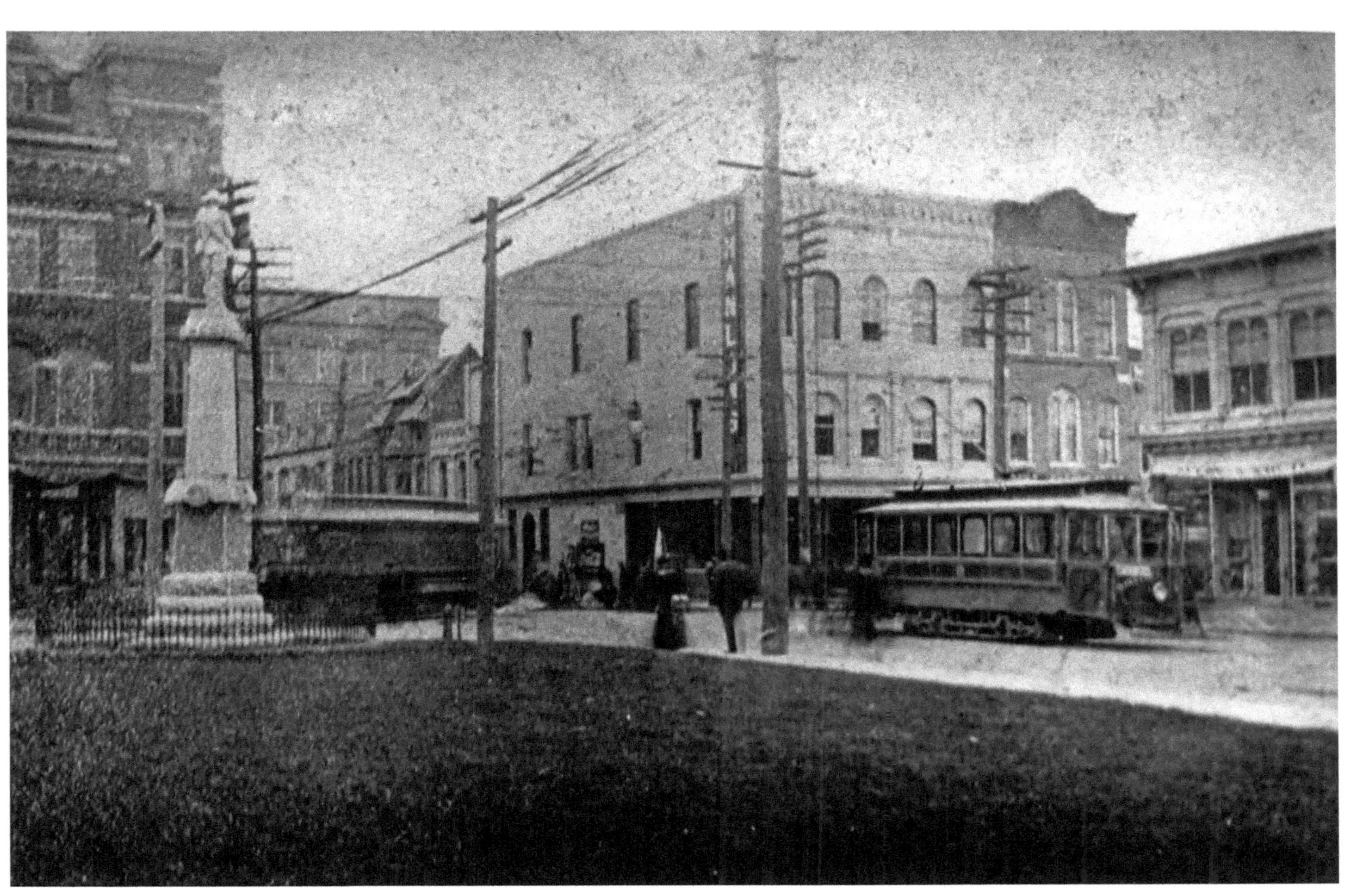

Snapped in 1909 from Courthouse Square, this photograph of Fourth and Liberty streets includes Forsyth County's Confederate Memorial, which was dedicated October 3, 1905.

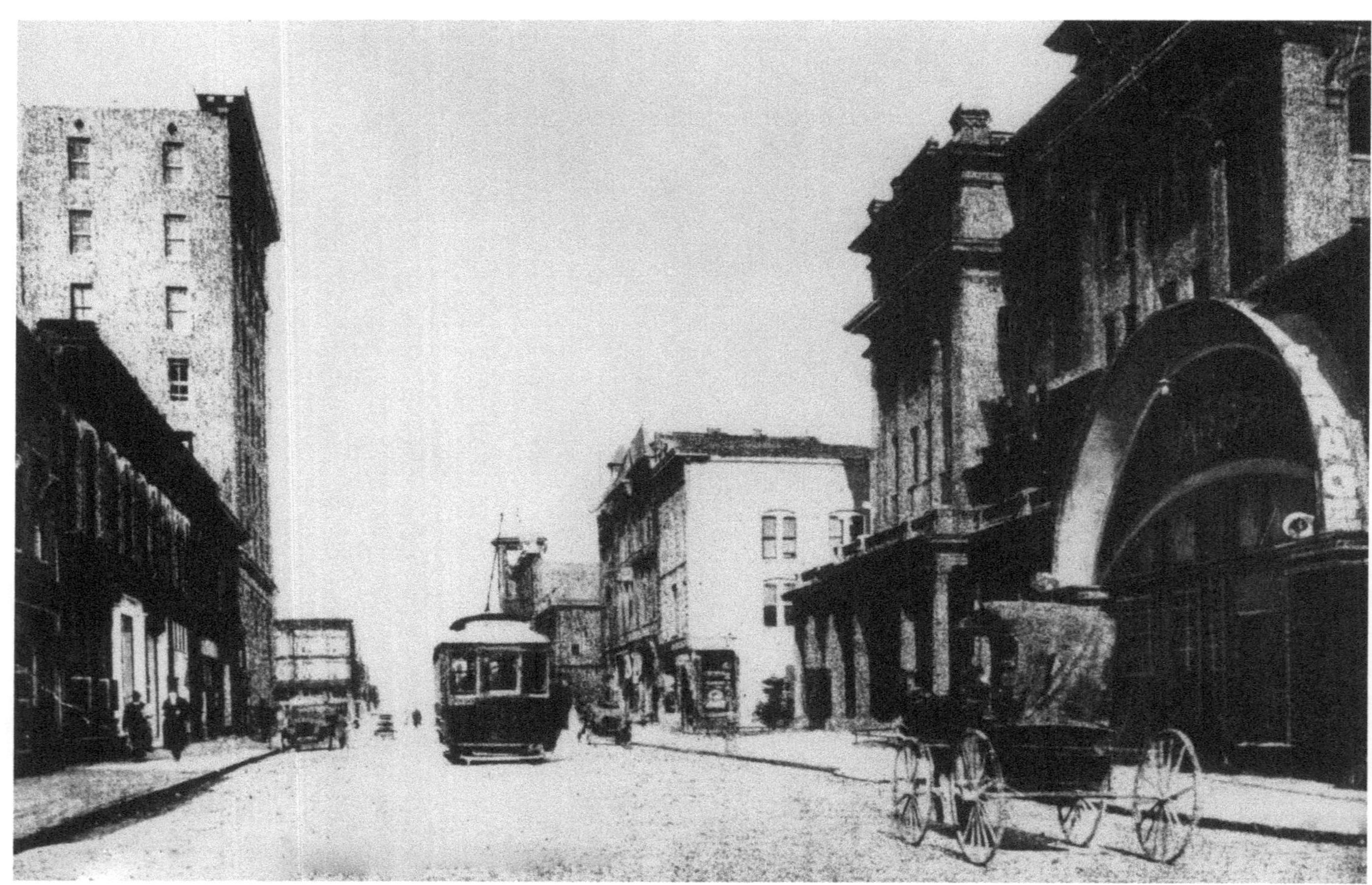

This Main Street view in 1910 captures the changes common to many American cities in the 1900s: on the right a horse and buggy plods along, in the center an electric trolley dependably moves citizens between work and play, and in the distance on the left is the automobile that will displace both horse and trolley.

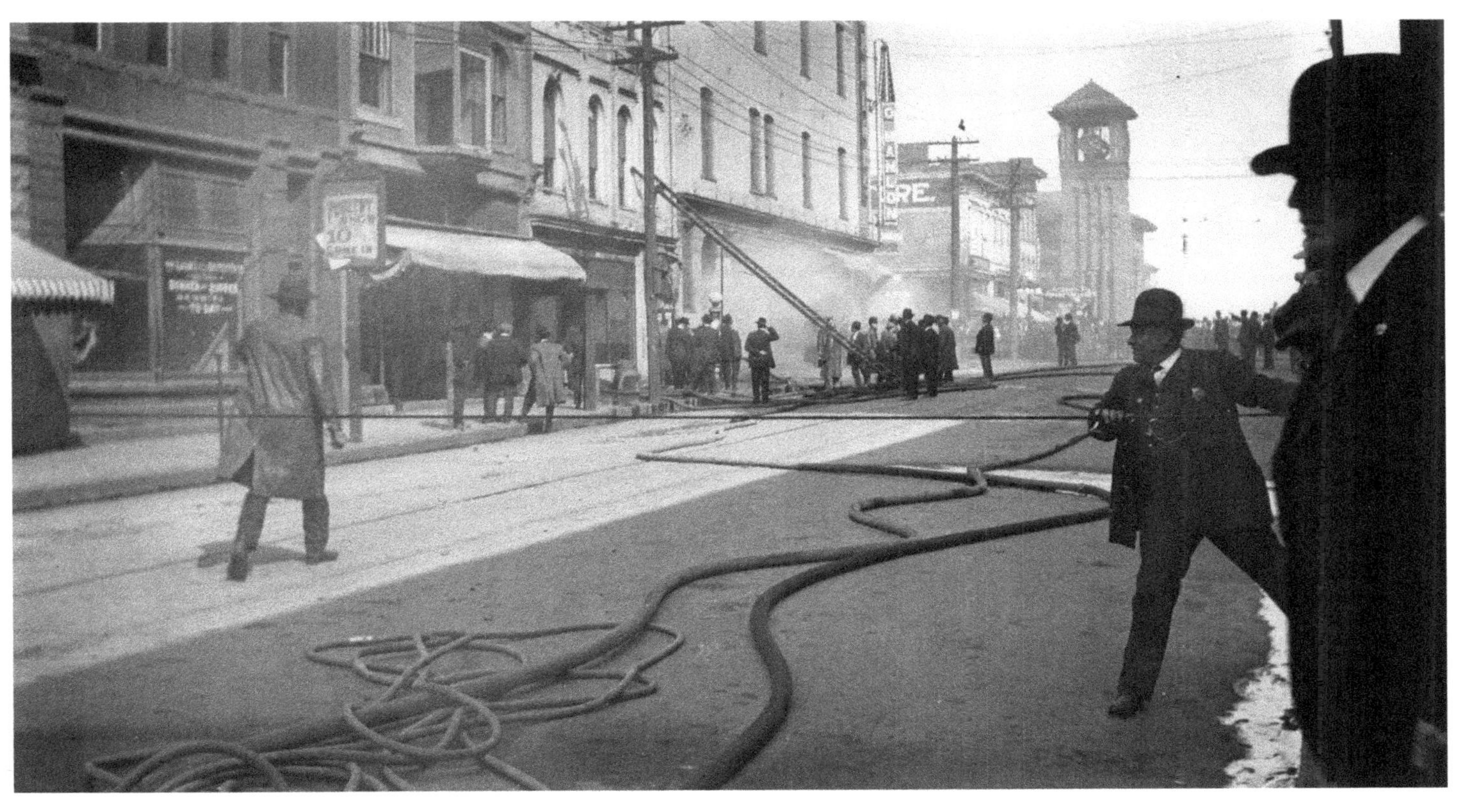

In 1913, the O'Hanlon Drug Store caught fire. Fortunately, the well-trained and well-equipped Winston-Salem Fire Department responded before the fire could jump to other buildings on Fourth Street.

Soon, however, traffic and citizens blocked access to the O'Hanlon fire. Unable to save the structure, firemen sought to control the blaze until additional units could arrive.

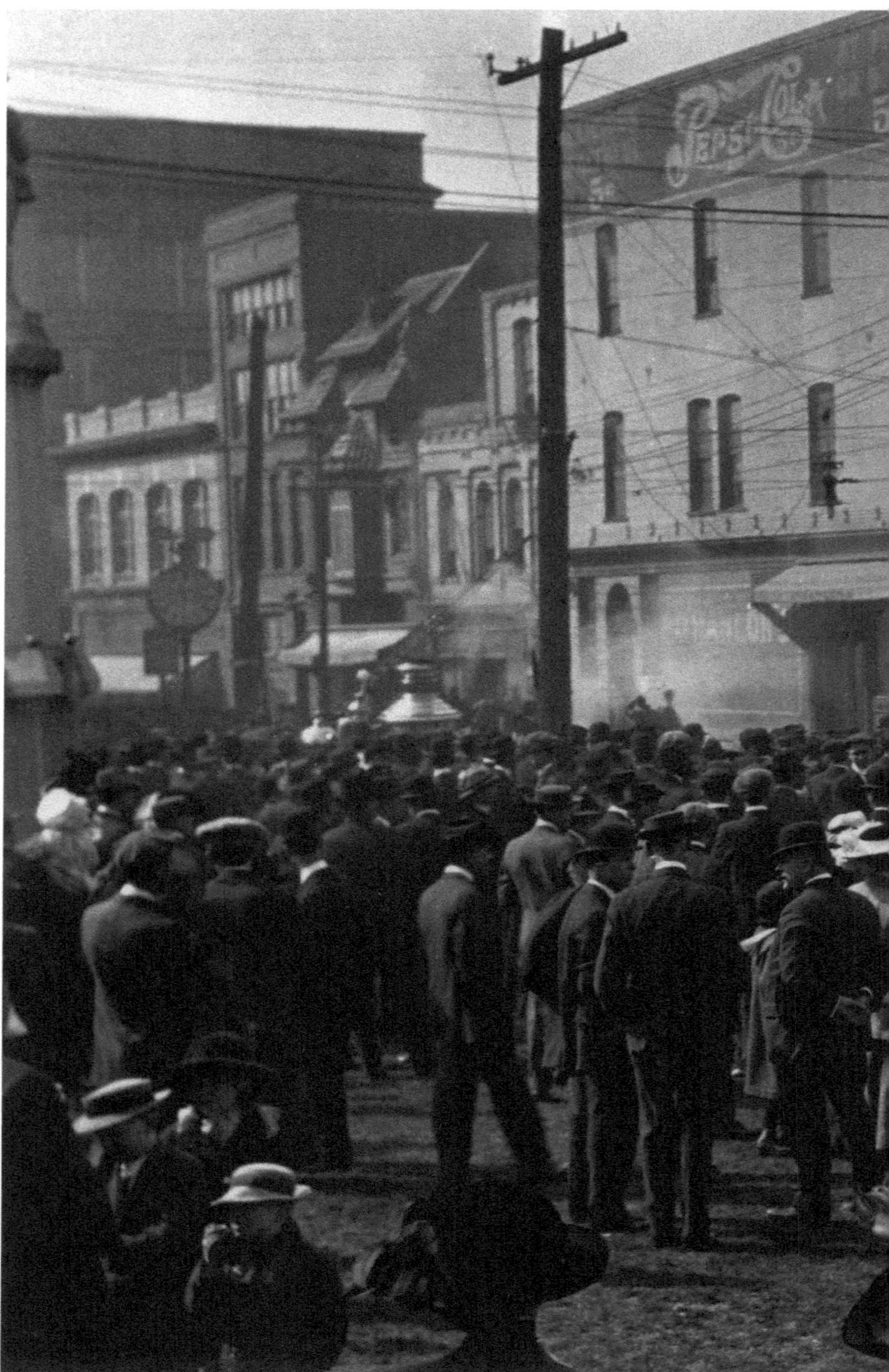

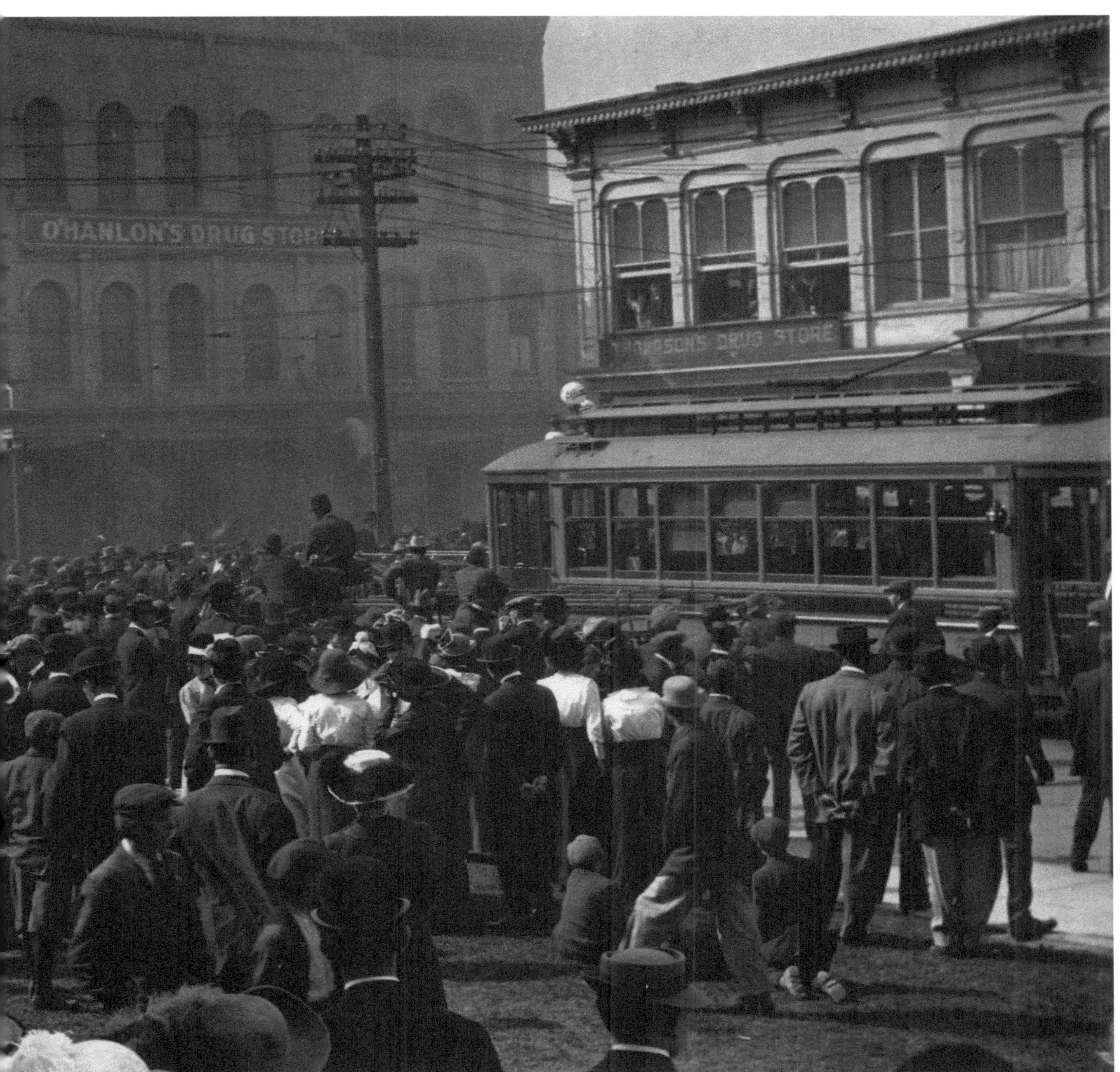
O'HANLON'S DRUG
DRUG STORE

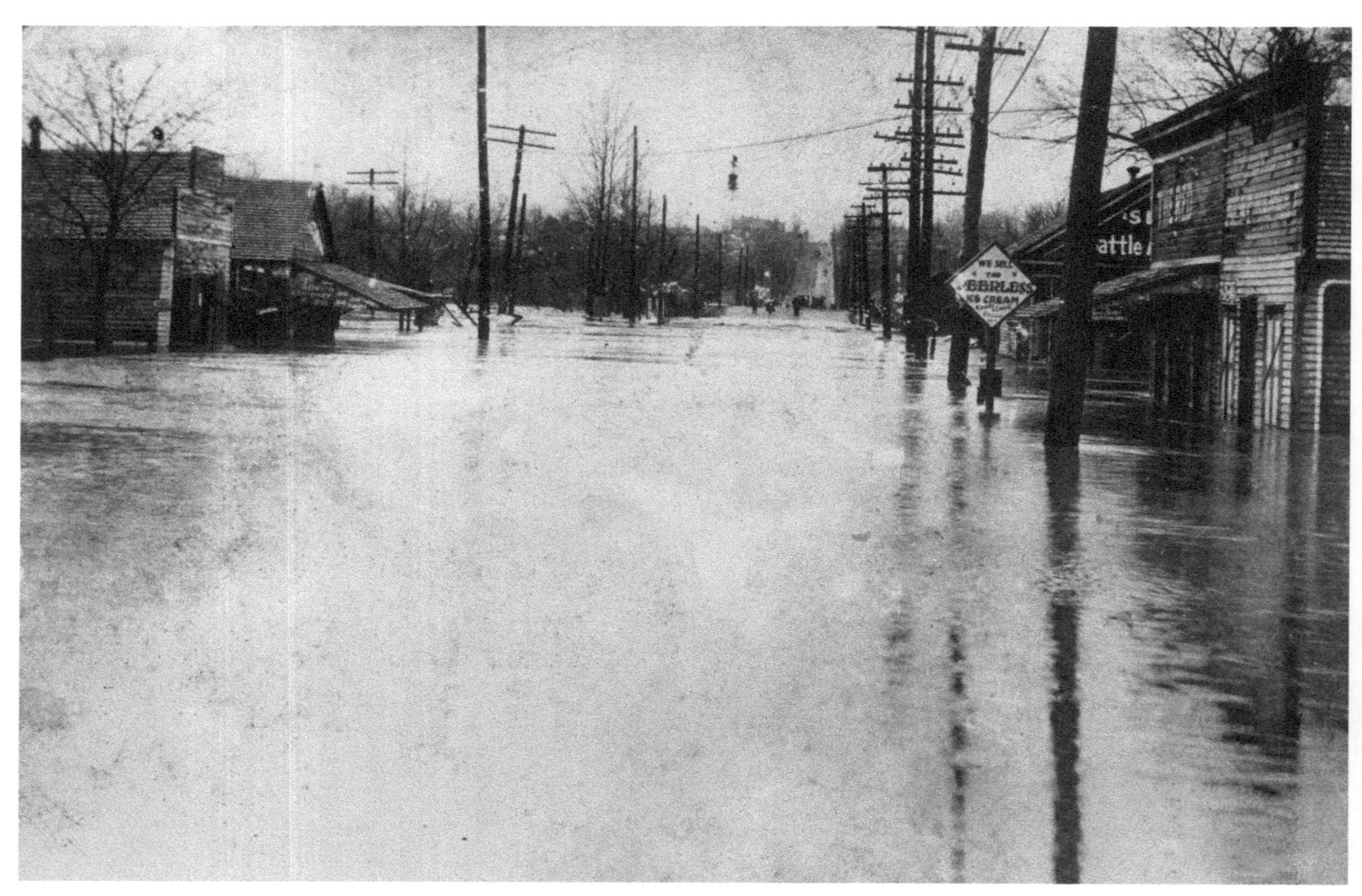

Flooding in North Carolina, such as the Salem Creek Flood of 1912, is not unusual. However, burgeoning metropolises often contributed to local flooding with poor or inadequate planning for expansion.

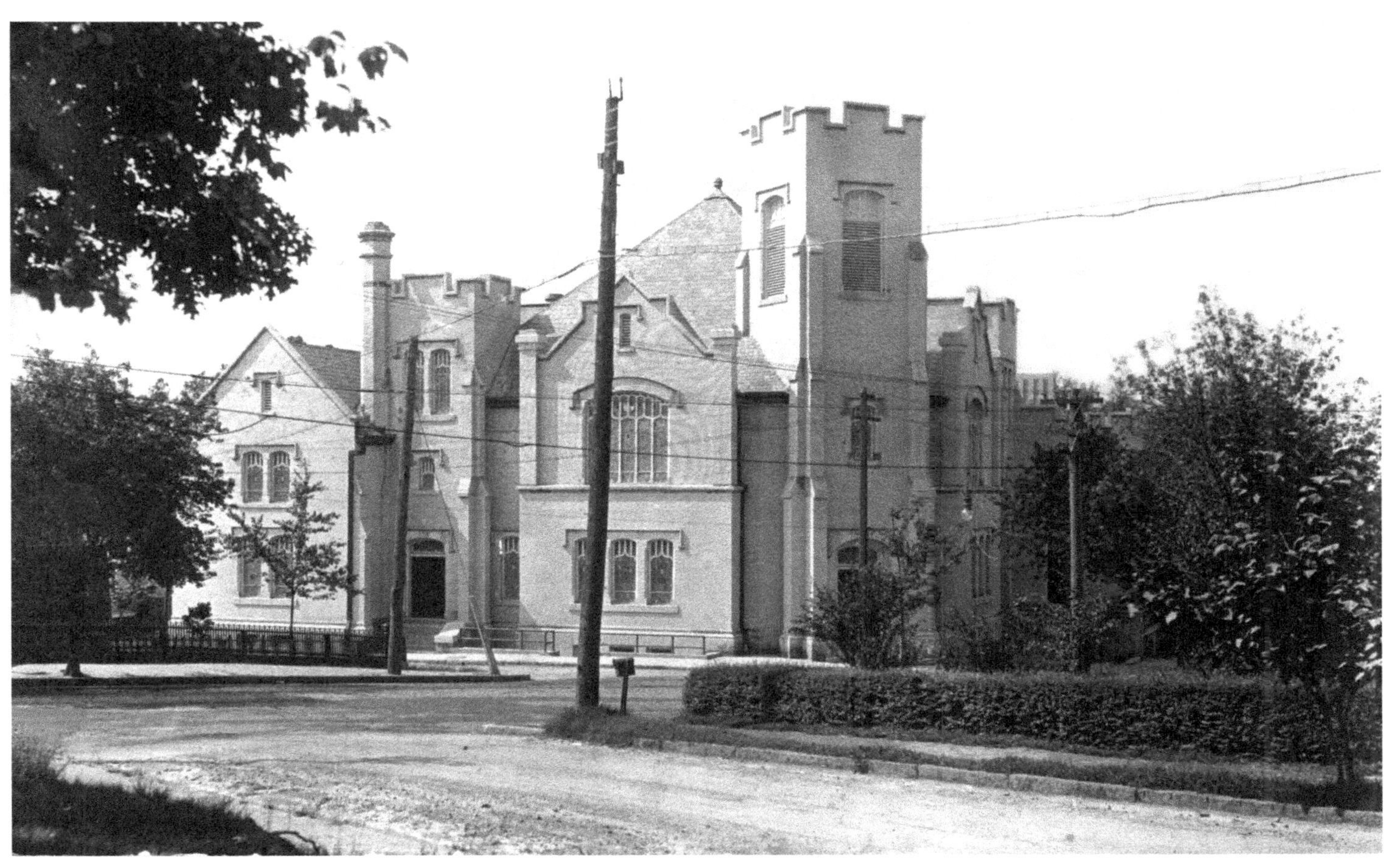

All denominations seemed to flourish in Winston-Salem, and many of the buildings reflected the wealth pouring into the region in the early 1900s. The beautiful architecture of West End Methodist Episcopal Church, photographed in 1913, is one example.

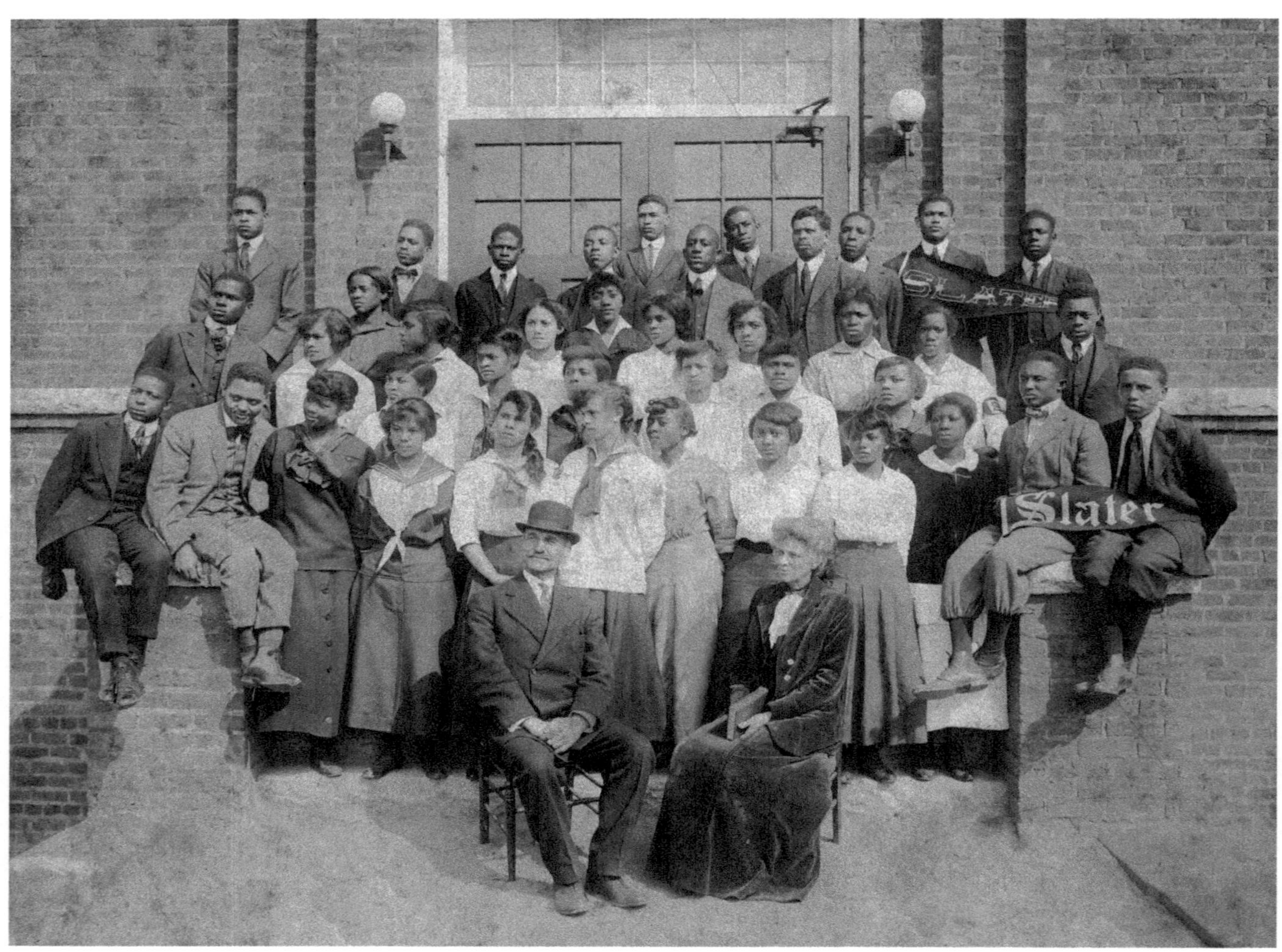


Slater Industrial Academy opened its doors in 1892 to offer continuing education to African Americans in segregated Winston-Salem. Over the years, it graduated many fine students, such as these pictured in 1915 with Simon Greene Atkins, the founder of the institution. In 1969, the college became Winston-Salem State University.

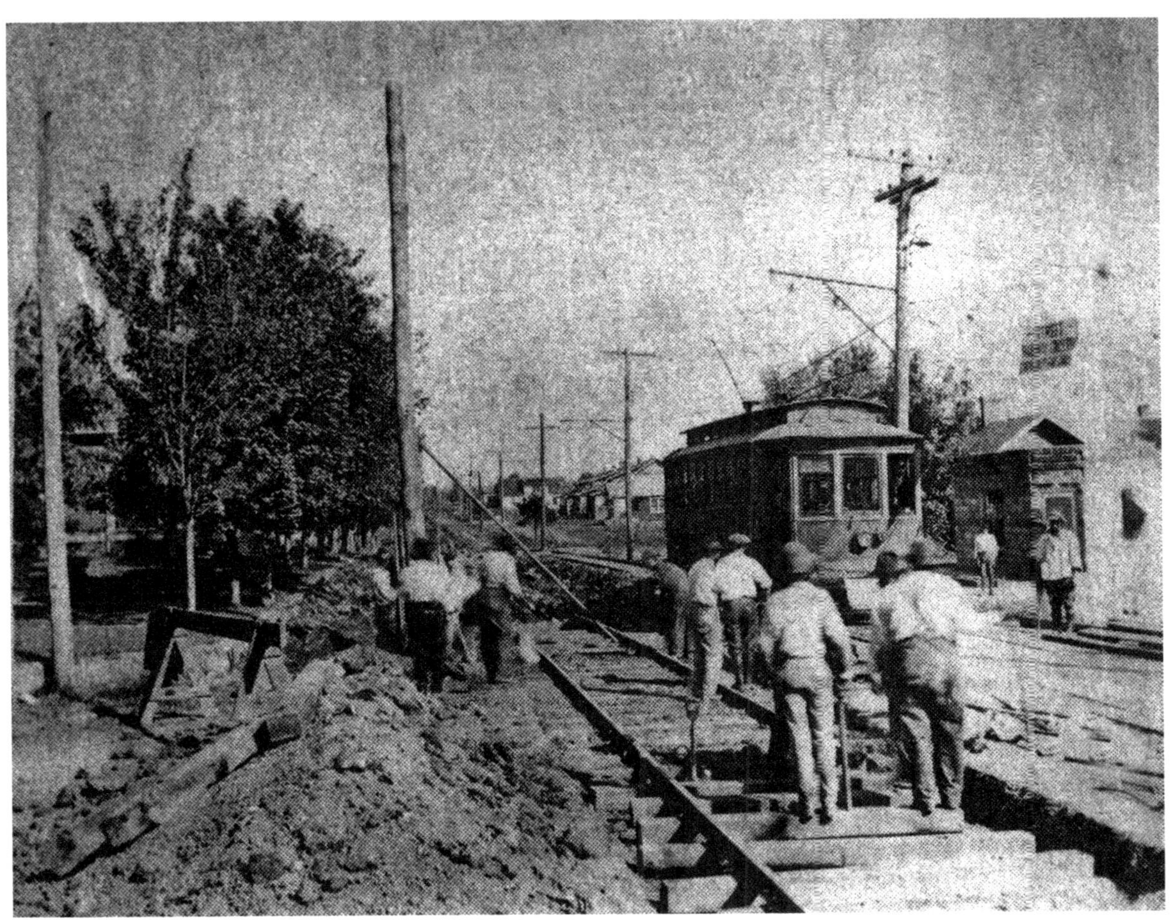

By the mid-1910s, old streetcar tracks, such as these on Sprague Street, demanded constant maintenance, but the struggle to keep the infrastructure functioning provided dependable, if low-paying, jobs for city employees.

If your favorite star was not showing at the Amuzu Theater, you could try here, the Pilot Theater, a few blocks away.

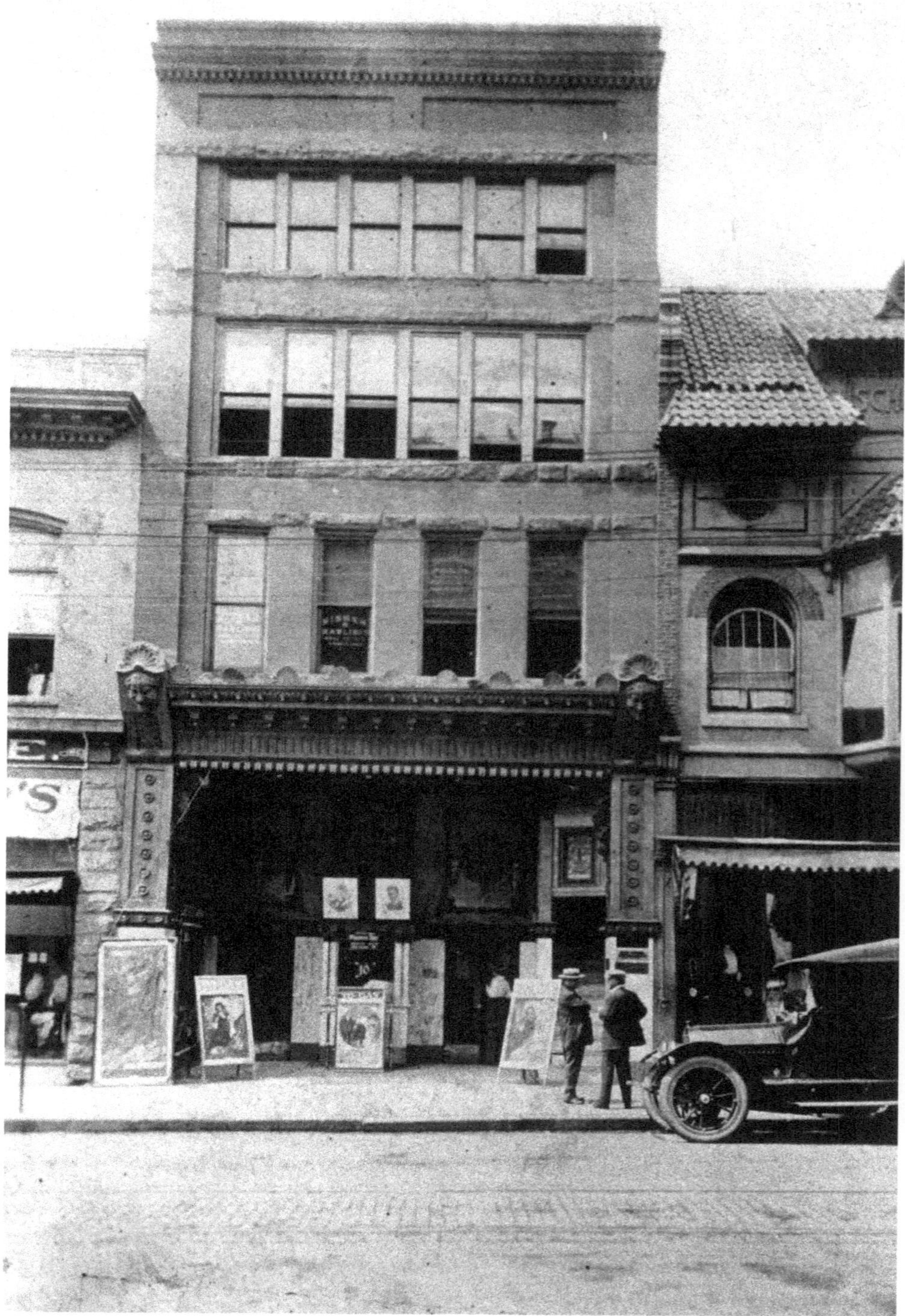

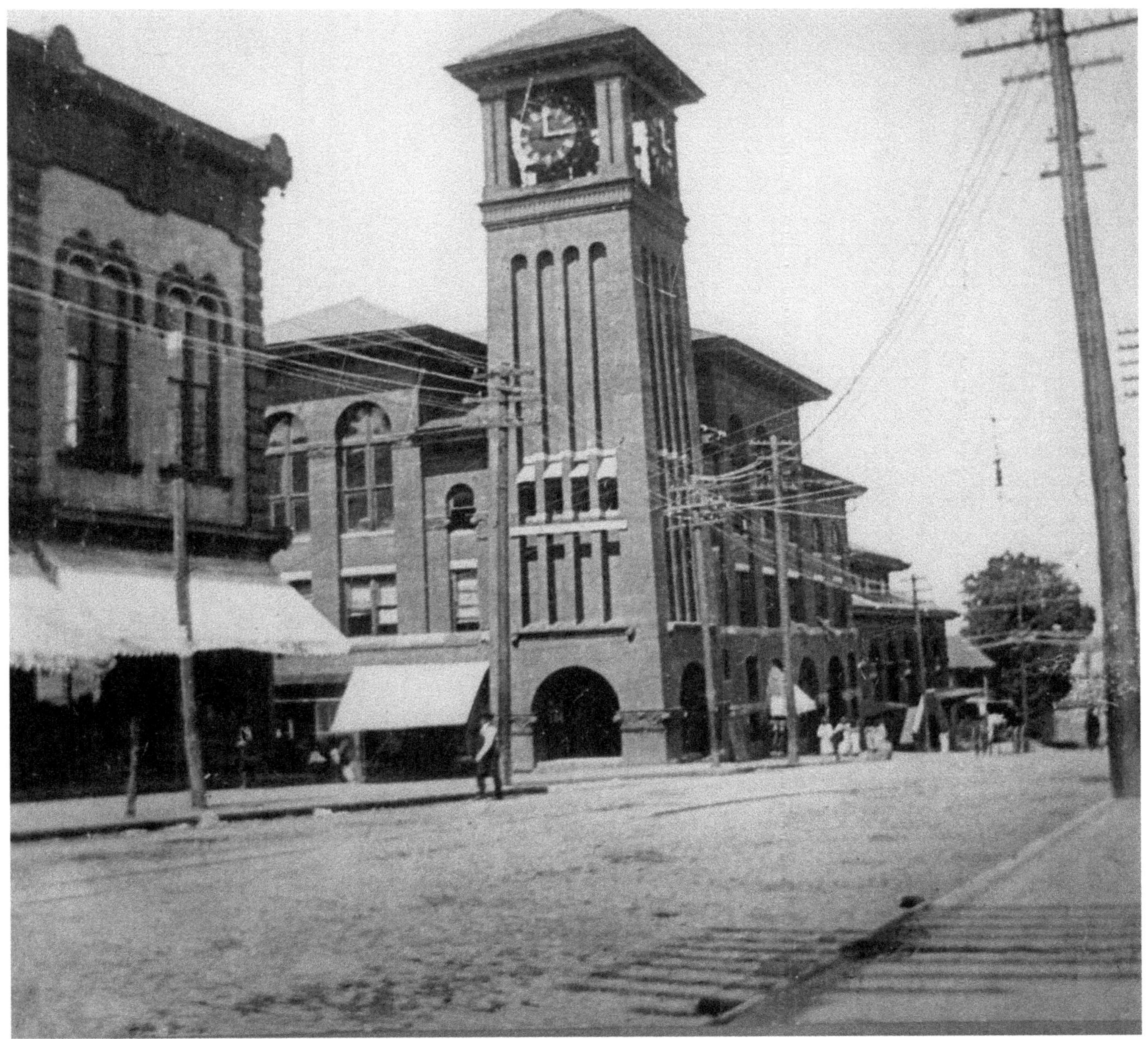

Winston Town Hall, with its outsized clock, became the town hall of Winston-Salem on March 18, 1913, when voters ratified the consolidation act and charter approved by the General Assembly on January 27, 1913.

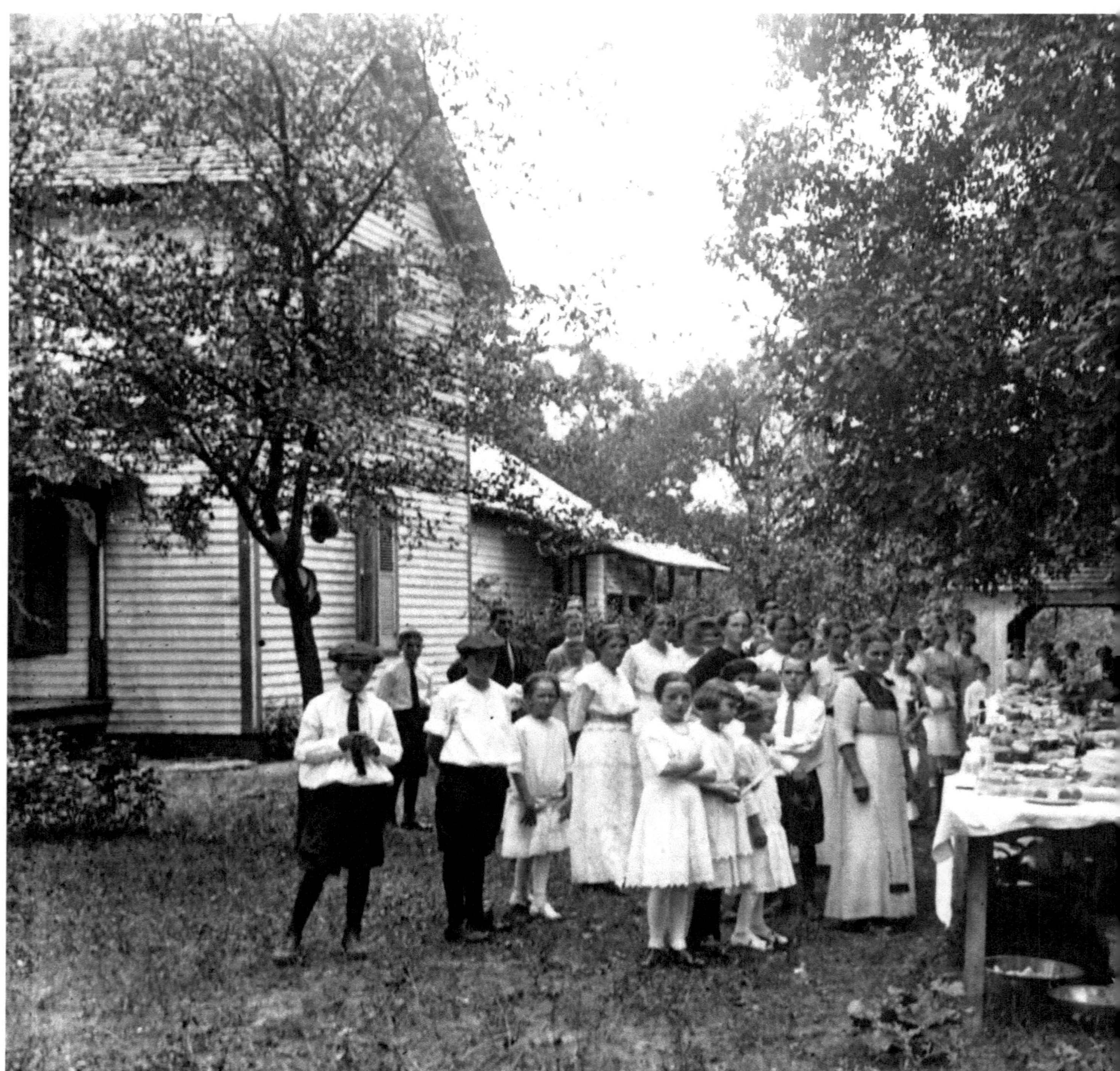

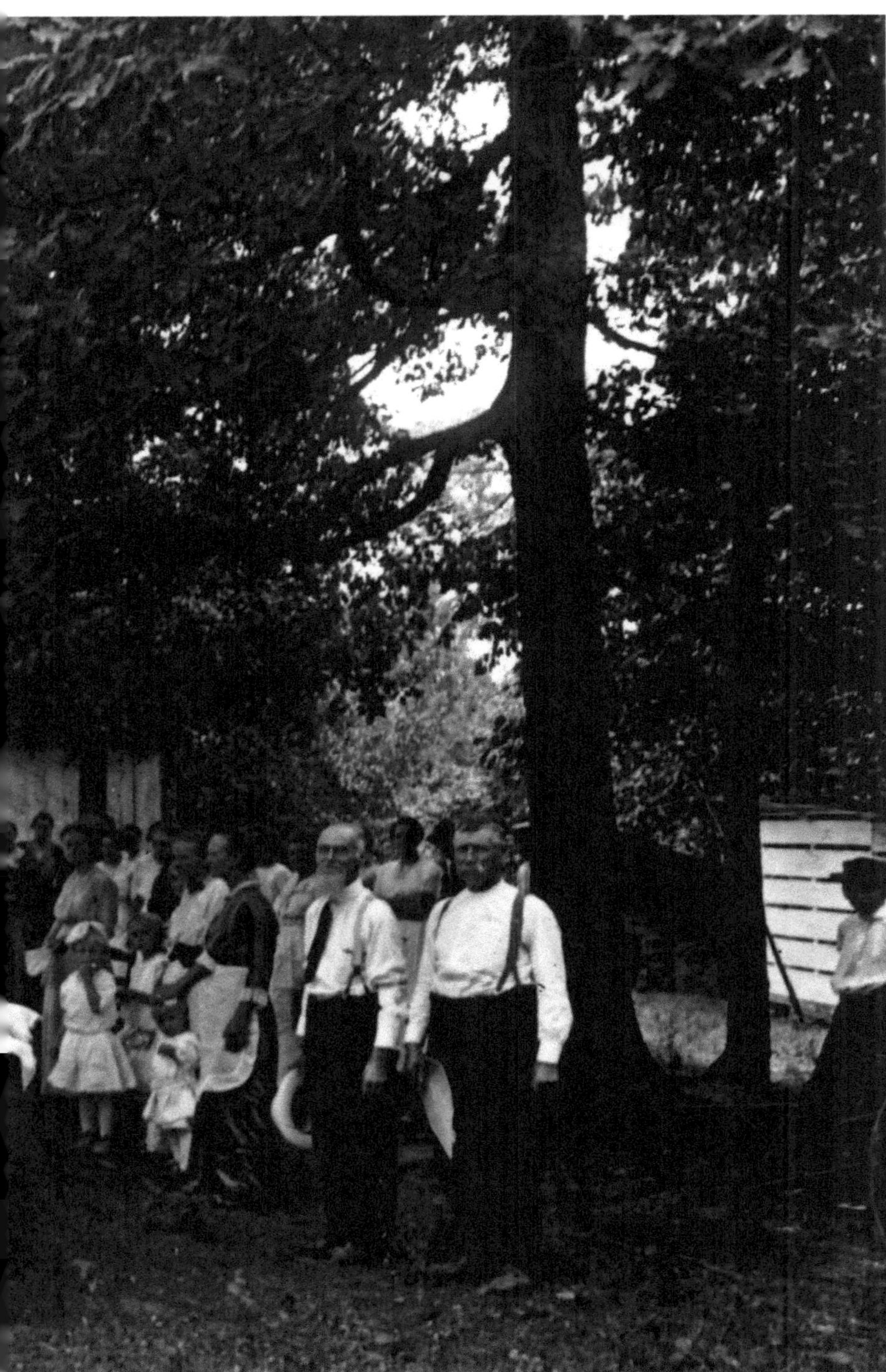

Children and adults together pose around a full picnic table at the R. J. Reynolds house on Fifth Street, around 1912.

Looking across Hanes Park from Silver Hill, one could see West End. By 1918, these were the suburbs of Winston-Salem, something made possible by the ever-expanding trolley system and the automobile.

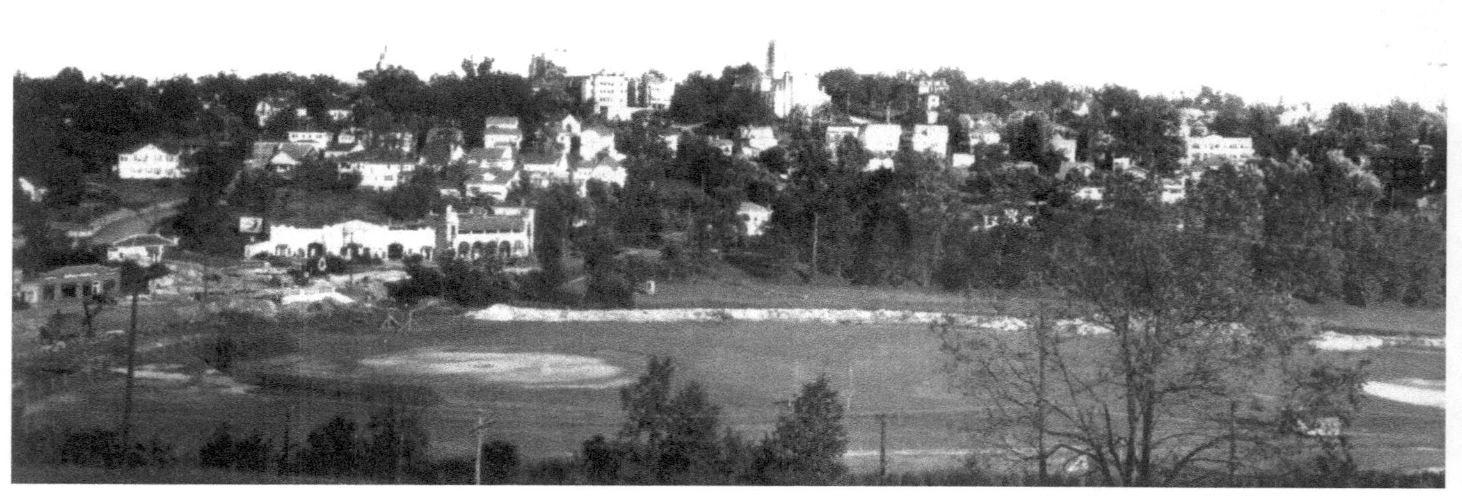

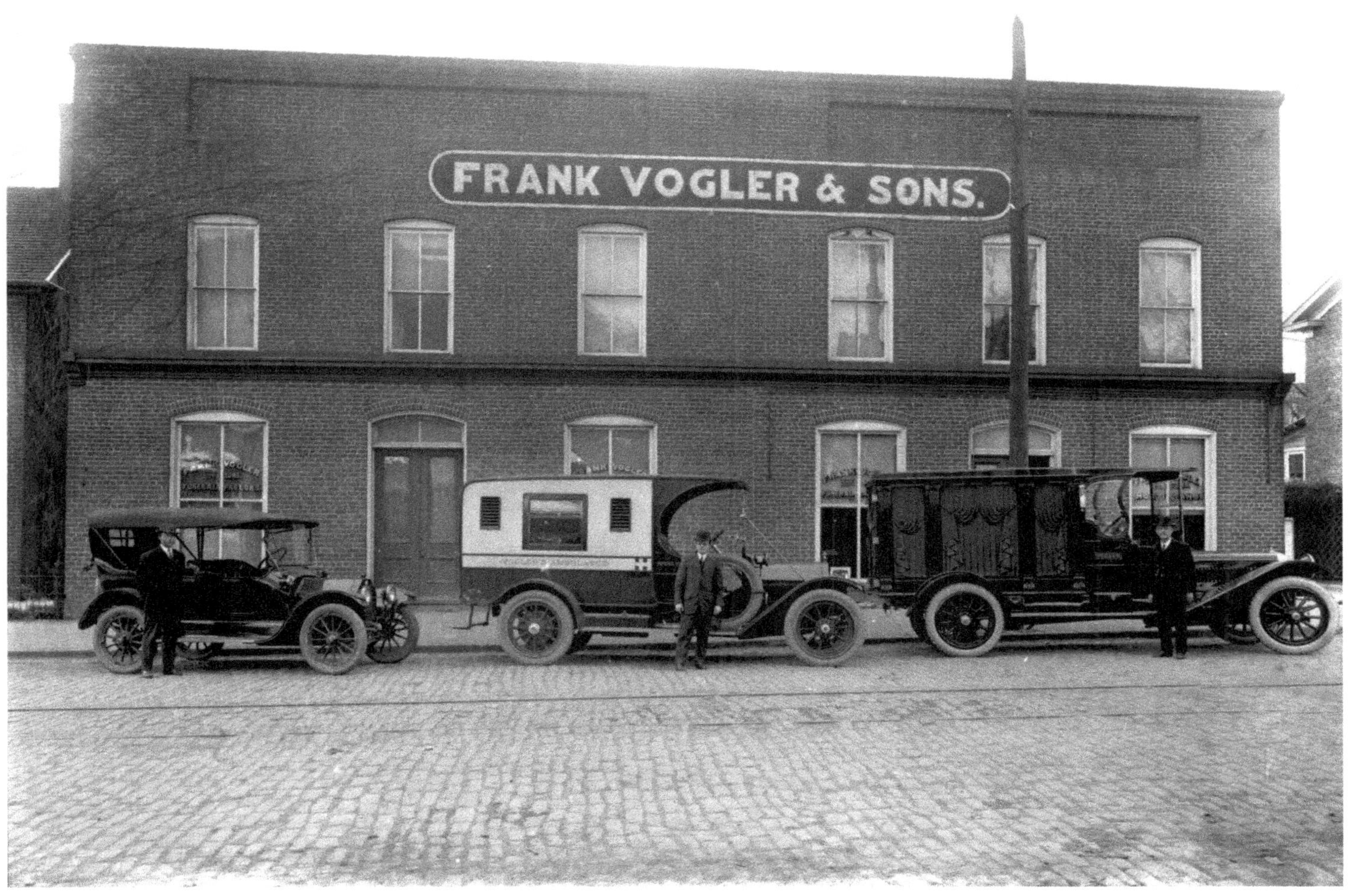


From 1858, Frank Vogler & Sons served as the premier undertakers, then funeral home, in Salem and Winston-Salem. A state-of-the-art hearse is parked in front of their business around 1918.

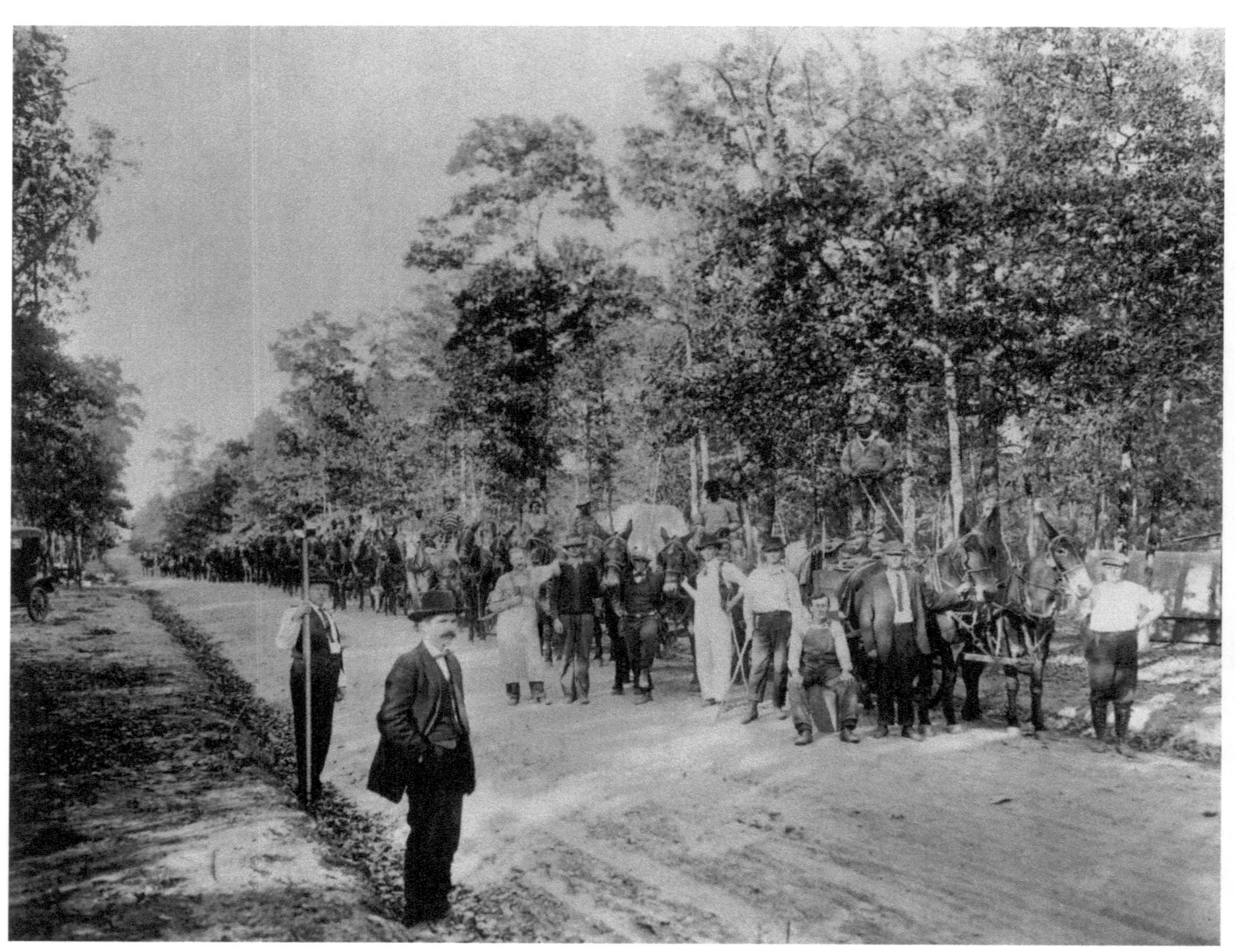

As with so many things in the city that bright leaf tobacco built, this road under construction in 1917 is named after R. J. Reynolds, or at least after his new estate, Reynolda, completed that same year.

The Elks Auditorium, on the corner of Fifth and Liberty streets, burned in 1916. The 1,800-seat State Auditorium opened in the same location the following year. It would remain the area's largest performance hall until the opening of R. J. Reynolds Auditorium in 1924.

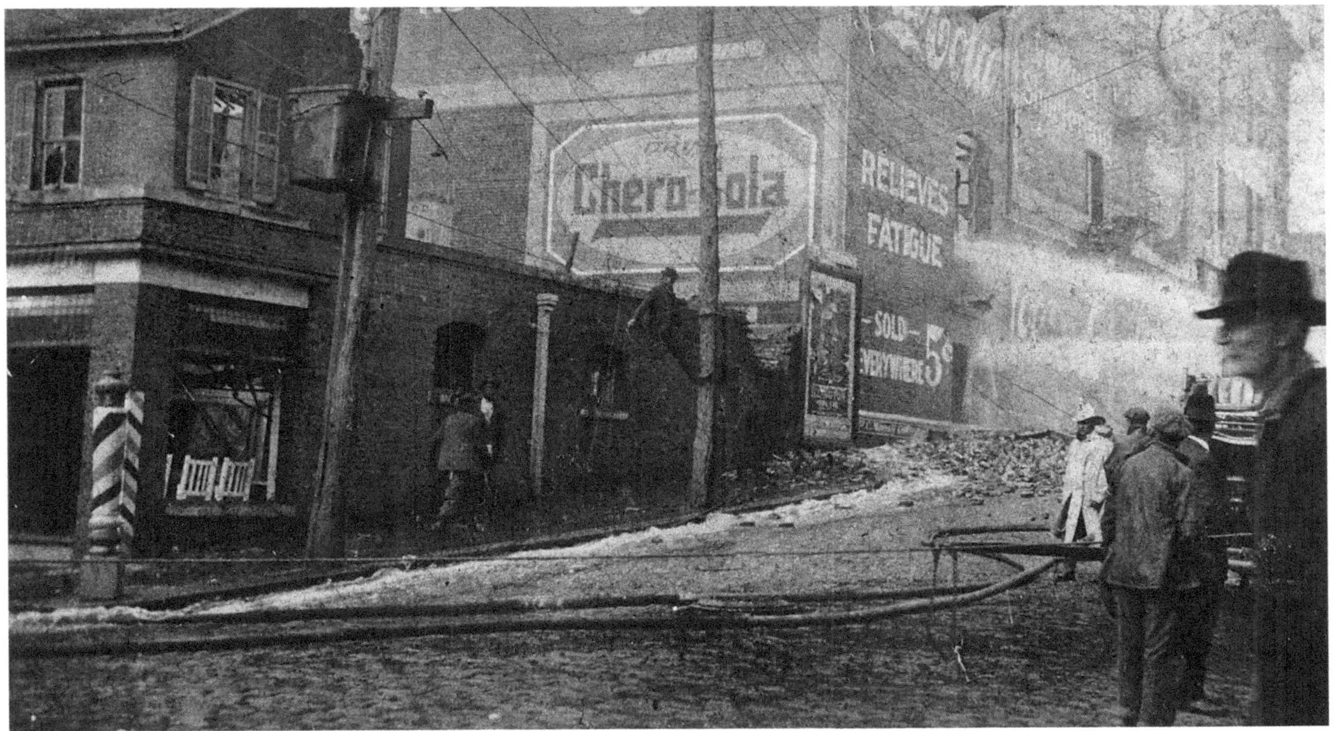

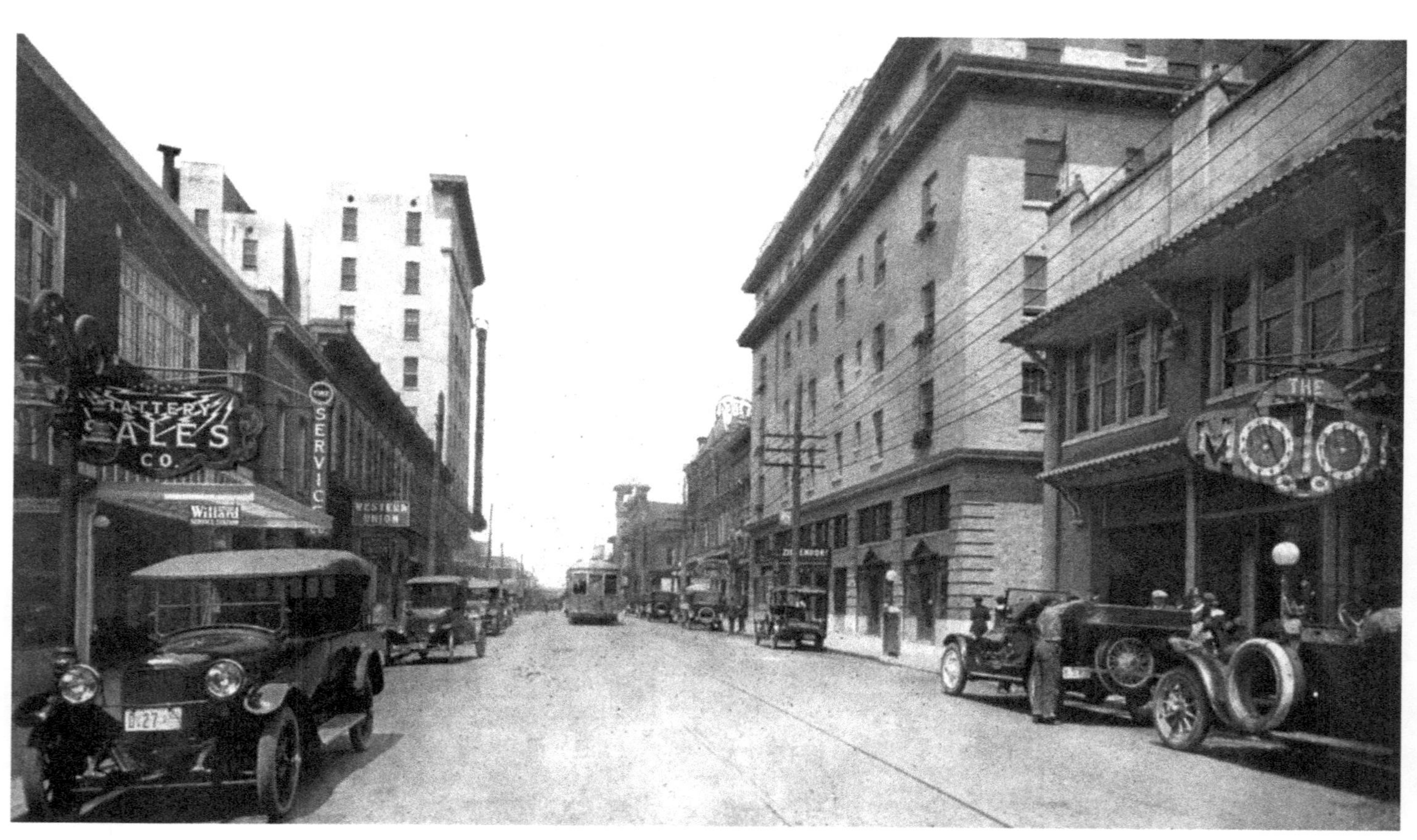


By 1918, on North Main Street, the horse and buggy of 1910 had been replaced by cars. The electric trolley remained—for another generation.

The corner of Fourth Street and Main, photographed on a quiet day in 1918.

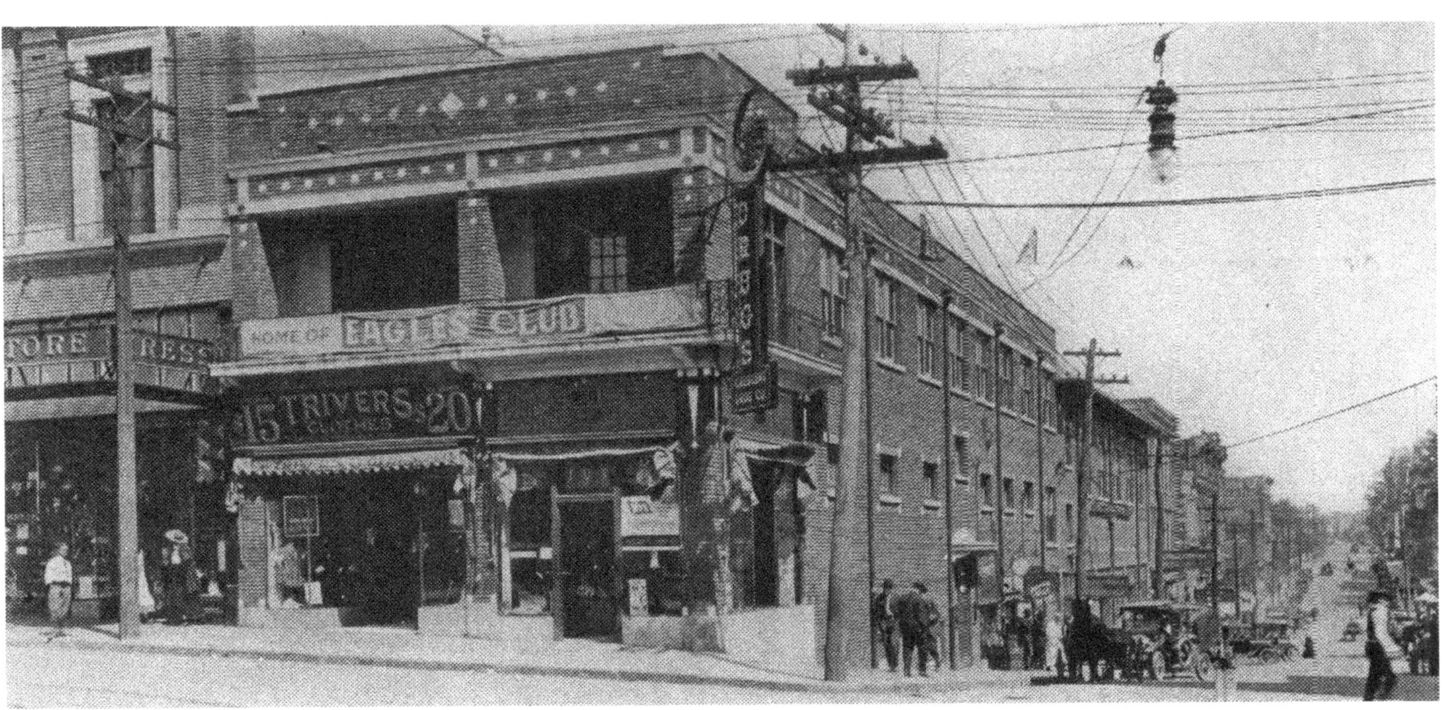

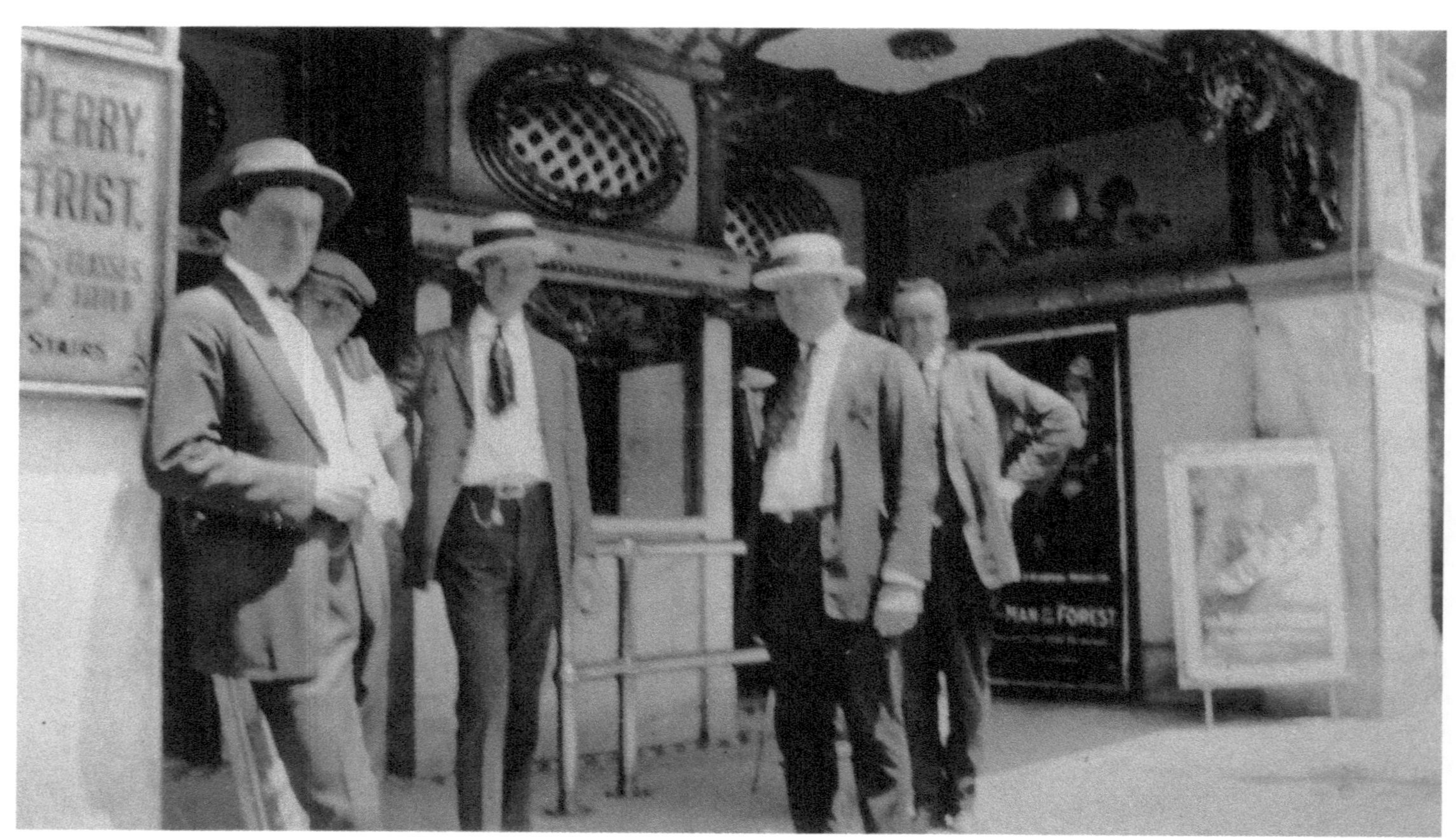


Men wait for the afternoon matinee at the Elmont Theater sometime in 1918.

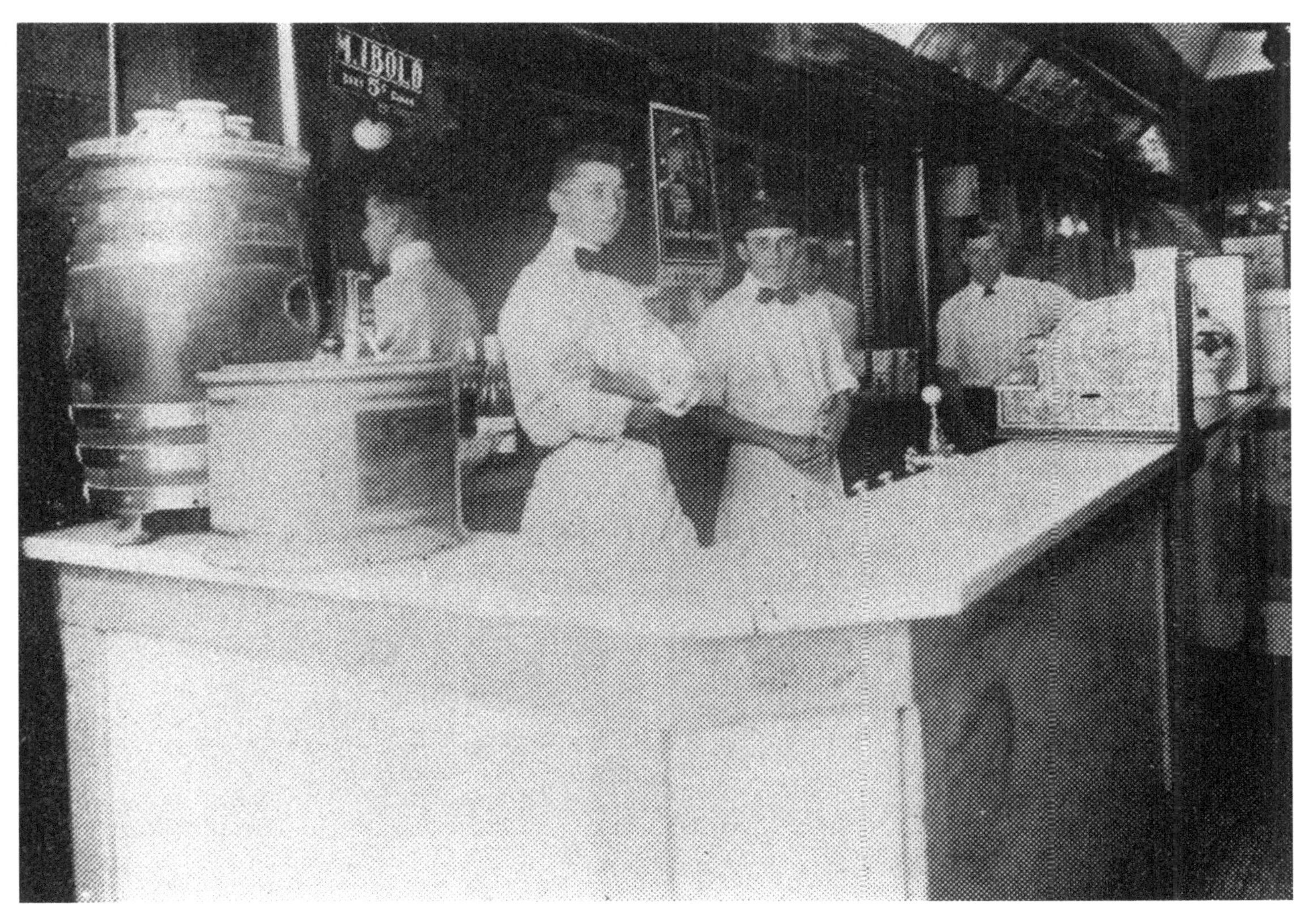

The Smokers Den was a popular hangout on Fourth Street in 1918.

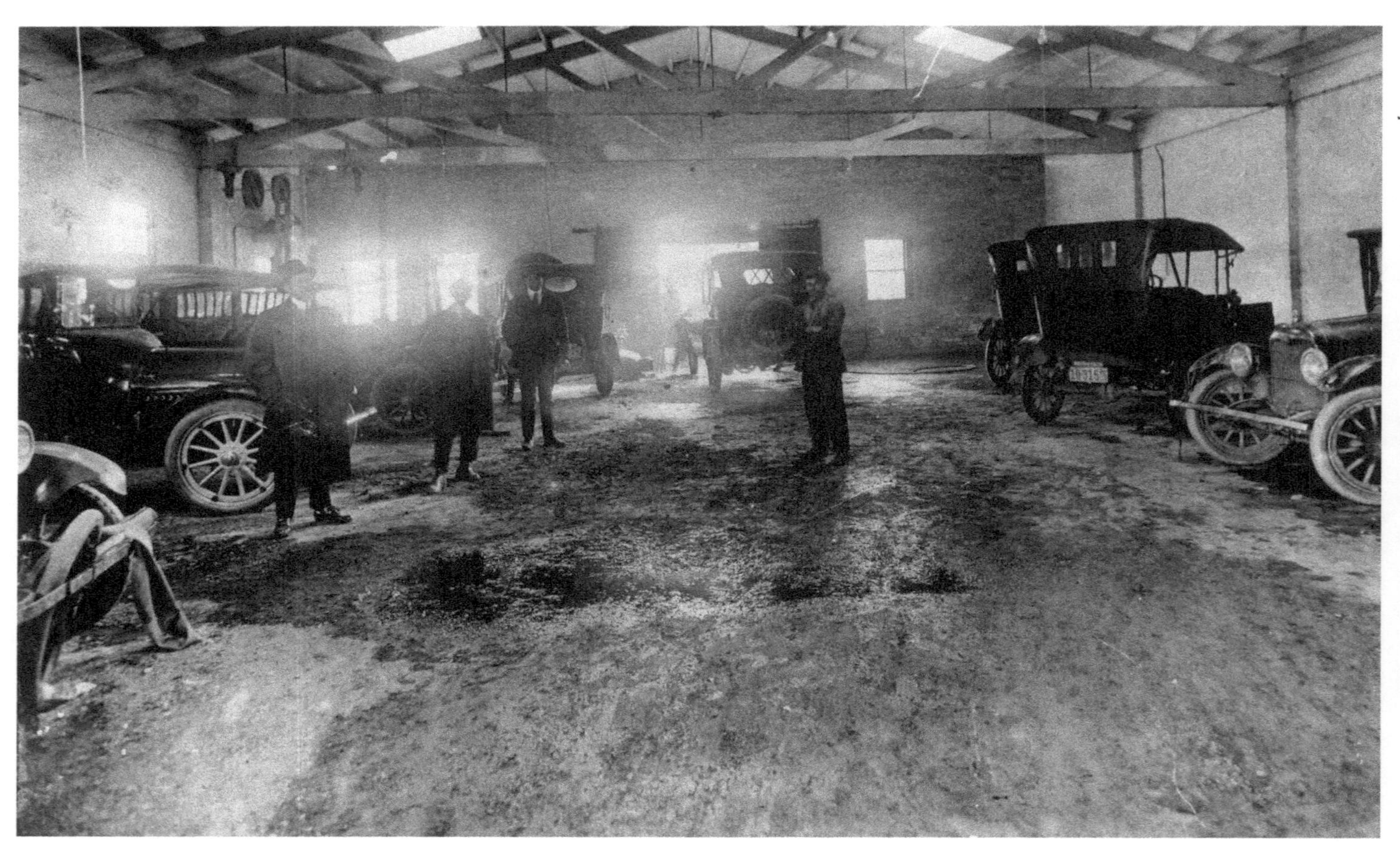

By 1918, a number of garages existed in downtown Winston-Salem.

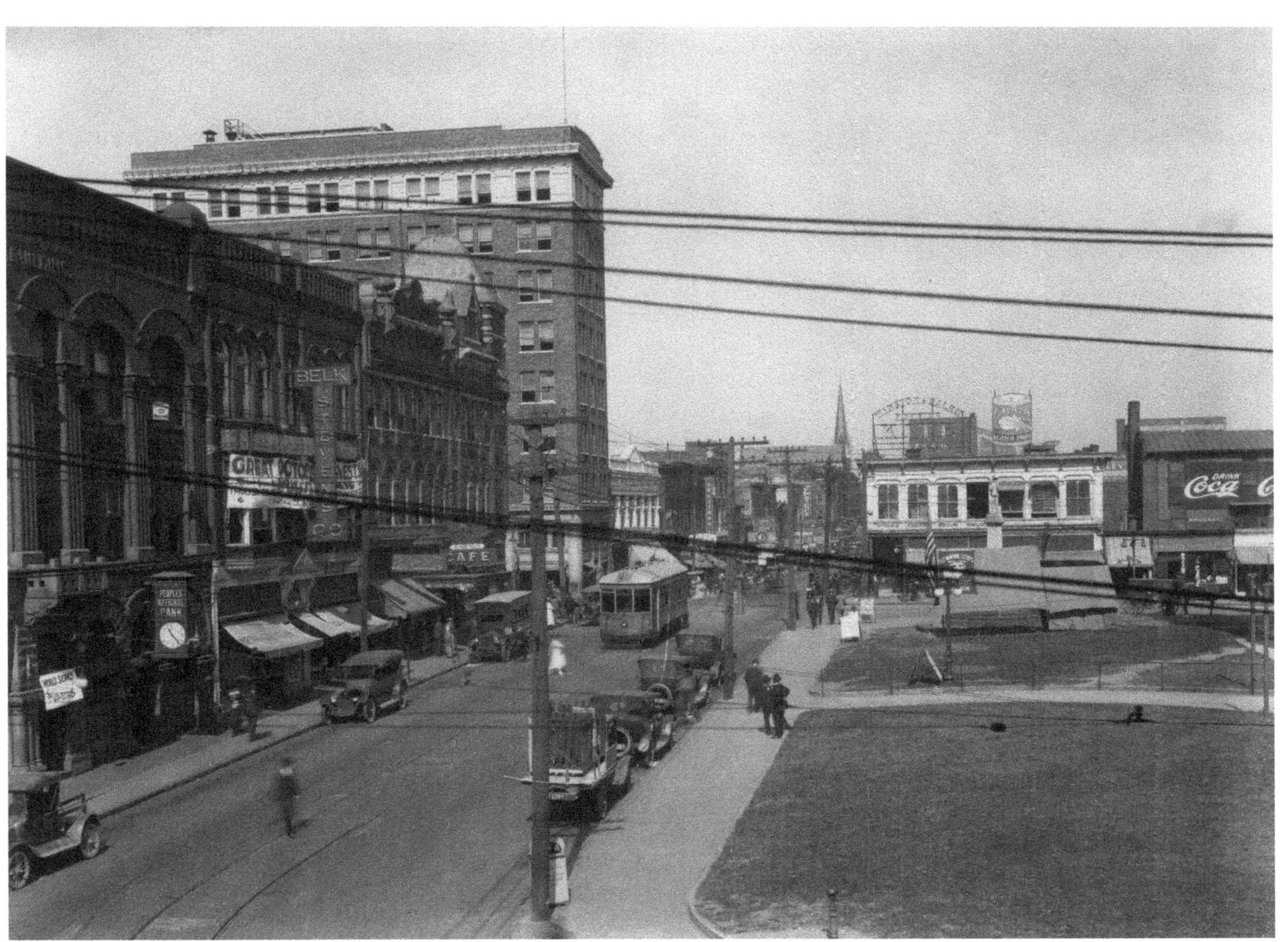


Five years after its predecessor burned, the replacement O'Hanlon Building towers over its fellows on North Liberty Street.

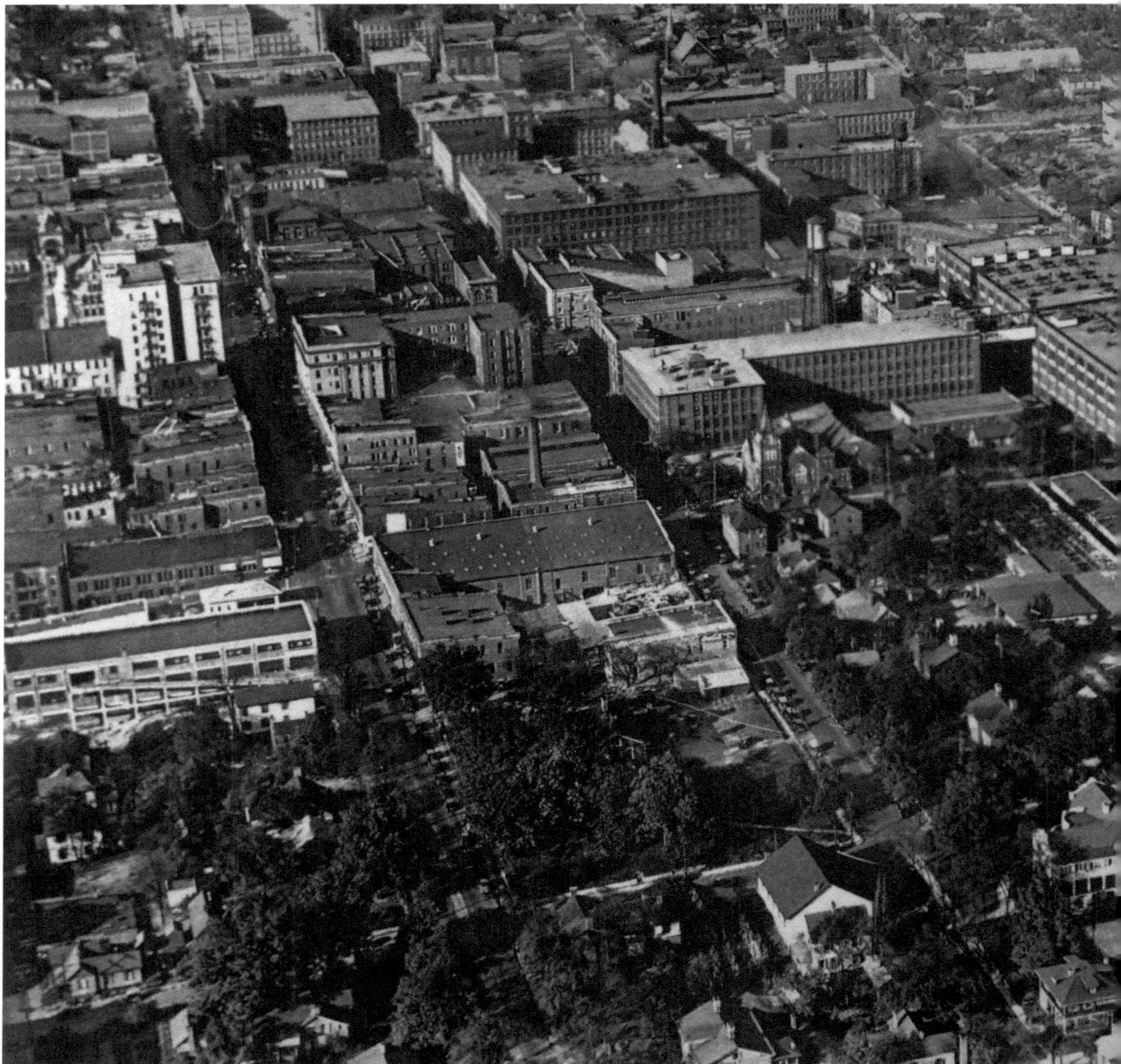

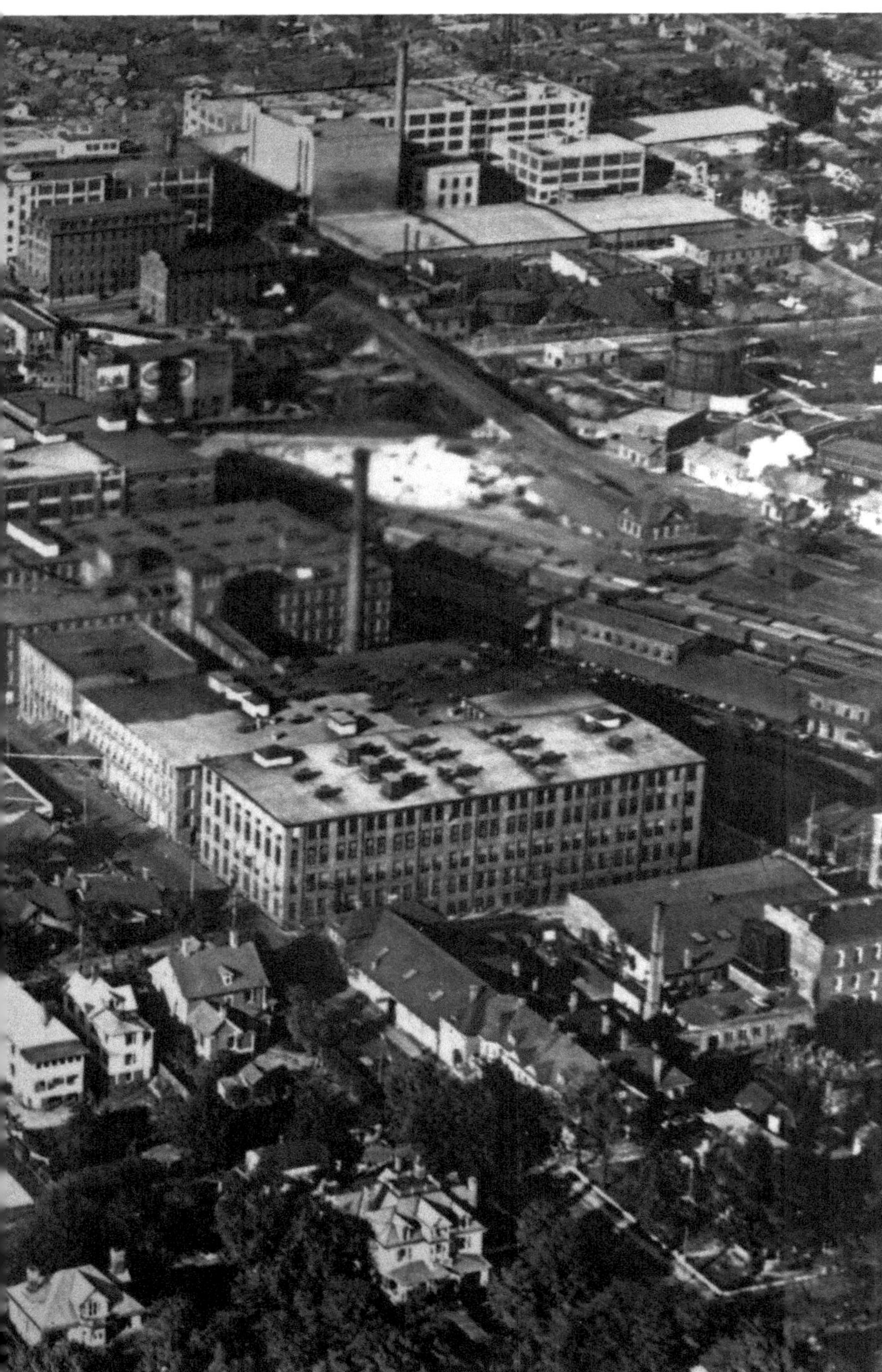

One of the earliest aerial photographs of Winston-Salem, taken in 1923, offers a view of a sprawling city replete with skyscrapers and massive factories. Winston-Salem stands ready as the Roaring Twenties commence.

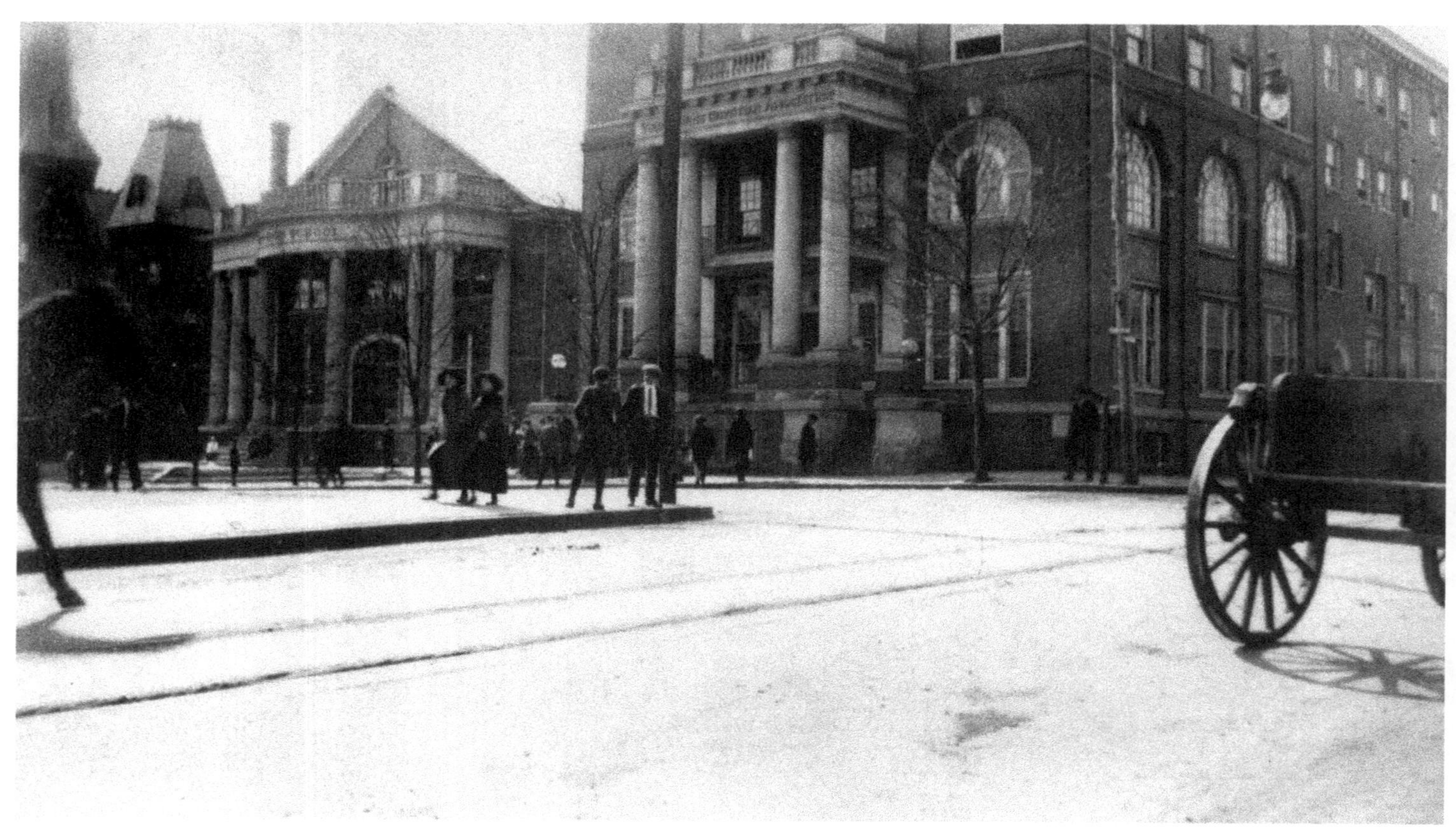

The YMCA Building, on the right, dominates this early 1920s tableau at the corner of Cherry and Fourth streets. The First Presbyterian Church stands at far left, and the center building is Winston High School, which would be destroyed by fire in 1923.

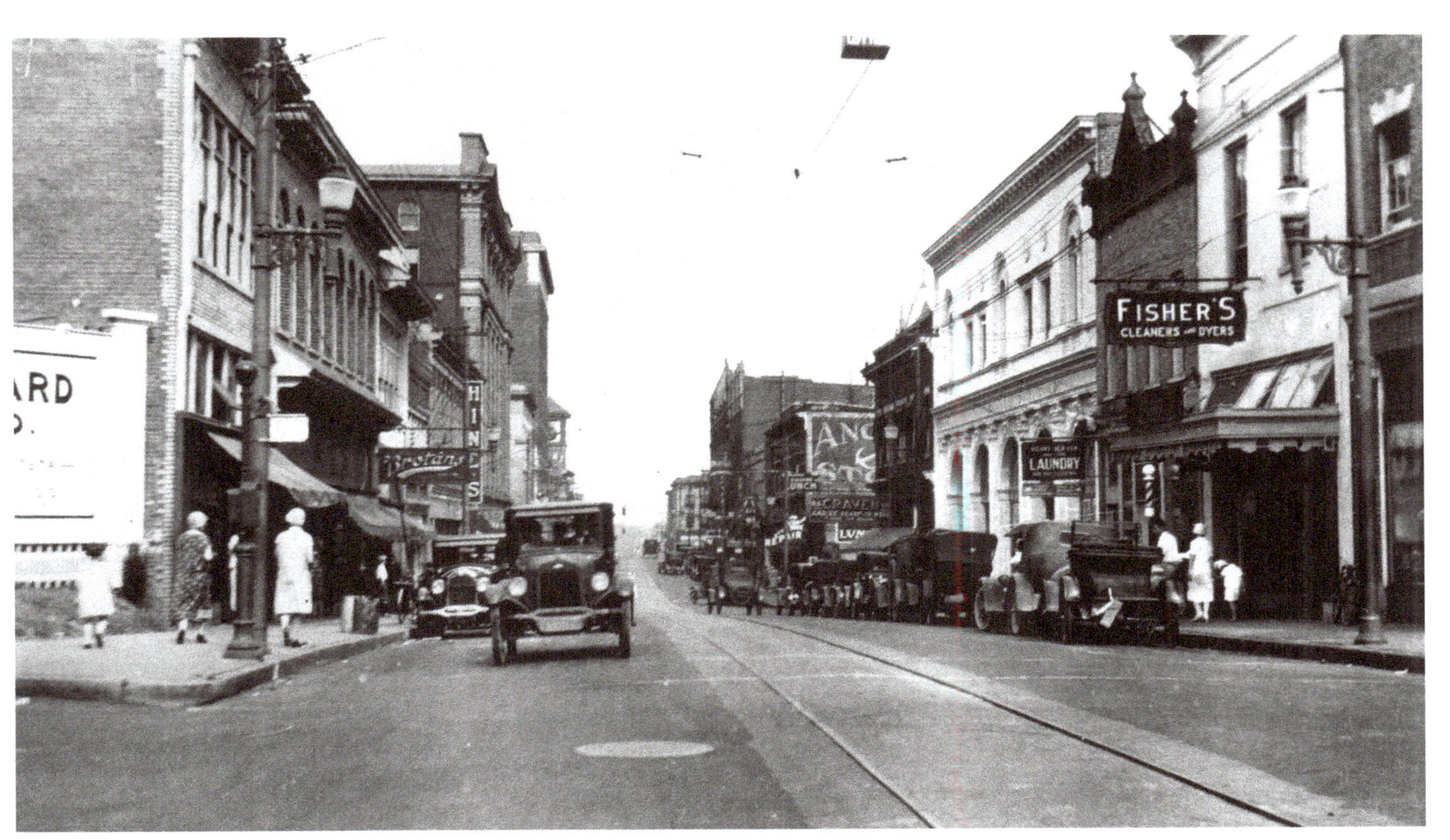


Cars line West Fourth Street beyond its intersection with Cherry Street in 1925.

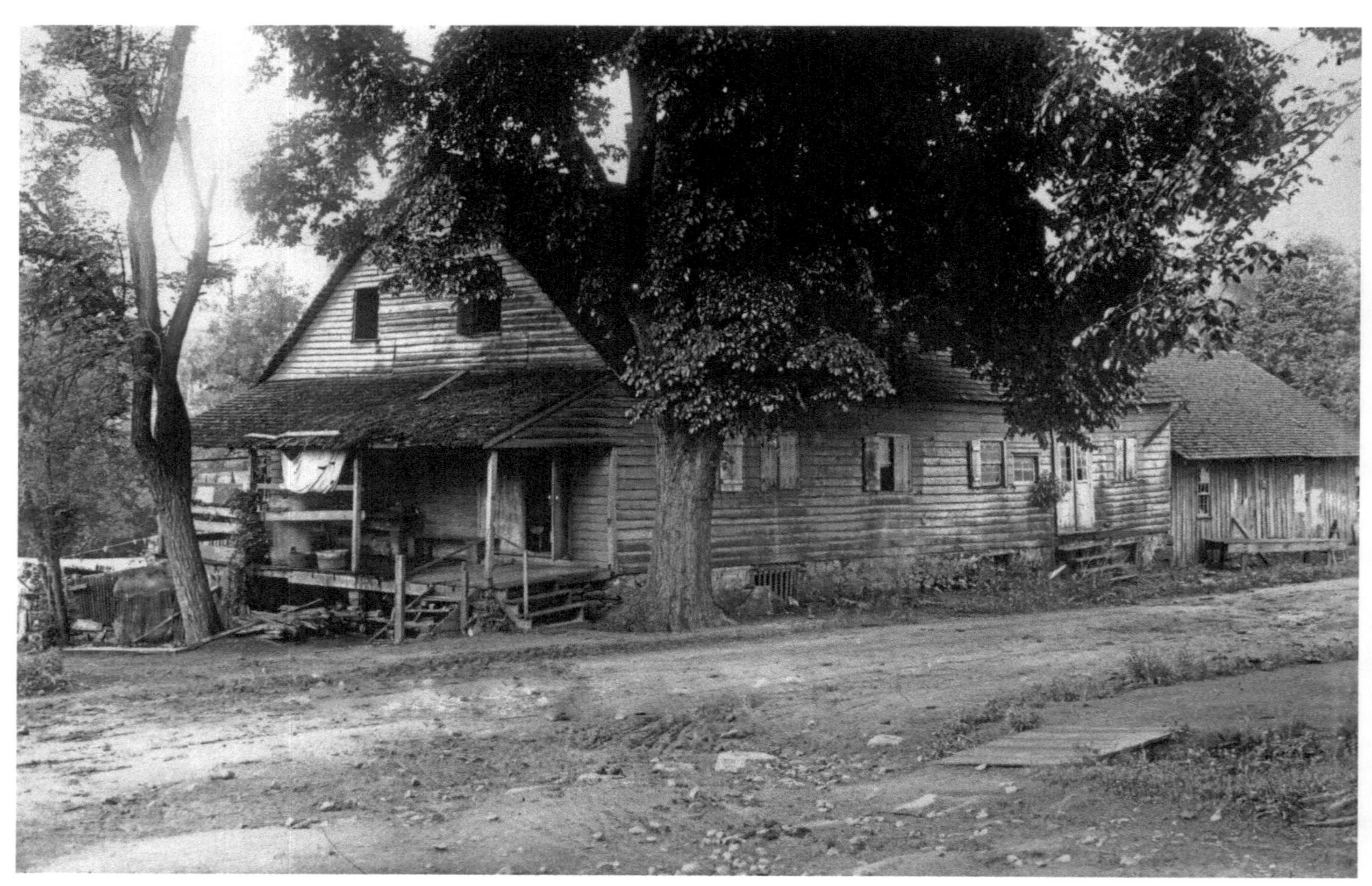

Sometime after 1920, the decaying Salem Brewery and Tan Yard stood silent, as did even more modern breweries, victims of Prohibition.

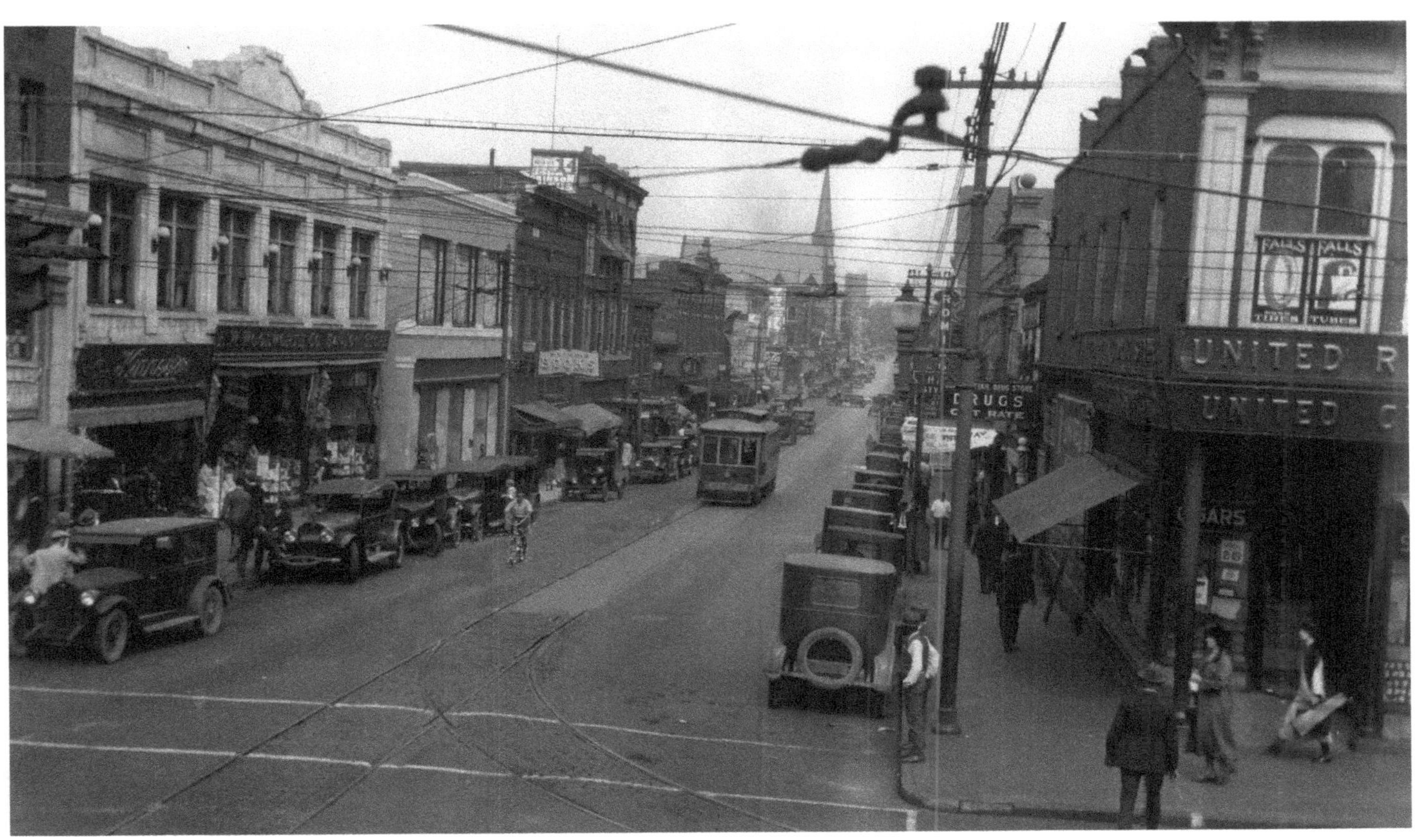


Viewed from its intersection with Liberty Street in 1925, Fourth Street reveals a dynamic downtown in Winston-Salem. People visit the bank or shop at department and specialty stores, or at the F. W. Woolworth store on the left, while their new cars lining the street reveal a level of prosperity enjoyed by few towns in North Carolina.

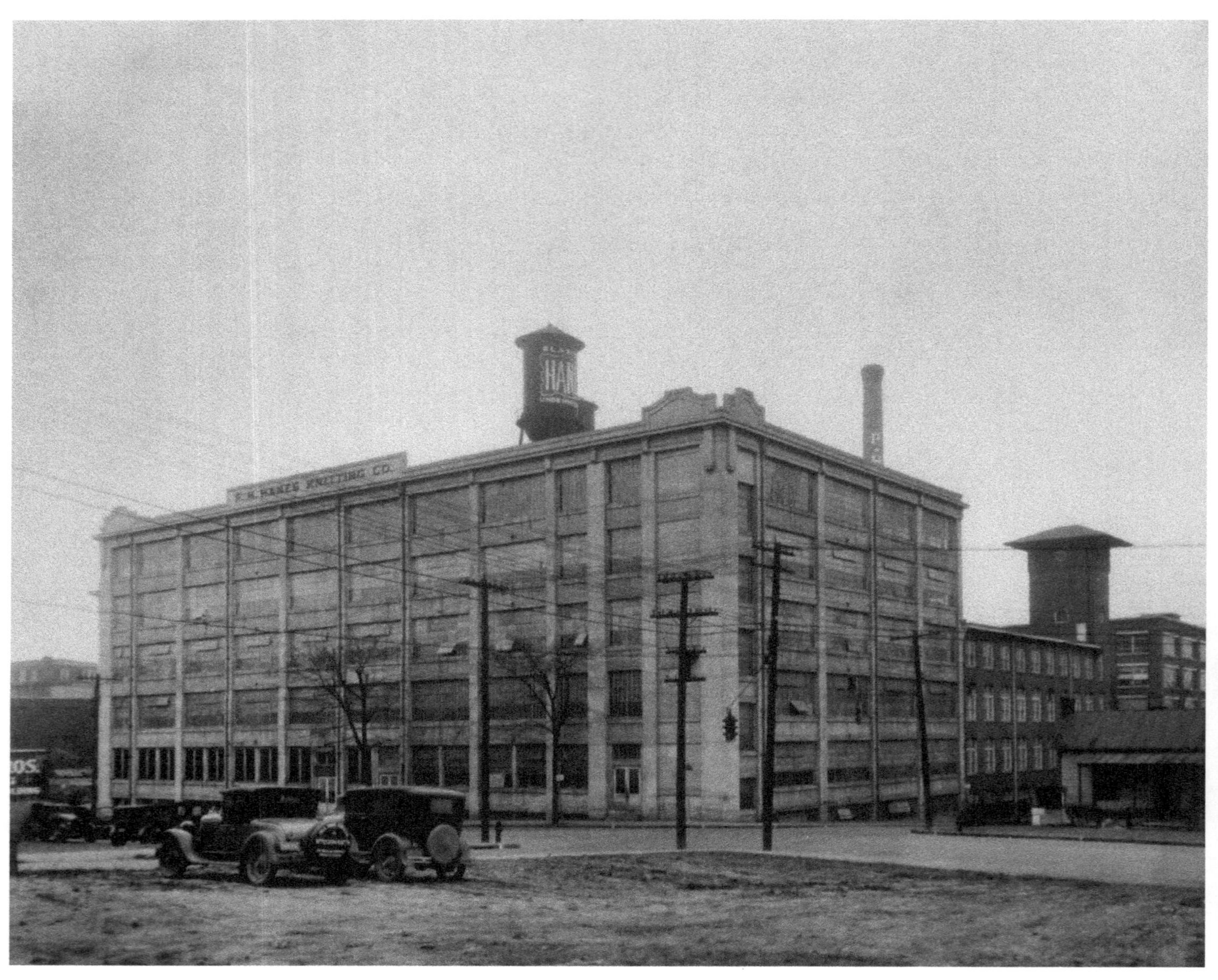

In the 1920s, the long-standing Hanes Knitting Company remained a vigorous Winston-Salem industry. By 1920, it had a new factory at Sixth and Main streets, as well as a cotton mill and a spinning mill, both located in Hane, the village the company built for its employees on the edge of Winston-Salem.

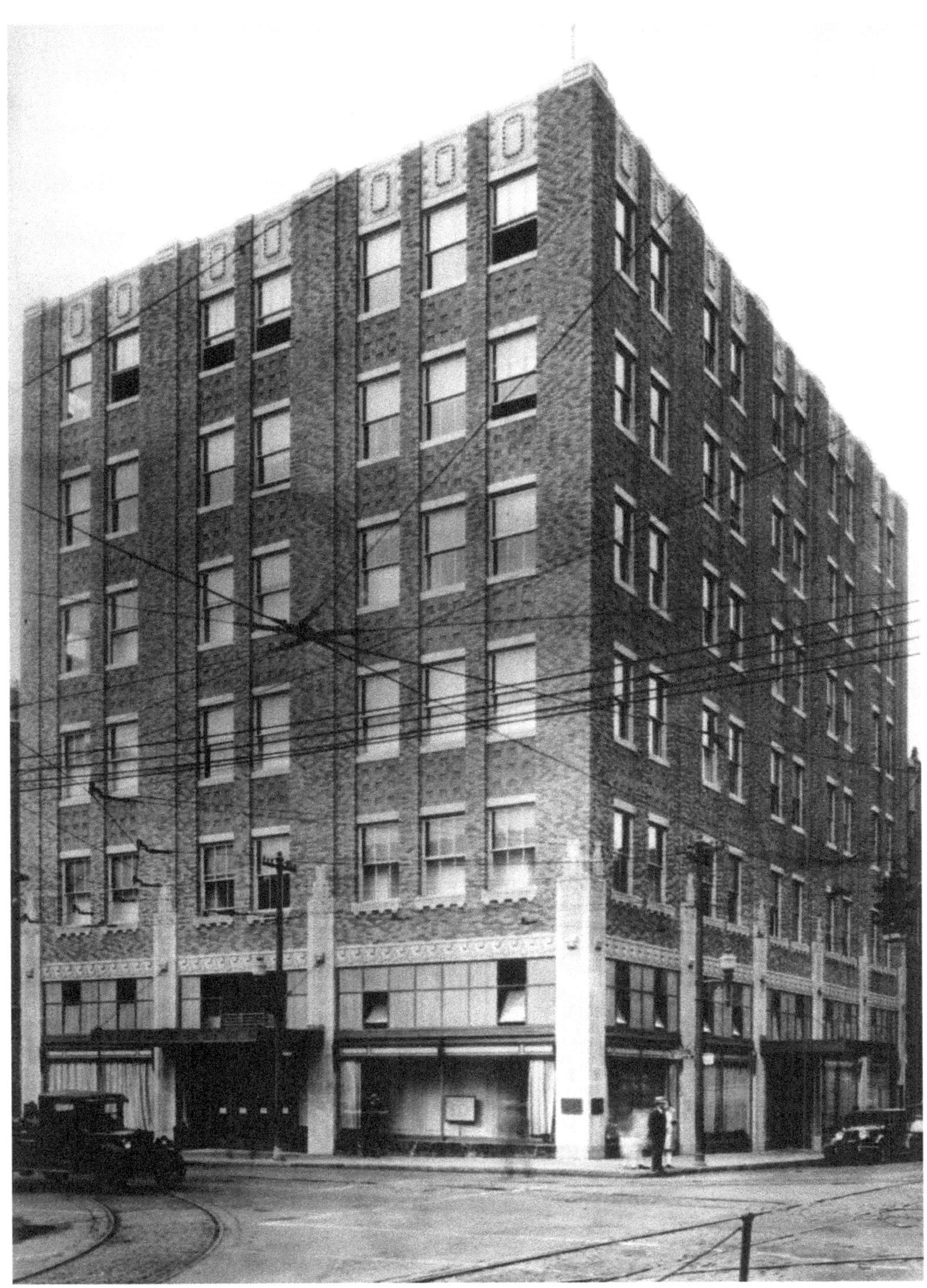

At the corner of Fourth and Liberty streets stands the Pepper Building. Completed in 1928, the impressive structure has been home to numerous enterprises since its opening. As of 2008, an effort is underway in Winston-Salem to save this superb example of early twentieth century architecture from demolition.

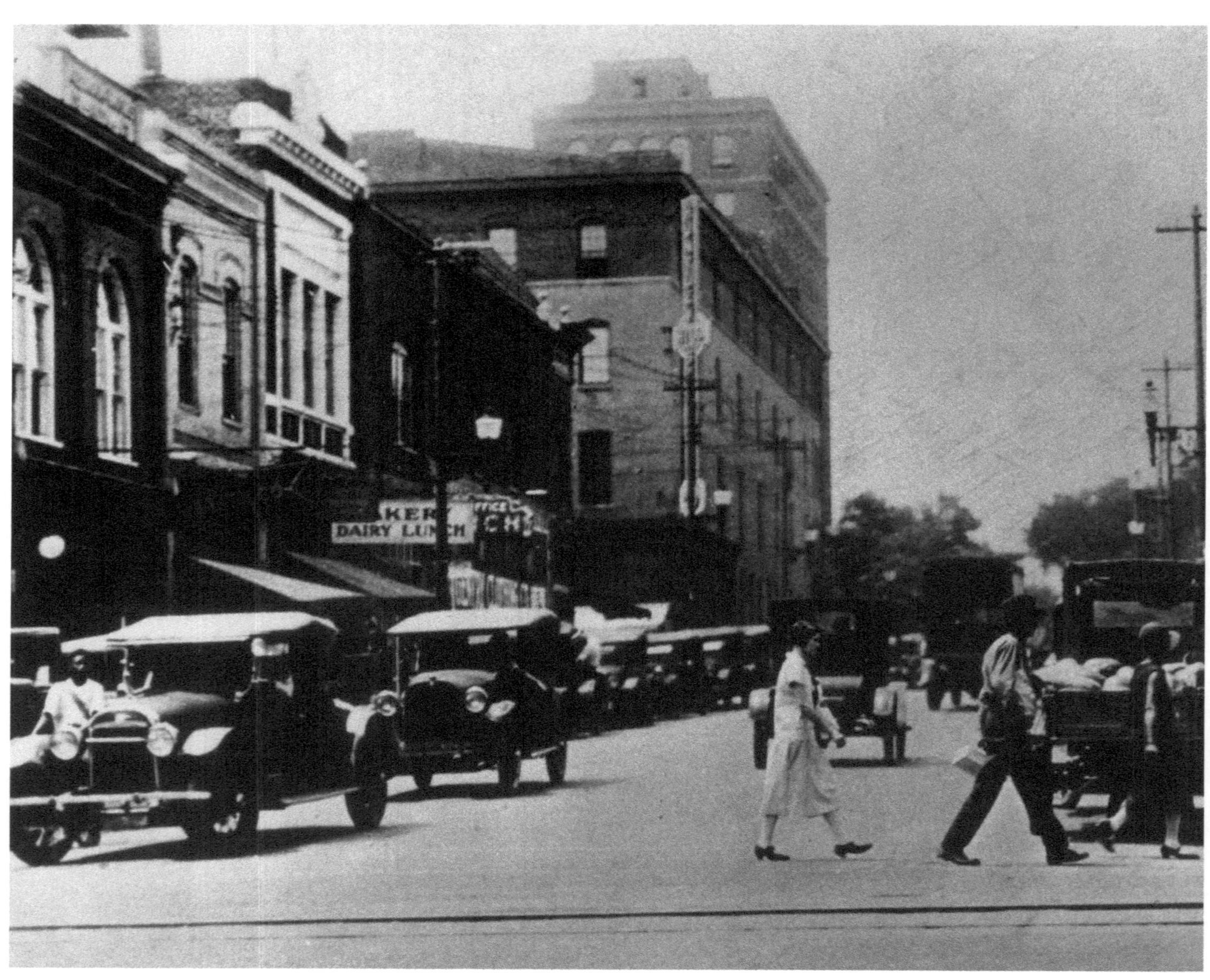


Prosperous citizens cross Fifth Street at its intersection with Liberty Street around 1928.

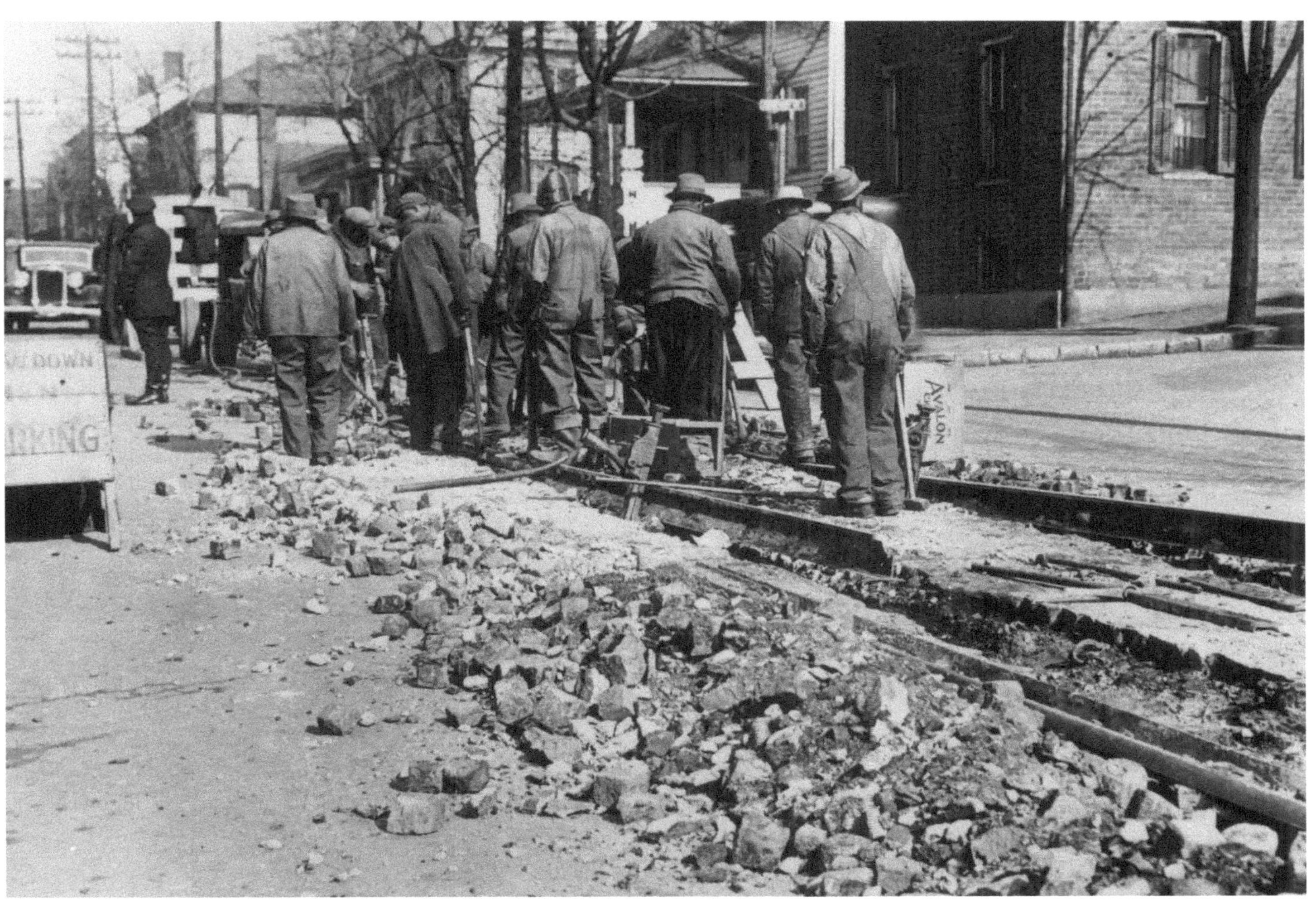


By the late 1920s, private bus companies began to take part of the load from the aging electric-trolley fleet. In this photograph, workmen repair or perhaps remove old trolley rails from the center of a Winston-Salem street.

Built in 1885, the Twin City Club thrived throughout the 1920s. Its dances, frequently held for teenagers, offered excellent opportunities to meet that special someone in chaperoned circumstances. The New Years Eve and Easter Monday dances were the social equivalent of "coming out" dances for local debutantes.

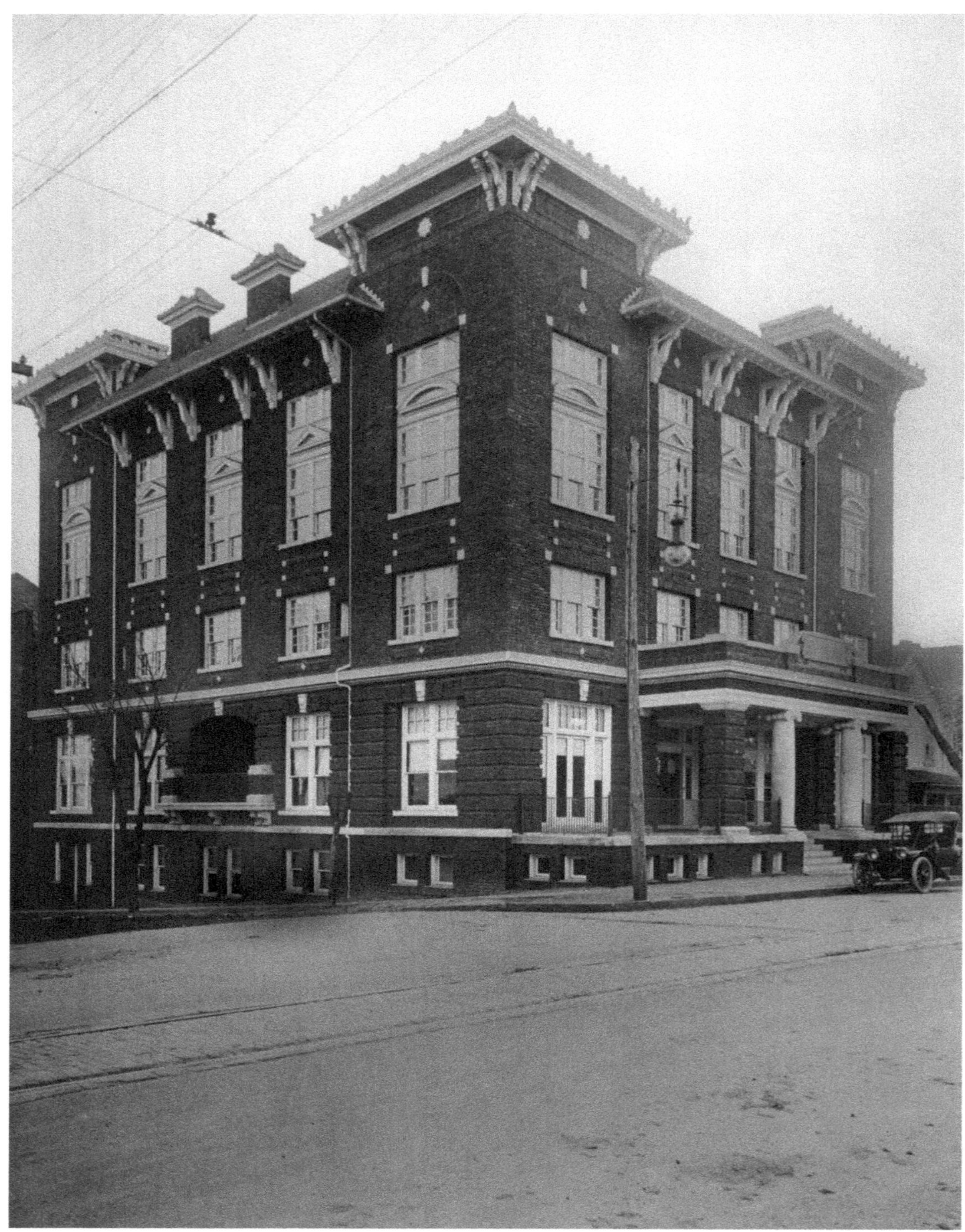

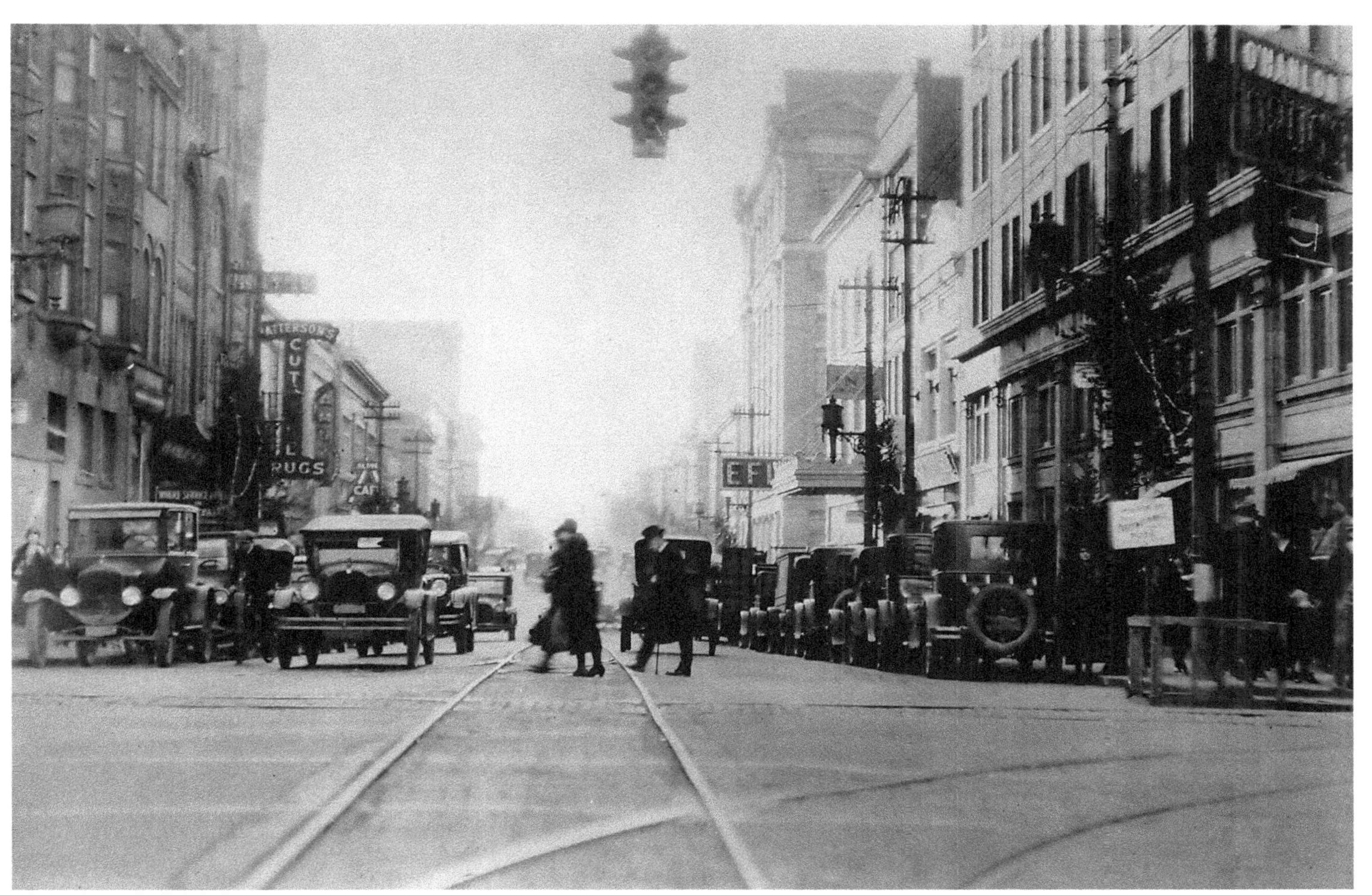


Pedestrians cross West Fourth Street at the intersection with Liberty Street on a cold, blustery day in the late 1920s. Note the traffic light swaying at the top-center of the photograph—a sure sign of increasing traffic in the city.

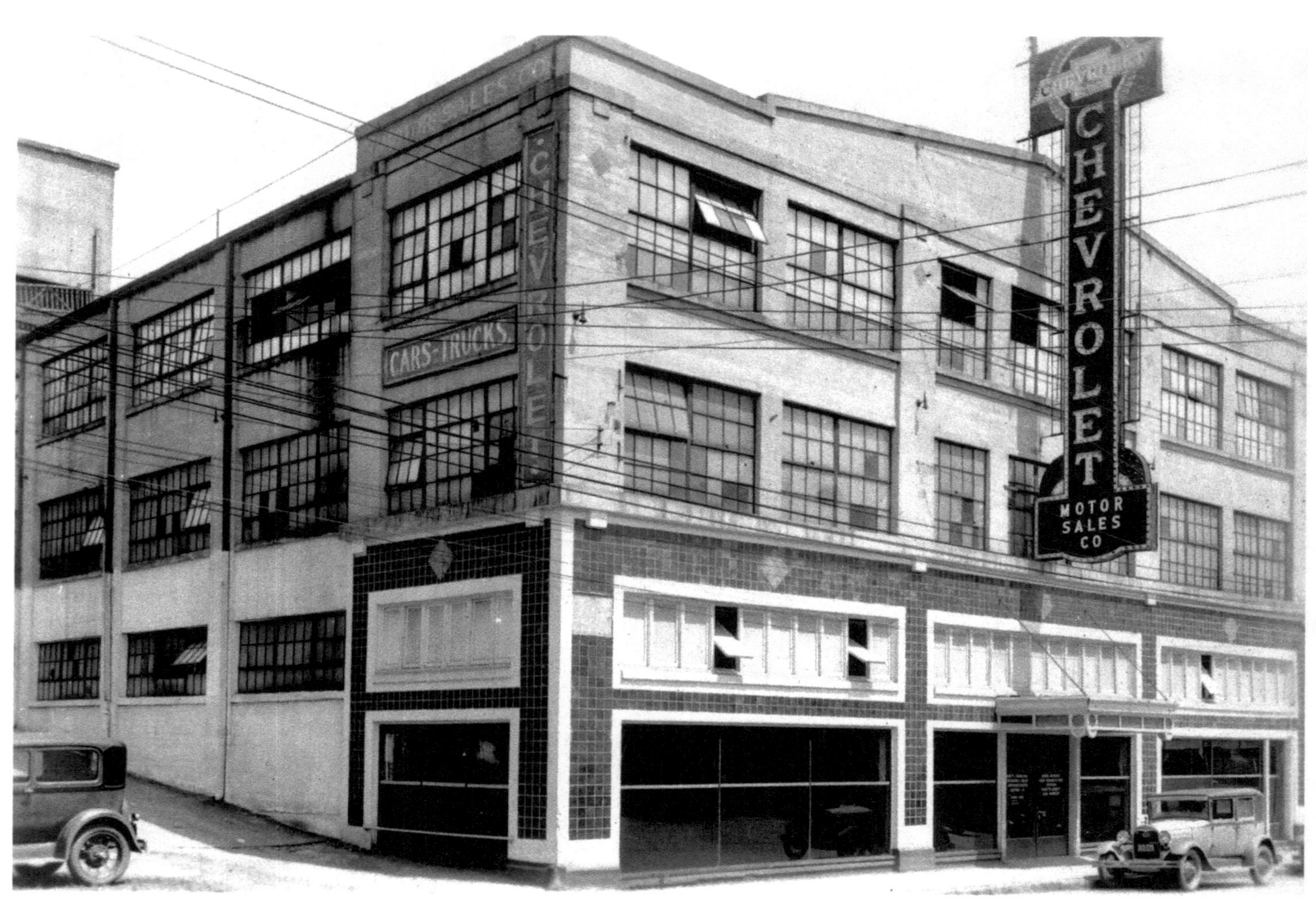


By the late 1920s, automobiles were big business—and were changing the face of the United States. Motor Sales Company was only one of many car dealerships that also offered automotive service to its customers.

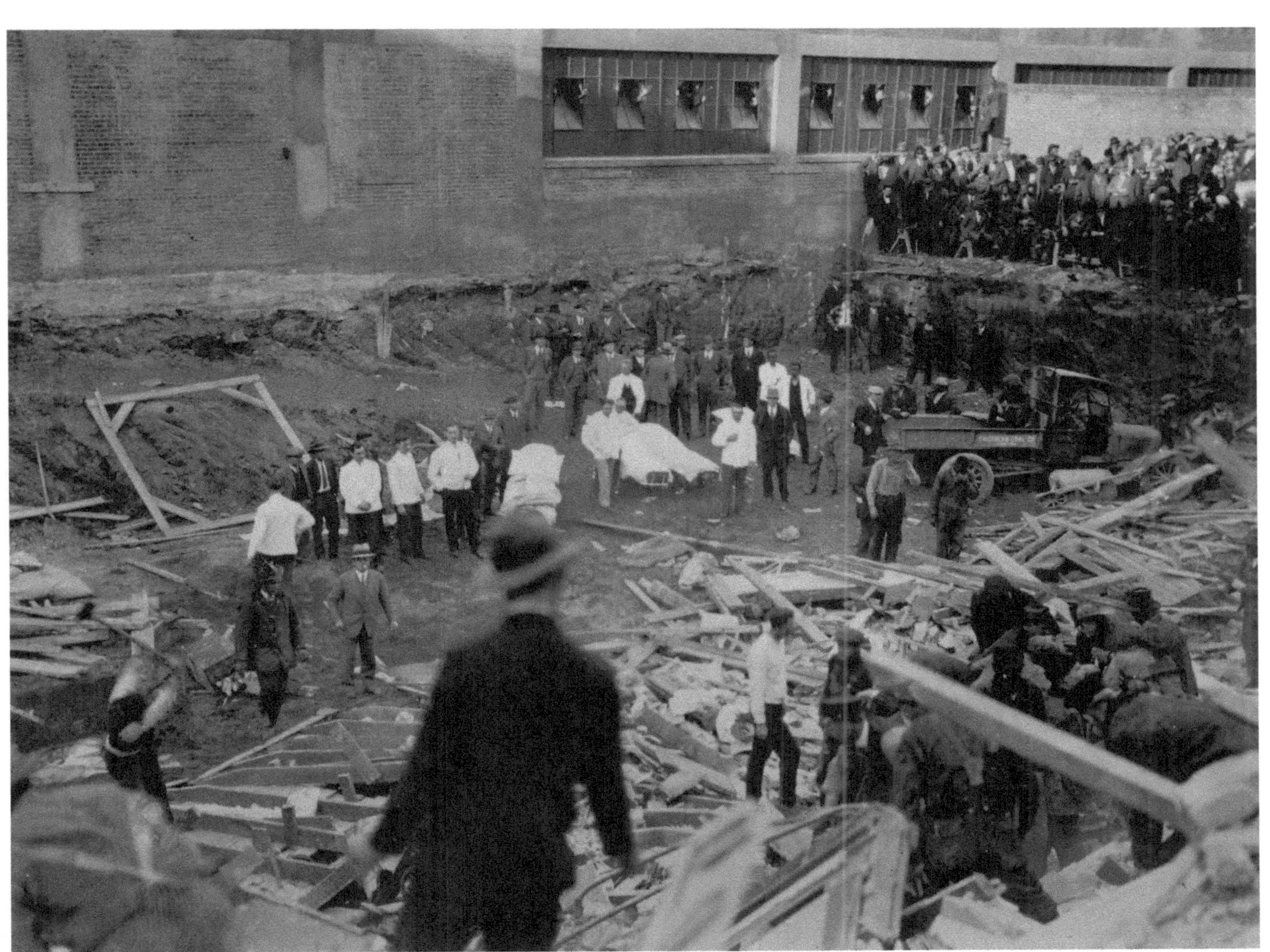

The collapse of the Urband Building on Main Street in 1927 shocked residents of Winston-Salem.

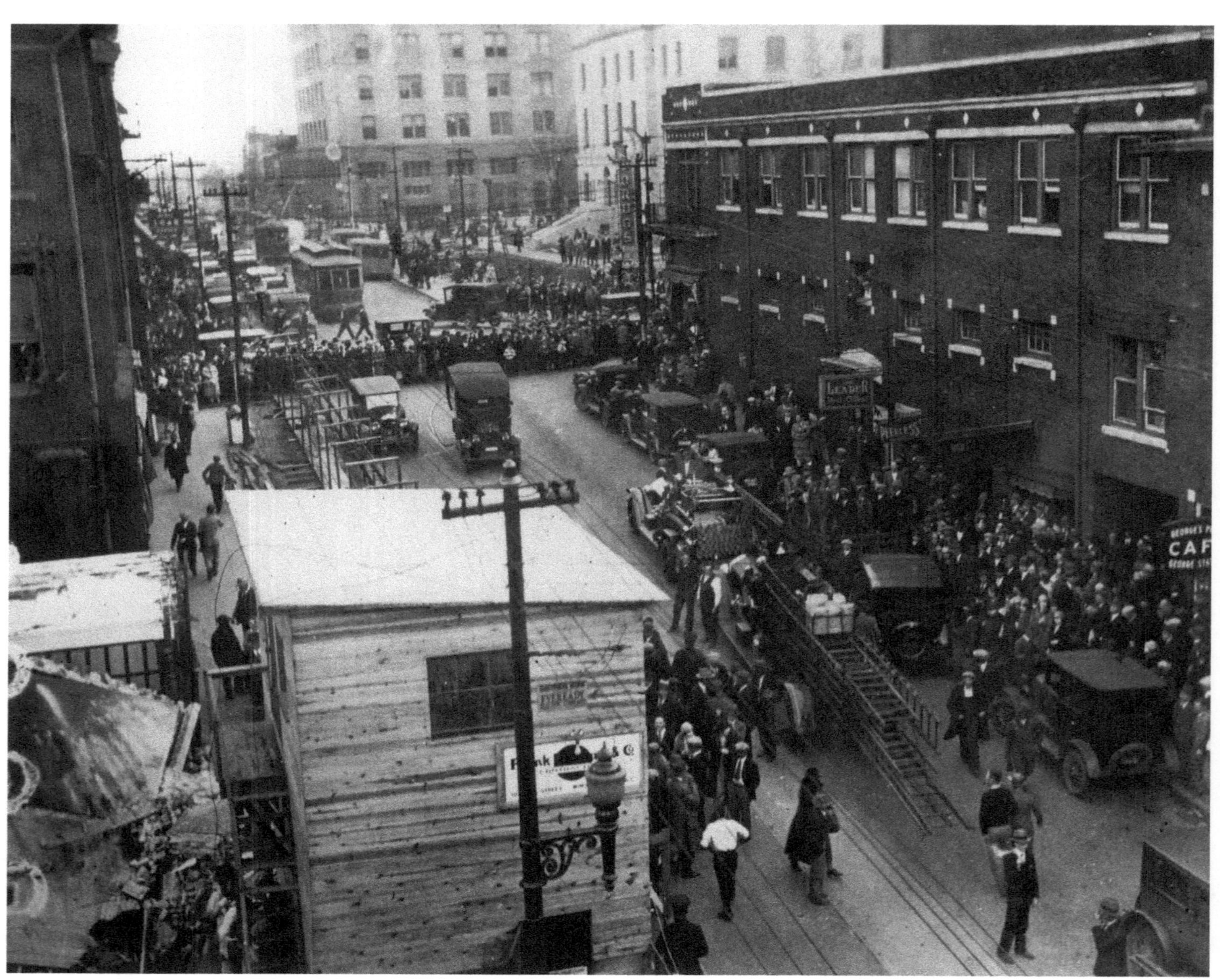

Citizens rush to assist after the collapse of the Urband Building on Main Street in 1927.

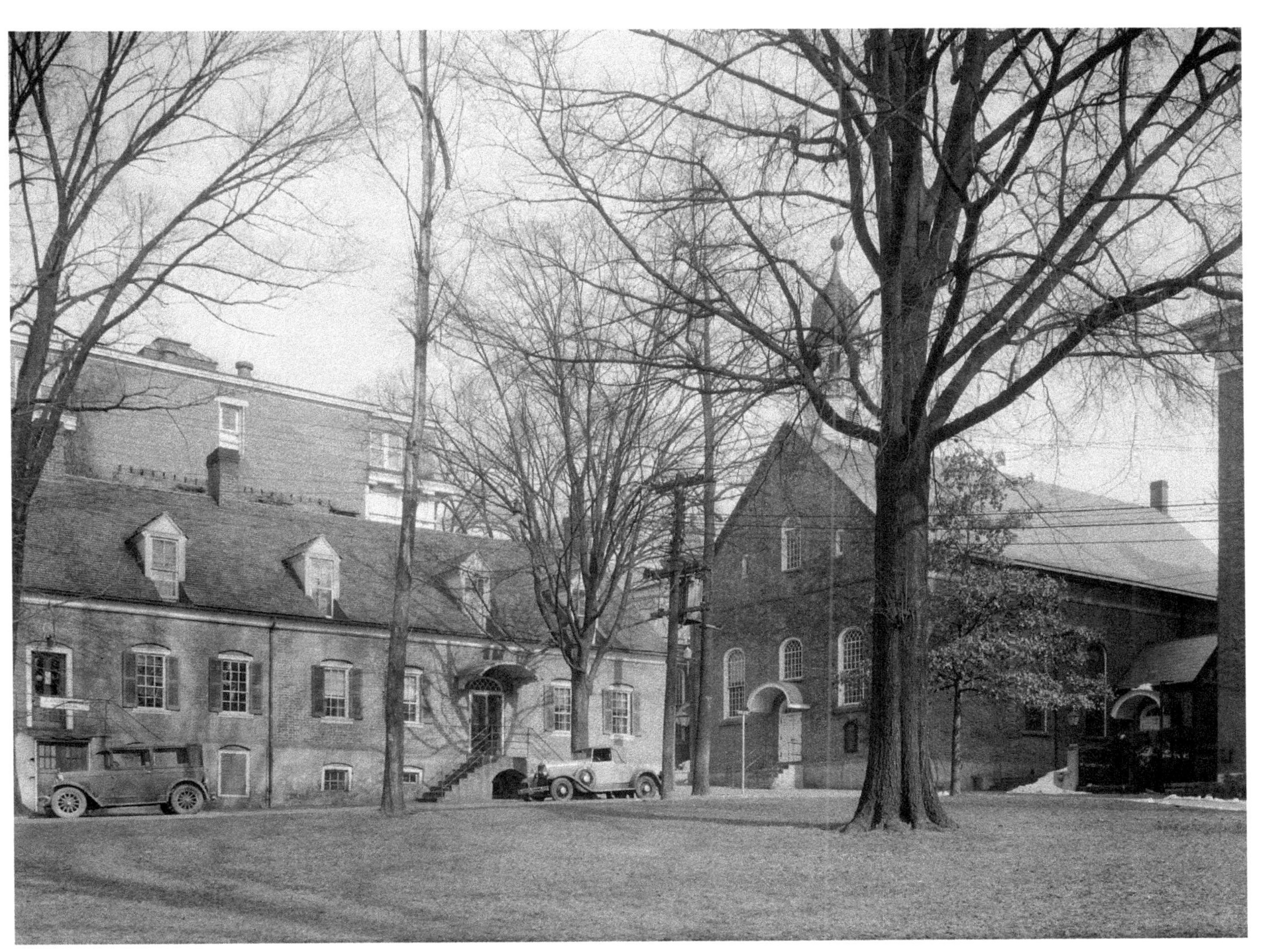

Buildings at Salem College as viewed across Salem Square around 1927.

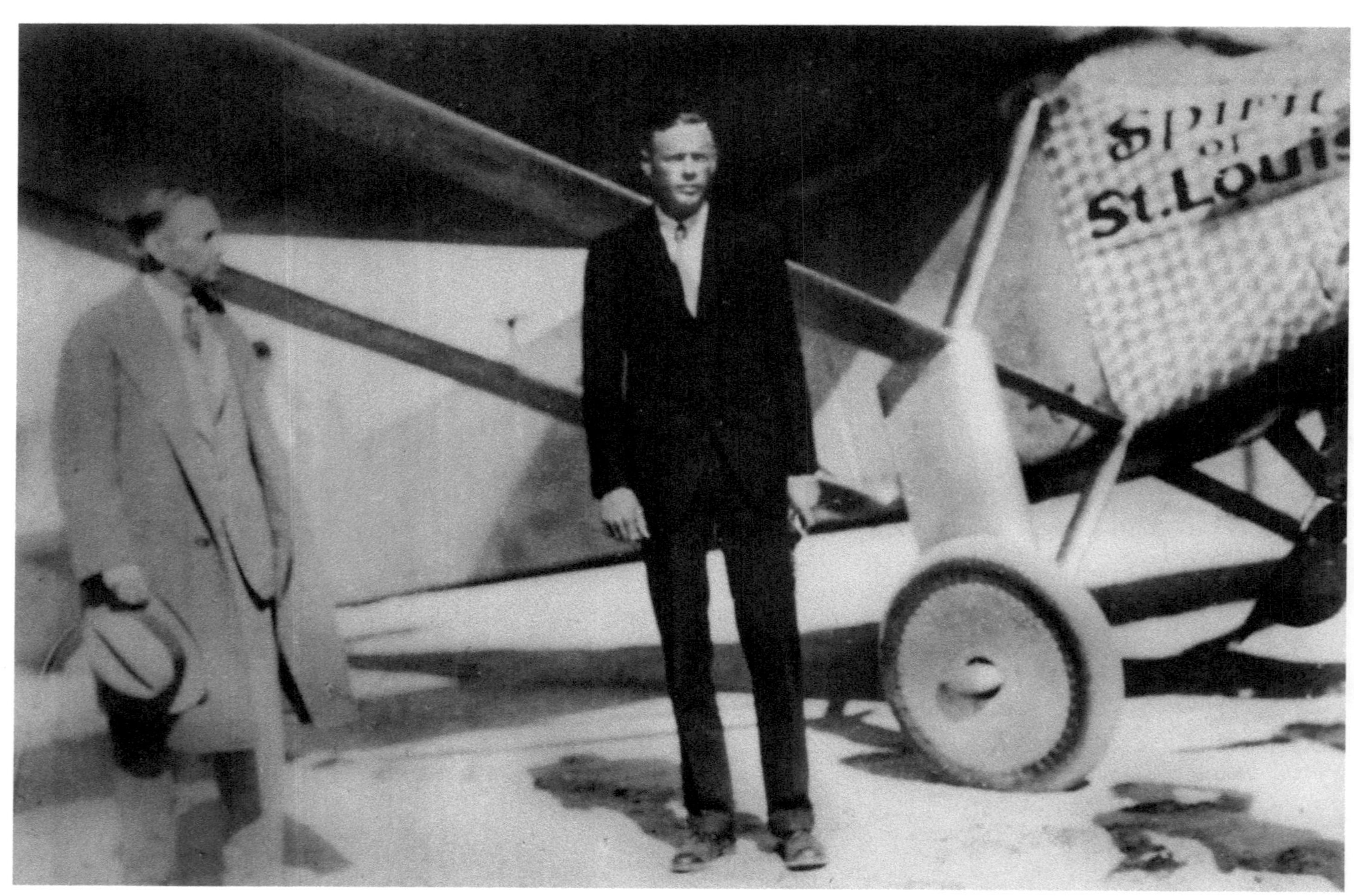


In 1927, Charles Lindbergh landed his famous *Spirit of St. Louis* at Miller Airport outside Winston-Salem. No doubt he inspired many youngsters while visiting the city.

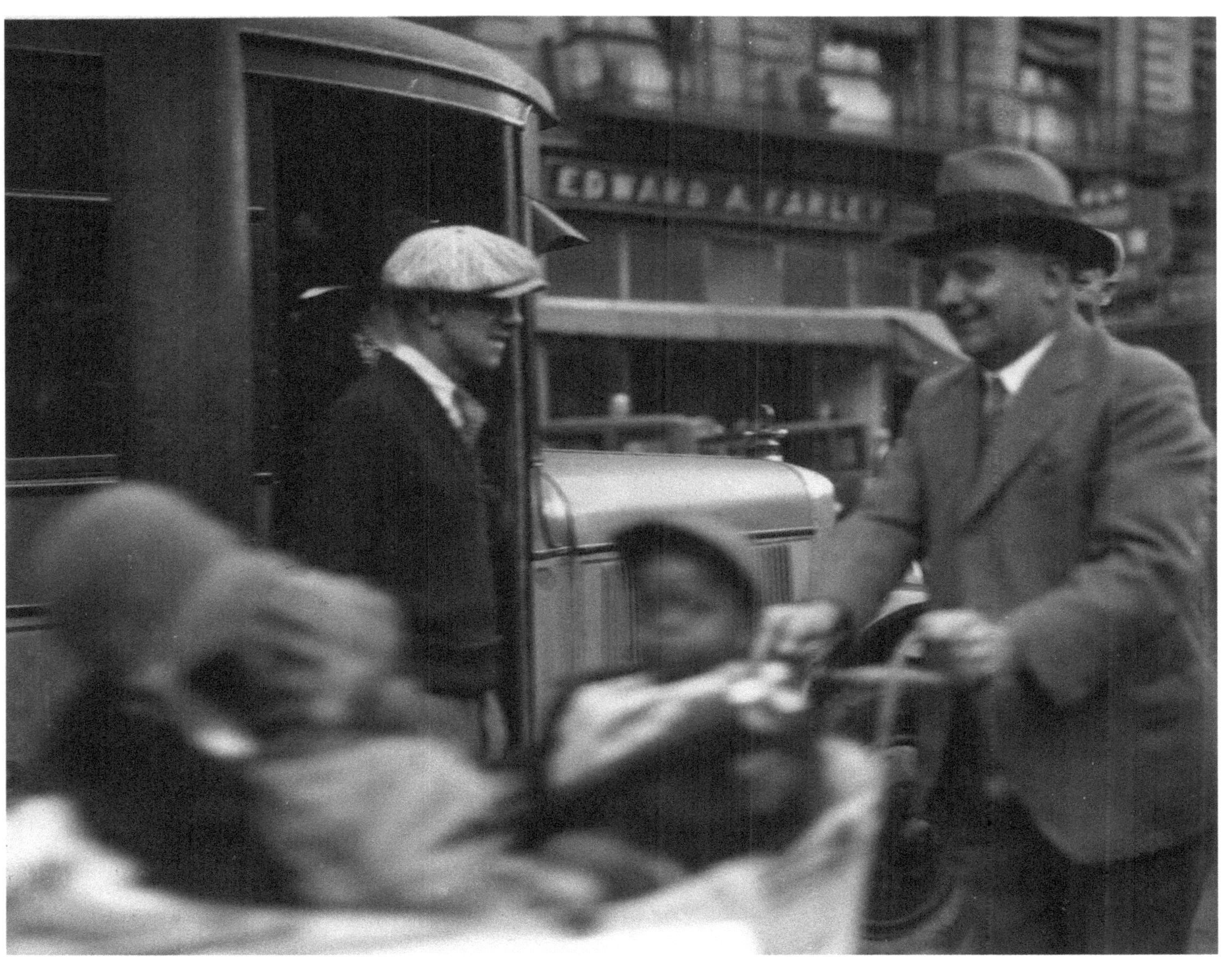


Two men smile in passing on a busy Main Street in 1928. Little did they suspect that their world was about to join the stock market in a mighty crash.

The completion of the twenty-two-story Reynolds Building on North Main Street in 1929 marked an end to new skyscrapers and significant changes in the downtown skyline, at least for a time. The dominating Reynolds Building would survive the coming Great Depression and continues to add character to the Winston-Salem skyline to this day.

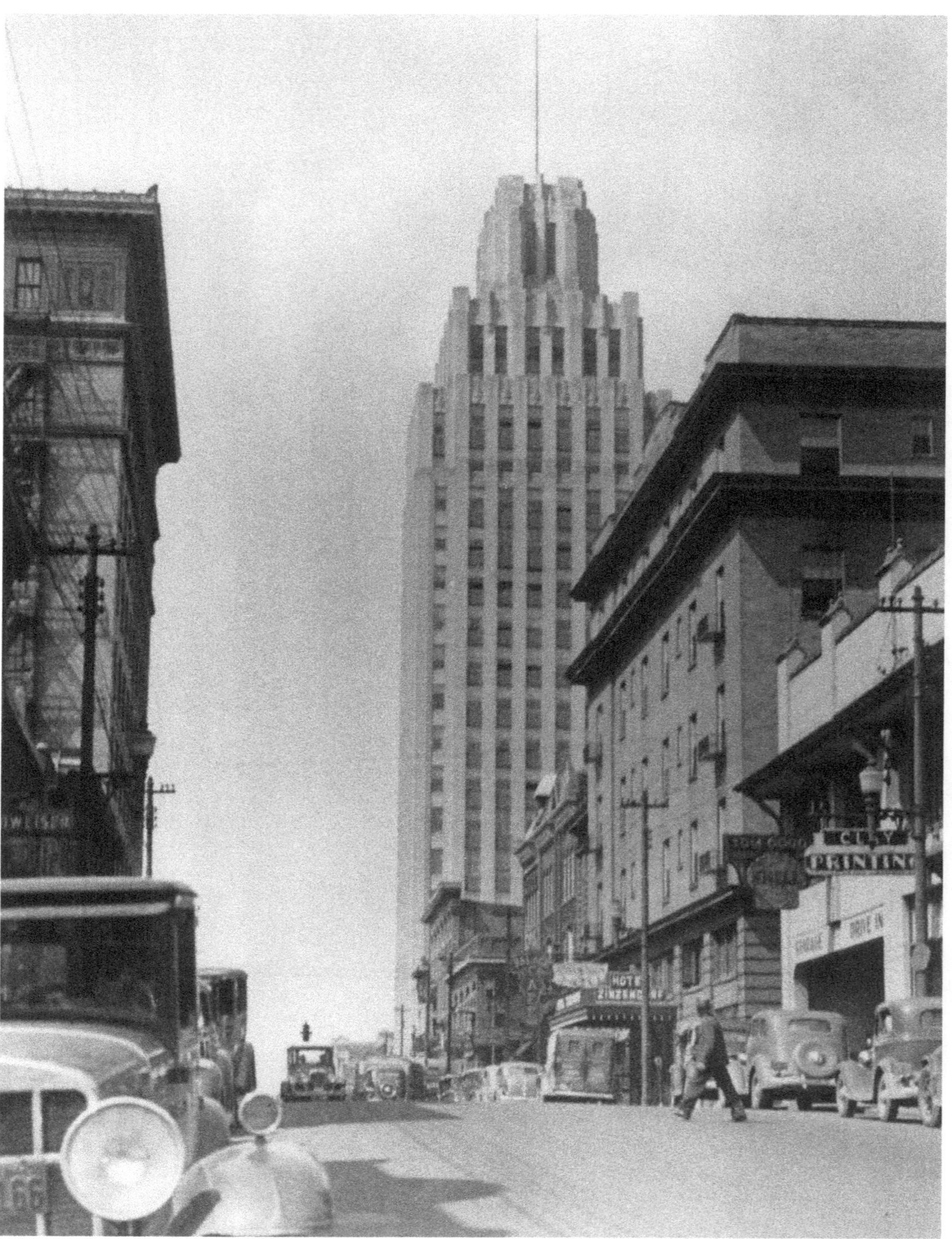

# The Hard Times

## (1930–1949)

Overproduction in industry, falling agricultural markets, and poor banking practices helped trigger the stock market crash in 1929 that signaled the beginning of a worldwide Great Depression. Winston-Salem suffered, but not to the extent of most cities in the United States. Tobacco and textile markets did not collapse, and Winston-Salem's banks managed to avoid closing their doors. The greatest blow to the city came when $1.5 million in street bonds, borrowed to pay for construction in the 1920s, came due around 1933. Fortunately for the city, its wealthiest citizens assisted with paying the bonds. Initially, the city council cut numerous jobs to balance the budget, with accompanying damage to city infrastructure when upkeep and preventative maintenance halted. But, as initial panic receded and extra money was found, the city took steps to help keep some money in people's pockets through job-sharing programs and public works projects, including the building of Bowman Gray Stadium with funds provided by the Gray family and the Works Progress Administration. The city also relocated hundreds of jobless and homeless families to empty farms in the county, where they could at least feed themselves.

On the heels of the Great Depression, an angry United States entered World War II. Winston-Salem sent its sons, and some daughters, to war: hundreds volunteered, and Forsyth County's Selective Service Board drafted over 13,000 men. For those who remained, there were jobs in plenty. From uniforms to foil chaff, production poured from the city's factories. Reynolds Tobacco actually employed German POWs to help make cigarettes. The prisoners returned to Germany in 1946; 301 citizens of Forsyth County did not return from the war.

Soldiers returning home after the war found a dirty, rundown, exhausted city. After years of penny-pinching, followed by war effort and labor shortage, potholes seemed more in evidence than pavement. Raw sewage flowed into streets in places, and slums had crept into Winston-Salem's nooks and crannies. Even as they celebrated an end to war in 1945, and the centennial of Forsyth County in 1949, the returning soldiers knew there was work to be done to restore the fading glory of their city.

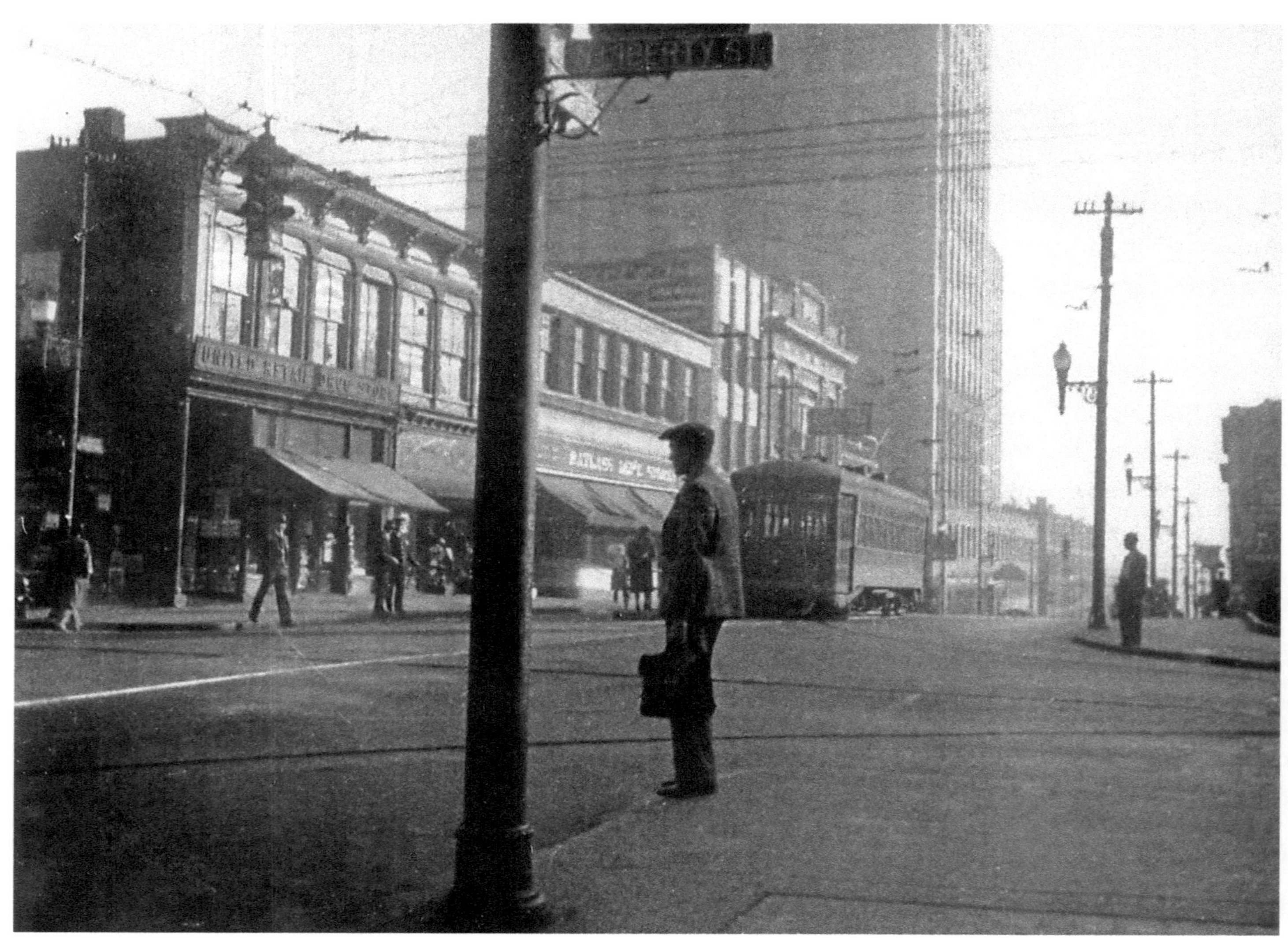

Liberty and Fourth streets, usually vibrant with pedestrian and automotive traffic, loom almost empty in 1931. Though Winston-Salem suffered less than many cities, few people in the early 1930s had excess wealth for luxuries—which included gas and tires for cars as well as new clothes and meals in restaurants. Small enterprises along these once bustling streets inevitably suffered, many closing their doors for good.

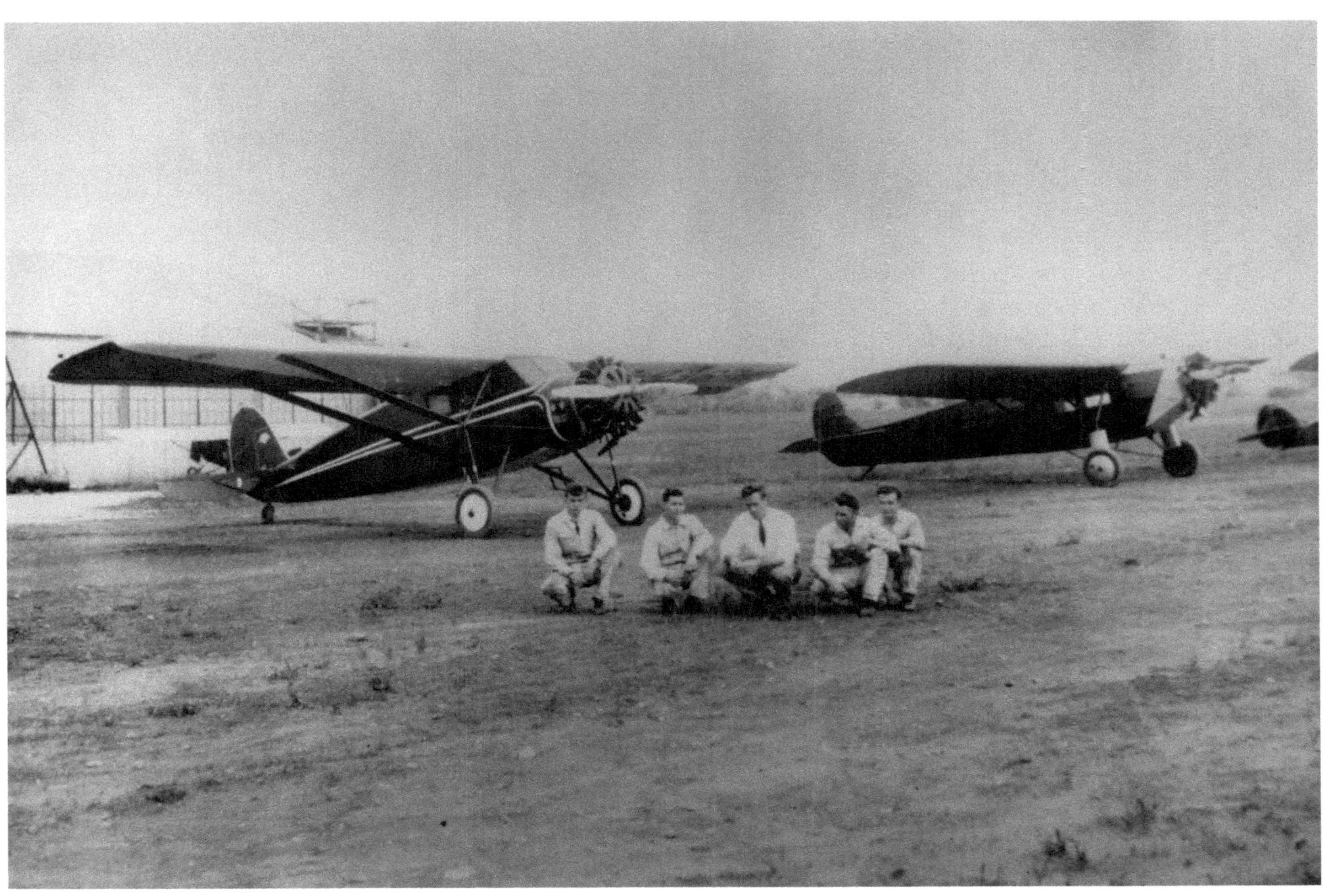

Because Winston-Salem's base industries (tobacco and textiles) remained in operation throughout the Great Depression, Miller Field continued to operate. Small planes, serviced by these mechanics in 1930, flew many corporate executives to meetings aimed at restoring the American economy.

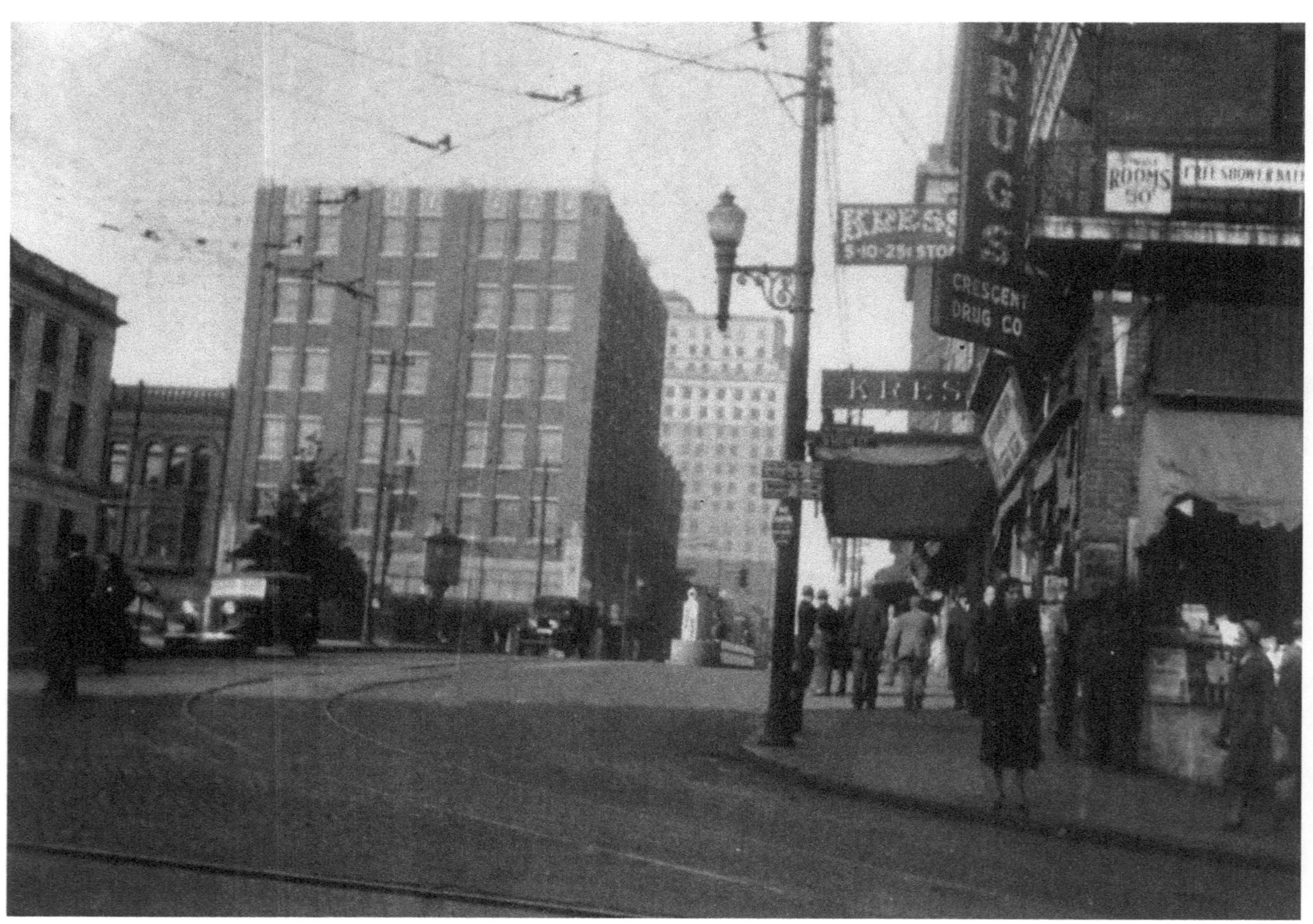


Pedestrians, shadowed by the proud skyscrapers built in the 1920s, wait at the corner of West Fourth and Main streets in 1932. Some wait for the next streetcar while others visit the corner drugstore. Perhaps some of these people gossiped about the biggest news in Winston-Salem that year: aviator Z. Smith Reynolds, R. J. Reynolds's youngest son, died in a mysterious shooting at the family home at age 32.

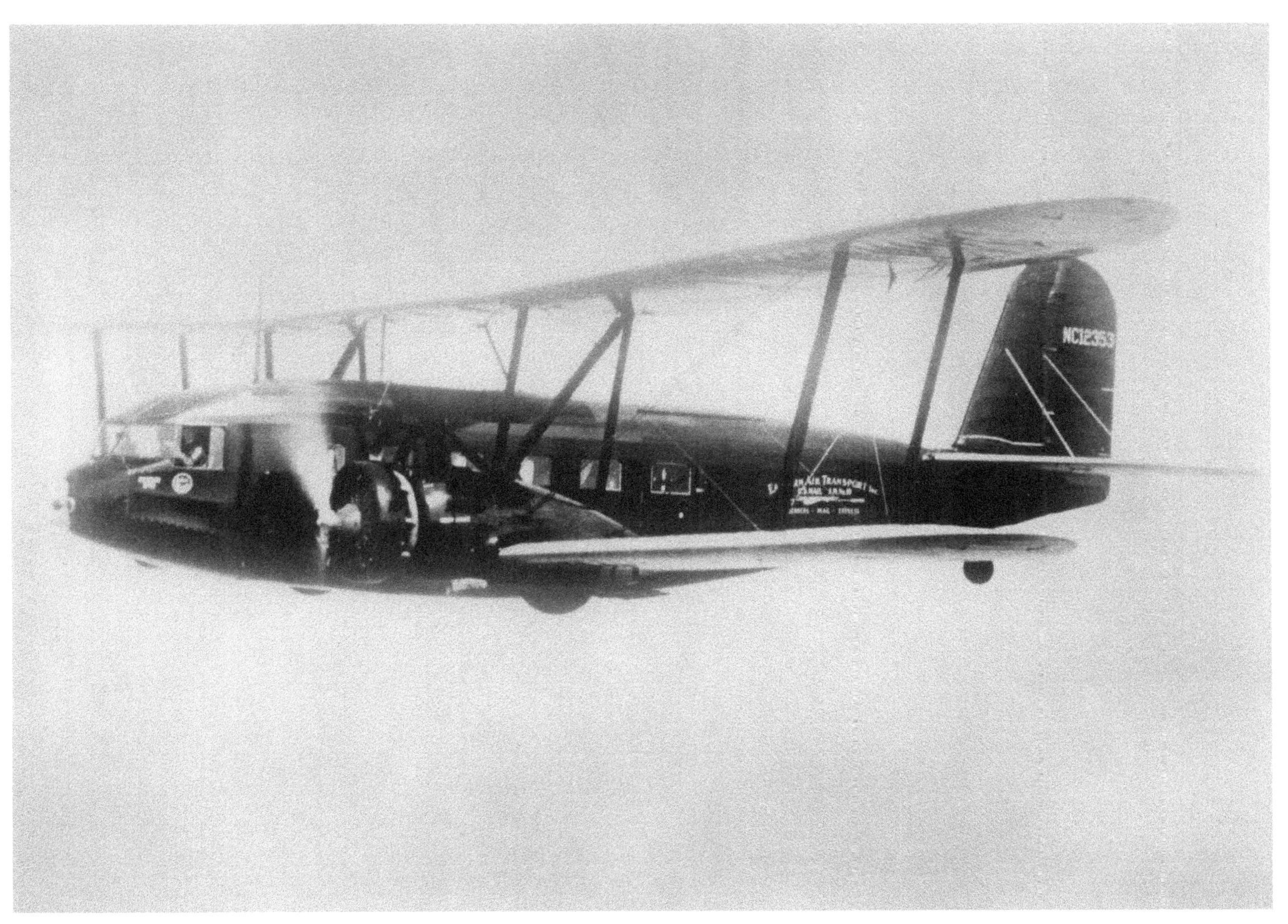


In 1935, Eastern Airlines established passenger flights into Miller Field, using planes such as this Curtiss Condor. Unfortunately, the field could not handle the large planes. Eastern suspended service later that year, and only in 1941 did regular commercial service return to Winston-Salem.

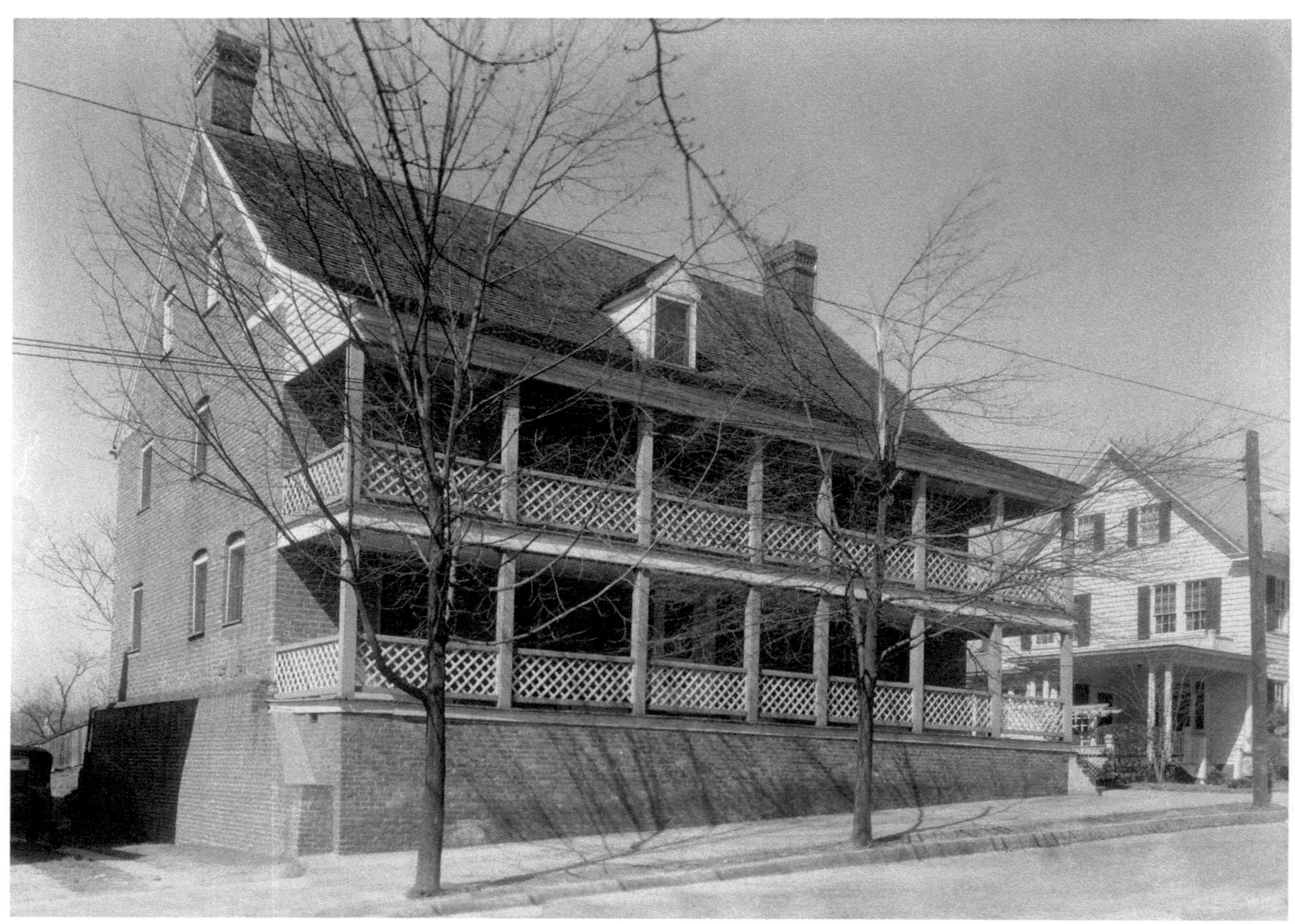

During the Great Depression, the federal government made many efforts to reduce unemployment, including hiring people to preserve American historical and cultural artifacts. Photographers participating in the Historical American Buildings Survey (HABS began in 1933) captured many Winston-Salem historic sites on film, such as Salem Tavern on South Main Street, dating from 1784 and photographed in 1934. There George Washington once enjoyed a peaceful evening, and probably a dram or two.

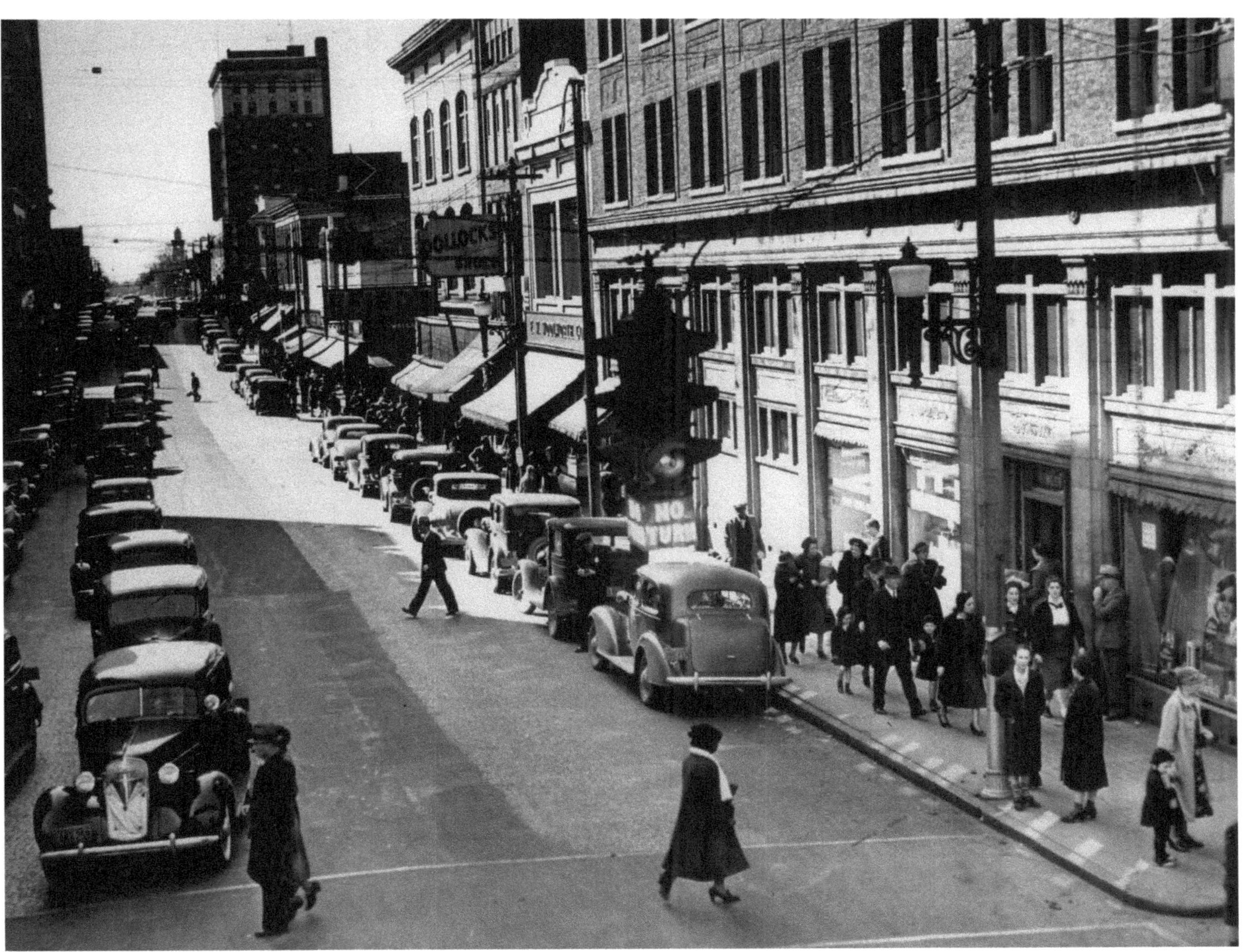

By 1935, Winston-Salem's economy began to recover, if slowly, from the early Depression. The Federal Reserve Board rated it as one of the top ten cities in the country in industrial production, while aggressive programs such as clean-up campaigns and job-sharing kept at least some money in most pockets. This view along West Fourth from Liberty Street seems little different from the busy streets of the late 1920s.

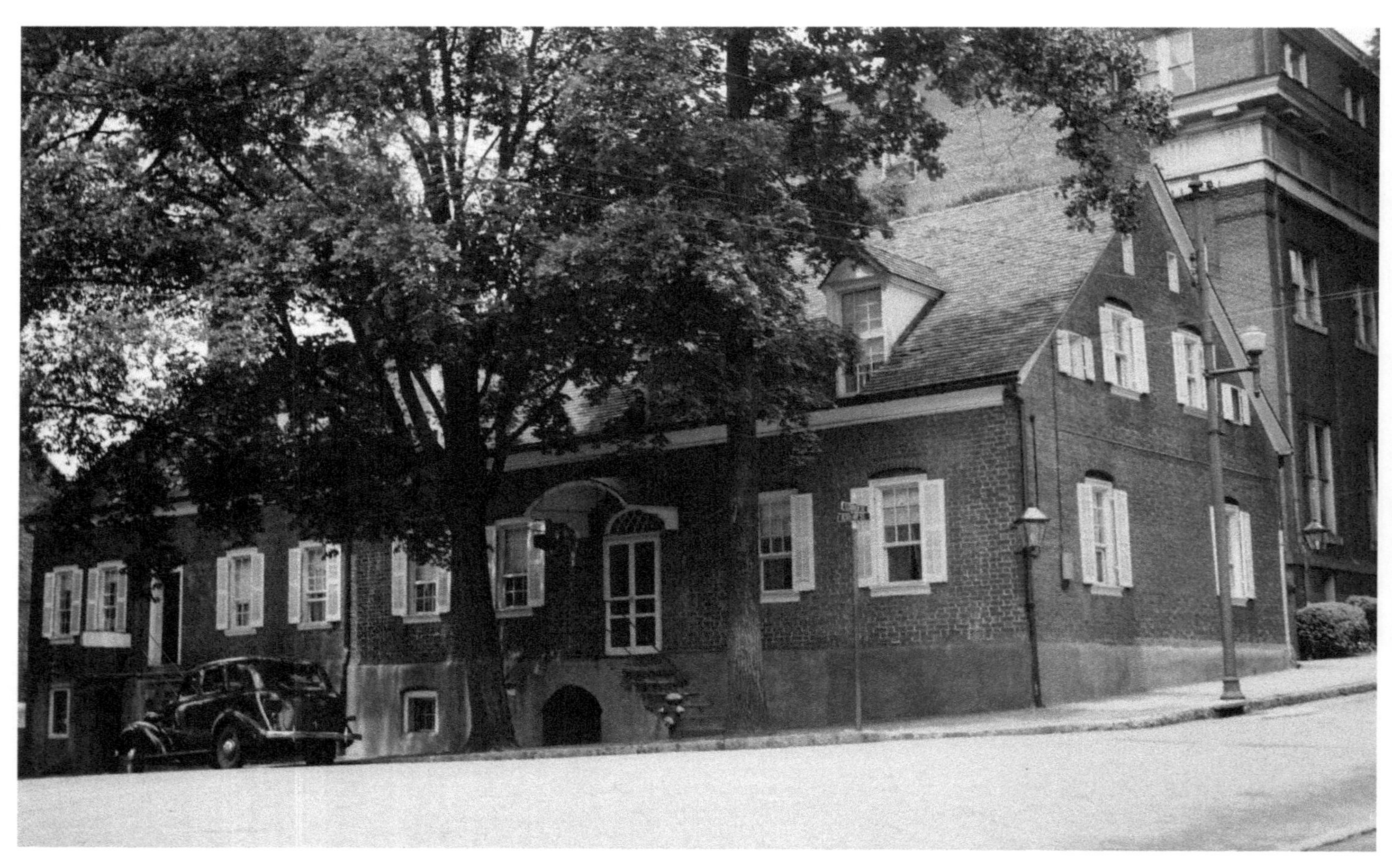

Situated on Academy Street, the Administration Building at Salem College, the thirteenth-oldest college in the United States, is seen here as it appeared in 1937.

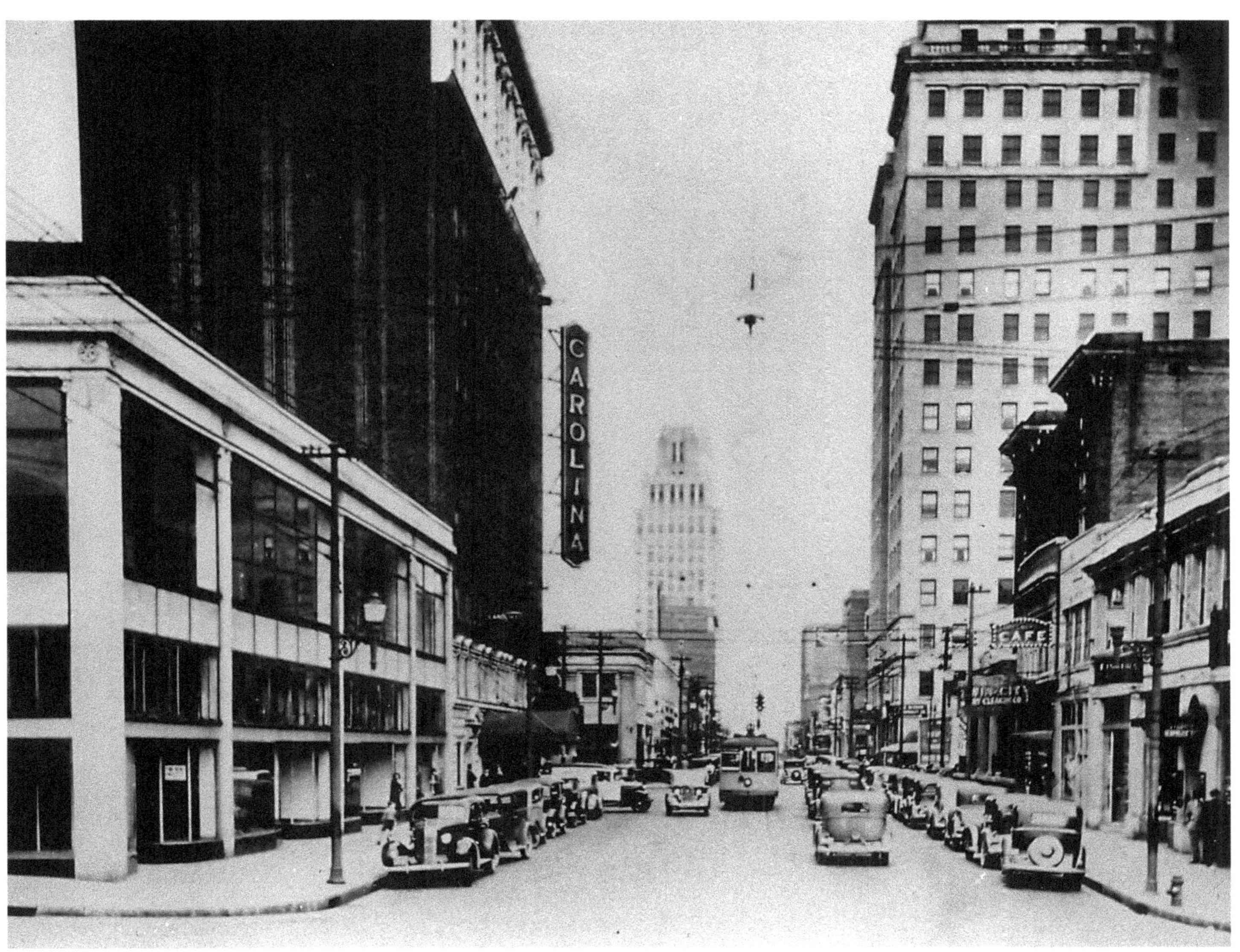


This view of busy West Fourth Street at Spruce Street, from around 1935, is dominated by the Carolina Hotel on the left, the Nissen Building on the right, and the R. J. Reynolds Building in the center.

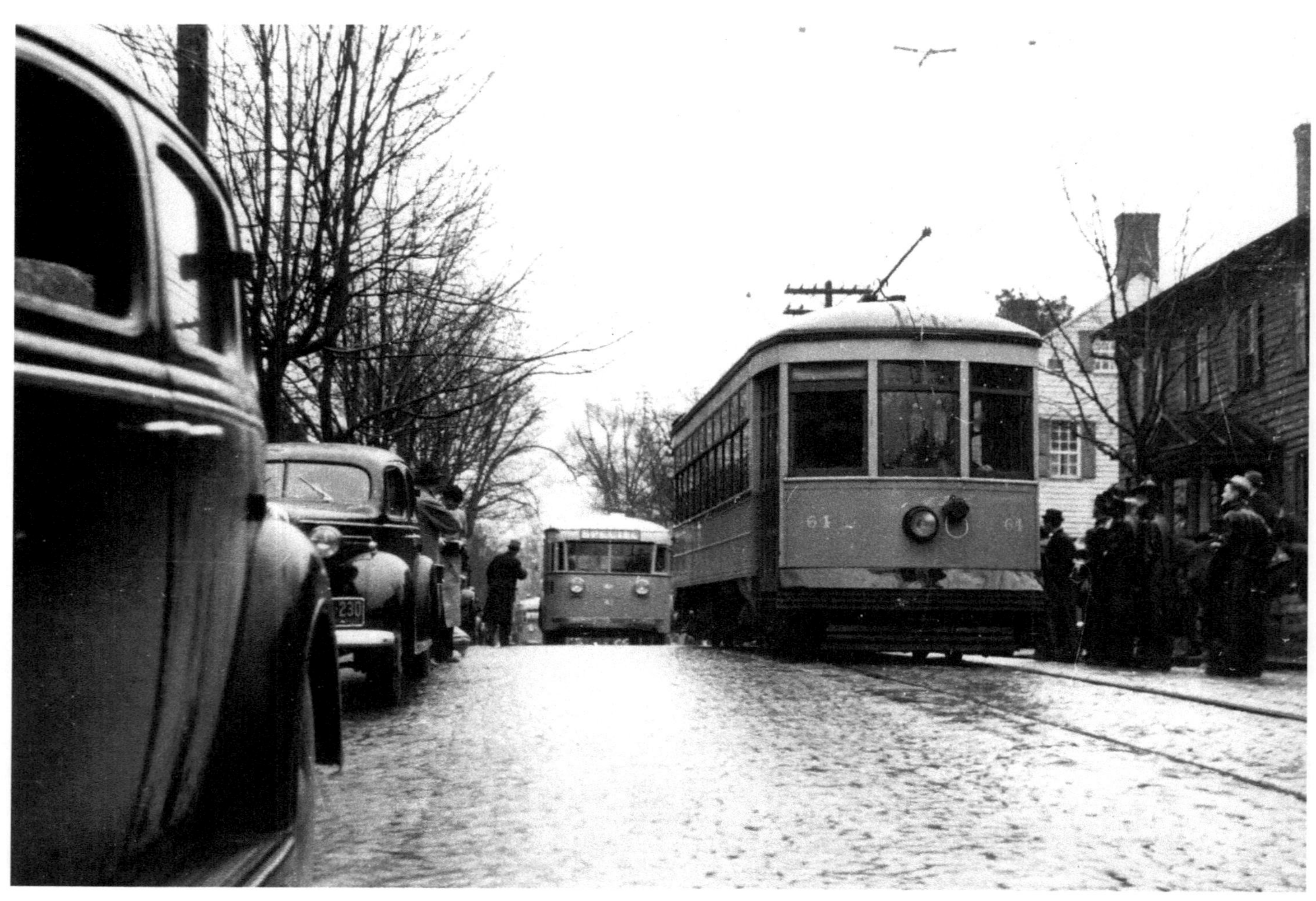

A new city bus passes an old streetcar in 1936. The streetcar seems to be doing more business; however, by the end of the year the old electric trolleys would go the way of the horse and buggy in Winston-Salem, another victim of the internal combustion engine.

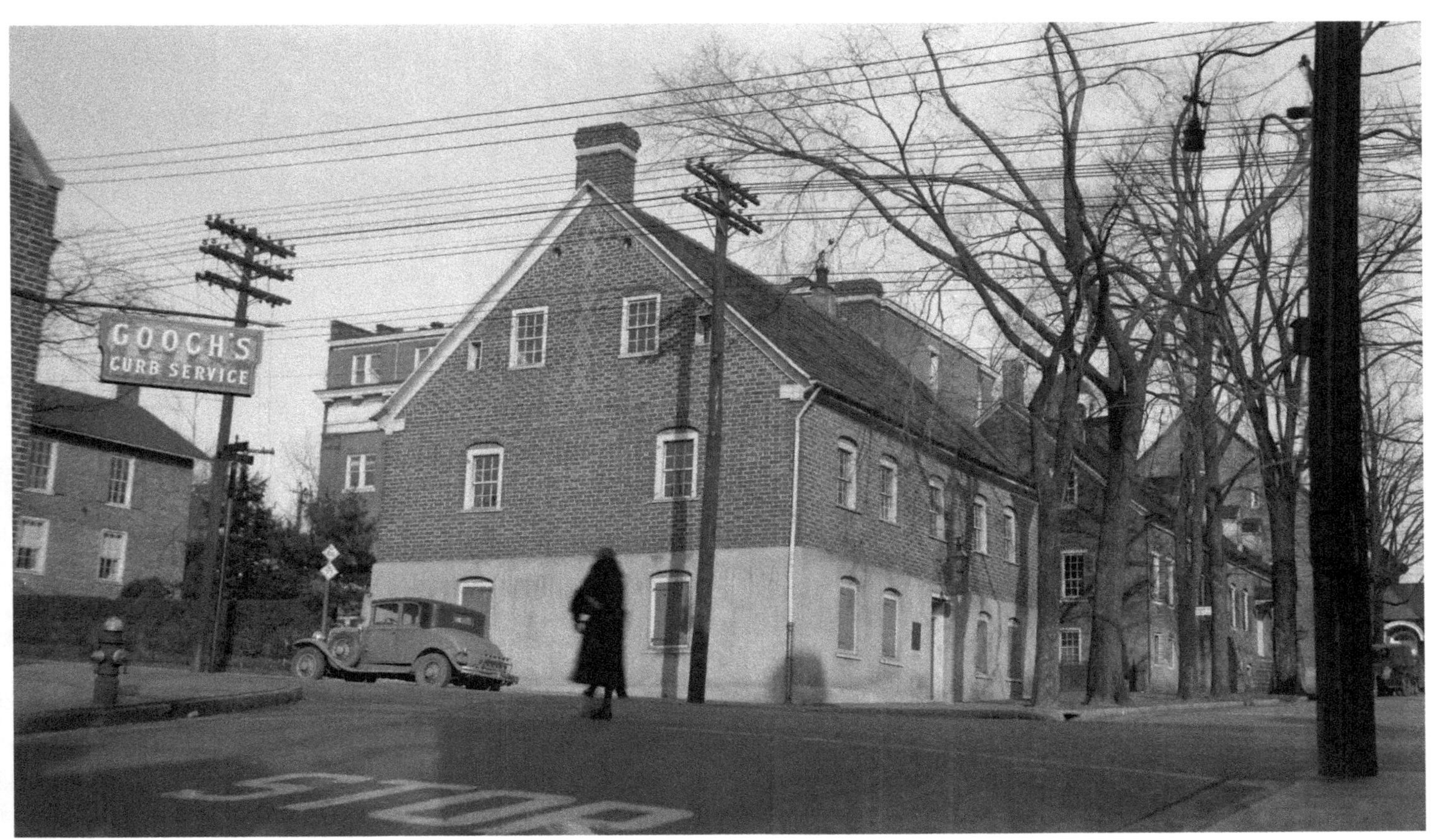


The Moravian community constructed the Salem Boys School at Main and Academy Streets in 1794. This photo, from 1934, does not show the Hall of History added to the structure in 1937 by the Wachovia Historical Society. Formed in 1895, the society deserves the thanks of every North Carolinian for its work to preserve the treasures of Old Salem.

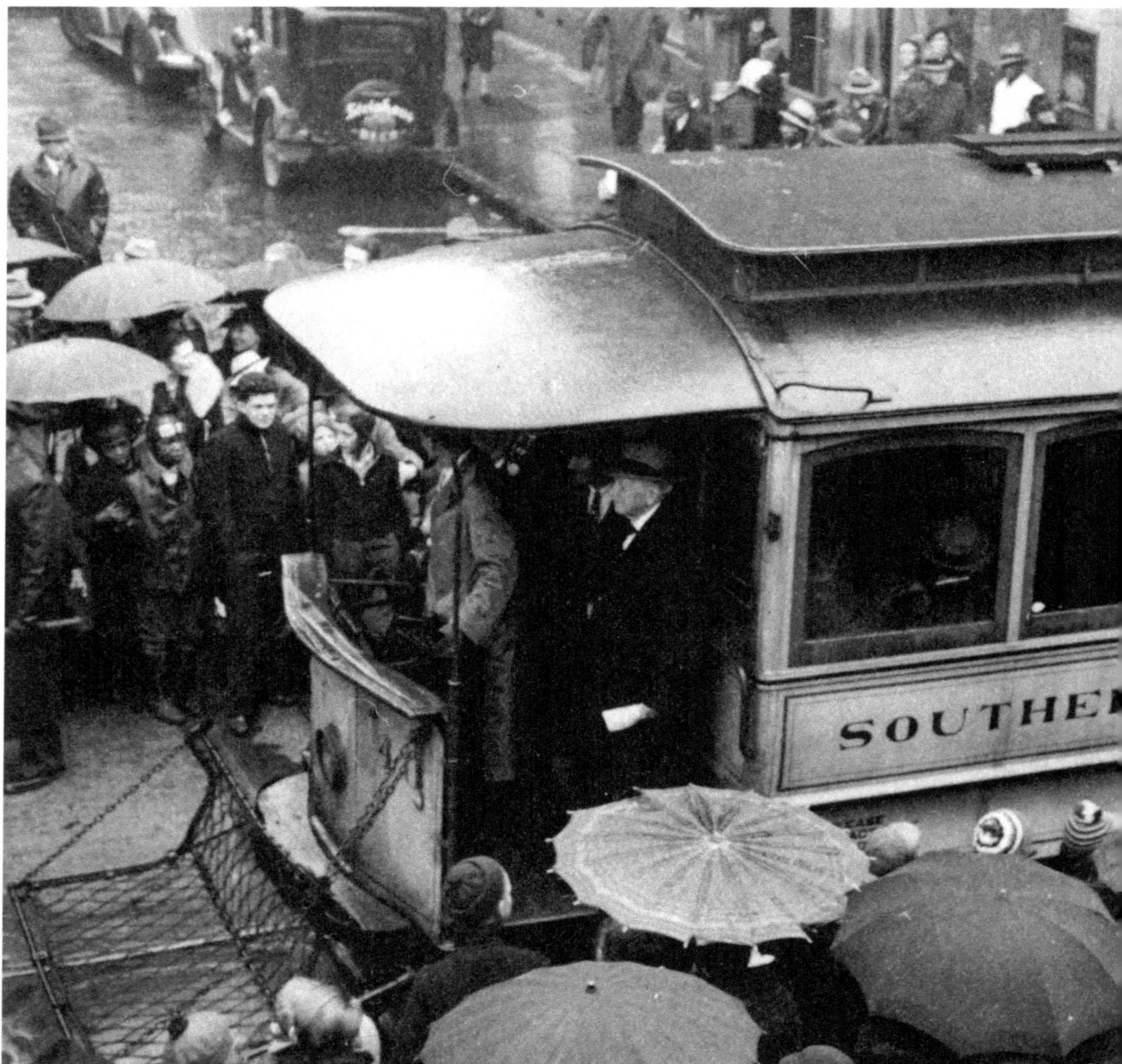
SOUTHE

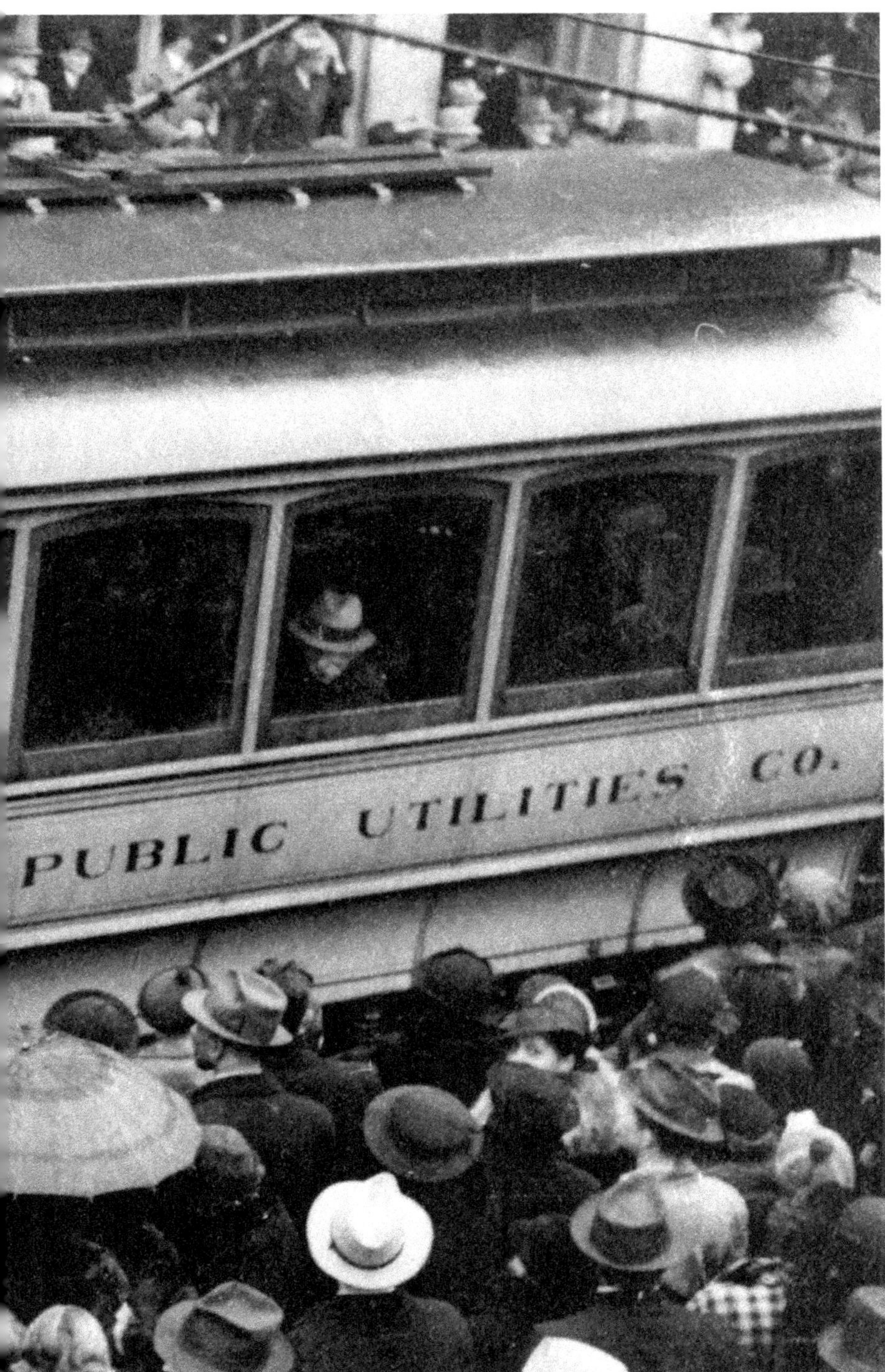


December 30, 1936, dawned cold and rainy, perhaps fitting weather for the elegiac "Romance of Transportation Parade" that marked the end of thirty-six years' of streetcar service in Winston-Salem. Henry E. Fries, who played a key role in beginning electric trolley service in 1890, stands beside the conductor of the car.

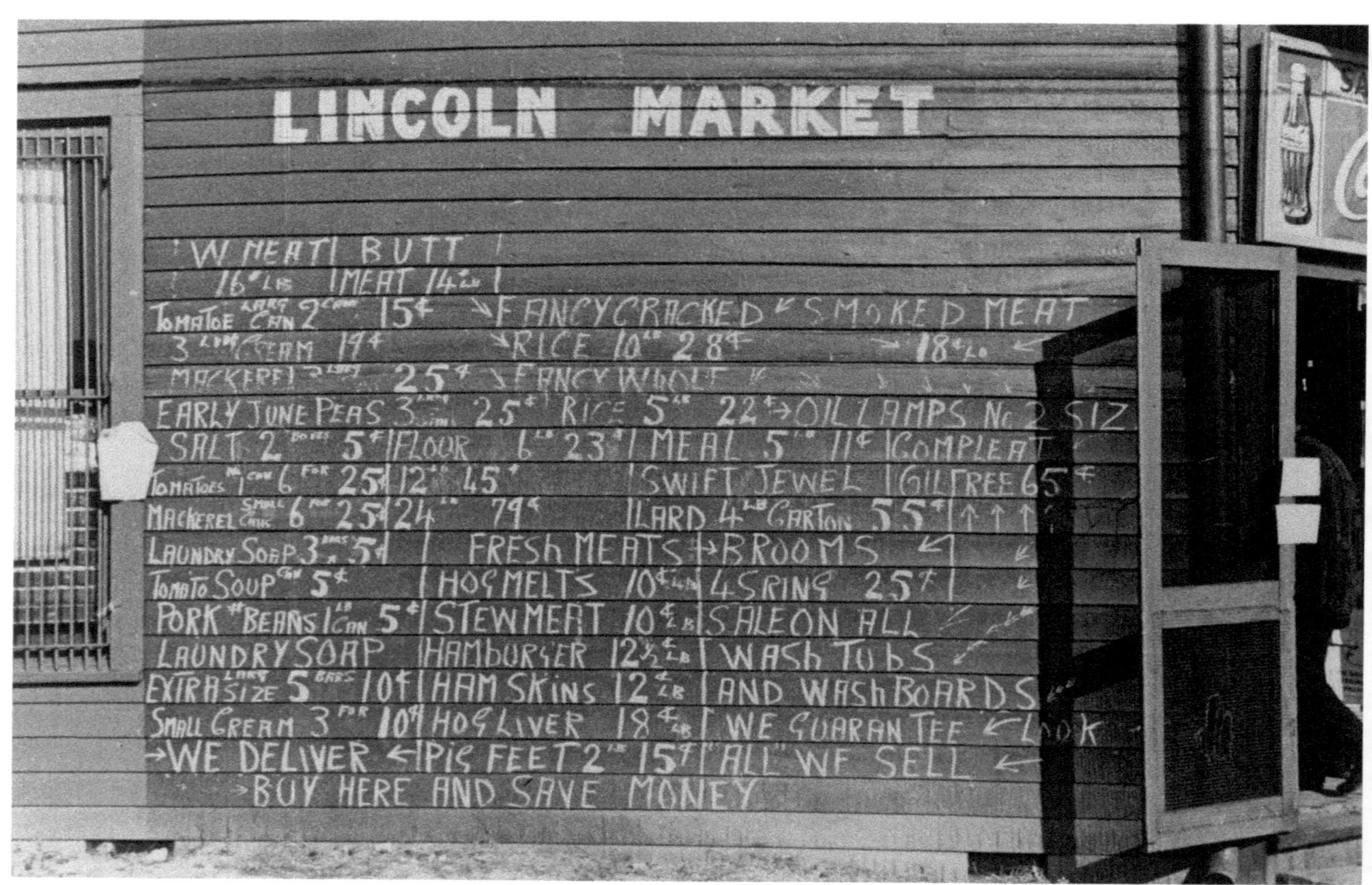


Typical of many corner grocery stores trying to survive in Winston-Salem in 1935, the Lincoln Market carried a variety of goods, from laundry soap to meats, at reasonable prices—reasonable, that is, for those who had money. The market's outdoor advertising caught the eye of famed photographer Walker Evans, who was working for the U.S. Resettlement Administration (predecessor of the Farm Security Administration) when he took this photo.

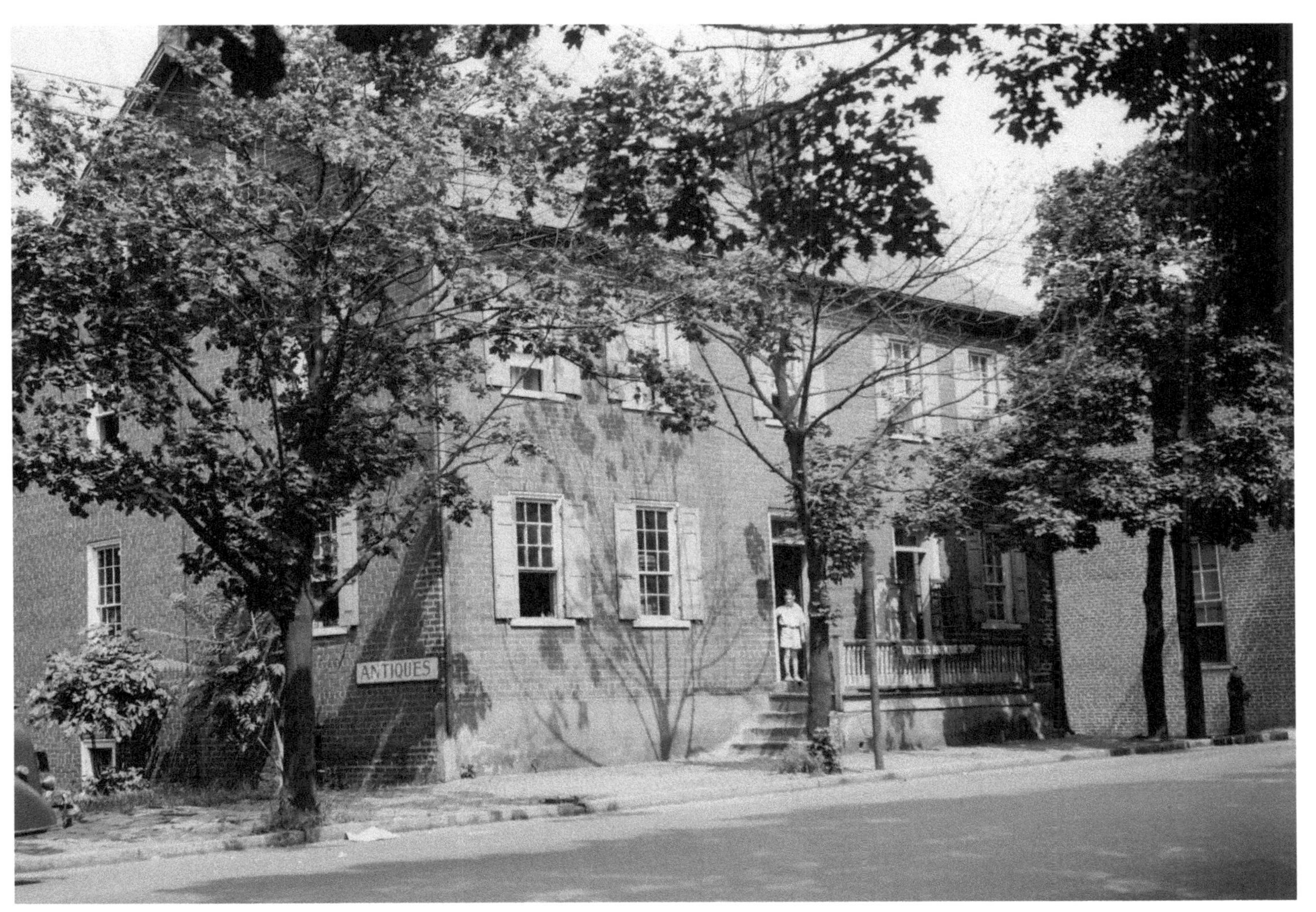


In 1937, the Israel Loesch Bank & House supported an antique business rather than the lending institution of the 1790s. The building is on South Main Street.

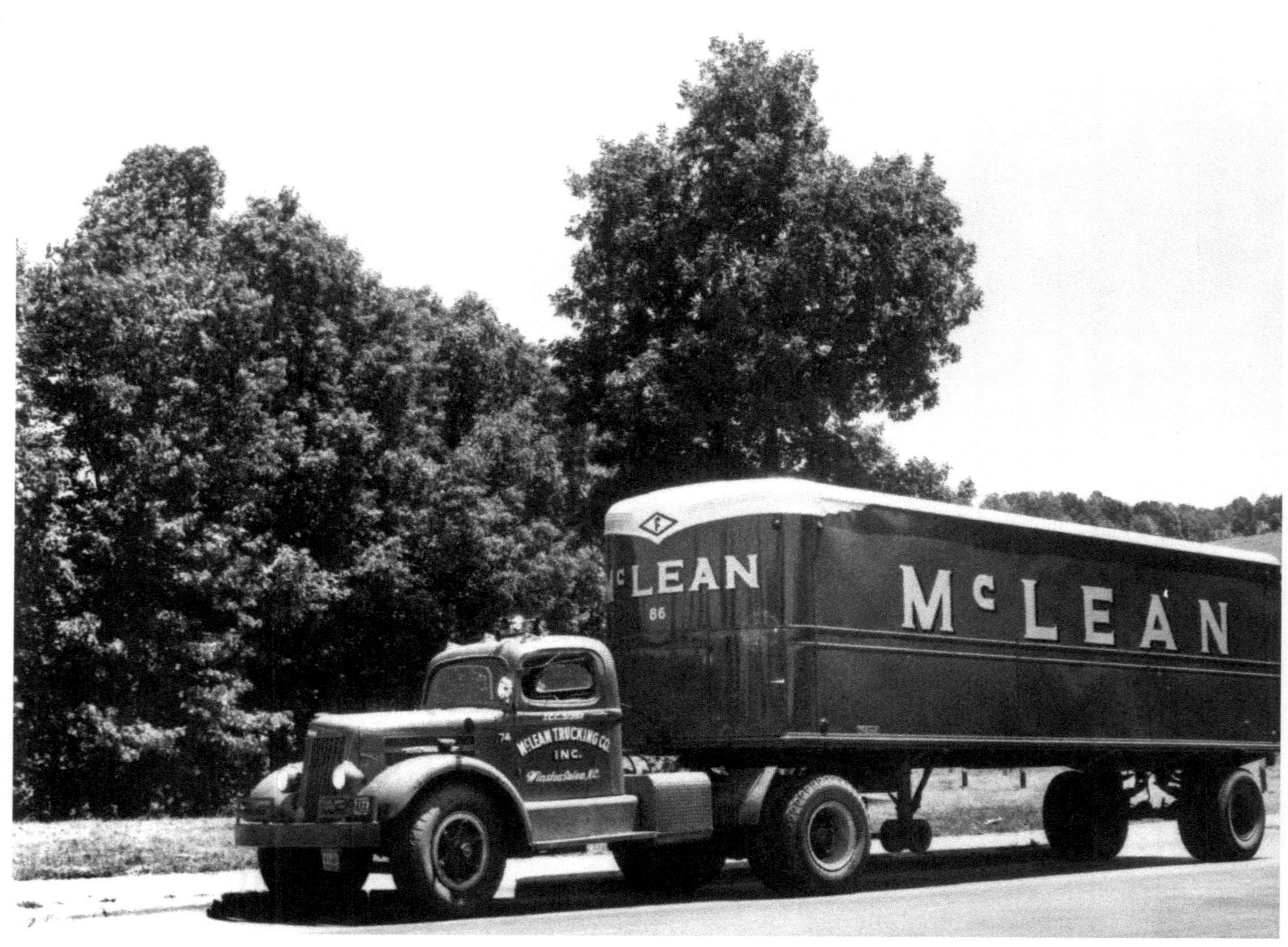


Malcolm P. McLean put his first truck in operation in 1934 and made his first profits from the fledgling business hauling empty tobacco barrels around Winston-Salem. In 1943, McLean Trucking established its headquarters in the city, the first of over forty trucking firms that would do so. Winston-Salem became a transportation center, and Malcolm McLean later achieved fame for his development of the concept of containerization.

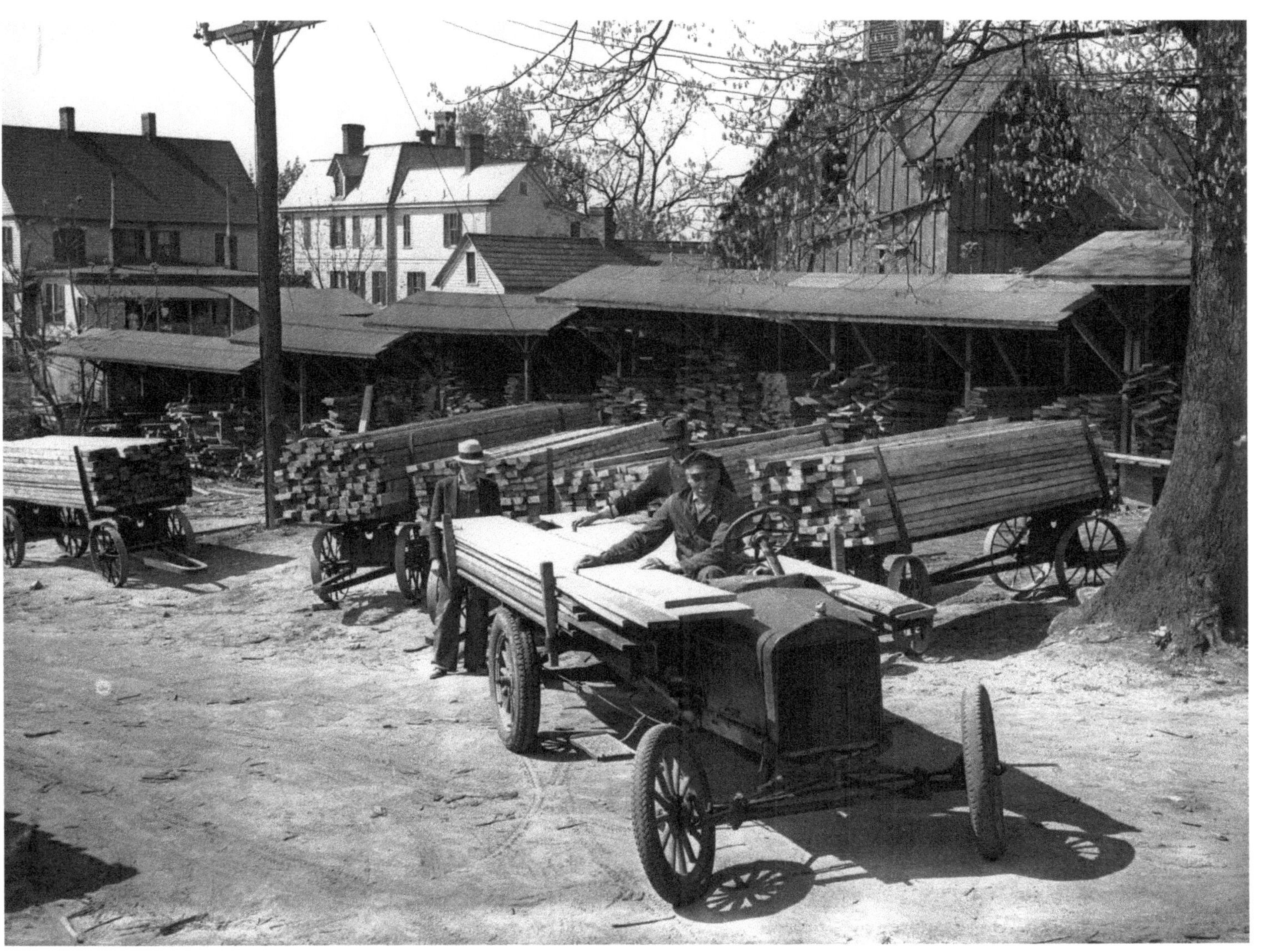

Fogle Brothers Lumber Company provided building materials and constructed homes in Forsyth County beginning in the 1800s. Sustained by assets and a name for dependability acquired during the Winston-Salem building boom and growth of 1900-29, Fogle Brothers survived the Great Depression, as evident by the activity visible here in 1938.

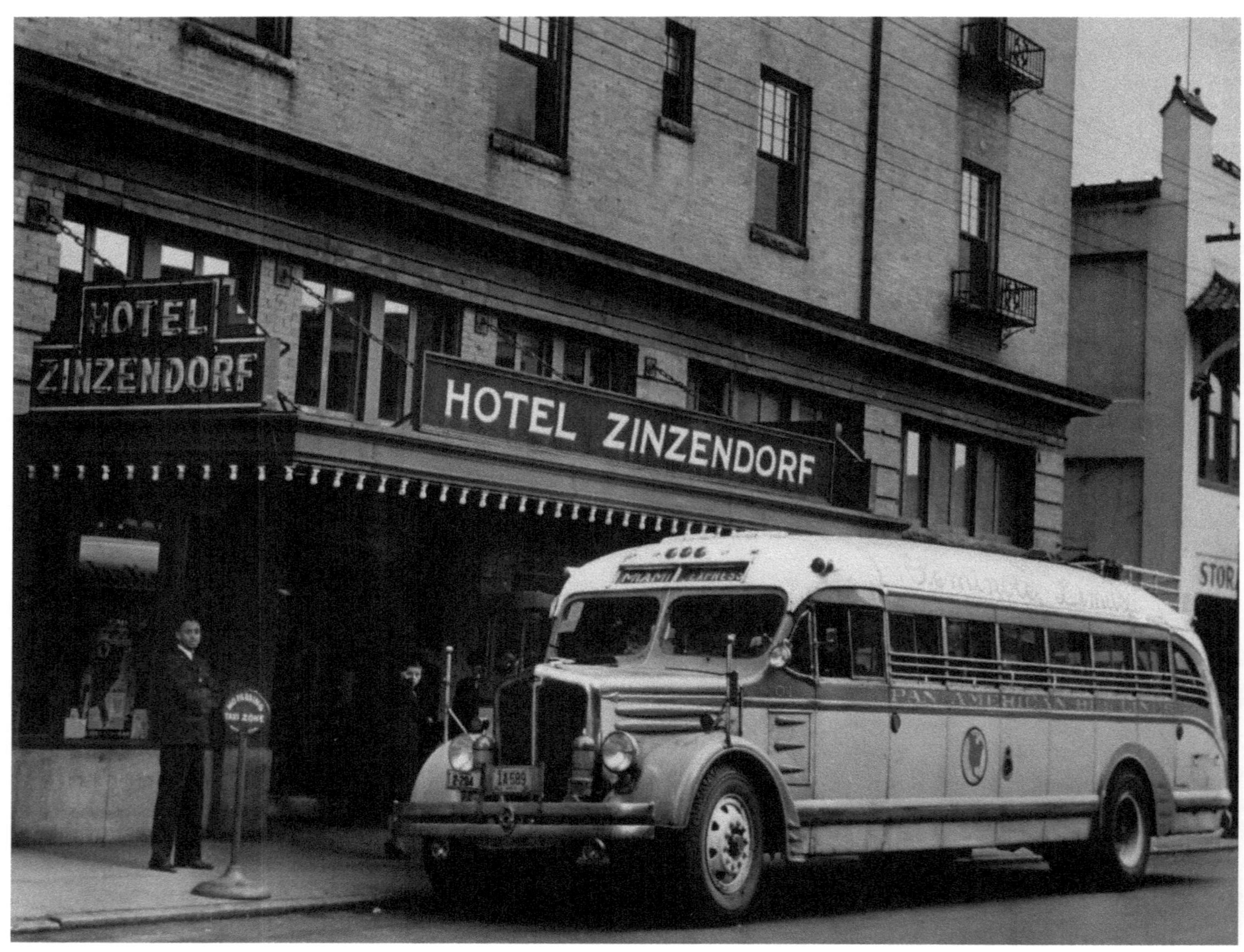


The Zinzendorf Hotel, namesake of the hotel that burned in 1892, stood on Main Street. Built on the site of the old Hotel Jones in 1906, the Zinzendorf featured 120 rooms, each with a telephone. Thirty rooms even had private baths with hot water. By 1938, when this city bus stopped in front, the hotel seemed dingy and worn, as did most of downtown Winston-Salem. Demolished in 1970, the hotel made way for the Federal Building, which now occupies the site.

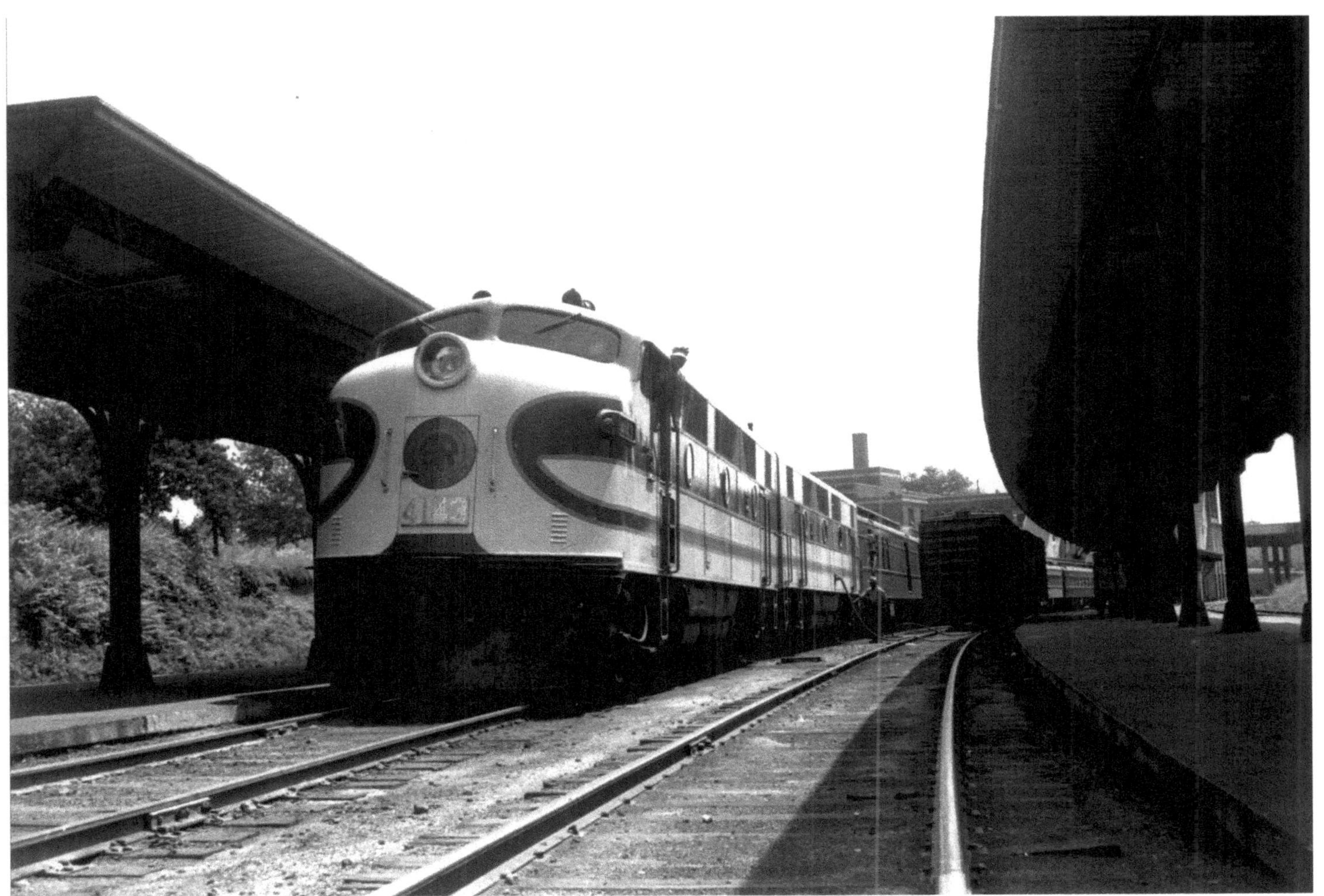

The coming of the railroad in the late 1800s allowed industry to concentrate in Winston. By the late 1930s, Winston-Salem still depended on the rails for shipment of goods, though steam locomotives had given way to diesel. In a very few years, passenger trains such as this one would begin moving the men and women of Winston-Salem to military training camps throughout the United States.

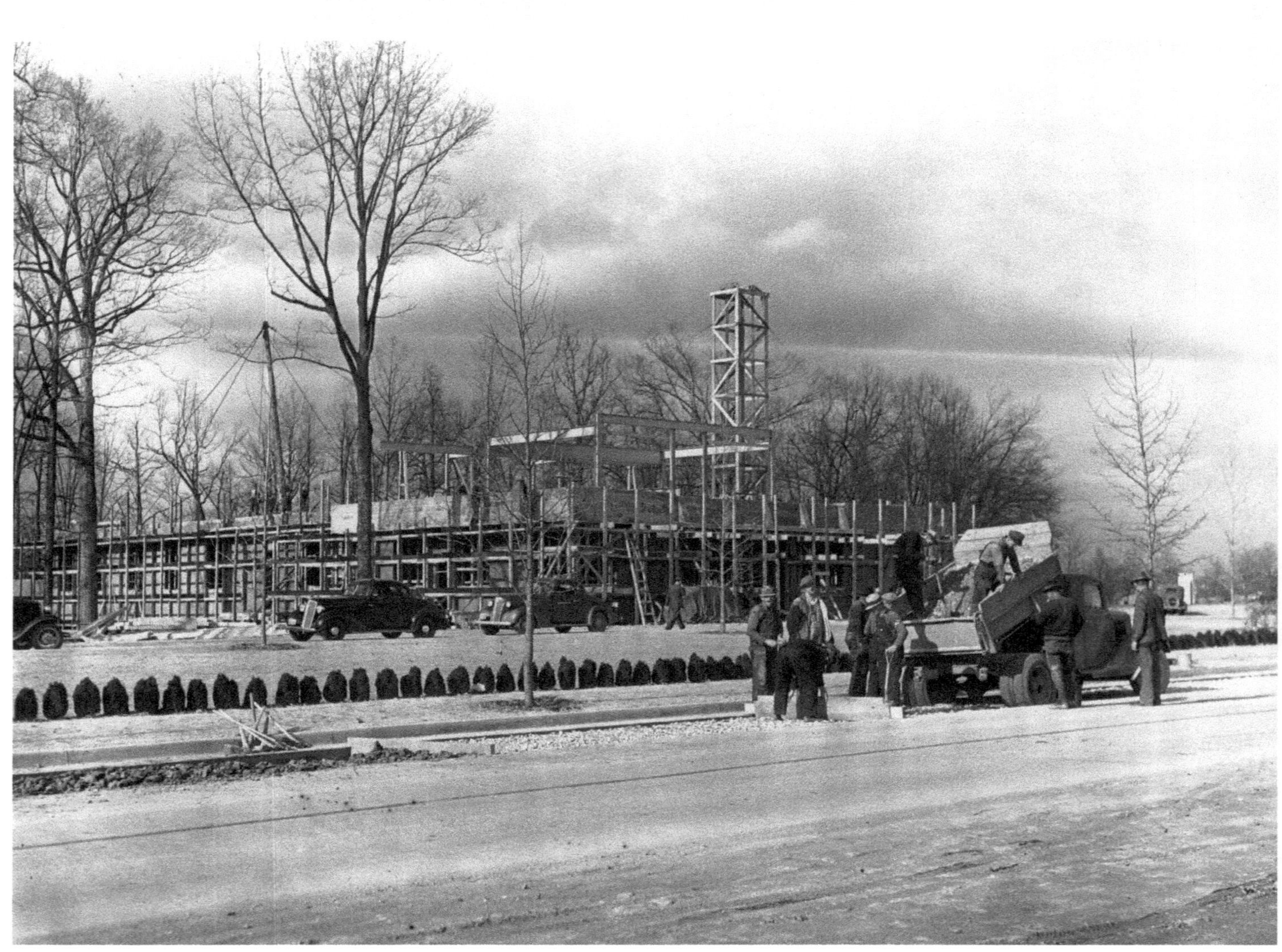

The owners of three dairy farms—Arden, Klondike, and Whit-Acres—joined their capital in 1937 to build Selected Dairies on South Stratford Road. The company would eventually draw on at least six local farms for raw milk. New industry meant jobs, not only for plant workers but also for these men working to complete construction of Selected Dairies in 1938.

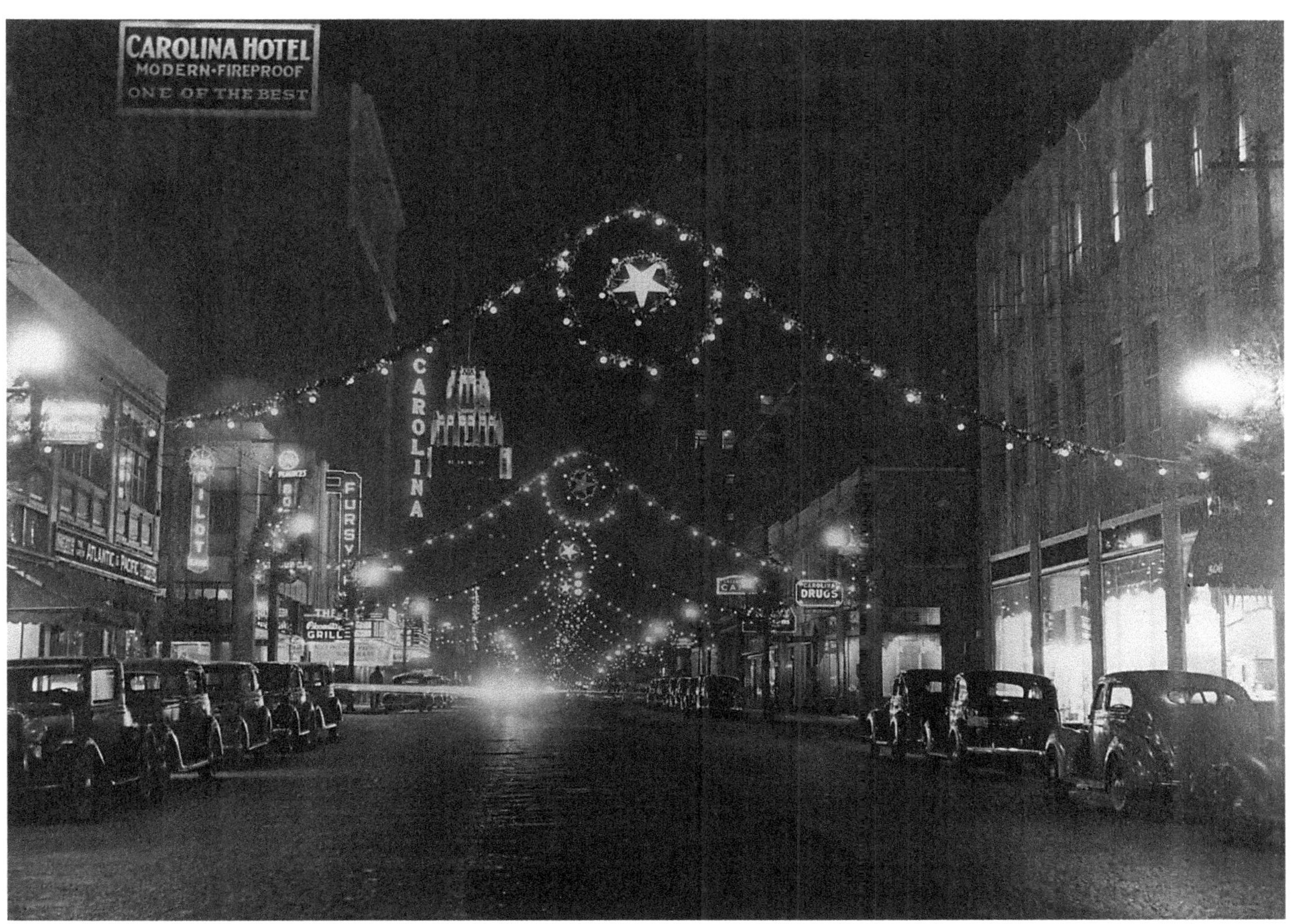


By Christmas of 1938, the future, like the twinkling lights of Christmas decorations on West Fourth Street, seemed a little brighter to residents of Winston-Salem. Though some shop fronts may have been empty, the Carolina Theater still attracted patrons, the Carolina Hotel still expected a Christmas rush, and the lights of the Reynolds Building, a symbol of industrial might, still glowed in the night.

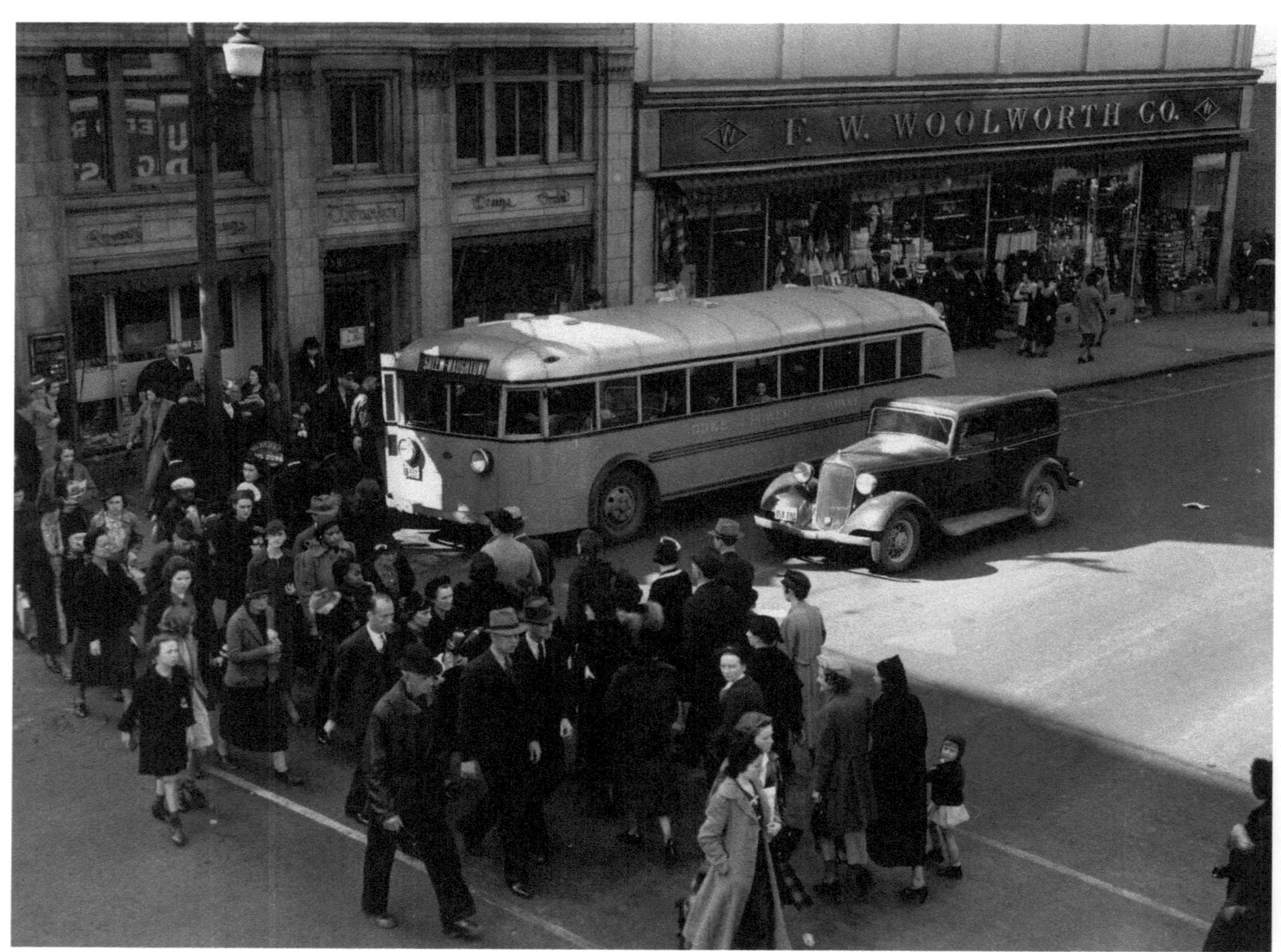


As winter approaches in 1938, a crowd of people, swelled by the emptying city transit bus, crosses Liberty Street at Fourth Street. Perhaps off to work, or maybe headed for some early morning shopping, some will cross the street again at noon to visit the lunch counter at the Woolworth store. Probably few, if any, of the walkers give a thought to the pavement in the center of the street where streetcar rails once twined.

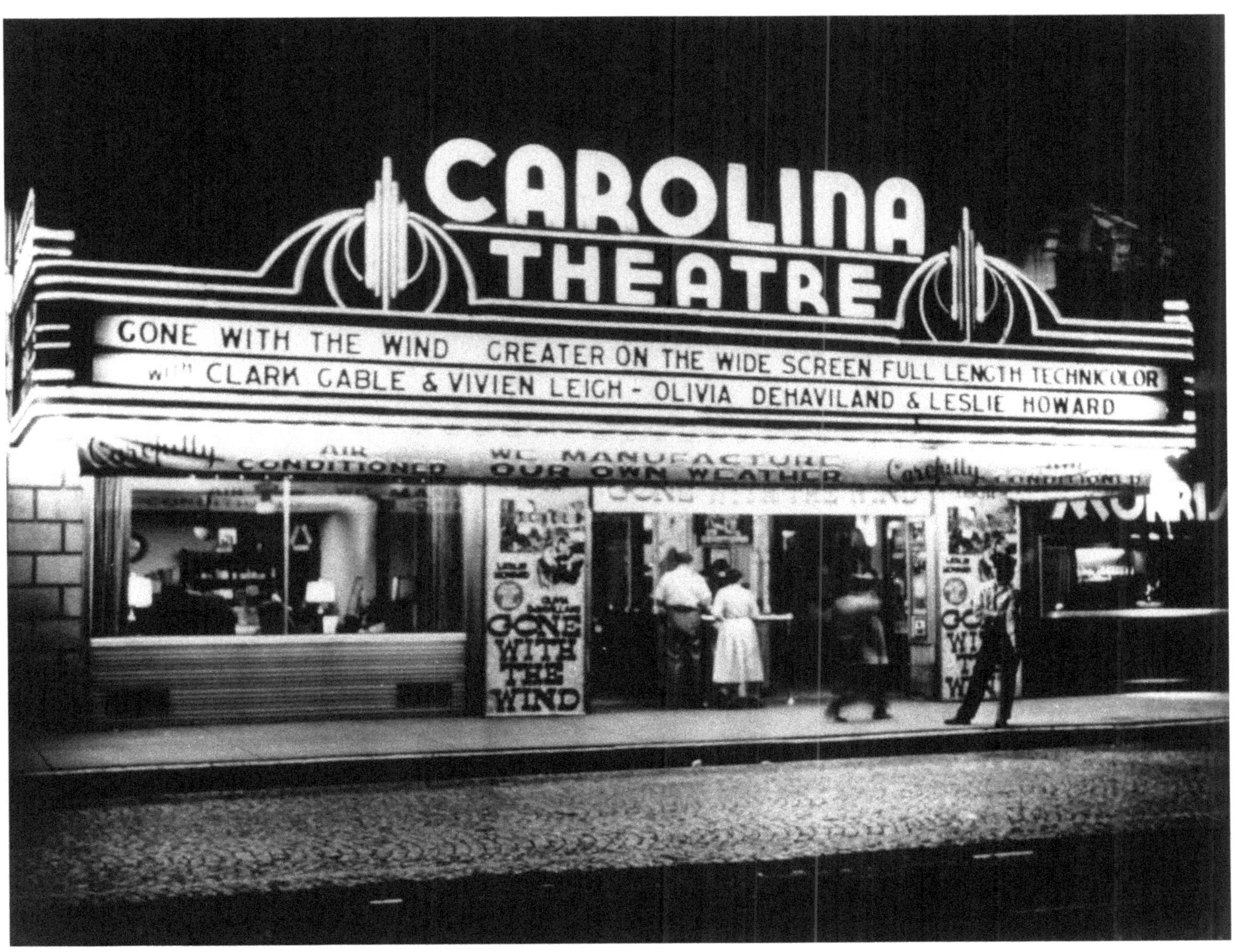


The Carolina Theatre opened for silent movies in 1929 at Fourth and Marshall Streets with seating for 2,500. By 1939 and the premiere of *Gone with the Wind*, movies captured the hearts, minds, and imaginations of Americans everywhere. Perhaps the grandchildren of these moviegoers still visit the site, though extensive remodeling in 1983 turned the Carolina into the Roger L. Stevens Center for performing arts in an attempt to revitalize the downtown area.

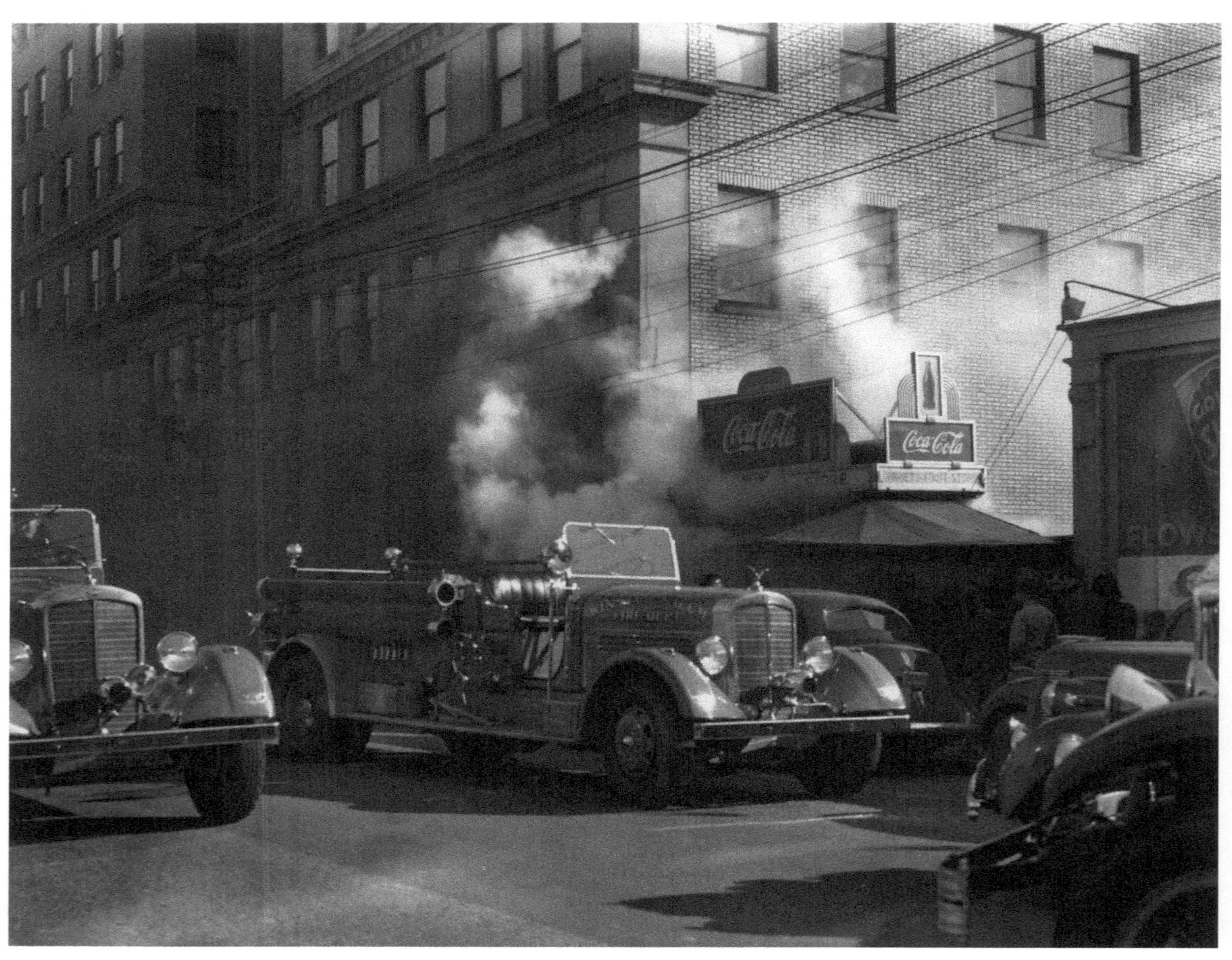


Firemen respond to a blaze at an eatery on West Fourth Street in 1940. Within a year, the average age of firemen would increase dramatically, as volunteers flocked to the colors, and the draft pruned the numbers of those who remained behind.

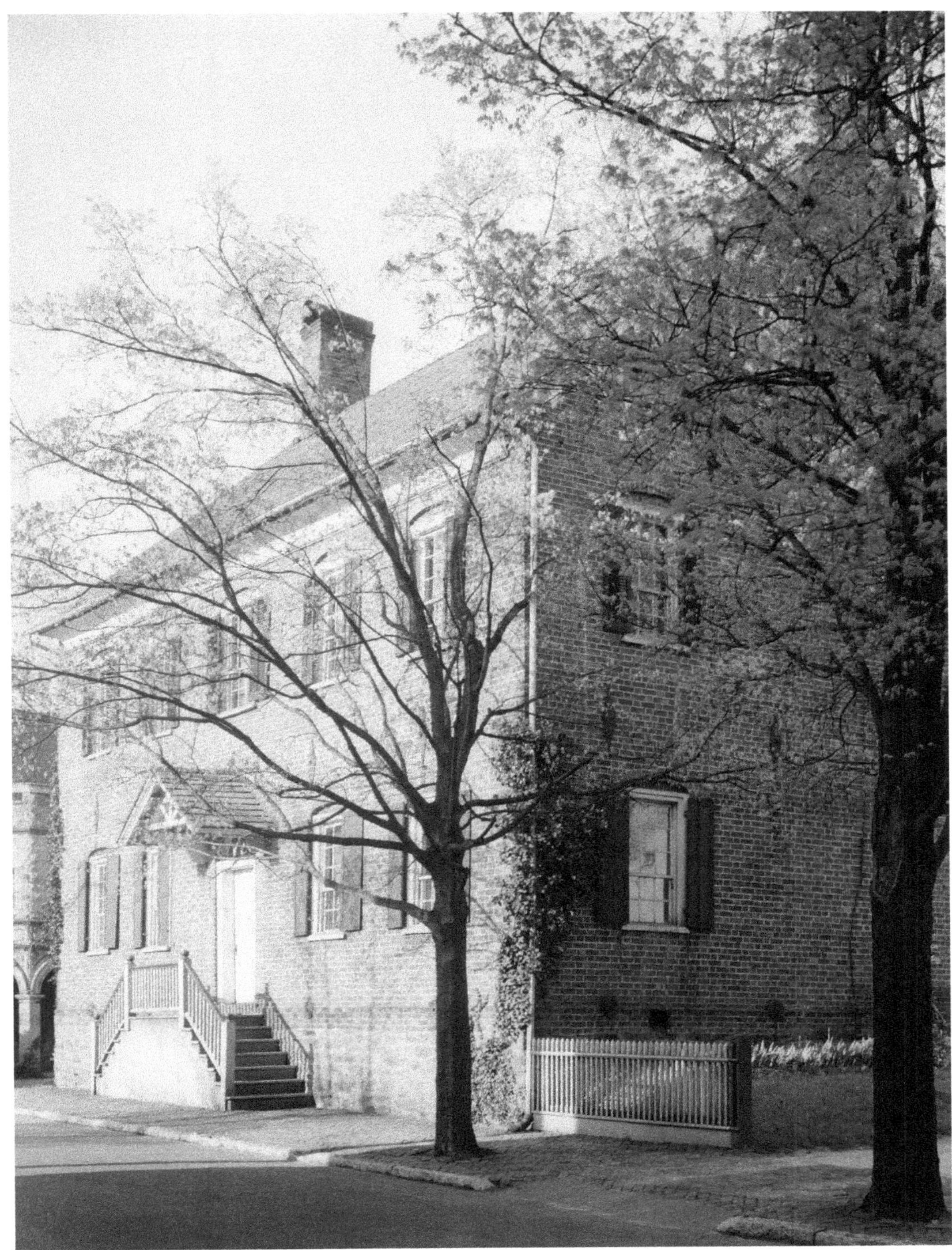

Photographed in 1940, the House of the Community Physician on South Church Street dated to 1800. It was the residence of a Salem physician, Dr. Vierling, whose instruments are on display in the Hall of History in Old Salem.

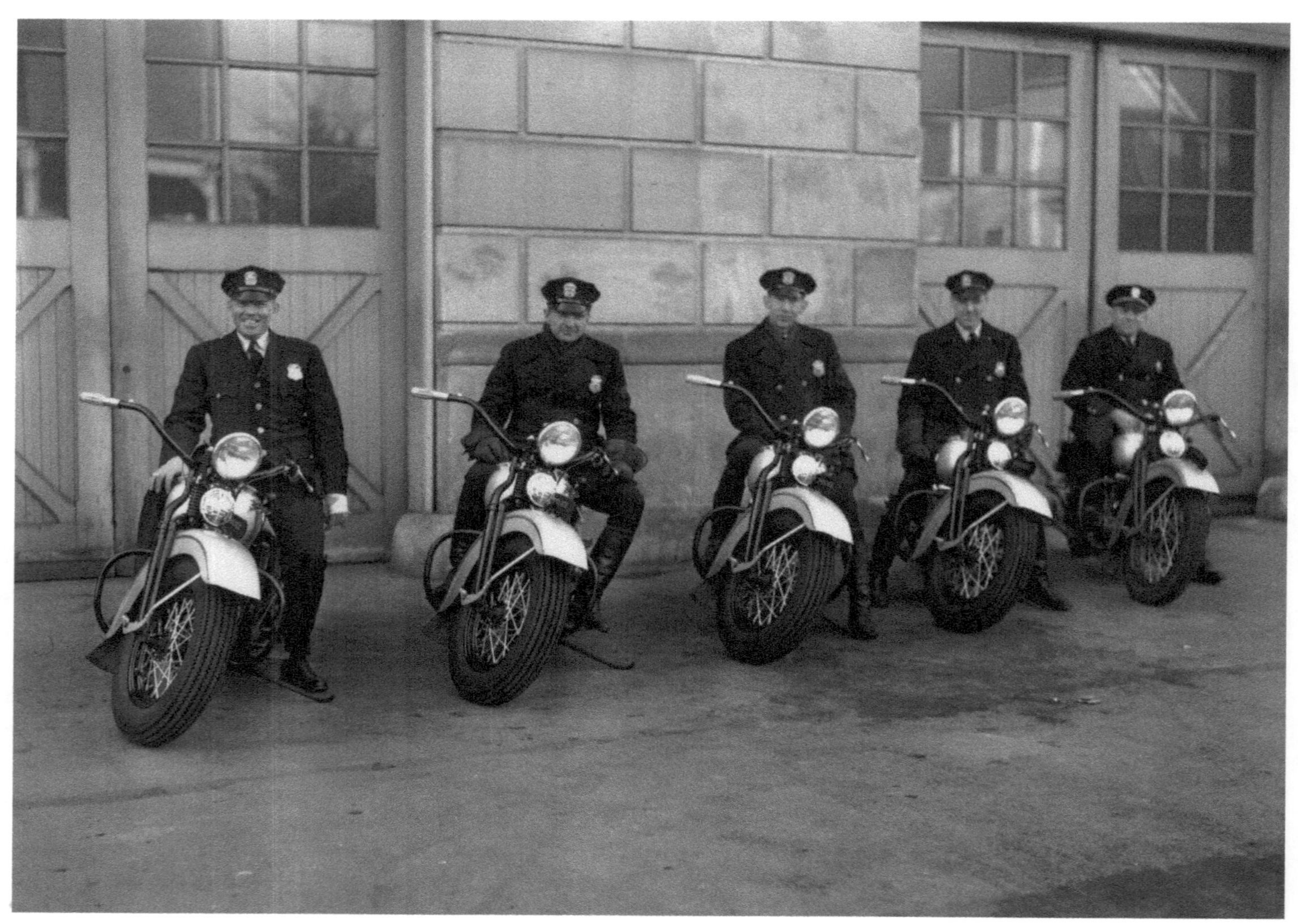

Adopted by the police forces of many towns during the Great Depression, motorcycles proved cost effective and highly maneuverable in urban settings. These Winston-Salem officers pose with theirs in 1940.

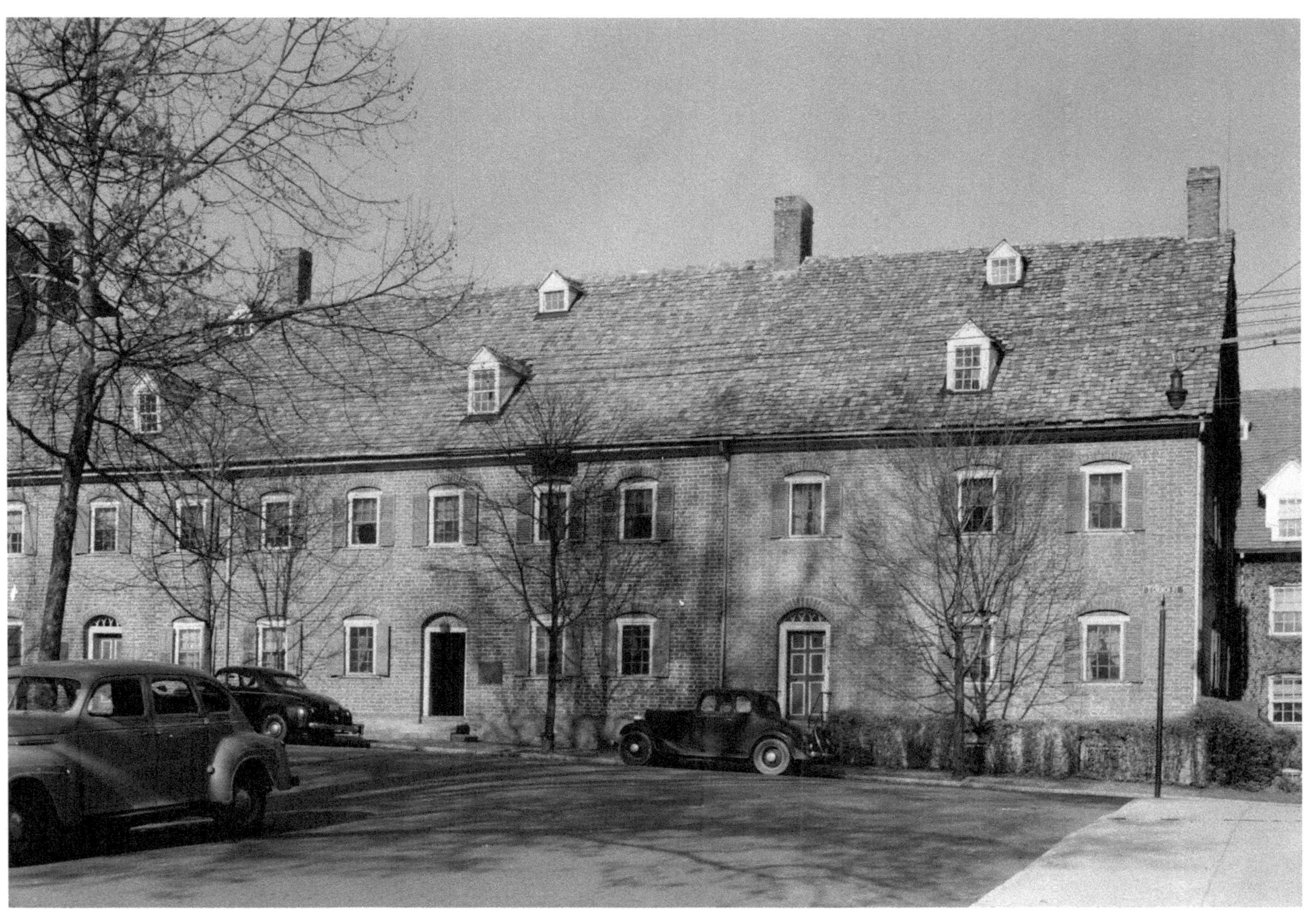

Seen here in 1940, the Sisters House of Salem College is on South Church Street. The oldest building on the Salem College campus, the Single Sisters House dates to 1785, with additions in 1819. The unmarried women of the Moravian community operated a school for young women inside this building, making it extremely important to the history of women's educational rights in America.

Built in 1927 on the corner of North Cherry and West Fourth streets, the Nissen Building, seen here in 1940, stood twenty stories tall. The family of W. M. Nissen, owner of Nissen Wagons (founded in 1787), lived on the top floor and leased space on the floors below to others. As this would be the first air-conditioned building in the Southeast, leasing went well. Recently, the building has been converted to a gorgeous apartment complex.

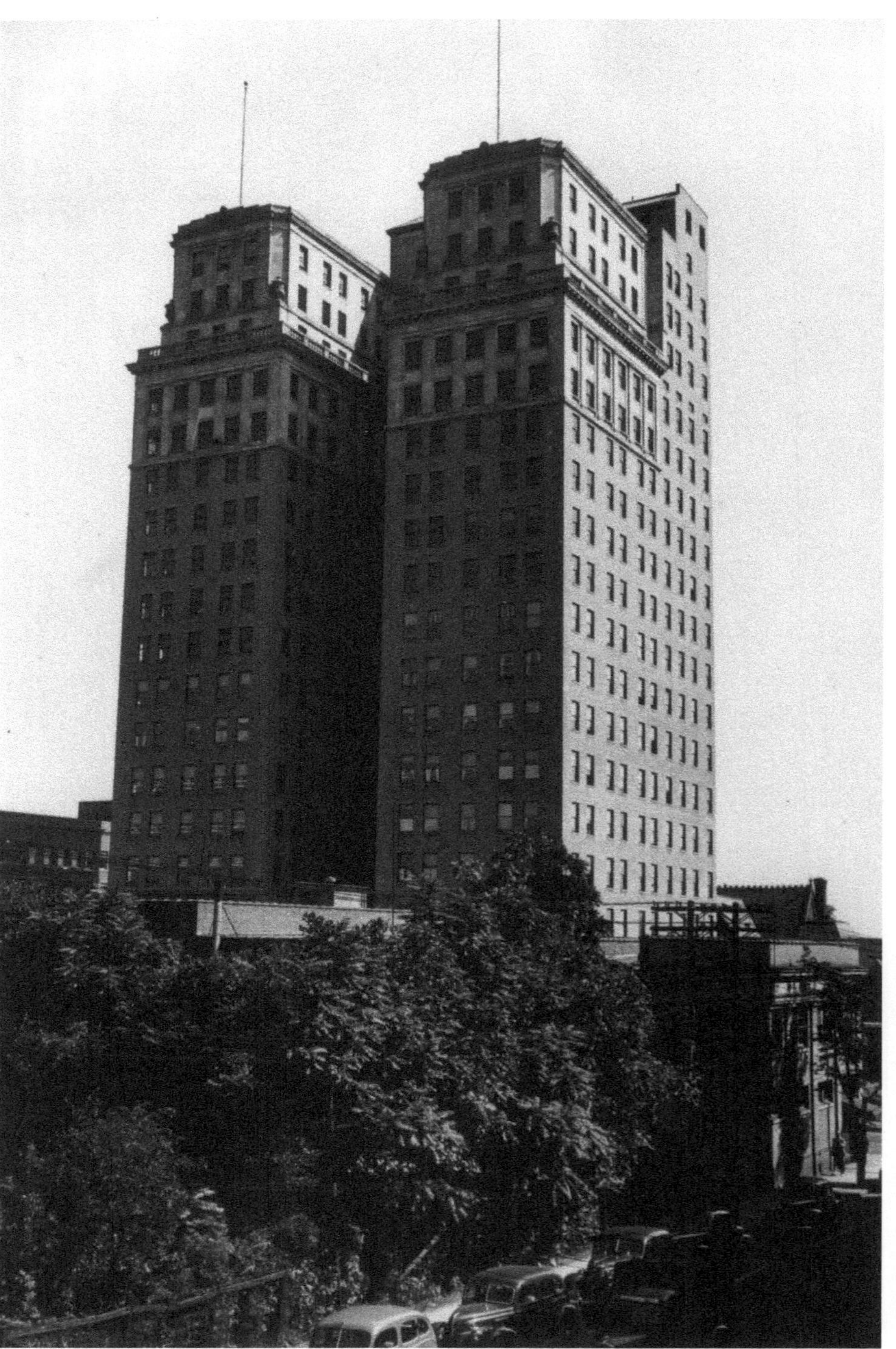

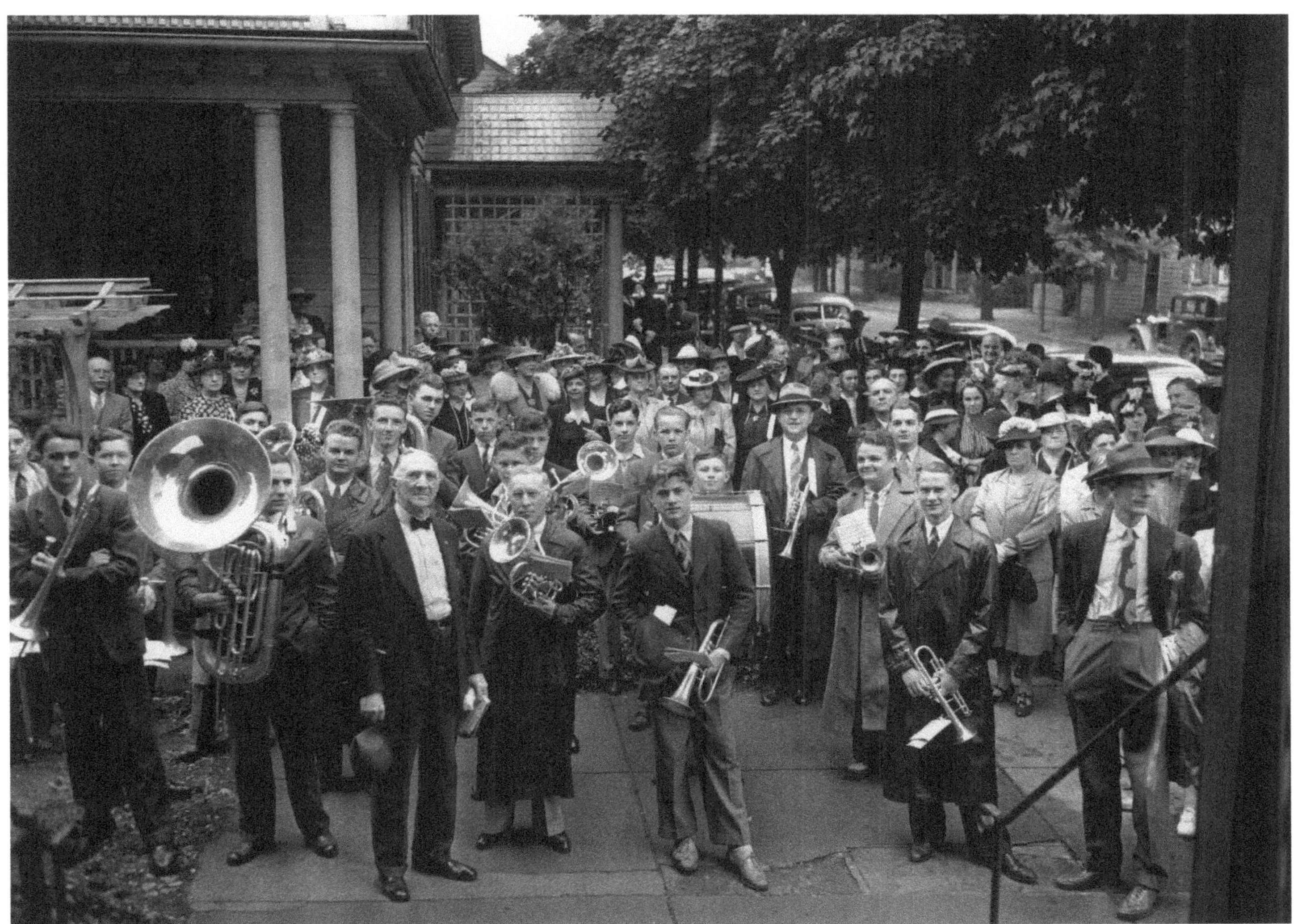

In 1941, Mayor R. J. Reynolds purchased Salem Tavern, built in 1784, and deeded it to the Wachovia Historical Society, which had been struggling to save the building from commercial developers. A dedication ceremony coincided with the 175th anniversary of Winston-Salem (the Moravians founded Salem in 1766). Short months later, an anonymous member of the WHS would write an "Inventory of Specimens in Wachovia Museum to be Moved to Place of Safety in Case of Attack."

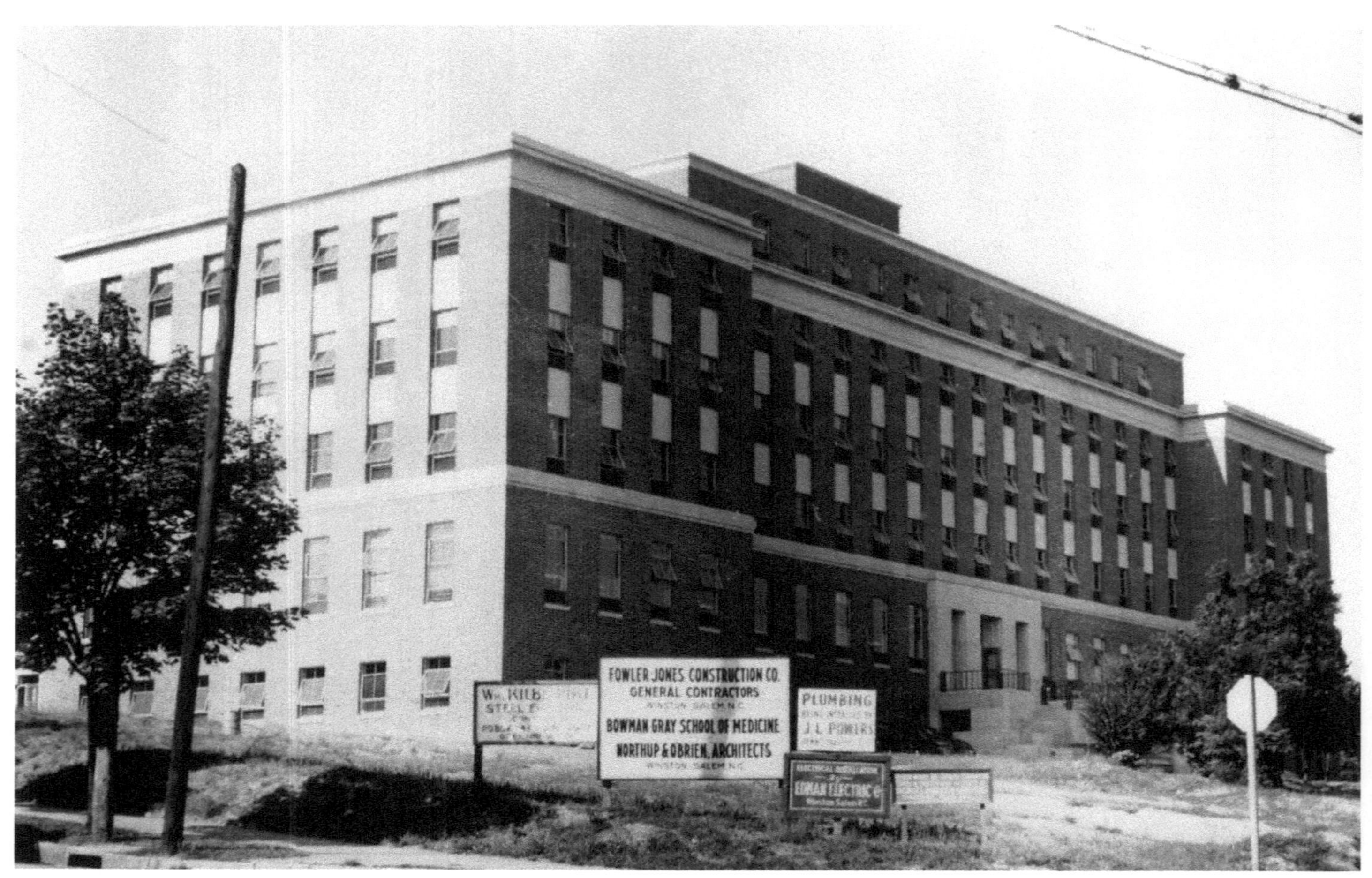


When Bowman Gray, Sr., former president of R. J. Reynolds Tobacco, died in 1935, he bequeathed $750,000 of R. J. Reynolds stock to Wake Forest College to establish a four-year medical school in Winston-Salem. Bowman Gray School of Medicine opened in 1941. This began the wooing of Wake Forest College (now Wake Forest University) by Winston-Salem. In 1956, the school's relocation from the town of Wake Forest provided Winston-Salem with a first-class research institution.

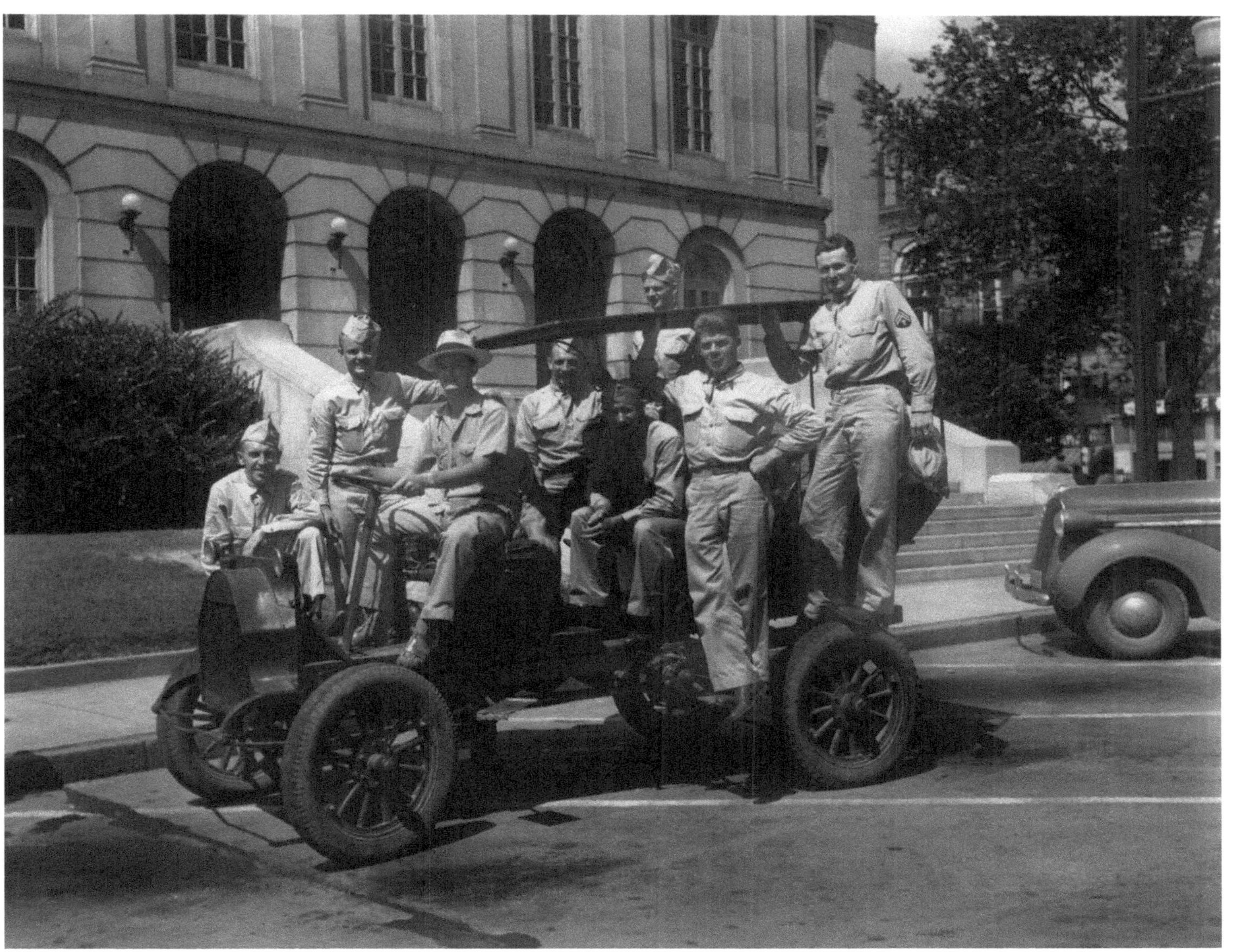

On the heels of the Great Depression, World War II called upon Winston-Salem to send its men and women to war. The *Winston-Salem Journal* had lost fifty-five employees to the military by 1942; area industries parted with hundreds of workers. In this photograph, snapped sometime during 1941 or 1942, soldiers pose in front of the courthouse.

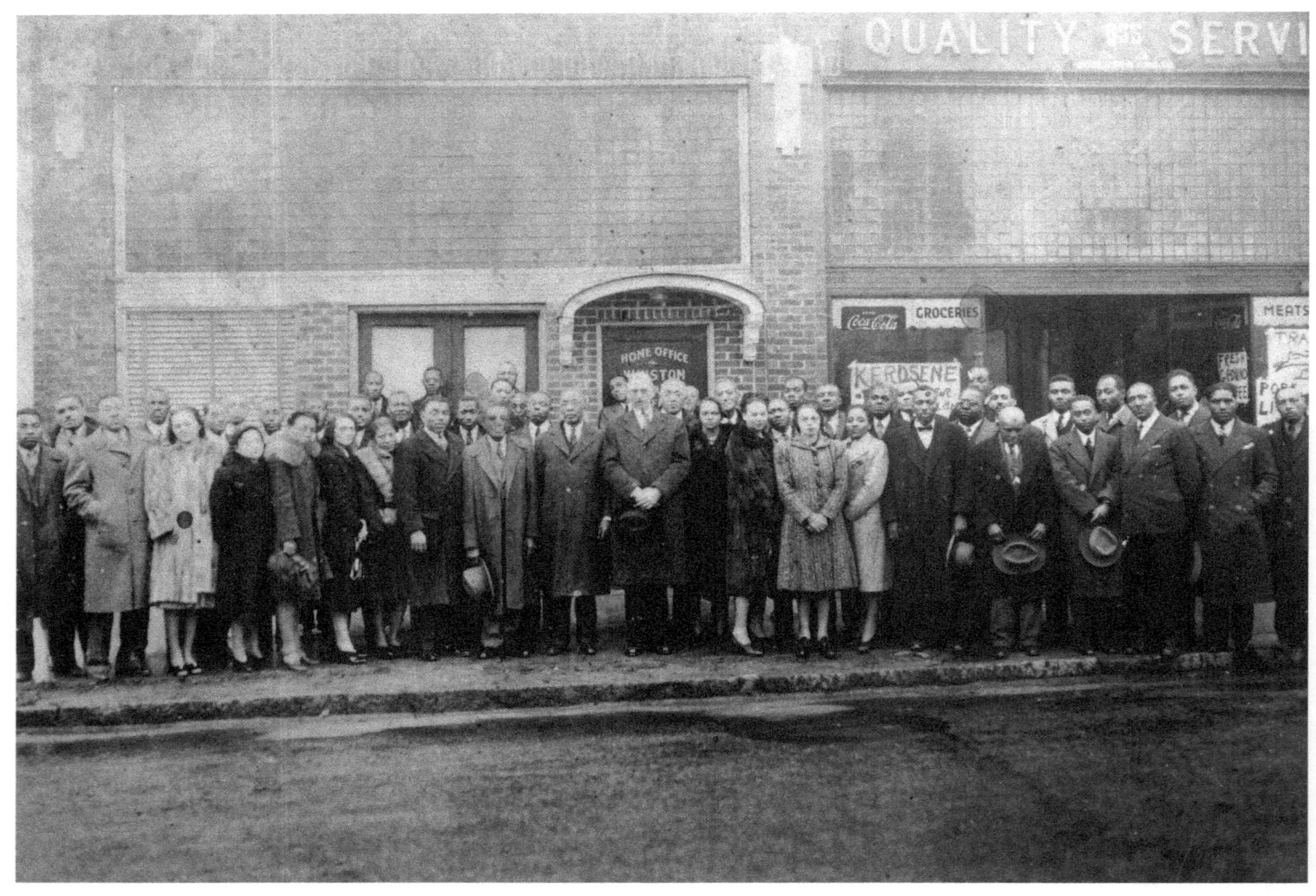


Founded in 1906 by George Washington Hill and other investors, Winston Mutual Life Insurance, a black-owned-and-operated business, has a record of long service to the African American community of Winston-Salem. This photograph taken in front of the company office dates to the early 1940s.

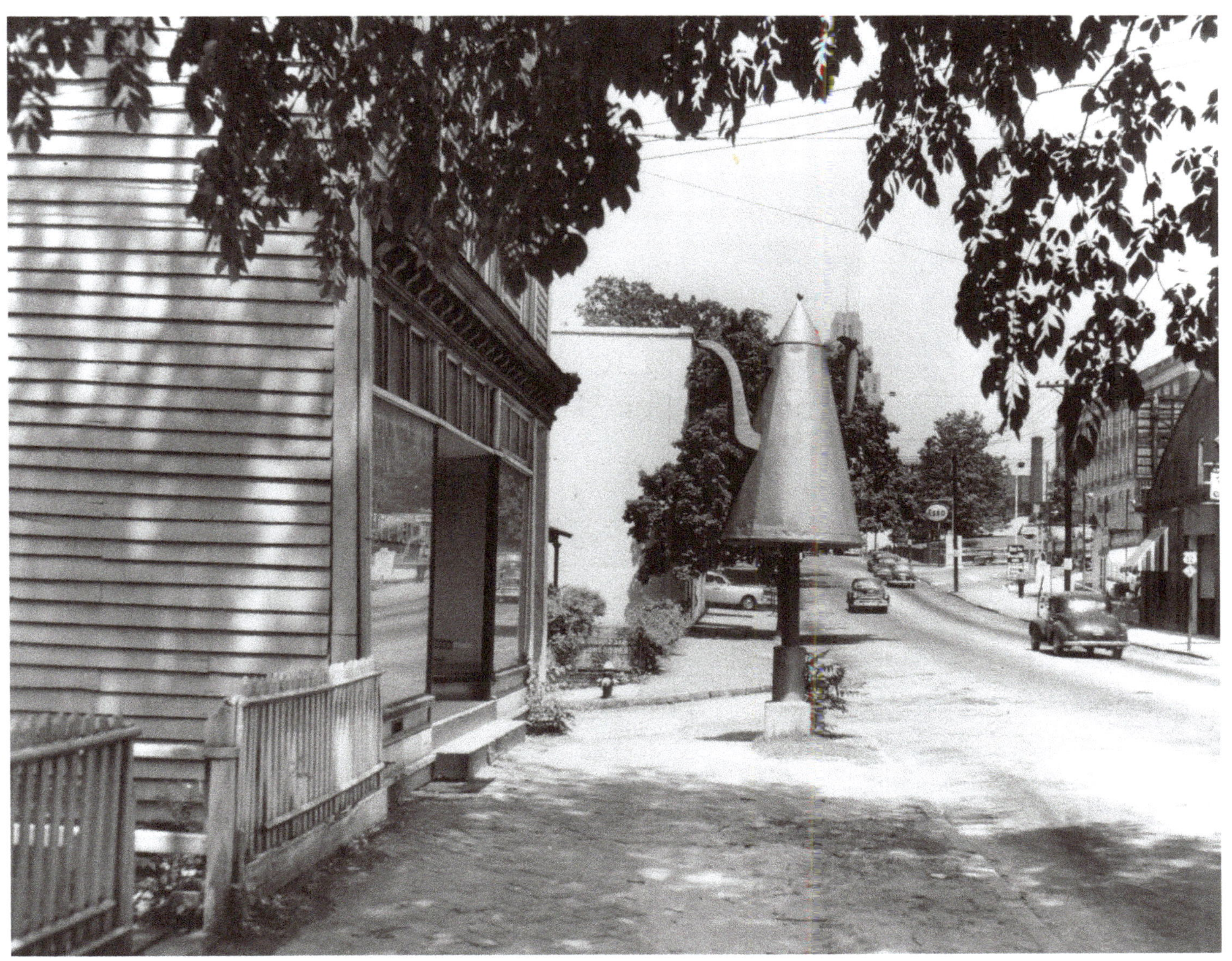


The giant-sized tin coffee pot remained a Main Street fixture in the 1940s. The following decade, the coffee pot would be relocated to a different spot on Main Street to make way for the East-West Expressway.

This "barometer" outside the county courthouse measured the money donated to build Memorial Coliseum, part and parcel of the wooing of Wake Forest College to Winston-Salem. The money was collected, and in 1955, the thudding of basketballs began to echo inside the new structure. Memorial Coliseum, with seating for 8,500, remained home court for the Demon Deacons until replaced by Joel Coliseum in 1989.

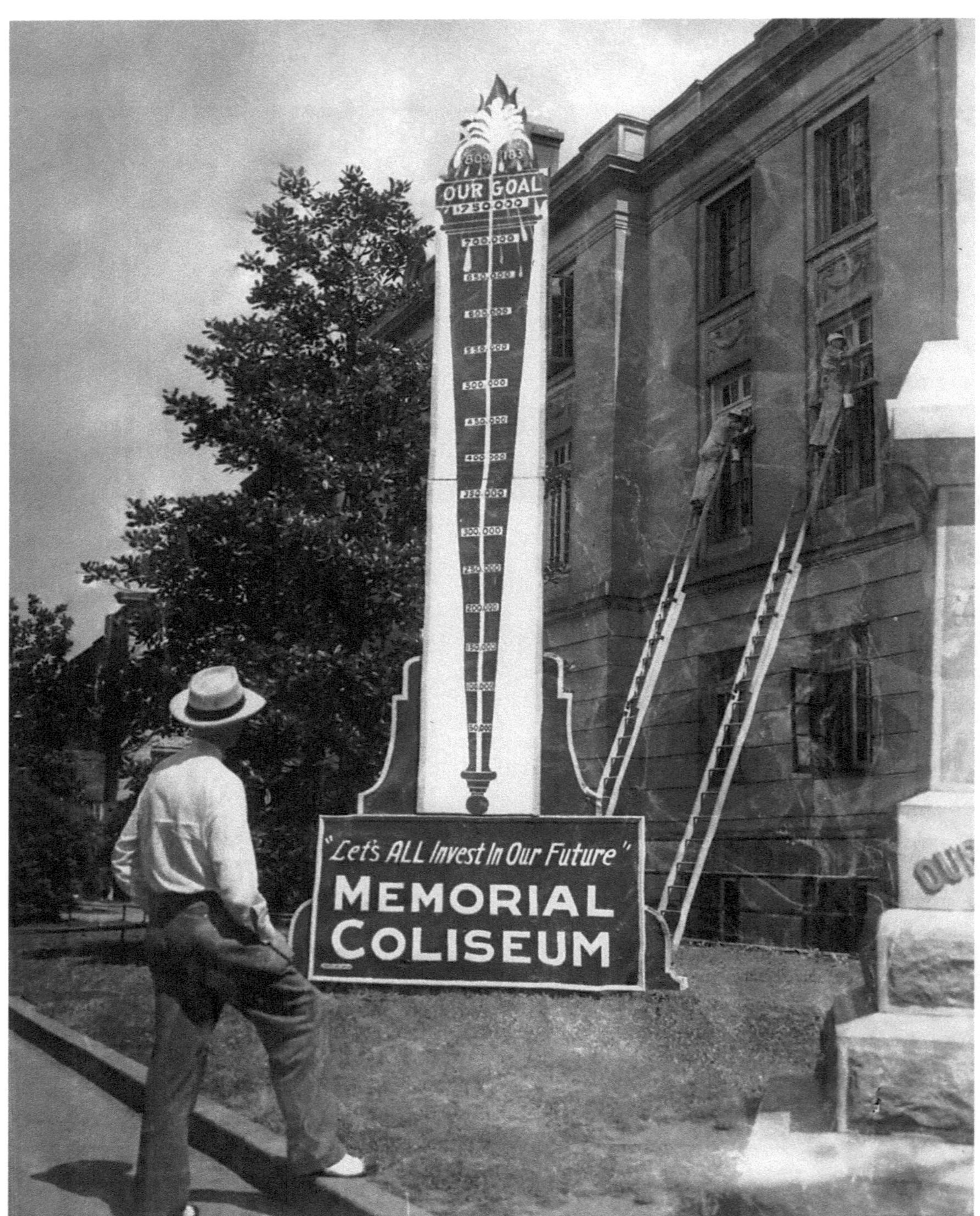

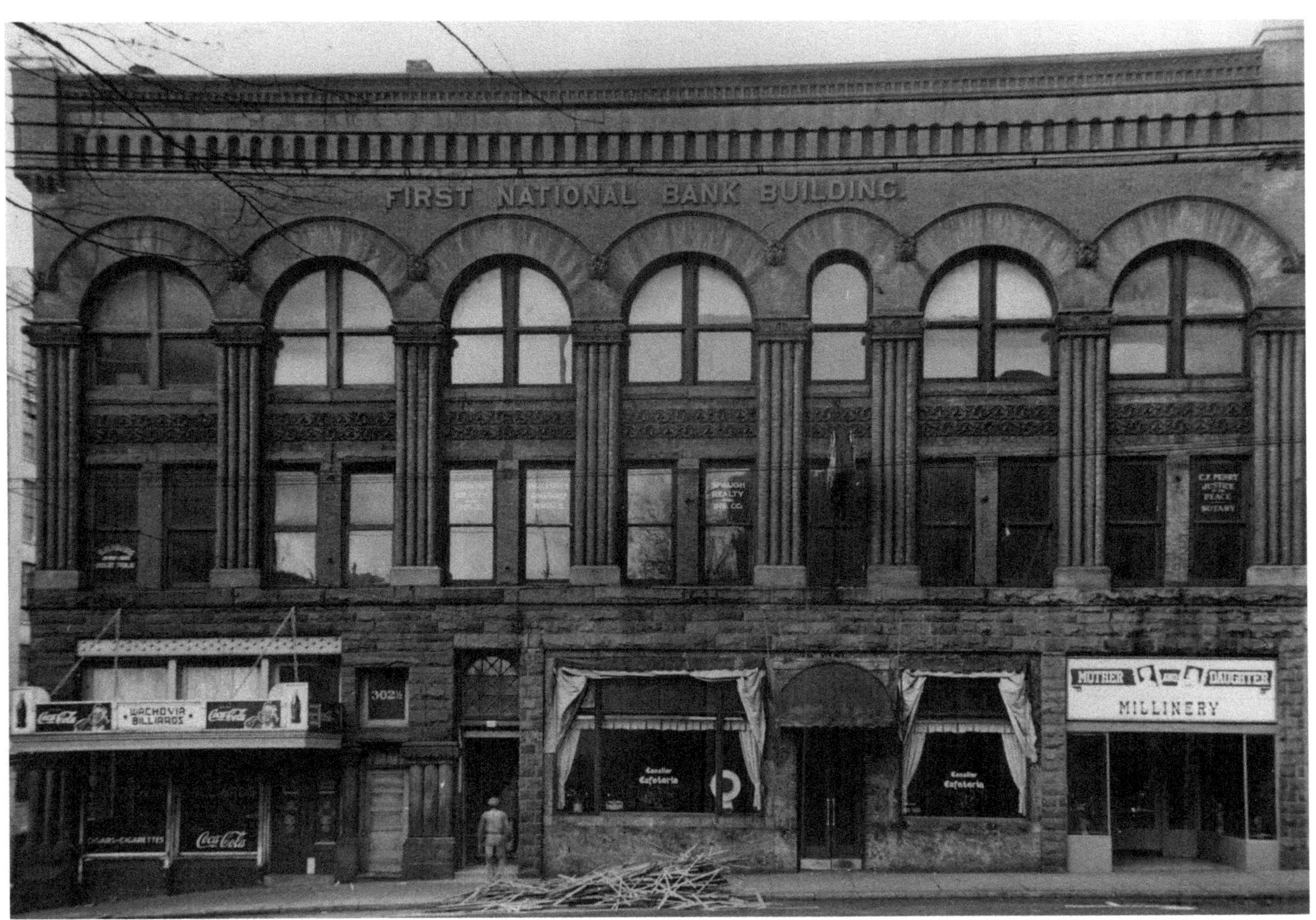


The First National Bank Building stood at the corner of Liberty and Third streets in 1946. Later, the banking enterprise moved across the street to the Universal Garage Building, where it remained until First National merged with North Carolina National Bank in 1961.

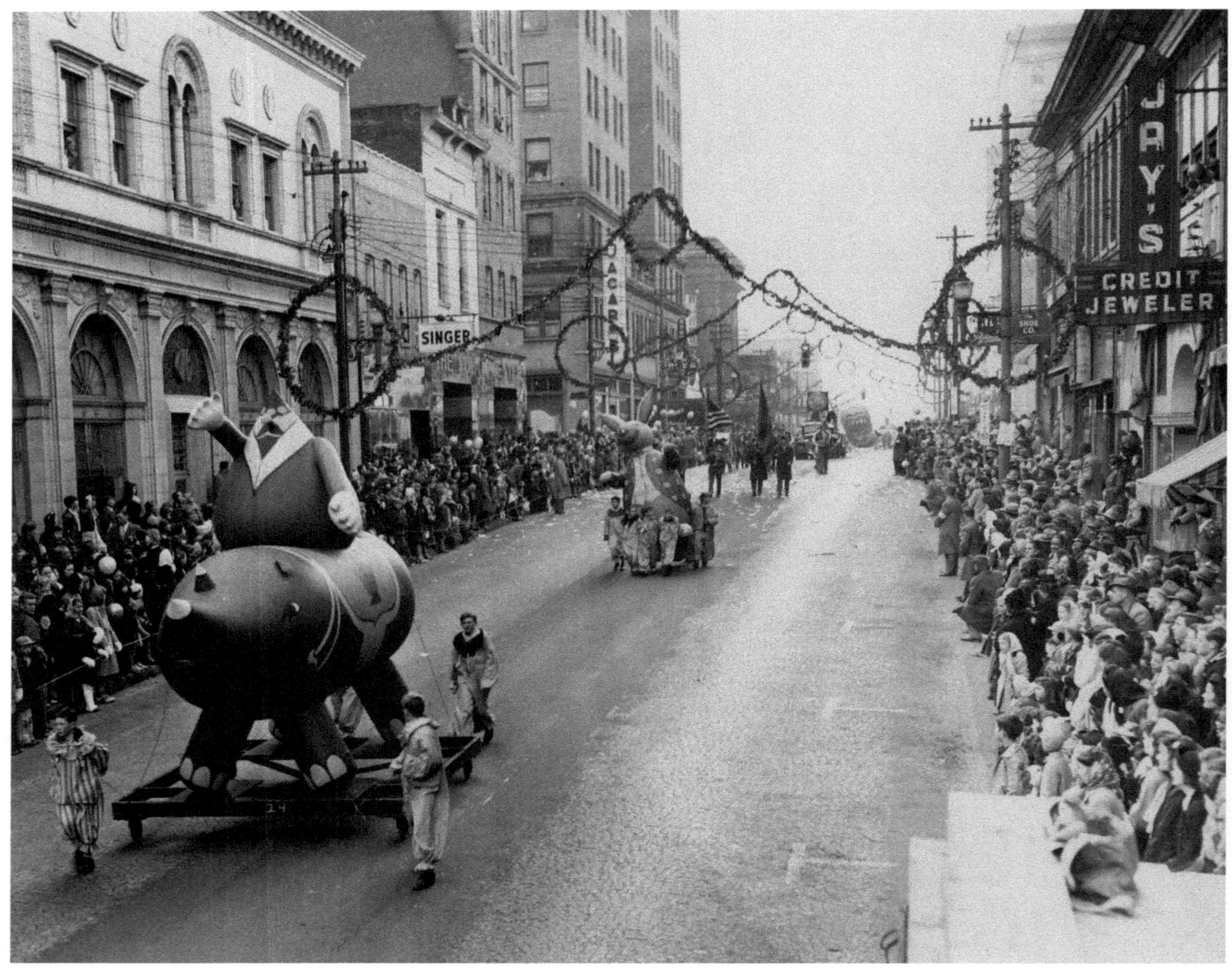


Impressive floats wended their way along crowded Fourth Street during the Christmas parade of 1947. New Christmas decorations for the city echoed a new attitude for the city. World War II had ended, most of the boys were home, and the first stirrings of the cold war to come were hardly noticed.

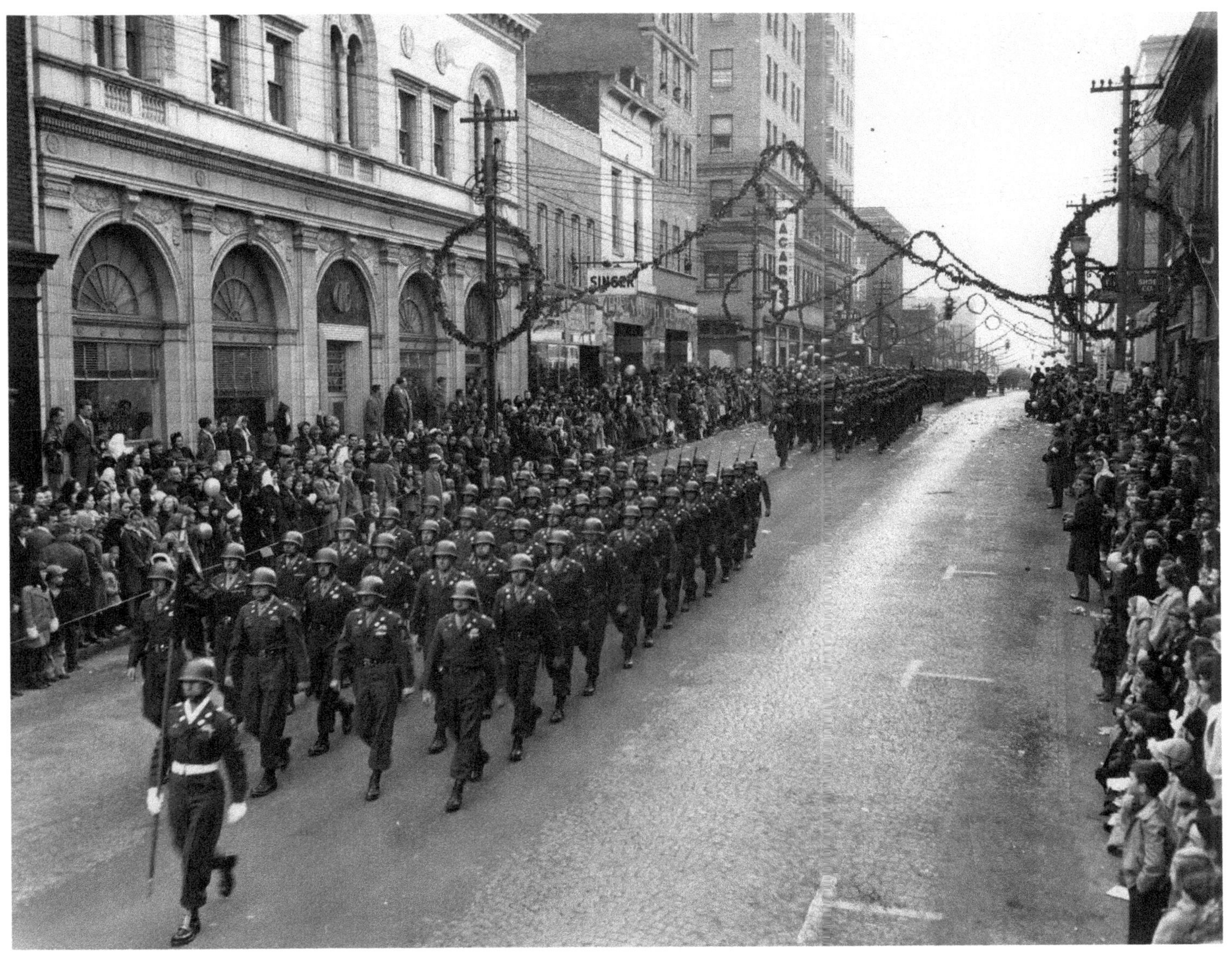


Veterans march along West Fourth Street in the 1947 Christmas parade, perhaps a last march in uniform for some, as they prepare to return to civilian life after serving garrison duties in Germany and Japan.

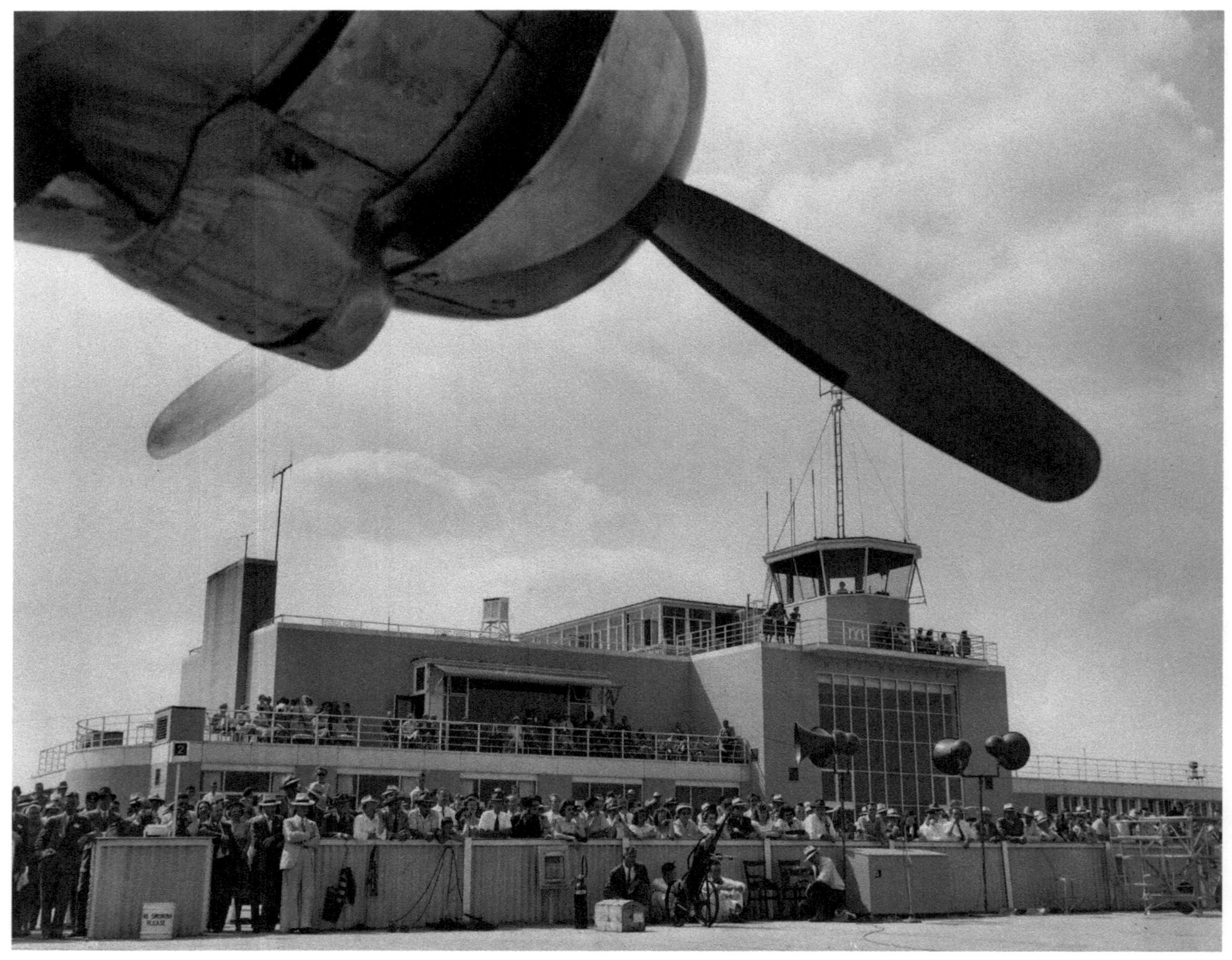

Having expanded constantly since the gift of a new terminal from the Reynolds family in 1942, Smith Reynolds Airport—named for the lost son of the family, Z. Smith Reynolds—stood second to none in North Carolina in 1947. In fact, Eastern Airlines representatives felt this was the finest terminal in the United States.

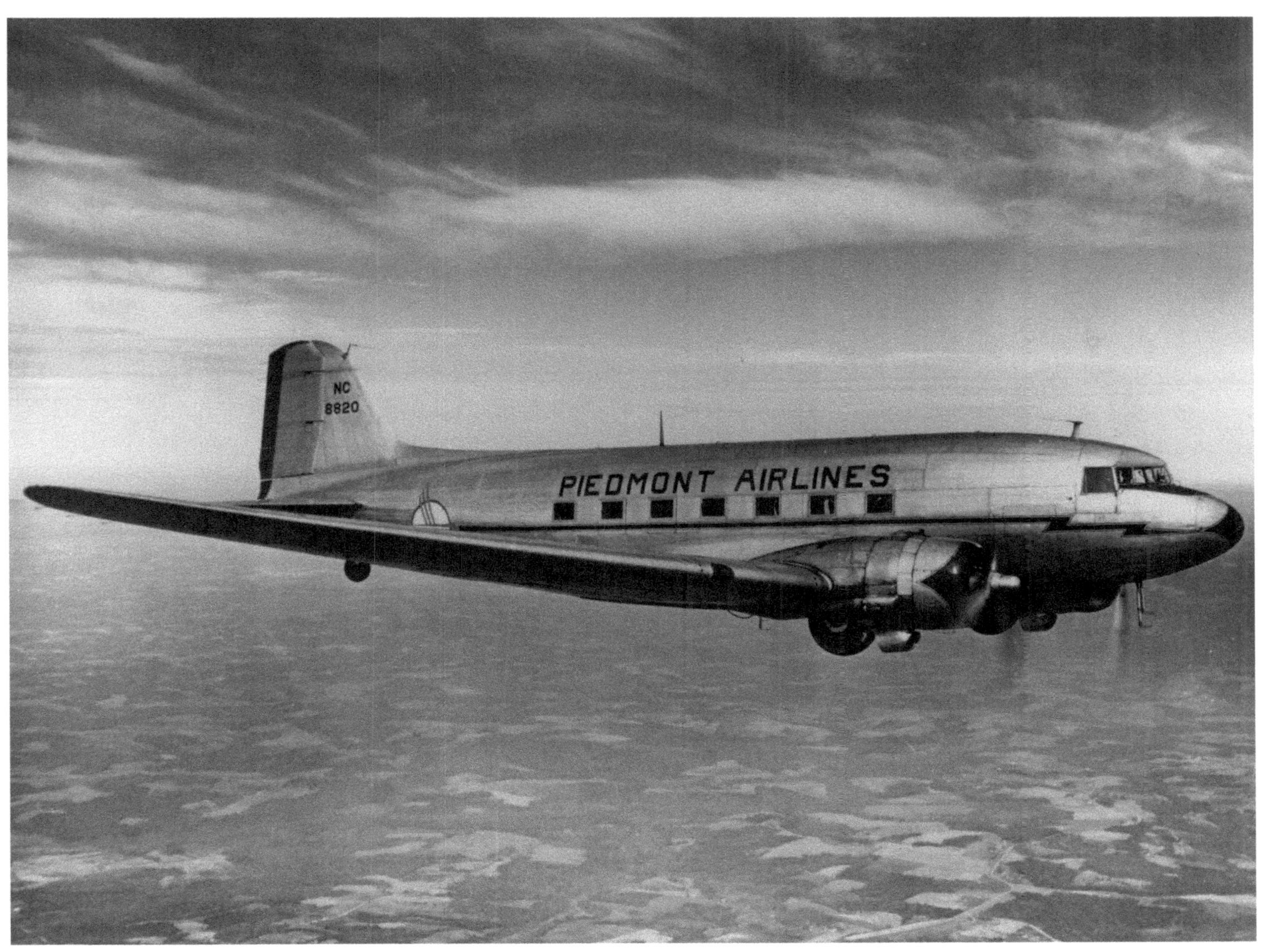


A Piedmont Airlines DC-3 wings through the skies, headed for parts unknown in the late 1940s. Based in Winston-Salem, the airline made its first commercial flight in 1948, flying (with stops) from Wilmington, North Carolina, to Cincinnati, Ohio, two of the 22 cities Piedmont served that year while transporting around 40,000 passengers.

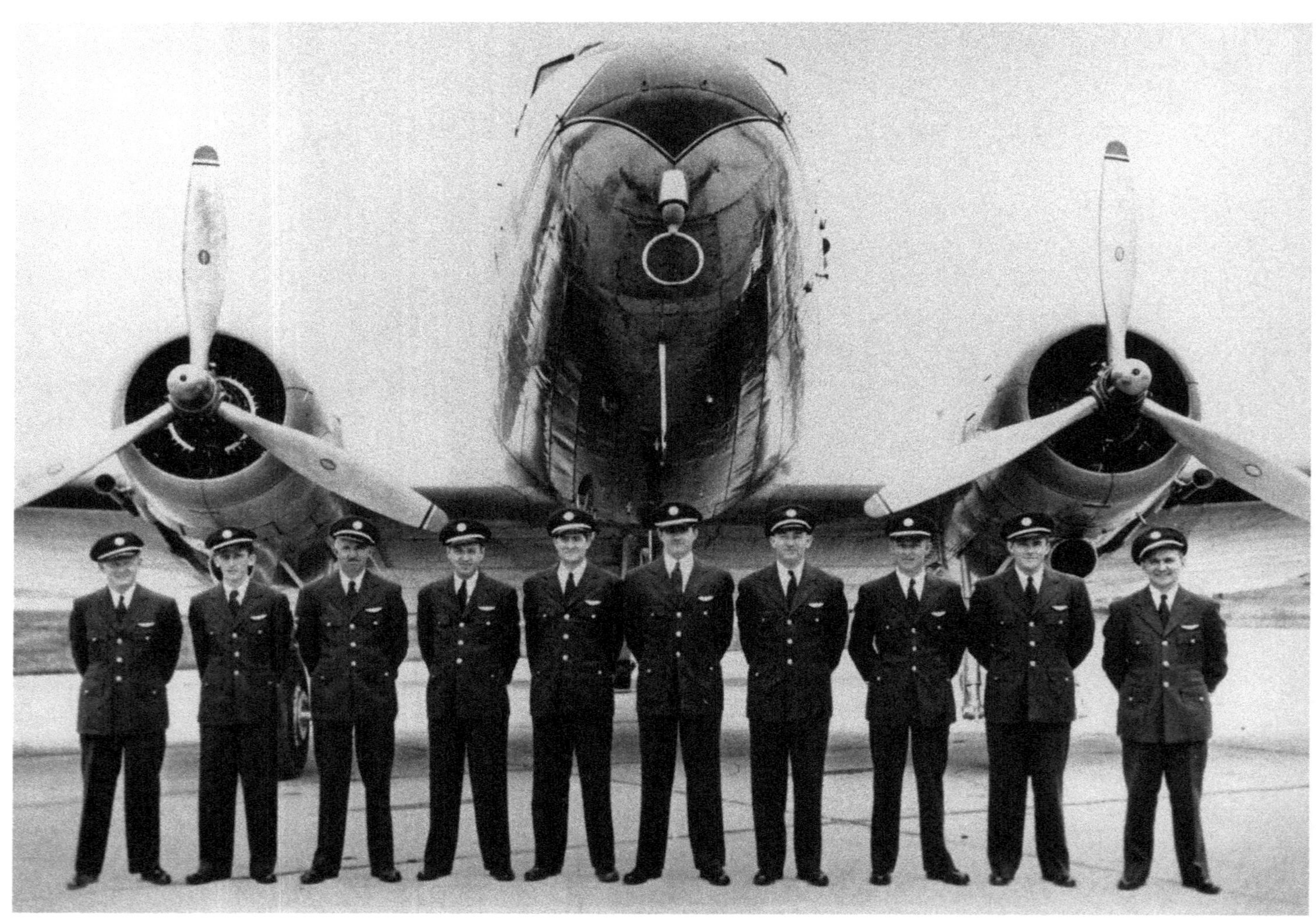

The first Piedmont Airlines pilots stand in front of a DC-3 at Smith Reynolds Airport in 1948. Winston-Salem would remain the headquarters of Piedmont until 1987, when US Air purchased the airline.

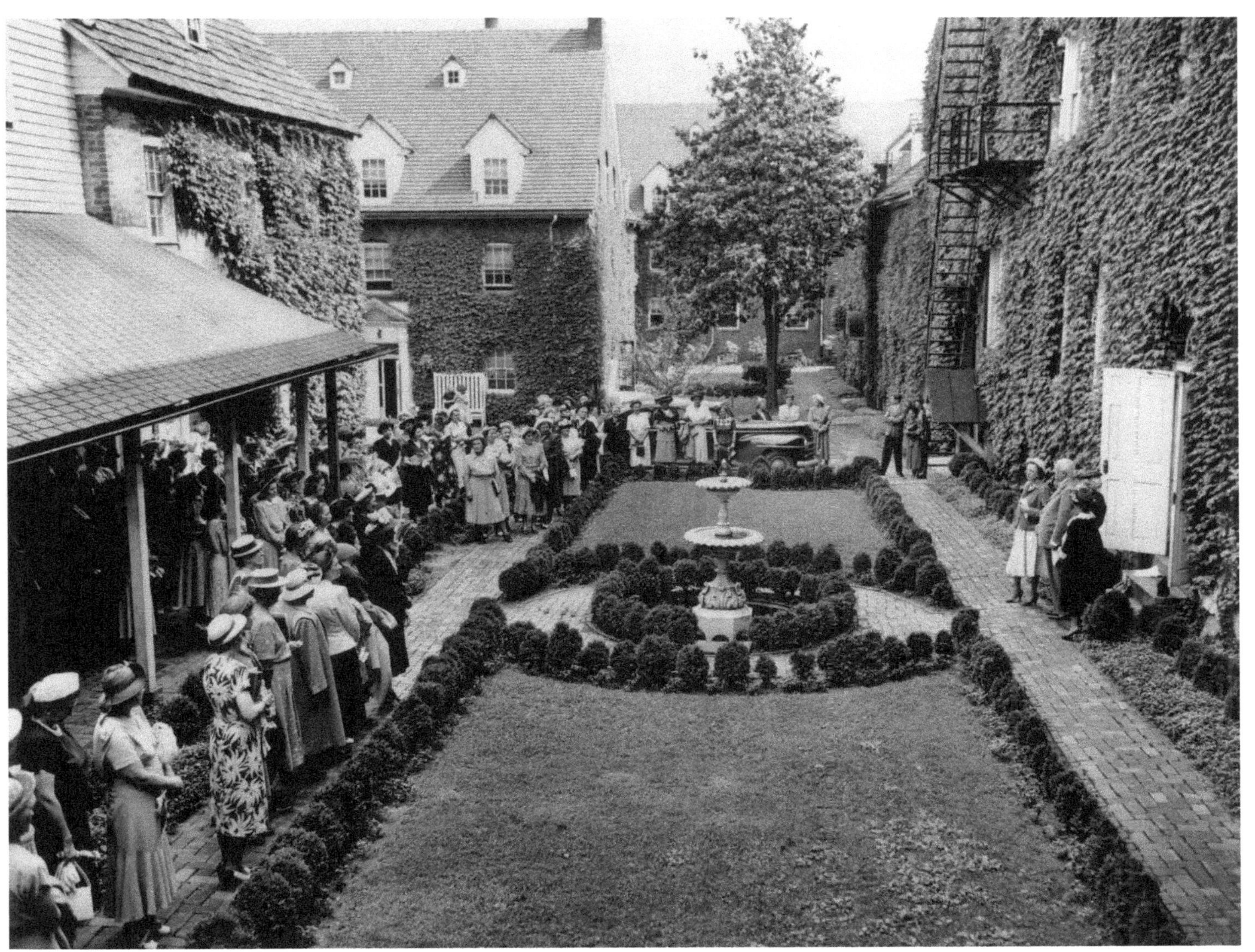

Salem College alumnae meet in May of 1948 to dedicate Alumnae Hall, the new building their generosity purchased for the school.

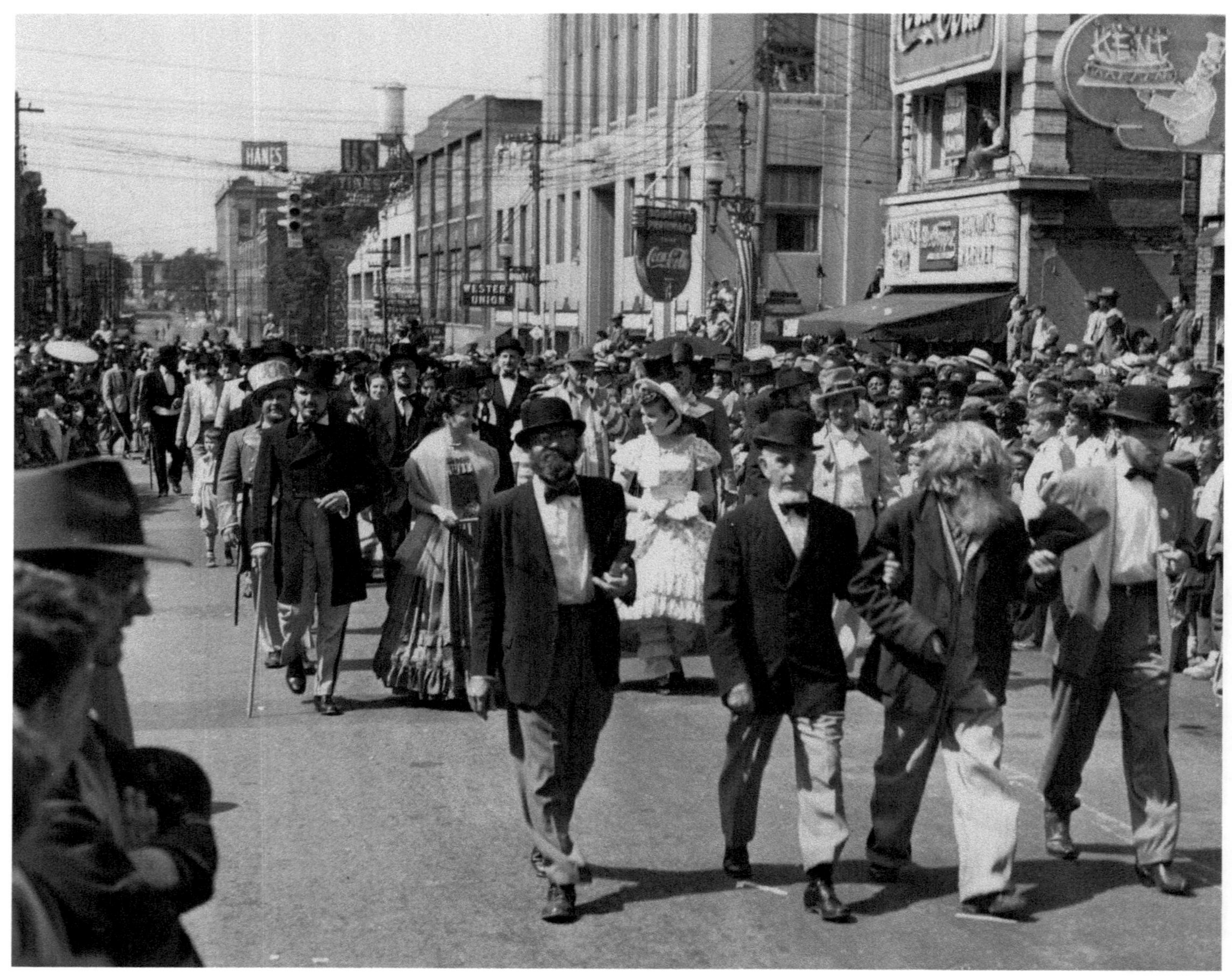


Forsyth County celebrated its centennial in May of 1949 with a parade that featured period costumes.

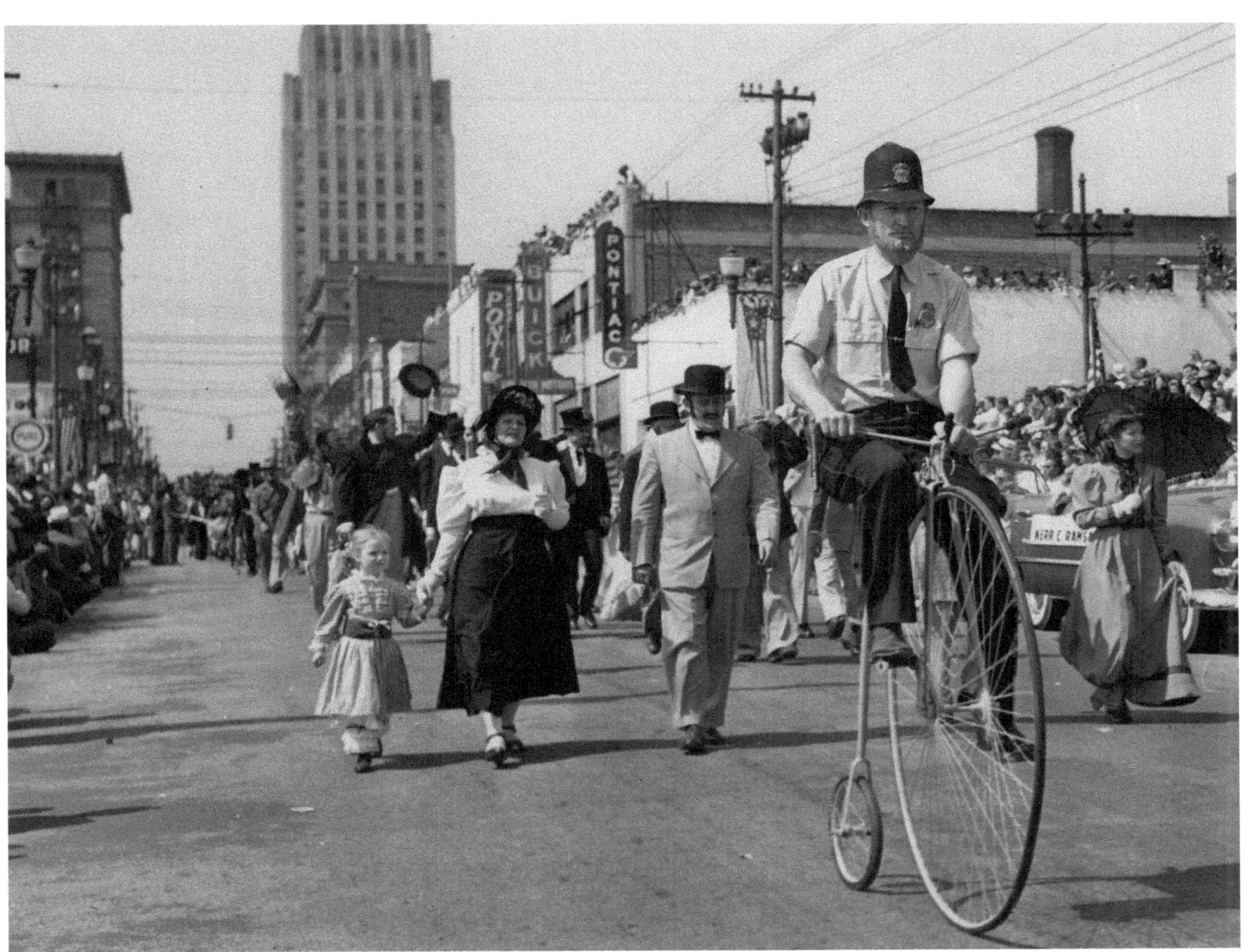


In addition to nineteenth-century clothing, the Forsyth County centennial parade brought out devices such as this vintage two-wheeler.

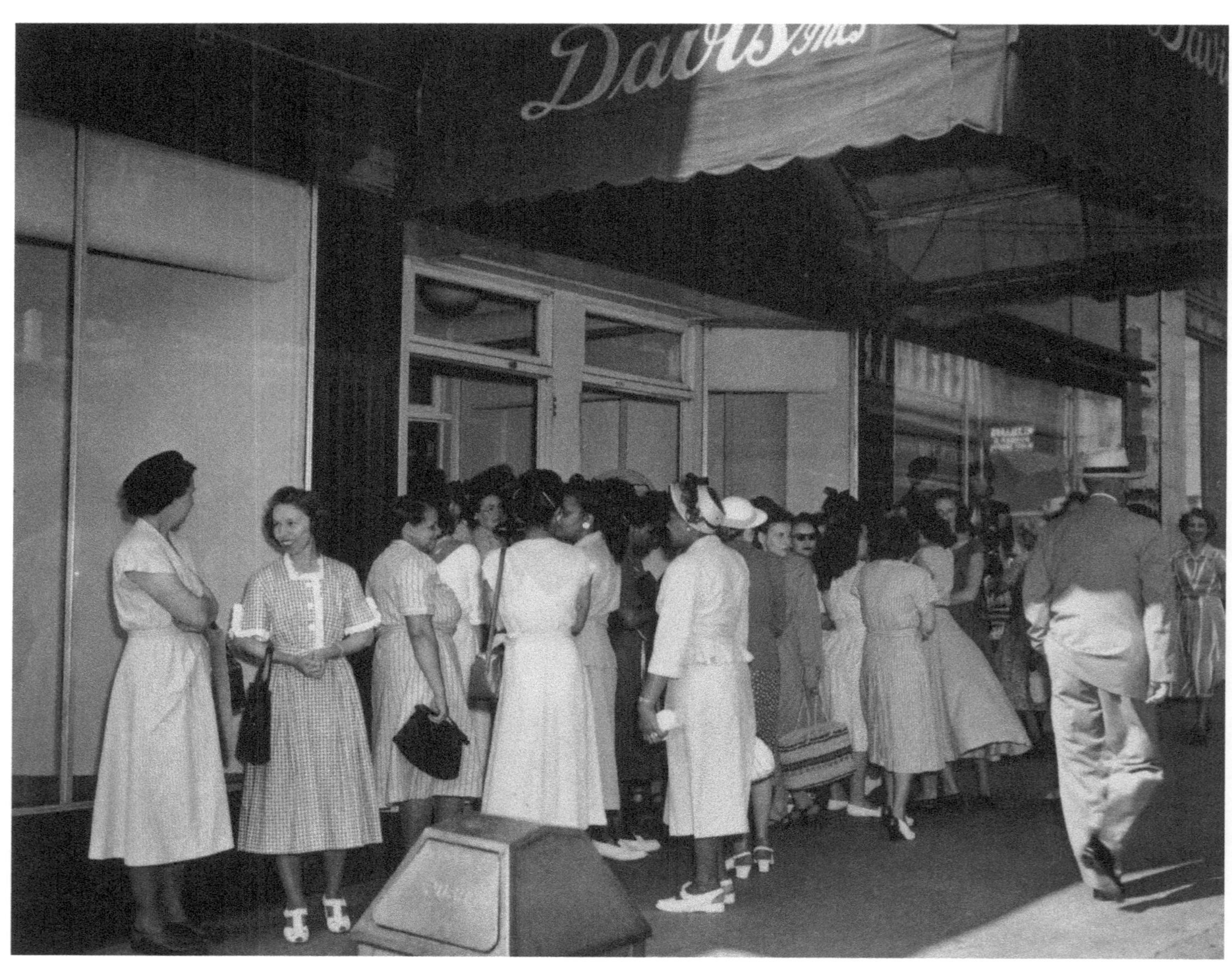

Built in 1910, Davis Department Store on Fourth Street served generations of shoppers, such as these ladies waiting for the doors to open and a sale to begin in 1948. As of 2008, the city is discussing razing the building for new construction in an attempt to revitalize downtown Winston-Salem.

# A City Redefined

## (1950–1979)

The story of Winston-Salem from 1950 to 1979 is, in part, the story of Mayor Marshall Kurfees, first elected to office in 1949 and serving until 1961. Mayor Kurfees, not always on the popular side of issues, tried to restore the downtown area to its pre-Depression luster, eliminated city slums, supported the preservation of Old Salem, worked to mesh the faculty and students of Wake Forest College into the community, and brought new roads to the city. He governed during the first stages of desegregation, a challenging time in every southern city. That Winston-Salem had largely recovered from two horrible decades by the mid-1950s is a testimony to his leadership. As proof of his efforts, Winston-Salem won an All-American City Award in 1959 (it would win another in 1964).

Such gains did not come without pain and trepidation. Slum clearance and urban renewal struck hardest in the traditional African American districts in town. Bulldozers destroyed more than tenements and old storefronts; they destroyed years of traditions and memories, and sometimes did so without consultation or planning for the future. Integration met resistance on all fronts; and though African Americans eventually won key roles in local governments, and the "Whites Only" signs disappeared, riots exploded three times in the 1960s, most seriously in 1967.

Stirrings of concern by the medical community over the dangers of smoking also brought fear to a city and a county long dependent on the fragrant, yellow leaves. The introduction of filtered cigarettes (Winstons and Salems, of course) by Reynolds Tobacco stopped the rumblings of neither the medical community nor of congressional hearings. But the market remained strong, at least through the 1970s.

Perhaps the greatest successes of this era came in education. Wake Forest College relocated to Winston-Salem, then became a university; Winston-Salem Teacher's College eventually became Winston-Salem State University; Salem College prospered; city and county schools consolidated; and integration finally confirmed that separate can never be equal. The quality and quantity of these institutions meant that a growing number of well-trained professionals stayed in the city. The end of the 1970s found Winston-Salem a stronger, more diverse city than at any other time in its history.

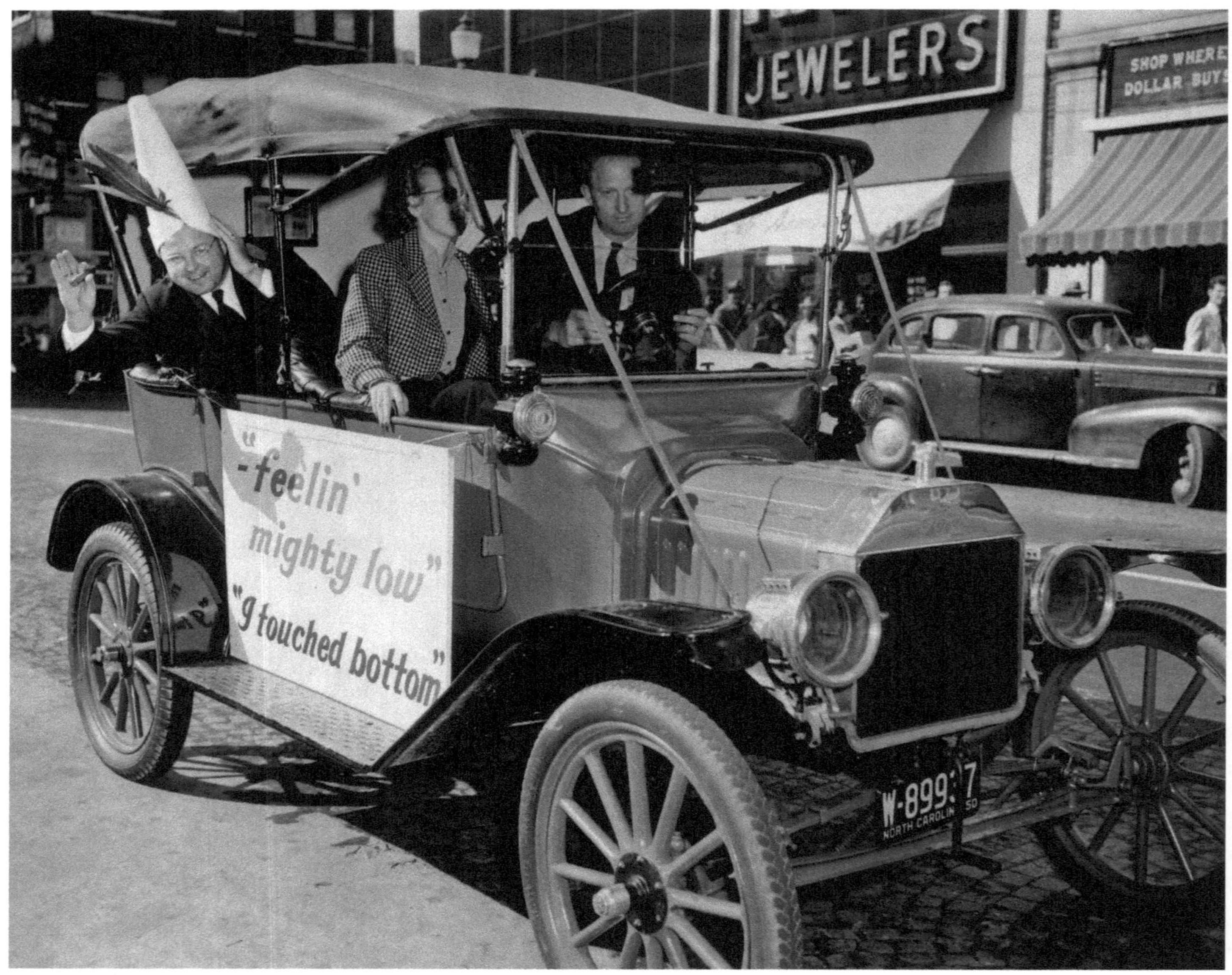


This driver of an antique car on West Fourth Street in 1950 may have "touched bottom" during the two previous decades, but like most Winston-Salem citizens, he probably believed they had turned the corner toward prosperity.

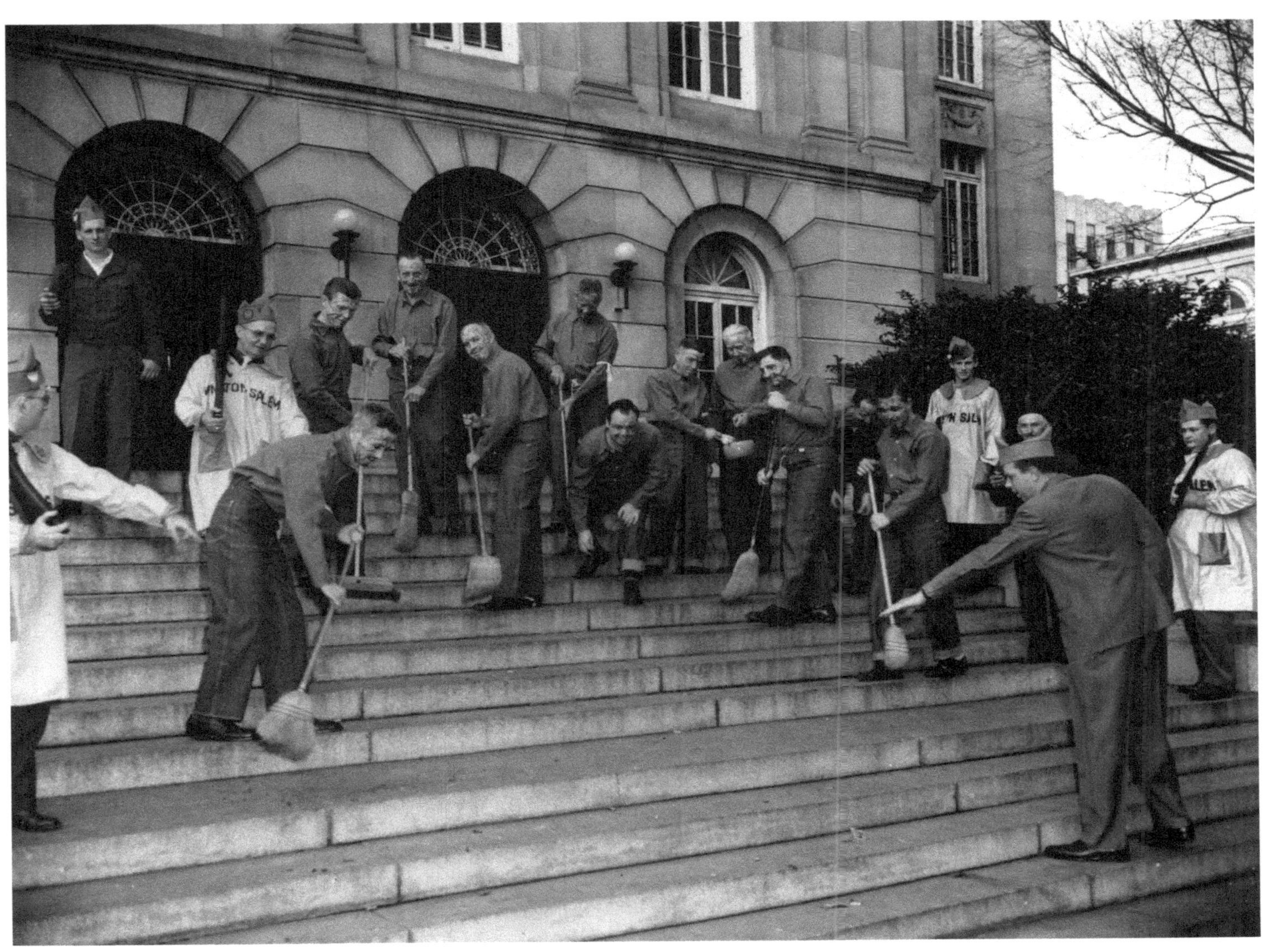

Veterans' organizations thrived after World War II and became central to many community activities. Here, American Legion members sweep the steps of City Hall in 1950.

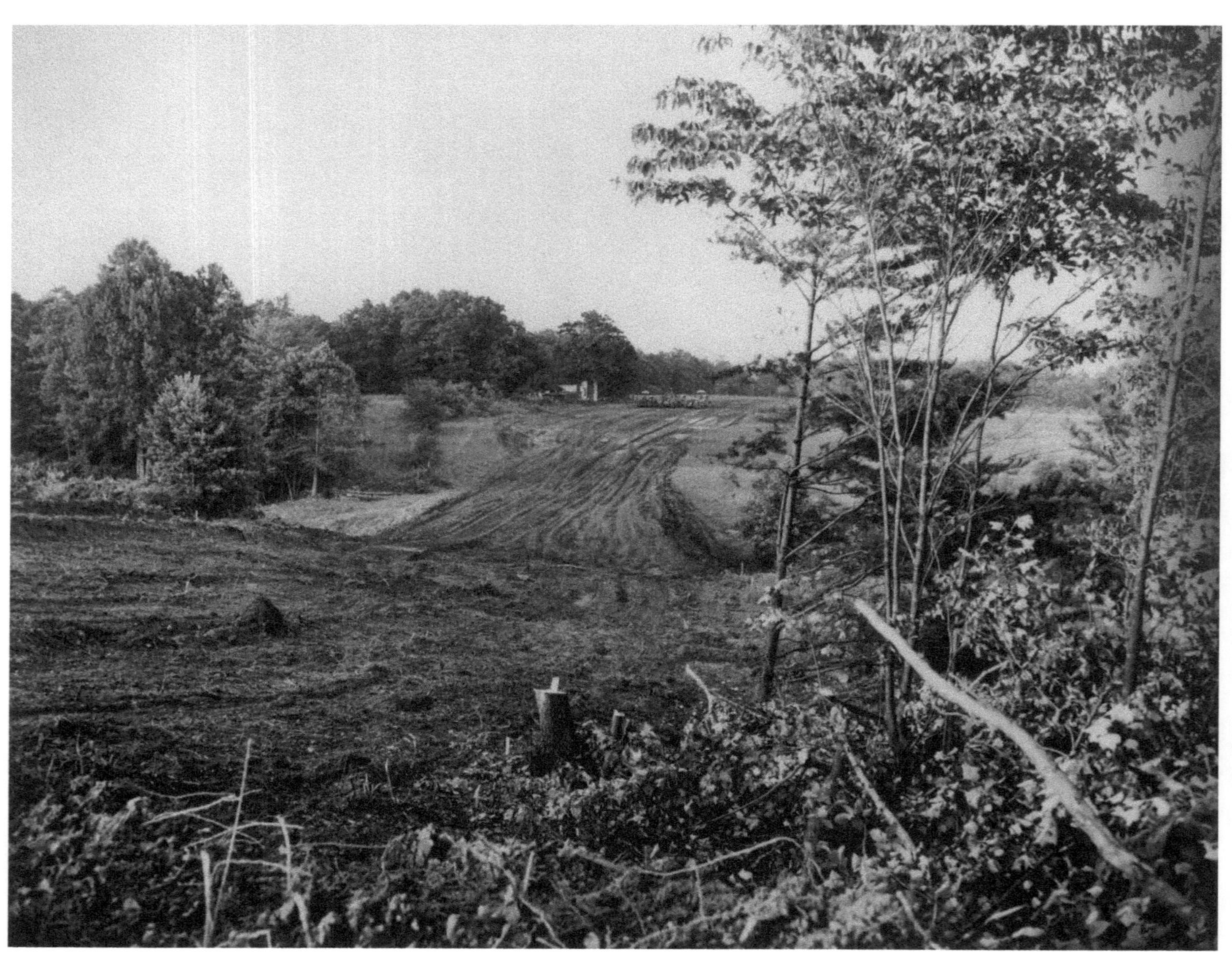

In 1946, unable to resist the incentives offered by Winston-Salem's leading families to relocate from the small town of Wake Forest to the big city, Wake Forest College's Board of Trustees and the Baptist State Convention approved the plan to do so. This is the east entrance to the Winston-Salem campus in 1951, five years before it opened—not quite as impressive as it is today!

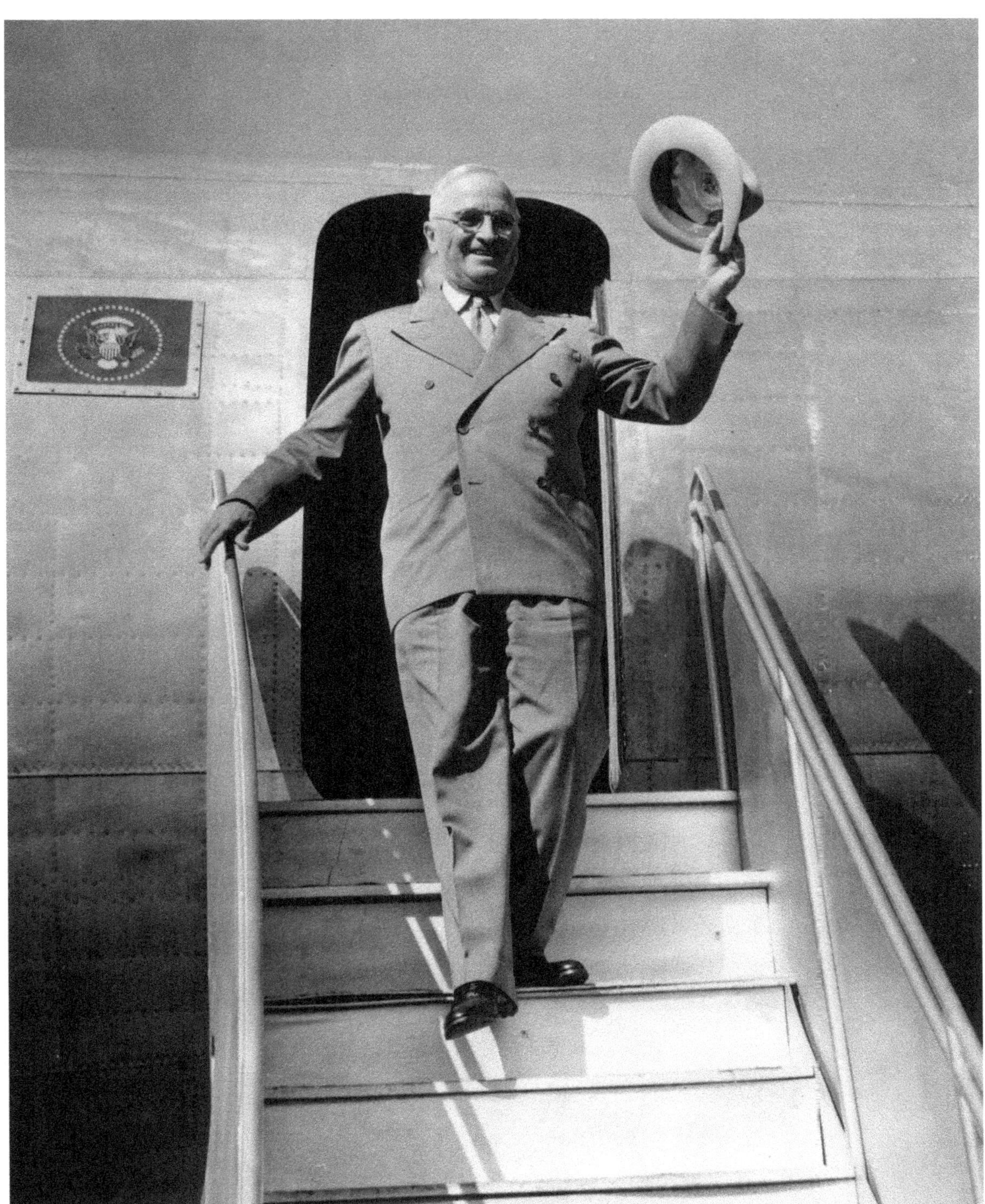

President Harry Truman flew into Winston-Salem for the Wake Forest College groundbreaking ceremonies. Here, he exits the presidential plane at Smith Reynolds Airport. On October 15, 1951, the president turned the first spade of earth to begin construction of the new facility.

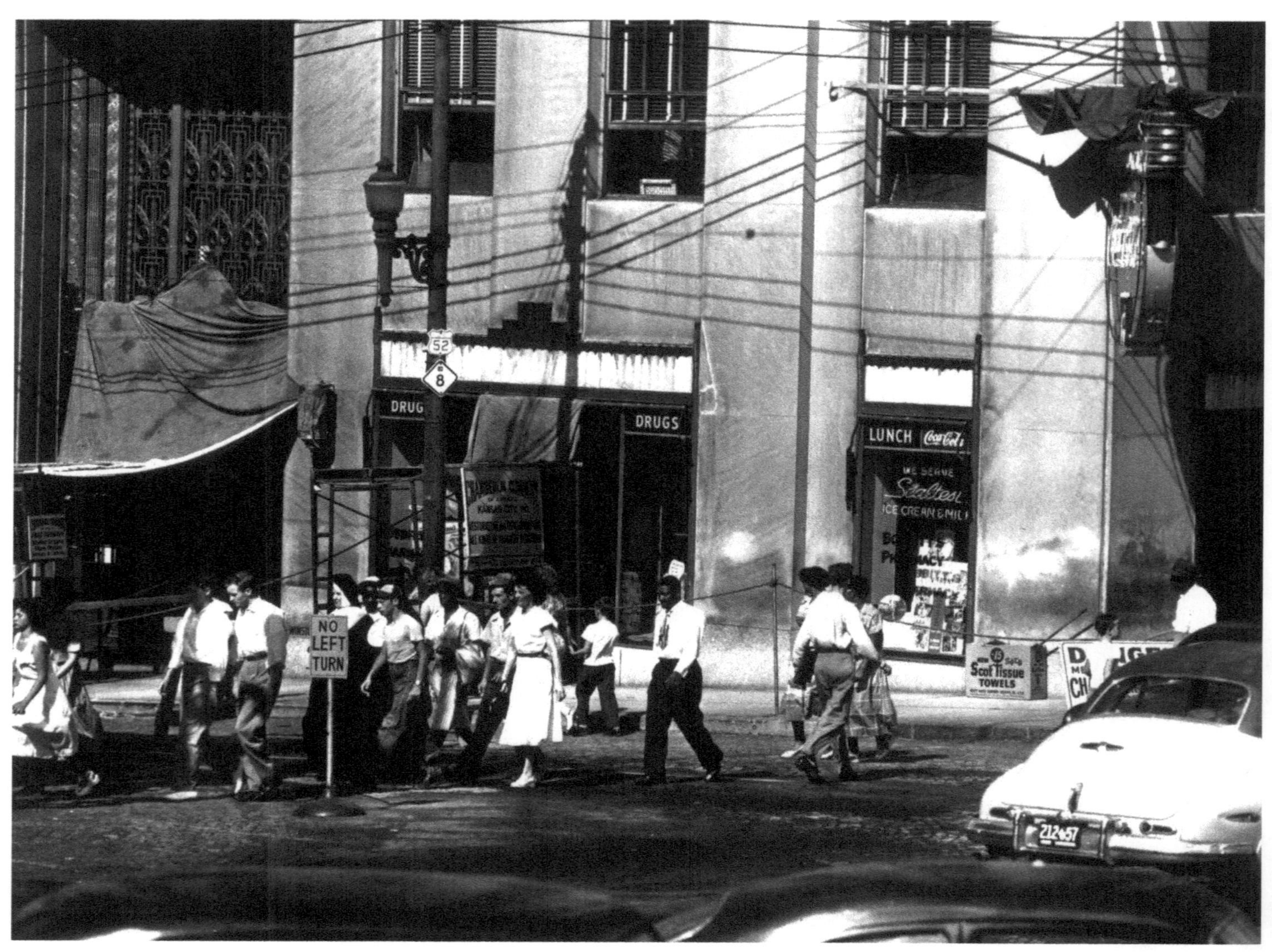


Pedestrians cross the street at West Fourth and Main on a warm day in 1950. Once prime real estate with spic-and-span family businesses lining the street, the district with its rundown, frequently changing storefronts had become reflective of downtown Winston-Salem's deterioration.

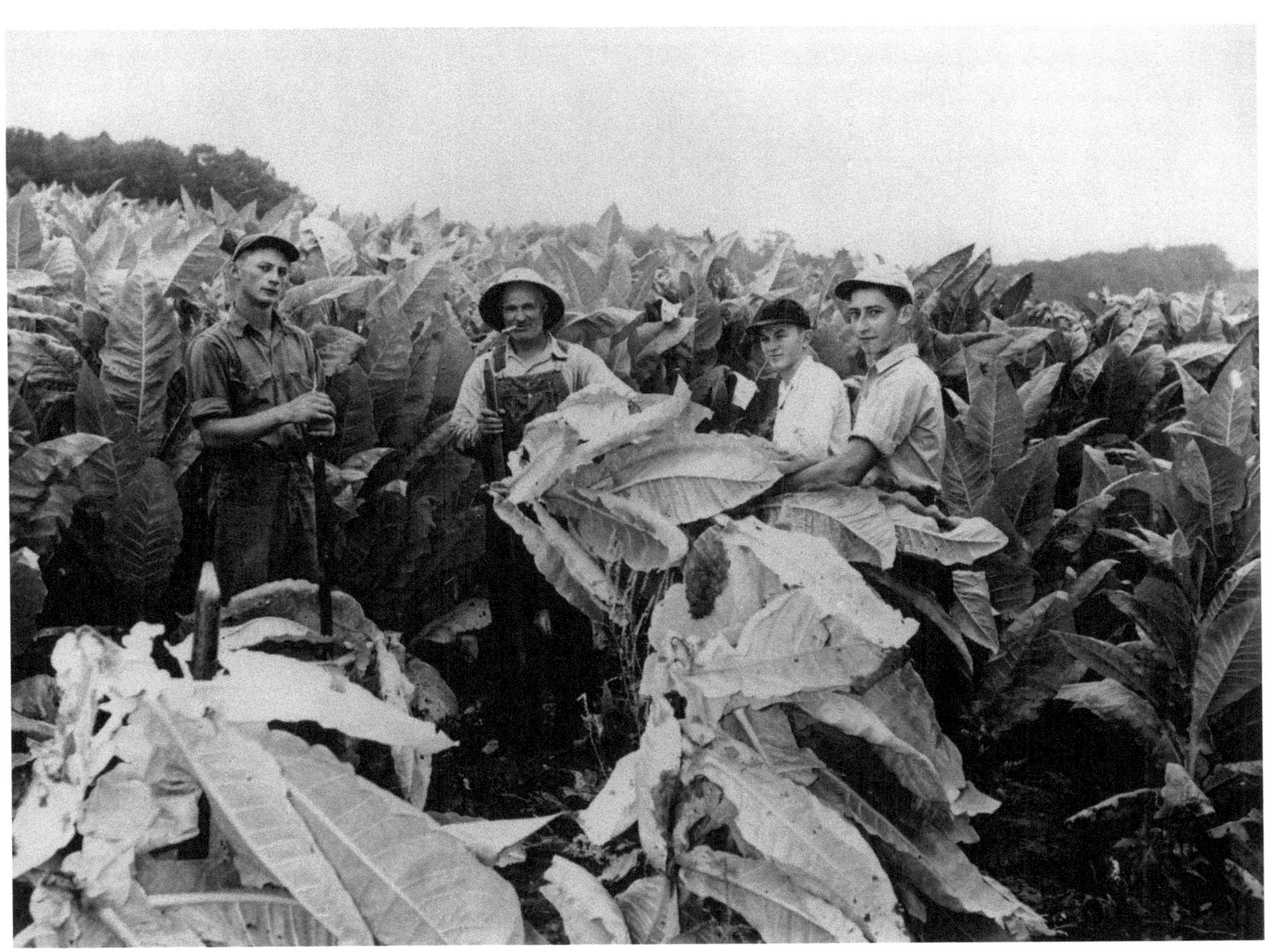

Farmers pause from "priming" tobacco in the summer of 1951. Their world seemed safe, and their future liable to continue in the same pattern of beds to fields to barns to market. Then, in 1954, medical scientists began to report findings of the hazards of smoking. From small farmers to CEOs of tobacco companies, there was now more to worry about than the weather.

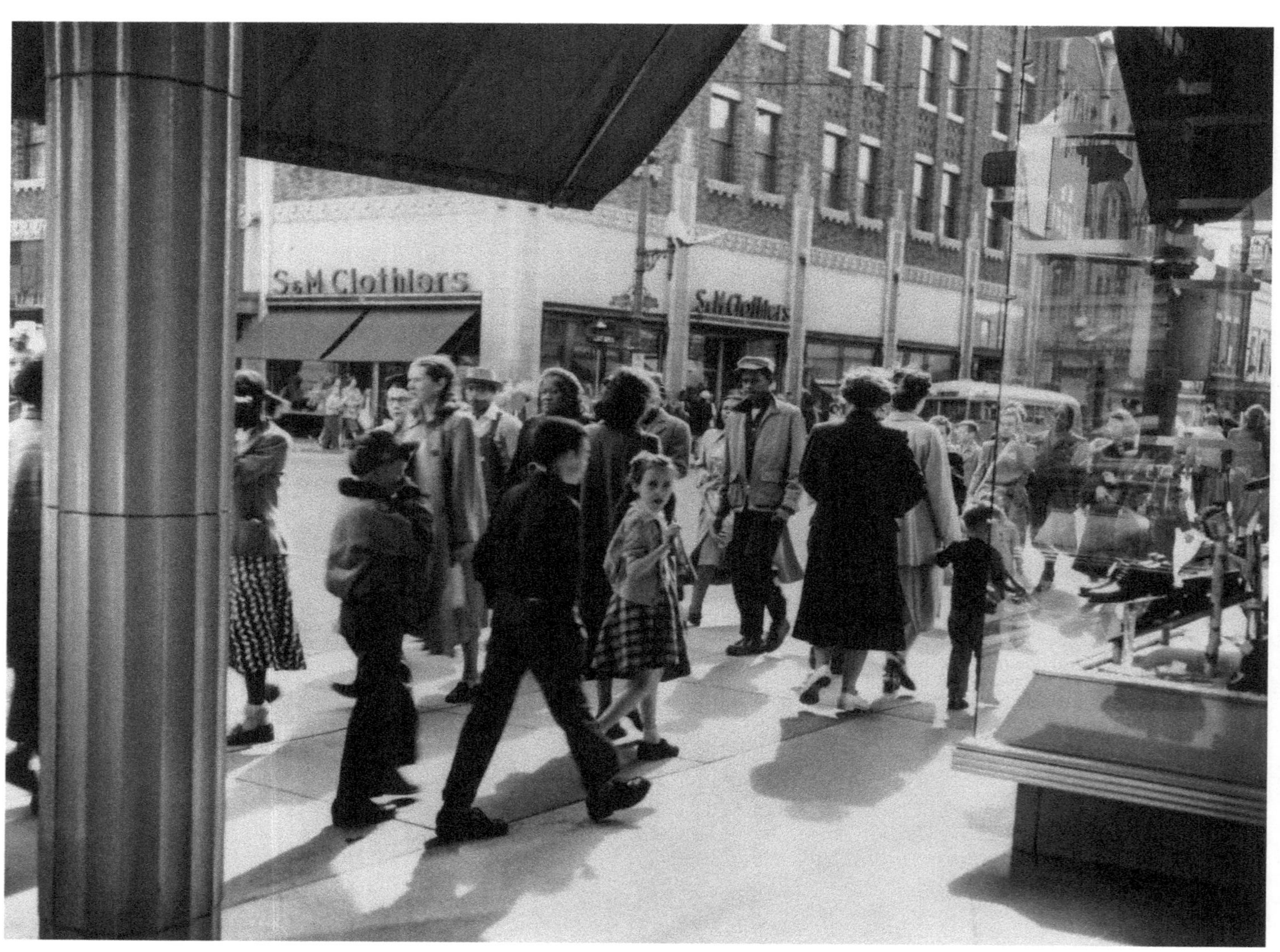


Easter shoppers promenade on Fourth Street in March 1951. Already, efforts to repair the aging infrastructure of the downtown area had begun showing some results with new stores, repaved streets, and repaired sidewalks.

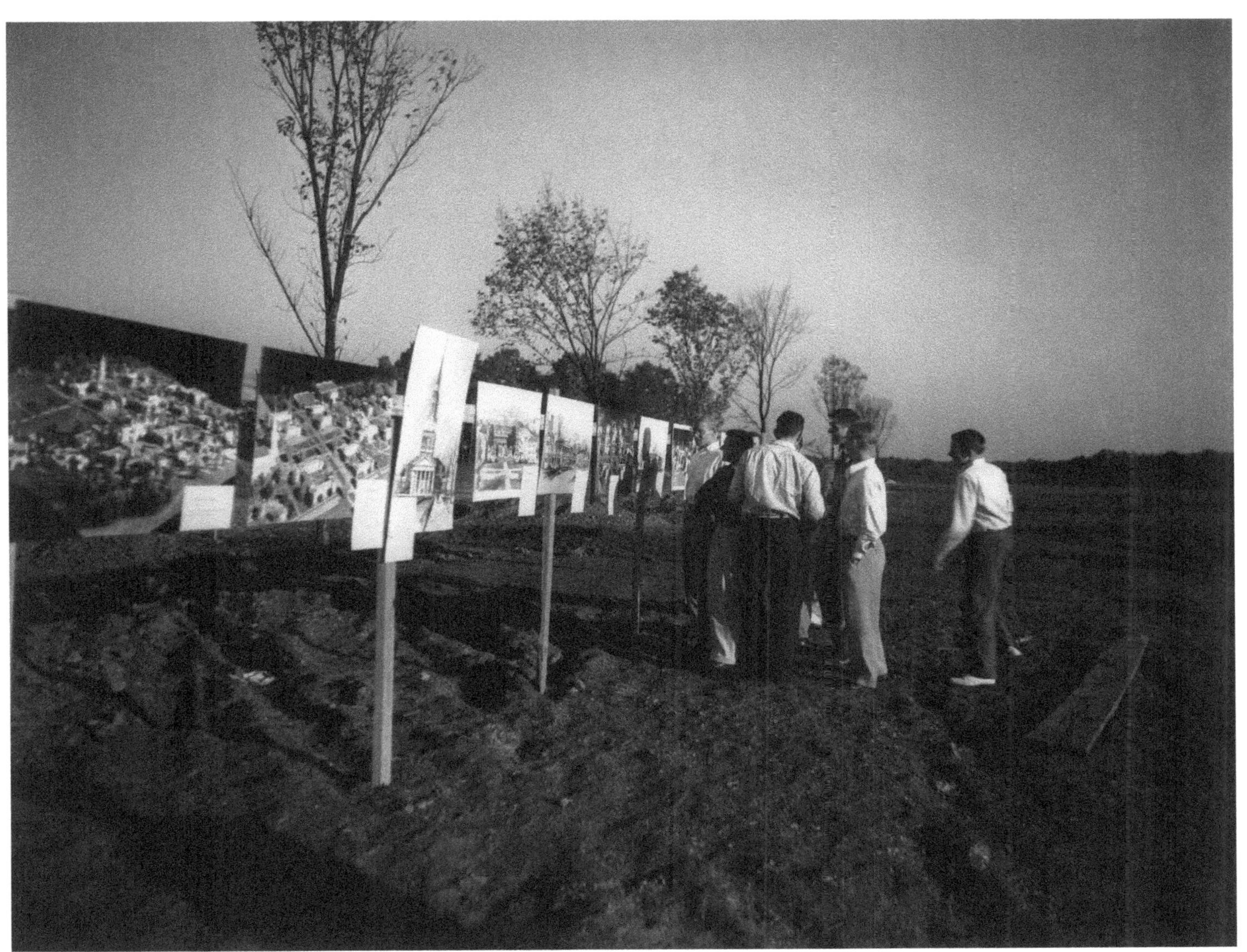

By 1952, students at Wake Forest College began appearing at the school's new location on the 320 acres of land donated to the school by Charles and Mary Reynolds Babcock. If the students in this picture were freshman, there is a good chance they were among the first to graduate in Winston-Salem, as the college did not finish its relocation until 1956.

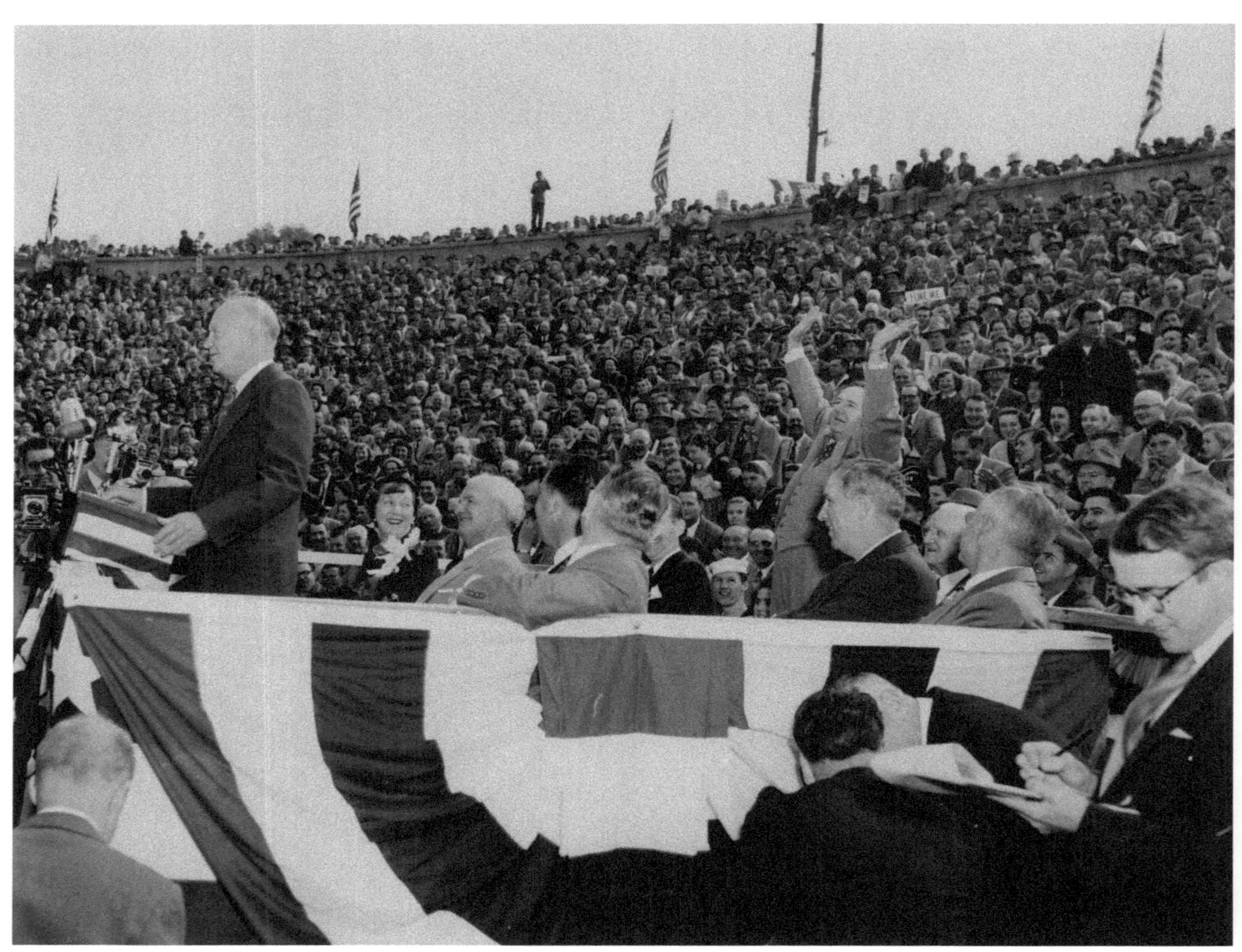

In 1952, General Dwight Eisenhower was hardly a stranger to Winston-Salem; his good friend Frank Swadley had managed the Robert E. Lee Hotel when General Eisenhower last visited in 1947. But a visit by President Truman in 1951 meant a follow-up stop on the campaign trail for Ike. This 1952 rally found cheering supporters filling Bowman Gray Stadium.

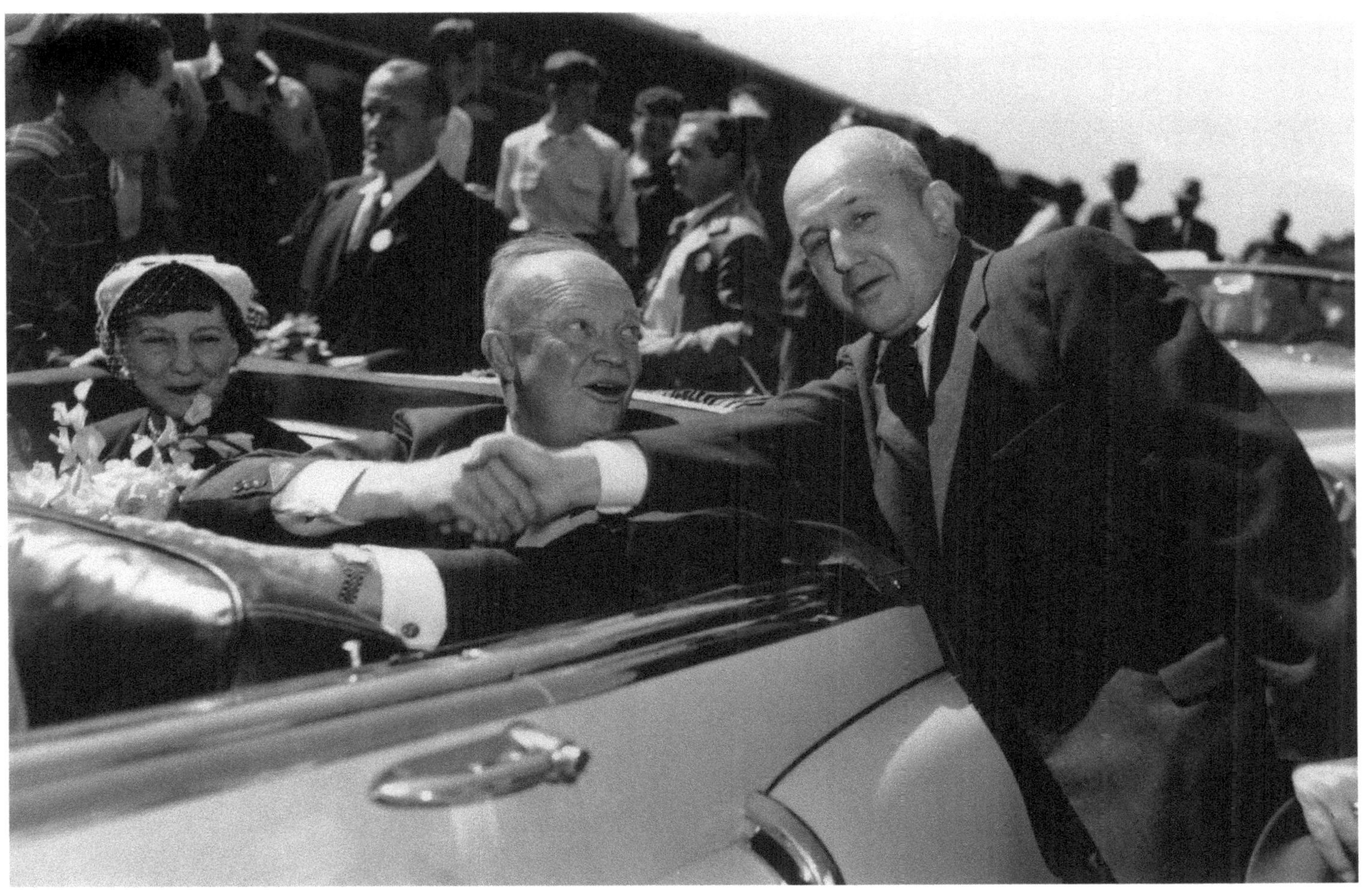

Before General and Mamie Eisenhower left the city in 1952, the mayor of Winston-Salem, Marshall Kurfees, extended his hand for a photo opportunity. First elected in 1950, Kurfees proved himself quite capable, if not always popular, as an administrator. He also kept his promises, including one to let the city vote to allow liquor stores. When the vote passed, the new ABC (Alcoholic Beverage Control) stores sprouting on corners were nicknamed "Kurfees drugstores."

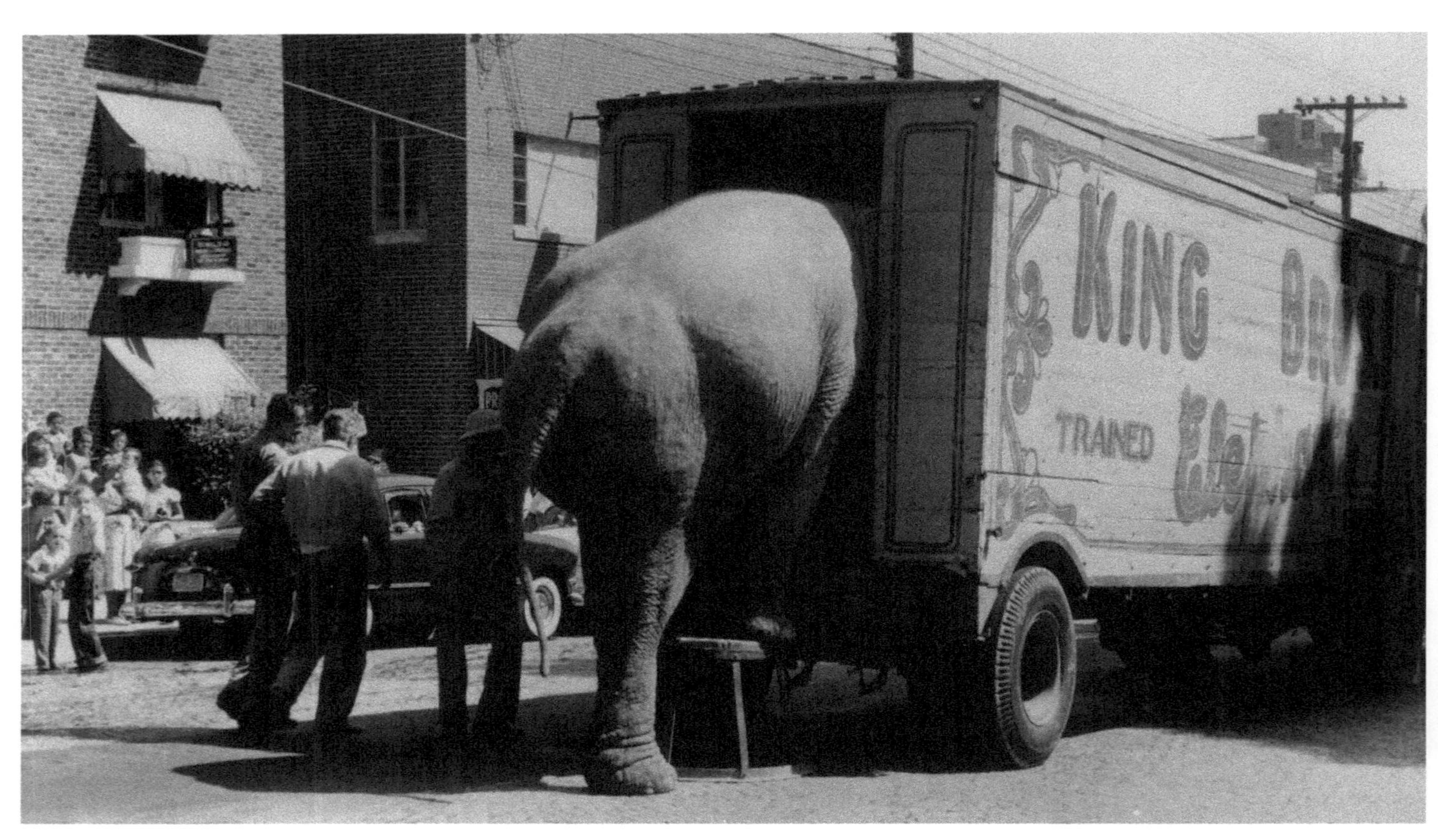


For generations, the circus caused excitement when it paraded through Winston-Salem. In 1954, the King Brothers Circus was no exception.

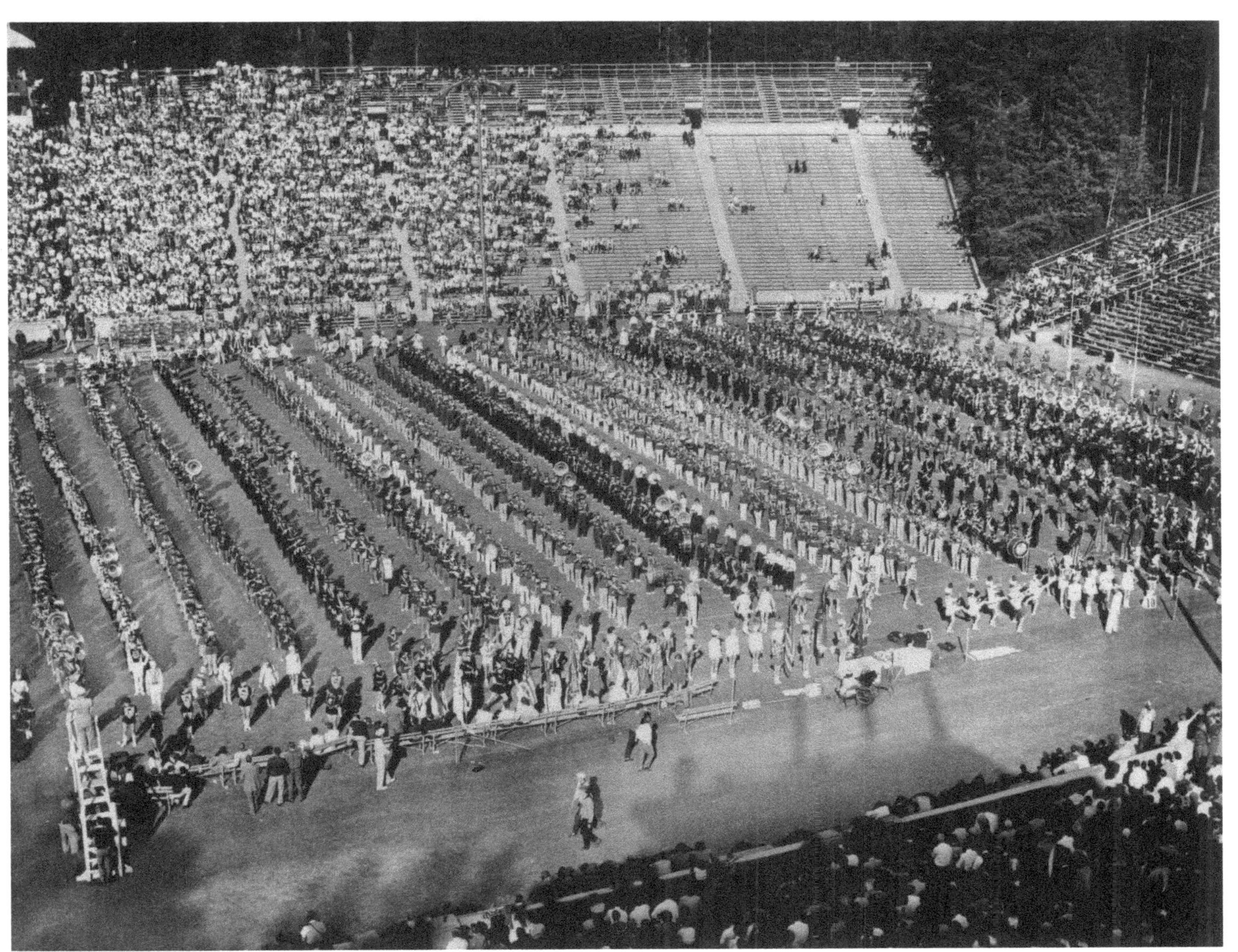

Band Day at the University of North Carolina, October 23, 1954, saw the Demon Deacons of Wake Forest drop a tough one to the Tar Heels, 14-7. With Wake Forest finishing the season 2-7-1 (1-4-1 in the Atlantic Coast Conference), some fans probably wondered if Coach Tom Rogers would be joining the team when it relocated to Winston-Salem in 1956.

Shoppers brave the drizzle on West Fourth Street in 1955, with the Reynolds Building dominating the skyline in the background. Storefronts stand full, traffic is buzzing, and at least this part of the city seems to have recovered from the hard years of the 1930s and 1940s.

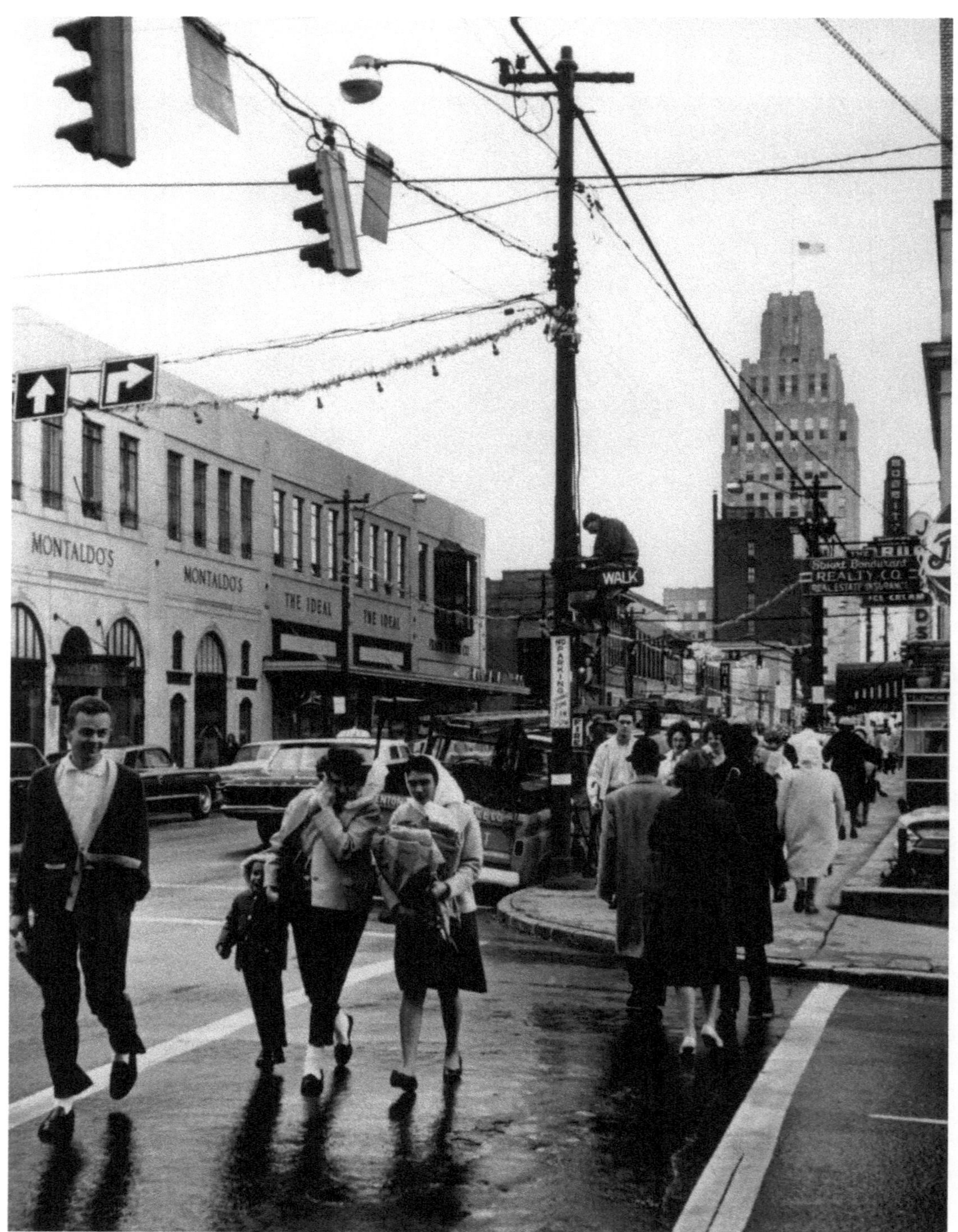

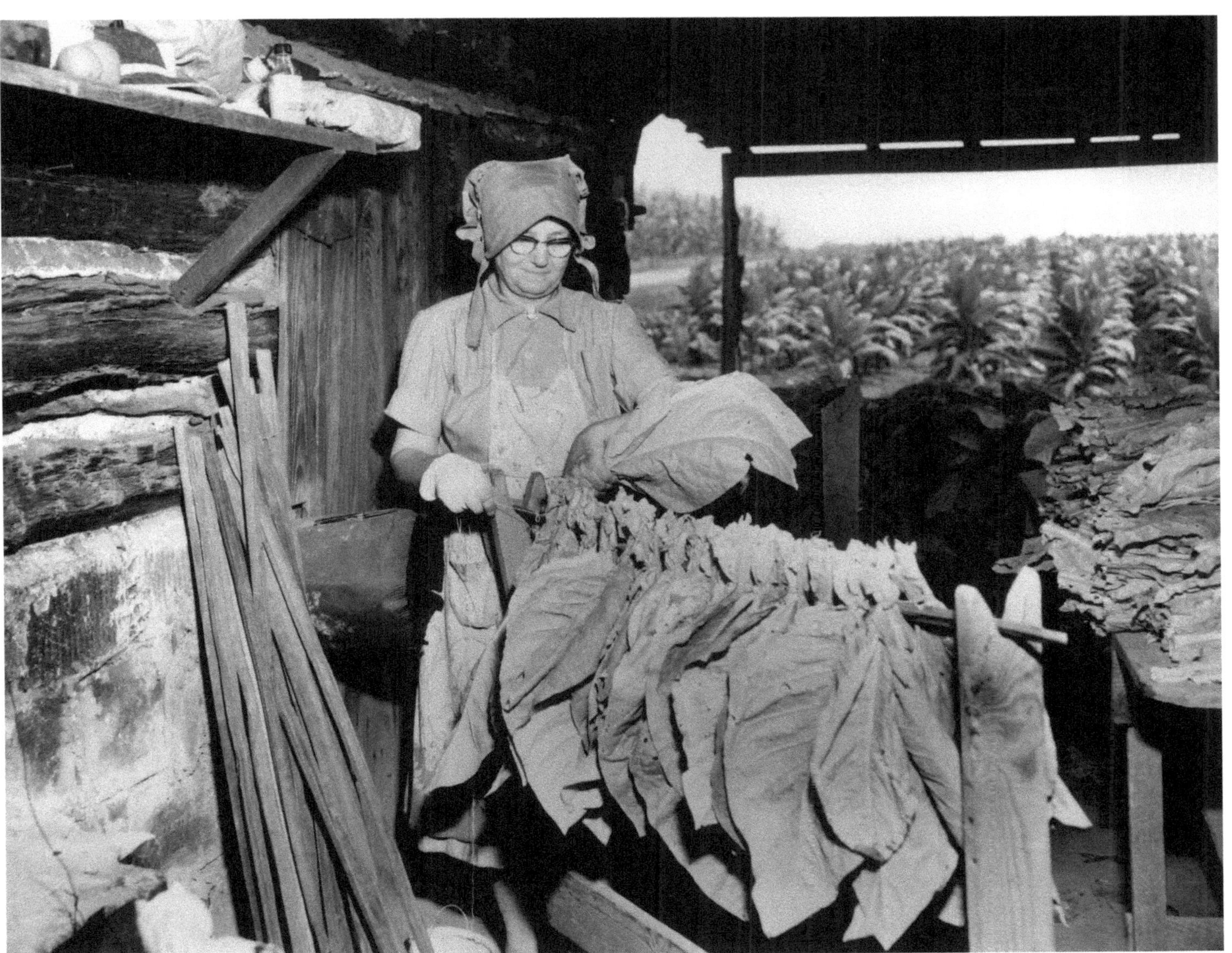

Of course, a day shopping in the drizzle on West Fourth Street beat a day stringing wet tobacco on the farm. The hard work had its payoff for Forsyth County's farmers, however, once those leaves turned golden brown and made their way to the markets in the city. Then, maybe, they could join the shopping throngs—if anything remained after paying mortgage, taxes, and loans.

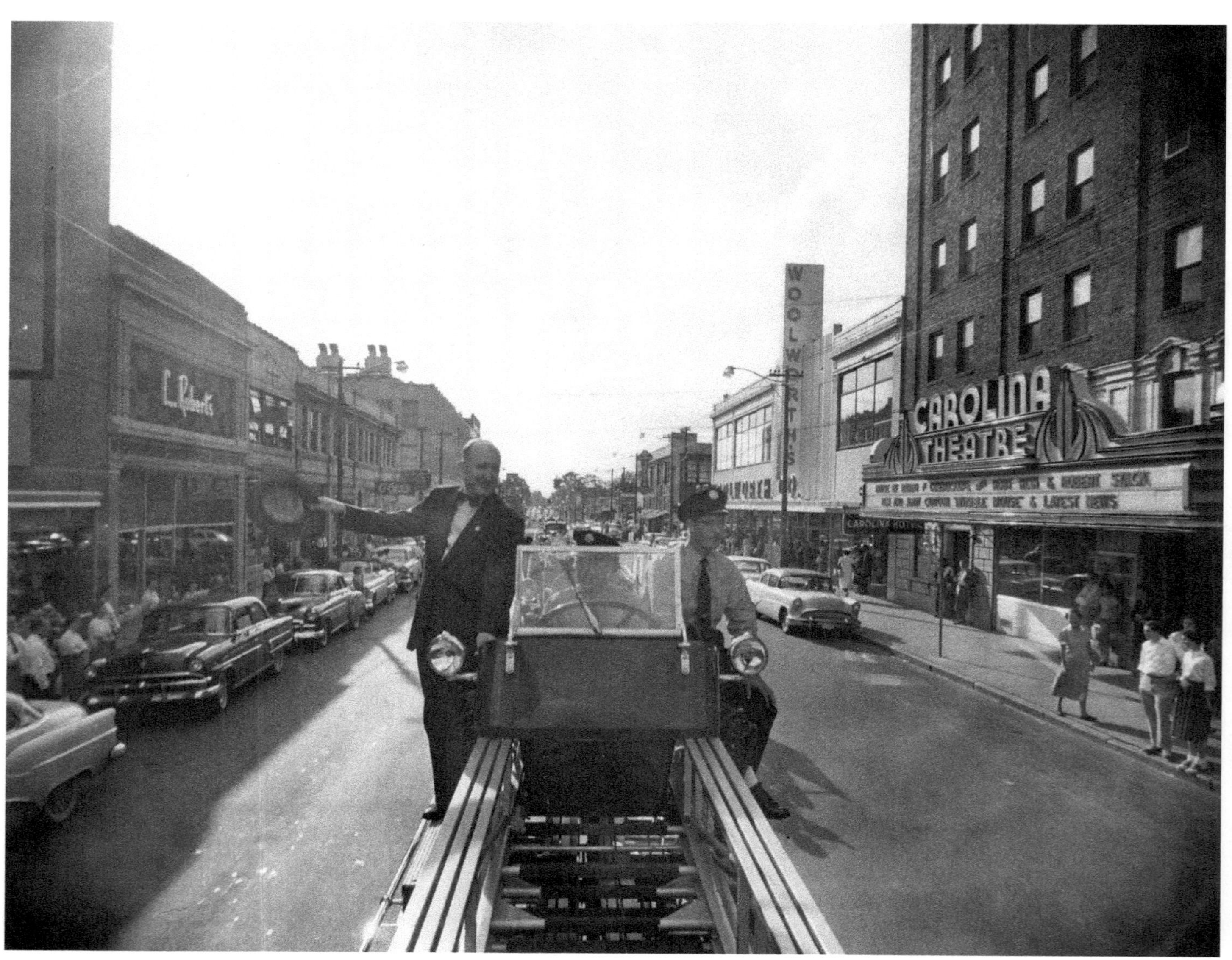


This Fire Prevention Week Parade seemed to draw few watchers as it drove past the Carolina Theatre on West Fourth Street in October of 1955.

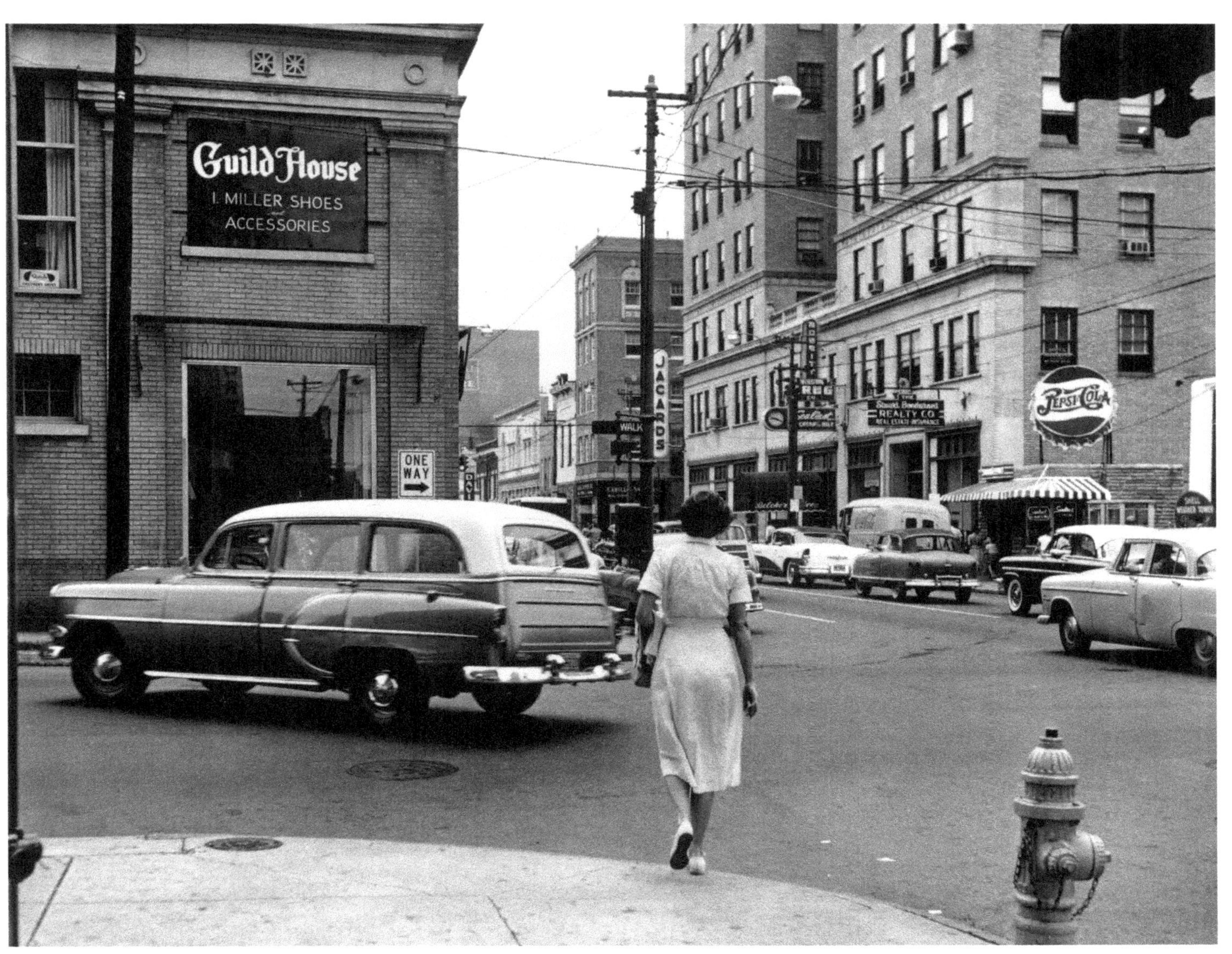


A woman crosses the street at Fourth and Marshall in the mid-1950s.

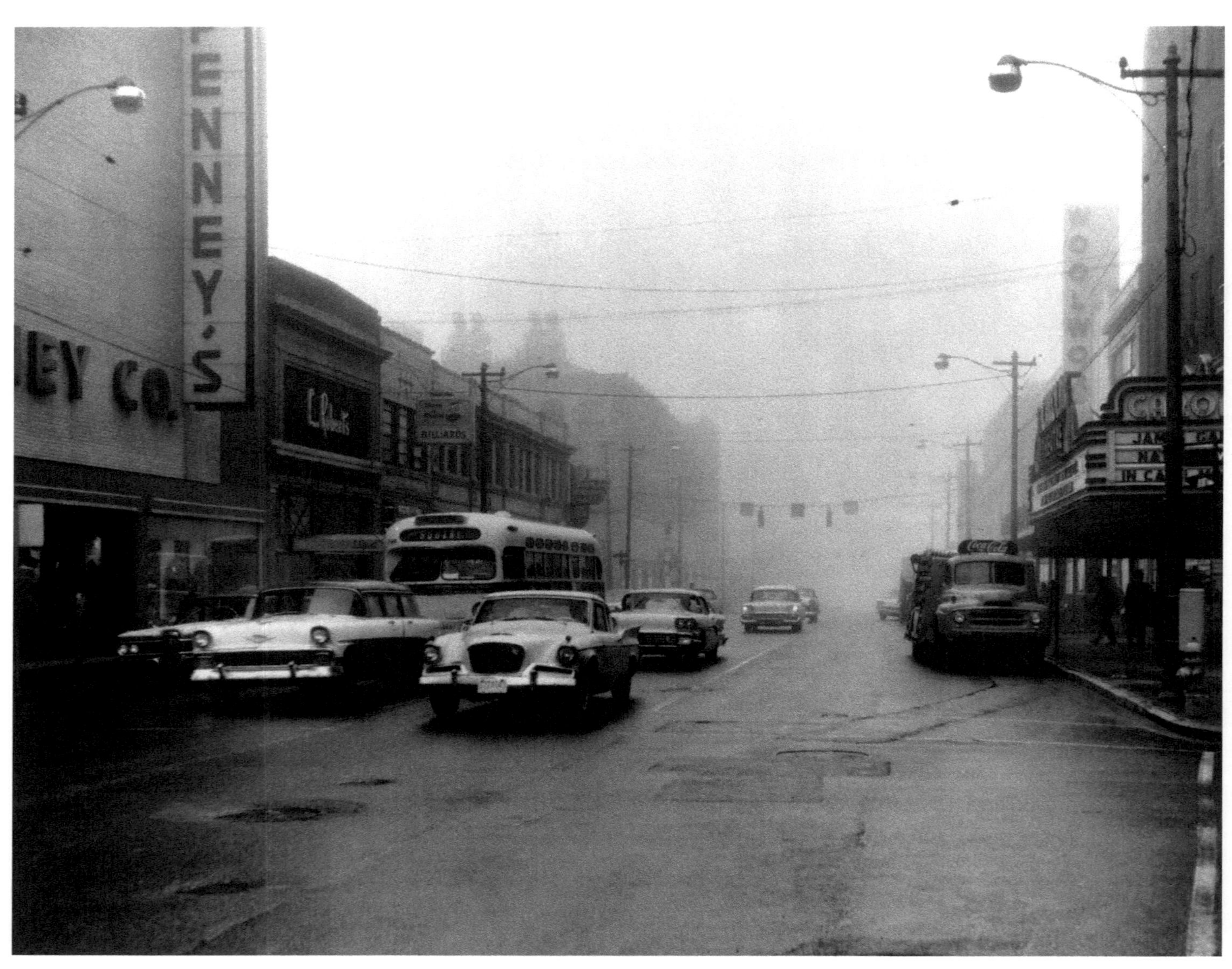

Traffic braves a wet Fourth Street at the intersection with Marshall Street in the mid-1950s. Note the new city transit bus on the left.

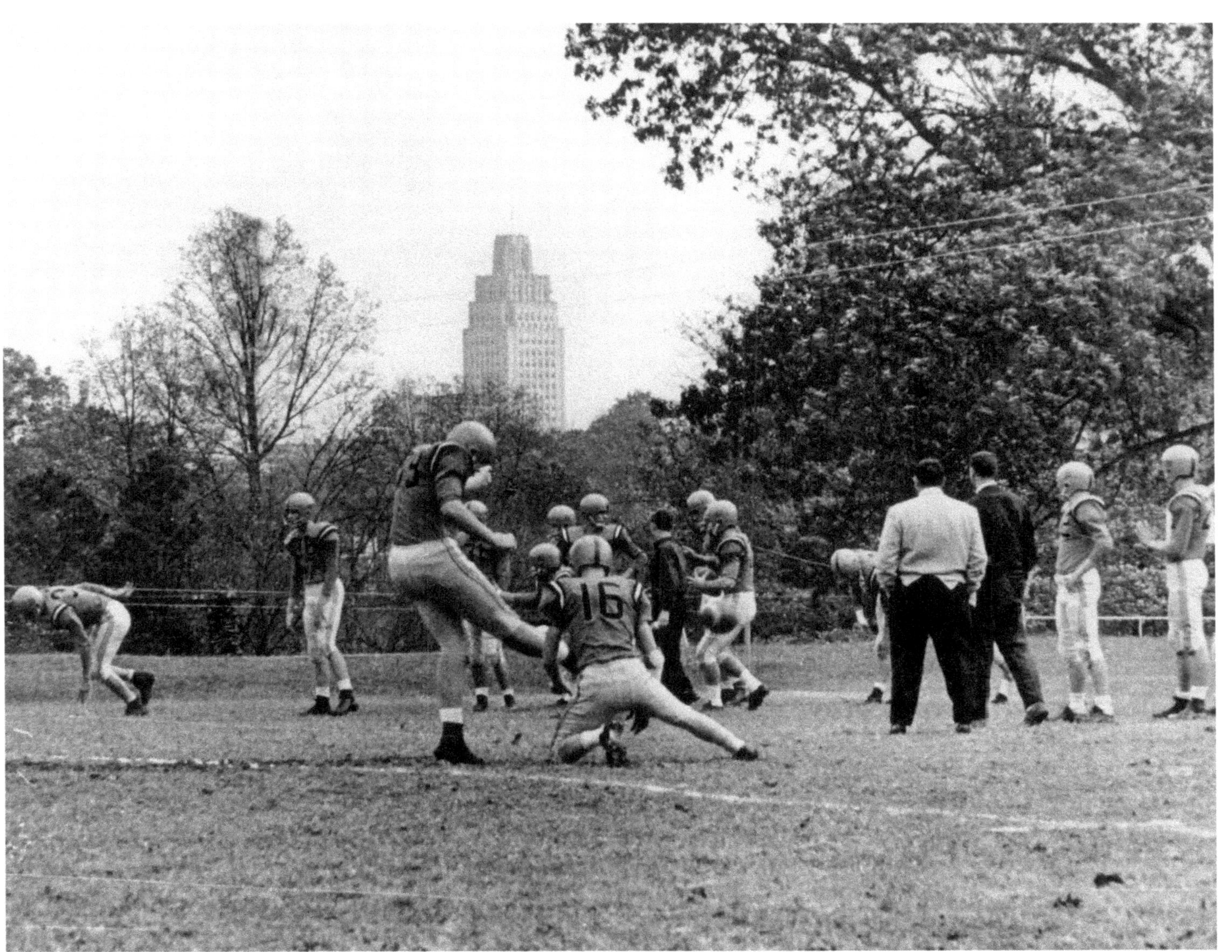


A mid-1950s football team practices at a high school field overlooked by the Reynolds Building in the distance. It is, perhaps, fitting, as the Reynolds family gave so much to the community in general and for education in particular. In doing so, they embodied that local claim of "the Winston Purse and the Salem Heart"—the combination of Winston's economic success coupled with the kindness to strangers traceable to Moravian Salem.

An officer appears to be writing a ticket in front of the Carolina Theatre during one of the mid-1950s Christmas seasons. Parking was obviously at a premium when the big names hit the marquee. Or was someone just trying to avoid the new parking meters?

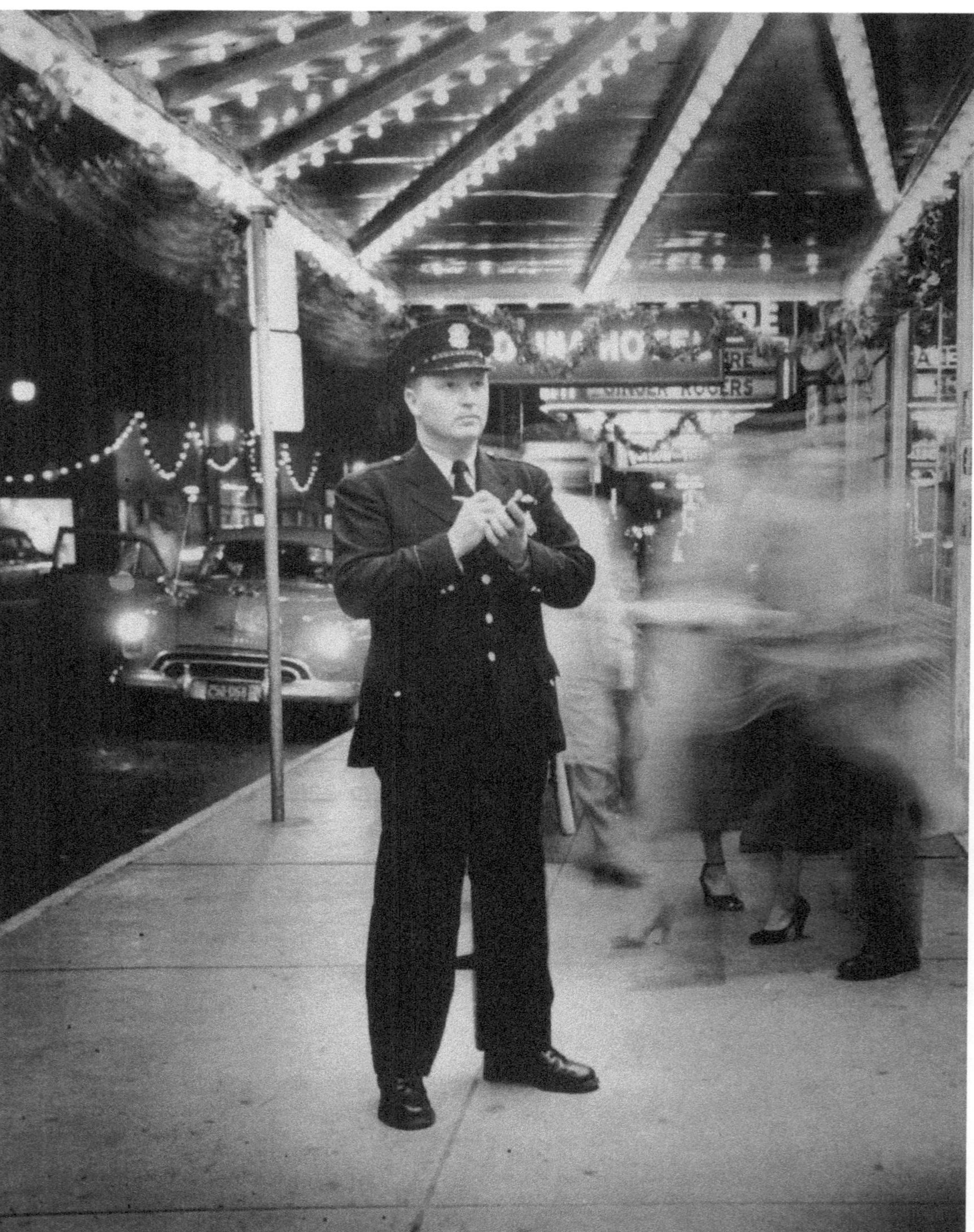

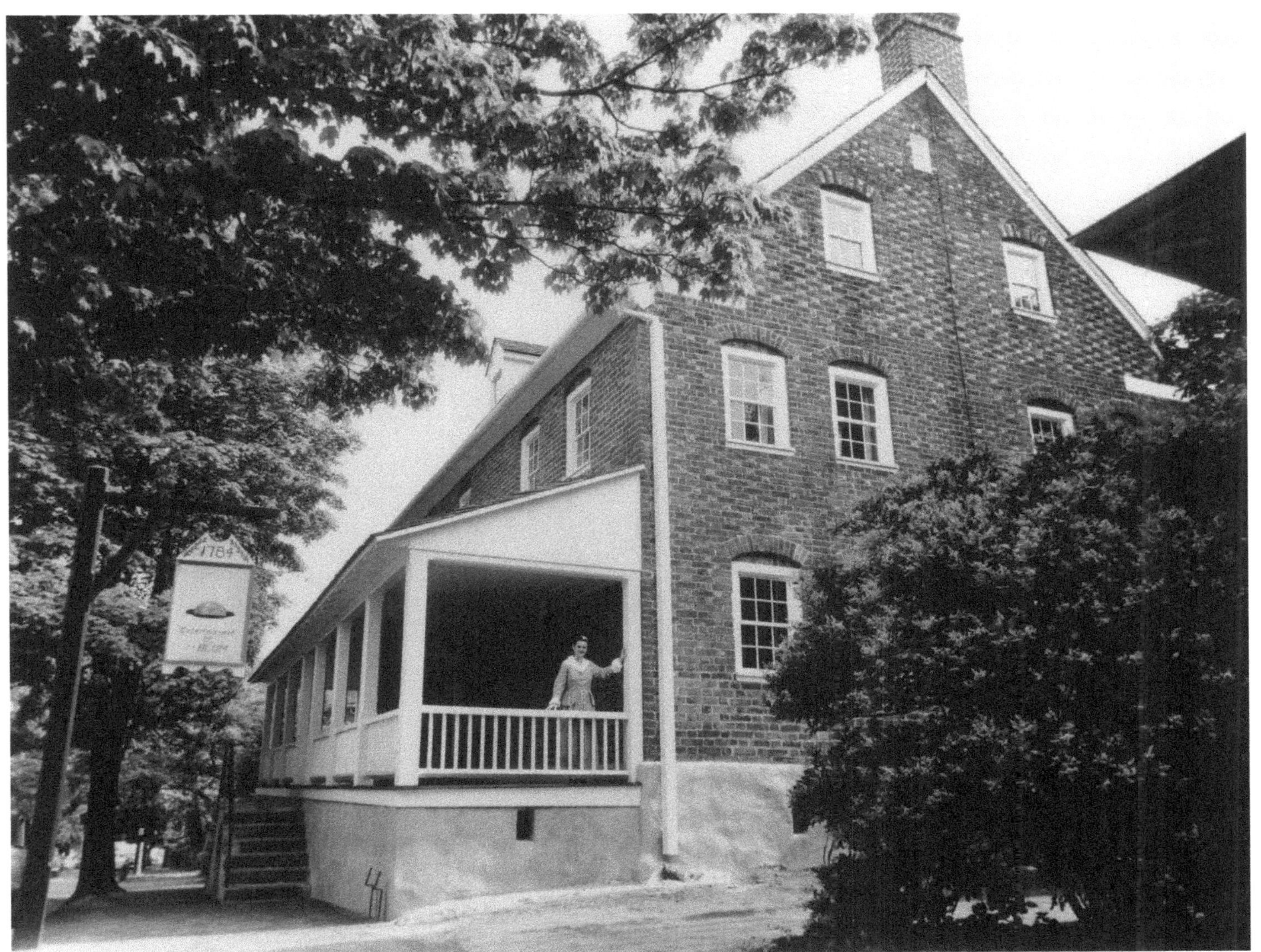


In 1947, a grocery store chain planned to demolish buildings and put a supermarket on Main Street in the middle of Old Salem. The city responded by establishing the Old and Historic Salem District and by banning new construction within the district boundaries. A non-profit corporation, Old Salem, Inc., formed in 1950, with plans to restore the district. Salem Tavern became the best-known building in Old Salem. By the time of this 1956 photograph, the Wachovia Historical Society had leased the tavern building to Old Salem, Inc.

Wait Chapel, designed as the centerpiece of the Wake Forest College campus, remains as beautiful today as when photographed here in the late 1950s.

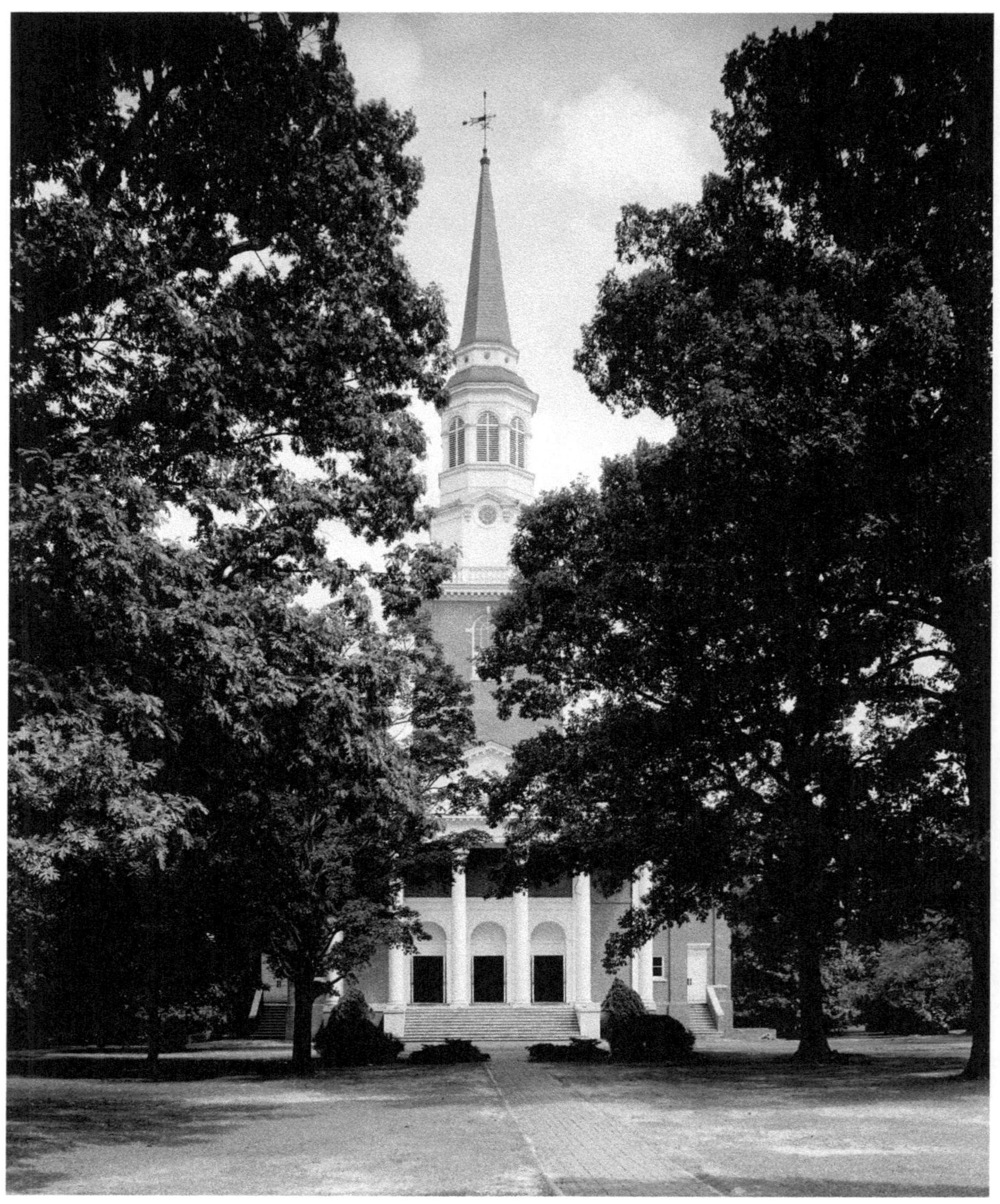

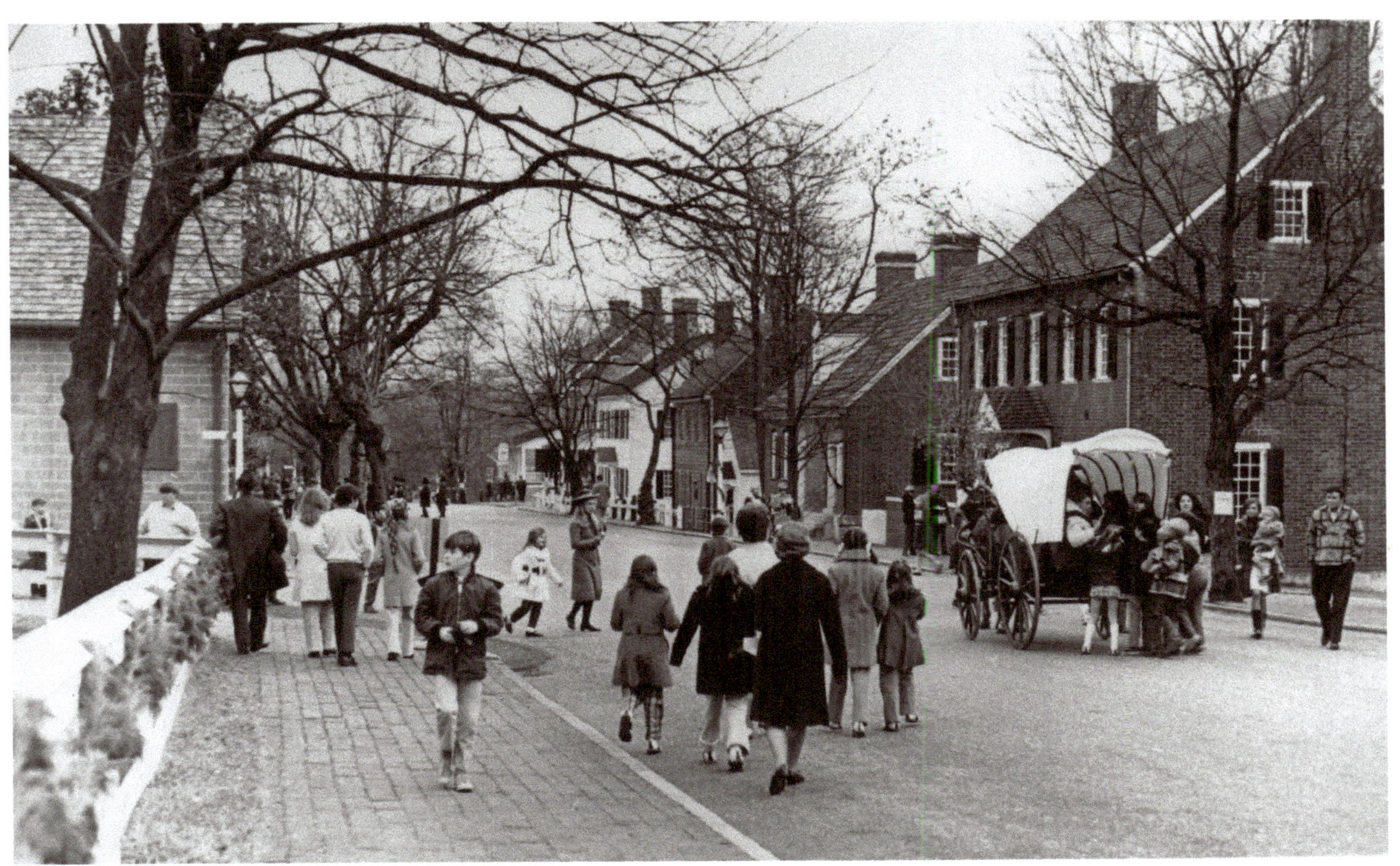

After the creation and development of Old Salem during the 1950s, the district continued to draw tourists and history buffs from around the United States.

As Wake Forest College prepared to open in Winston-Salem in 1956, the entrance arch, a gift from the Class of 1909, framed the campus.

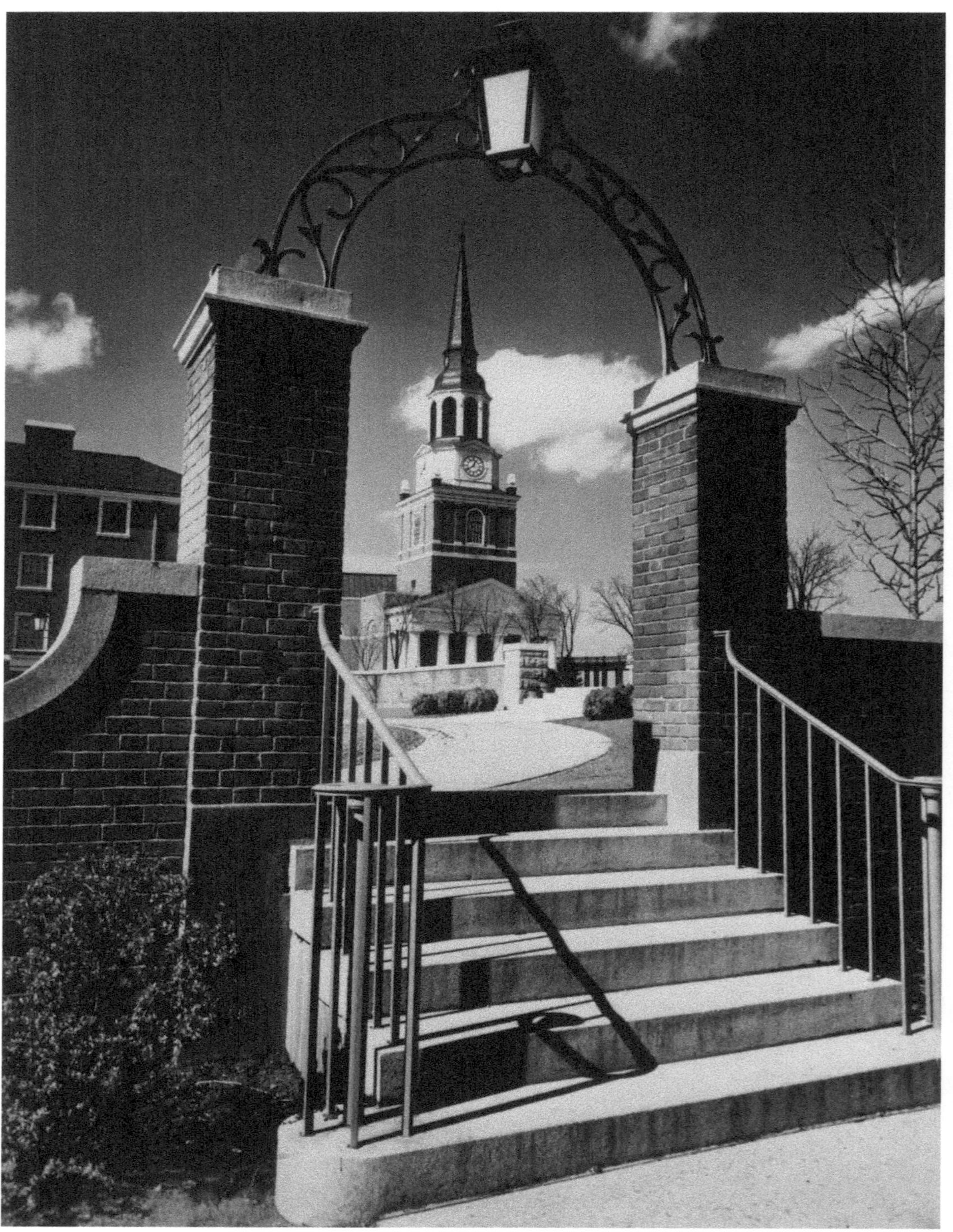

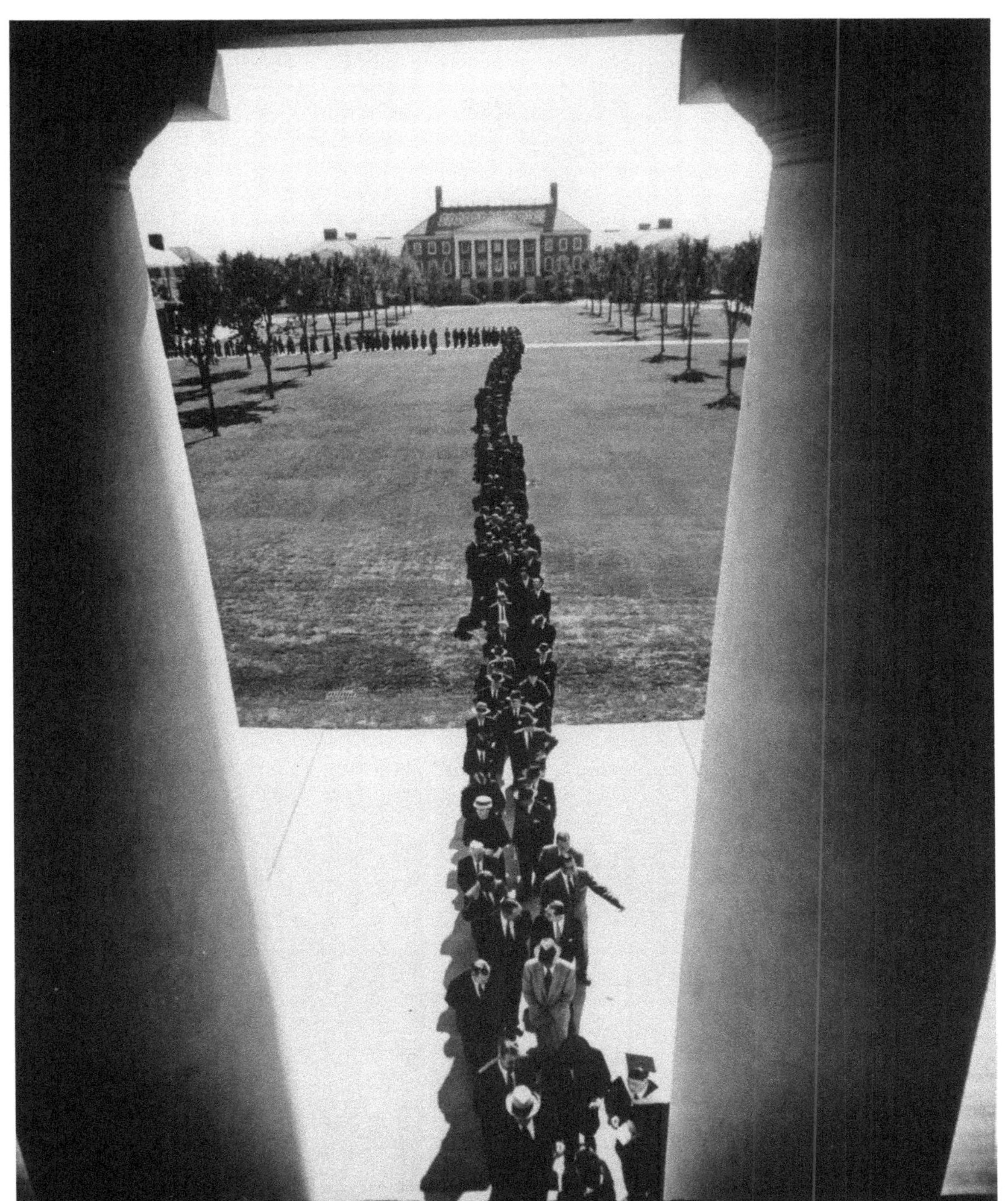

Viewed from the entrance of Wait Chapel, the processional for the 1956 dedication of Wake Forest College took place with Reynolda Hall in the background, across the plaza.

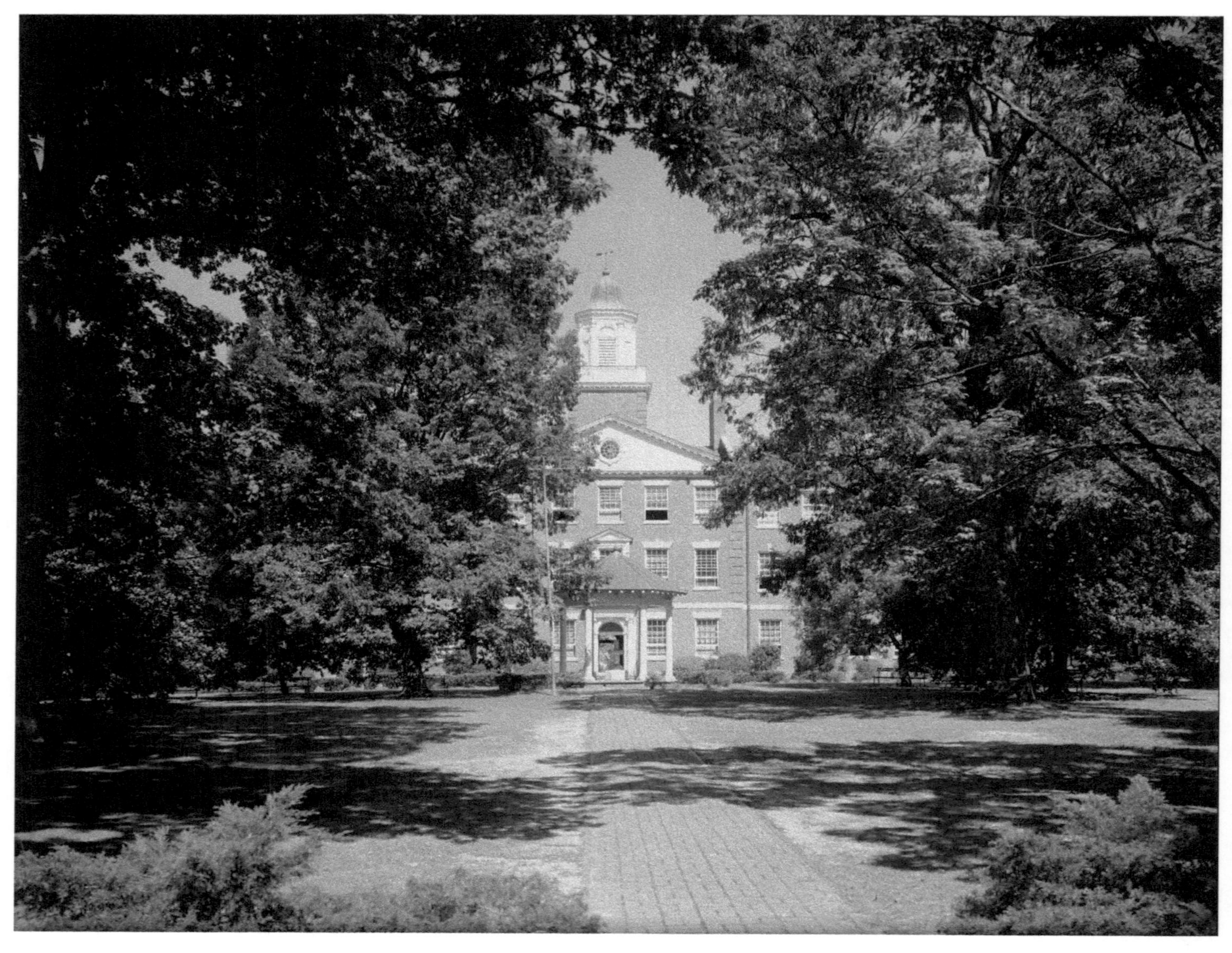

Z. Smith Reynolds Library at Wake Forest College remains a center of learning for Wake Forest University.

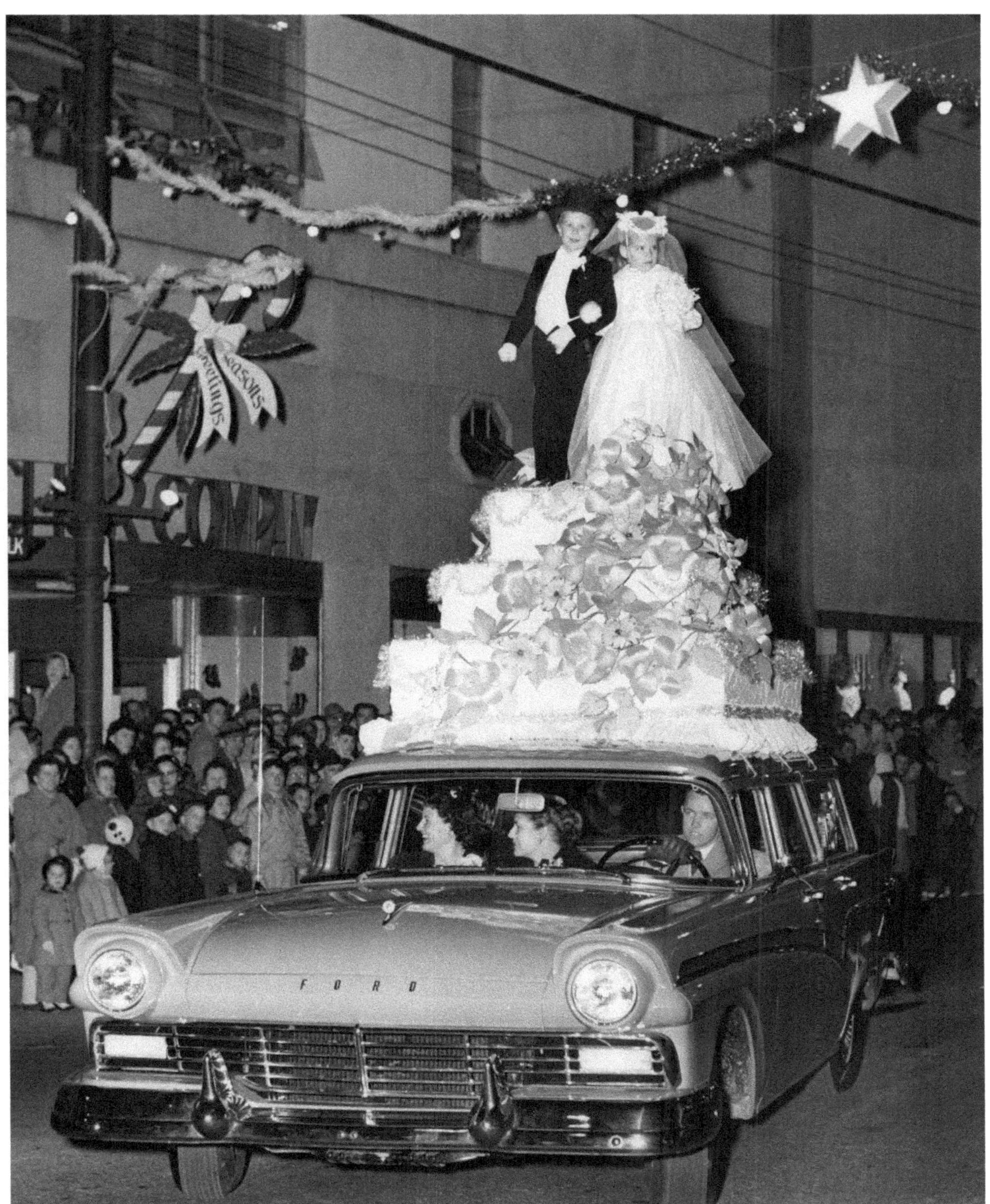


The 1956 Christmas Parade, held at night, drew a large crowd as it rumbled down Fourth Street.

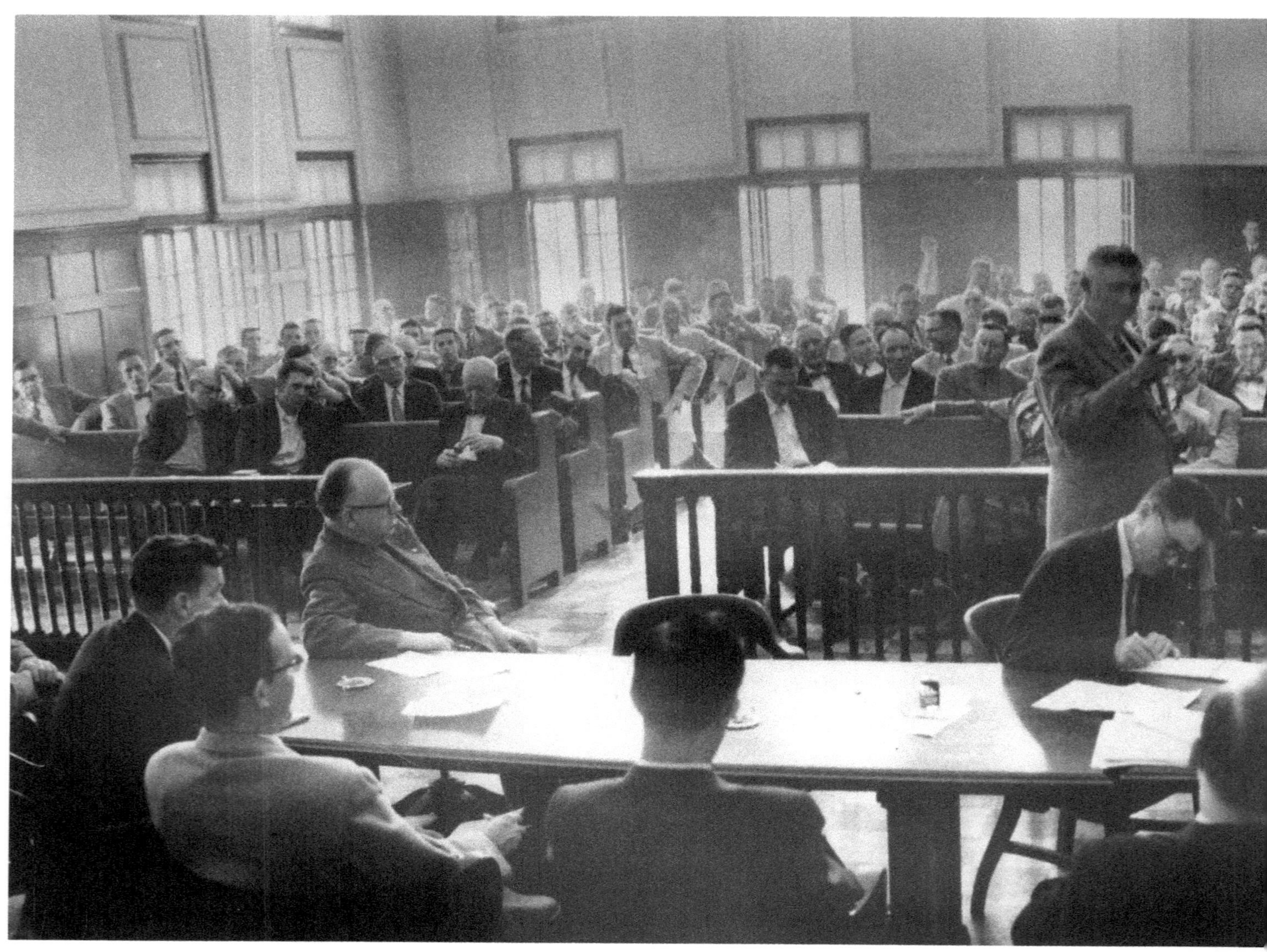

Concerns filled the air at these tobacco hearings in 1957 at the Forsyth County Courthouse. Studies linking smoking to lung cancer led to congressional investigations and, eventually, lawsuits. In an effort perceived incorrectly as reducing threats to health, Reynolds had introduced filtered cigarettes—Winstons in 1954 and menthol Salems in 1956. Both brands grabbed the leads in their respective markets.

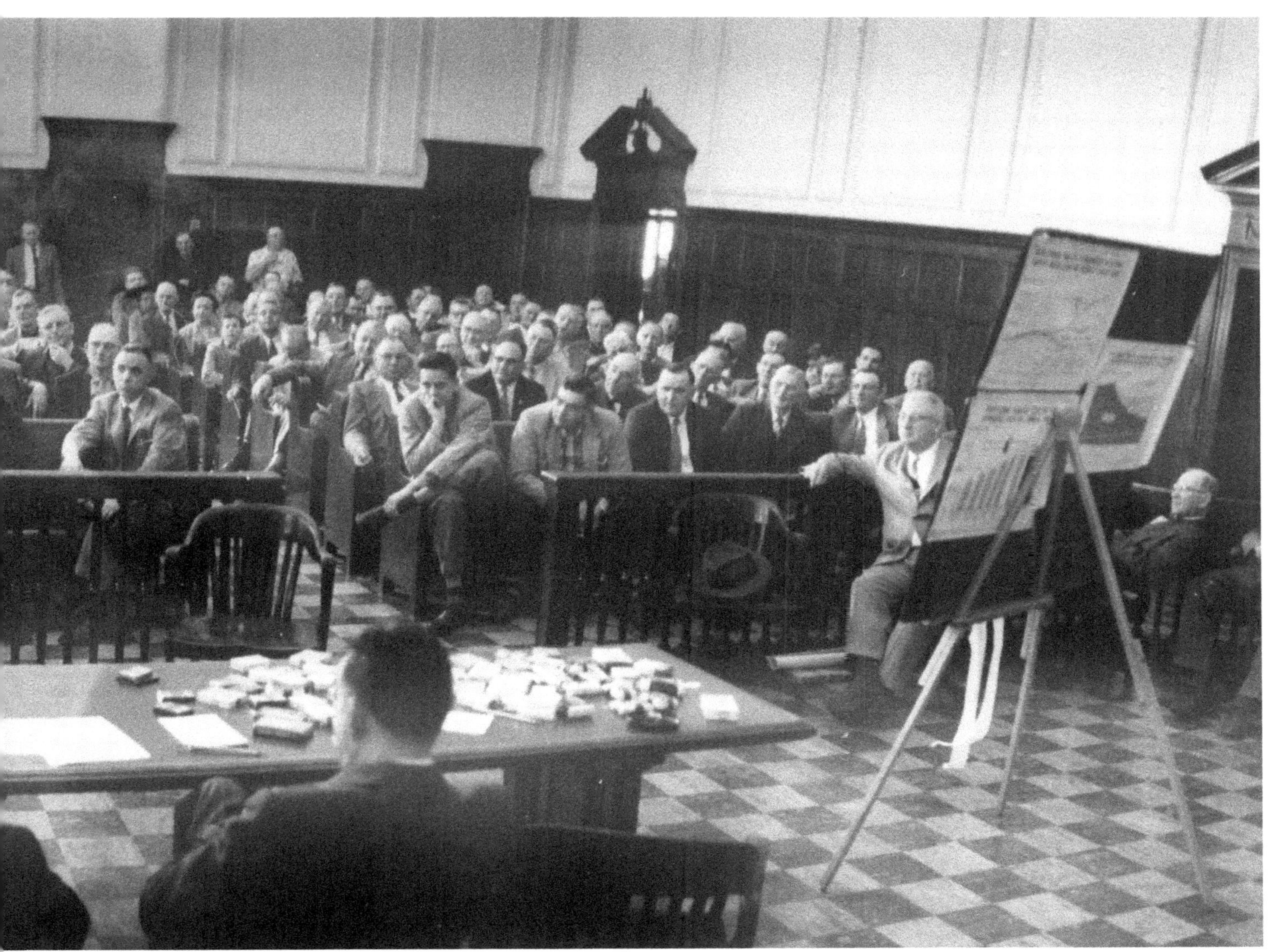

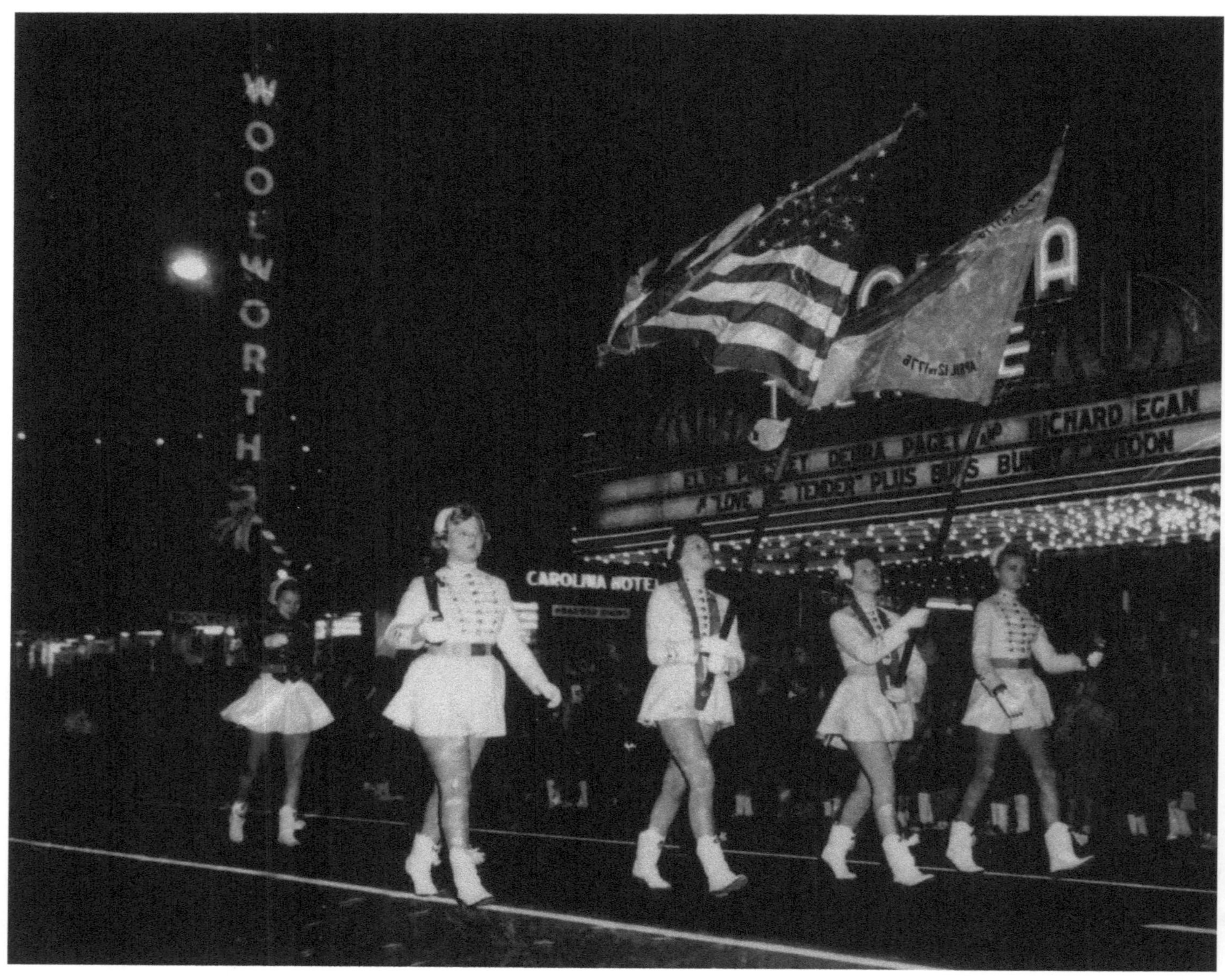


The 1956 Christmas Parade, led by this lovely color guard, passes by the Carolina Theatre, which is showing *Love Me Tender,* Elvis Presley's first movie.

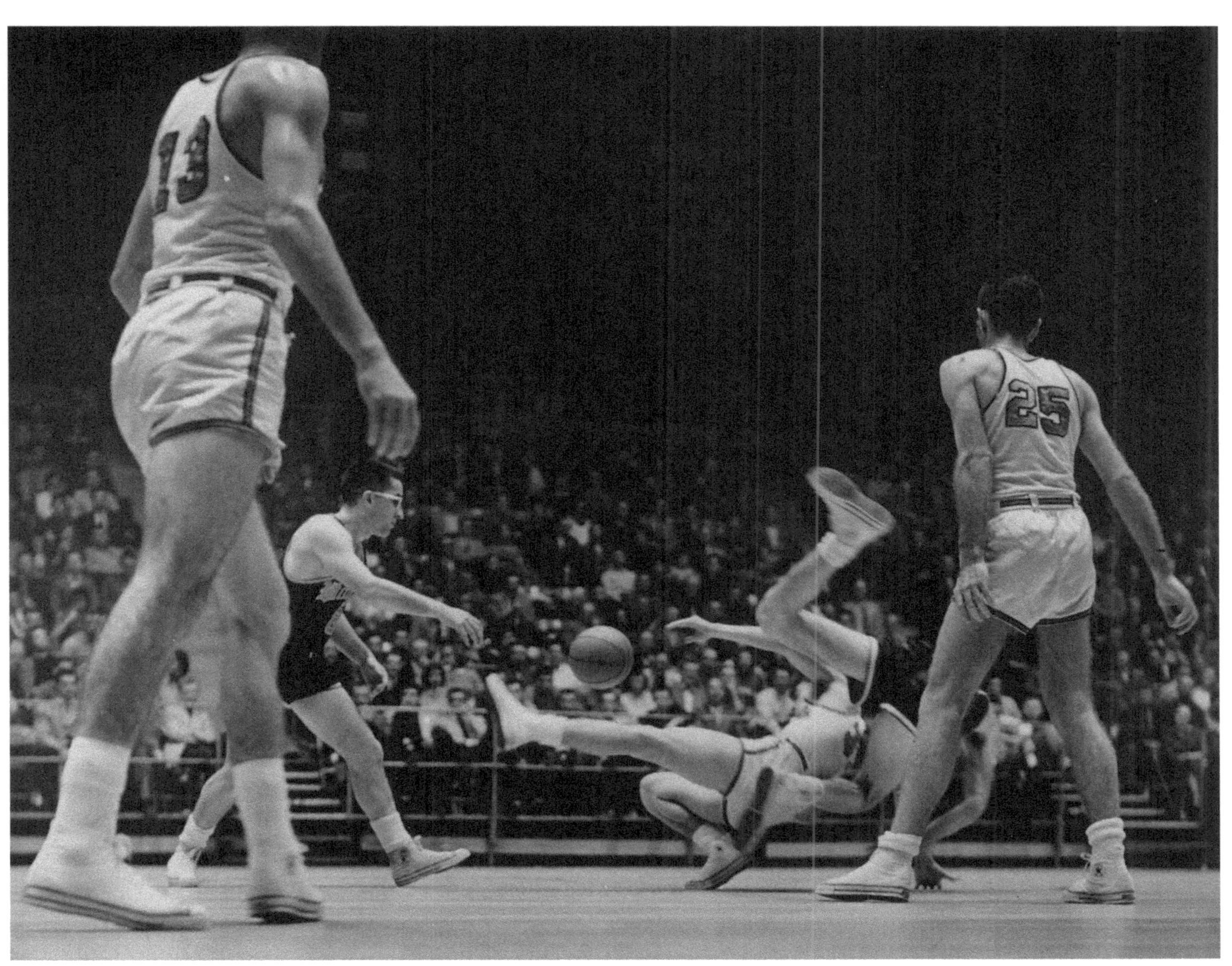

The Demon Deacons take on the University of Virginia Cavaliers in 1957—bet Wake Forest coach Bones McKinney was screaming over that collision!

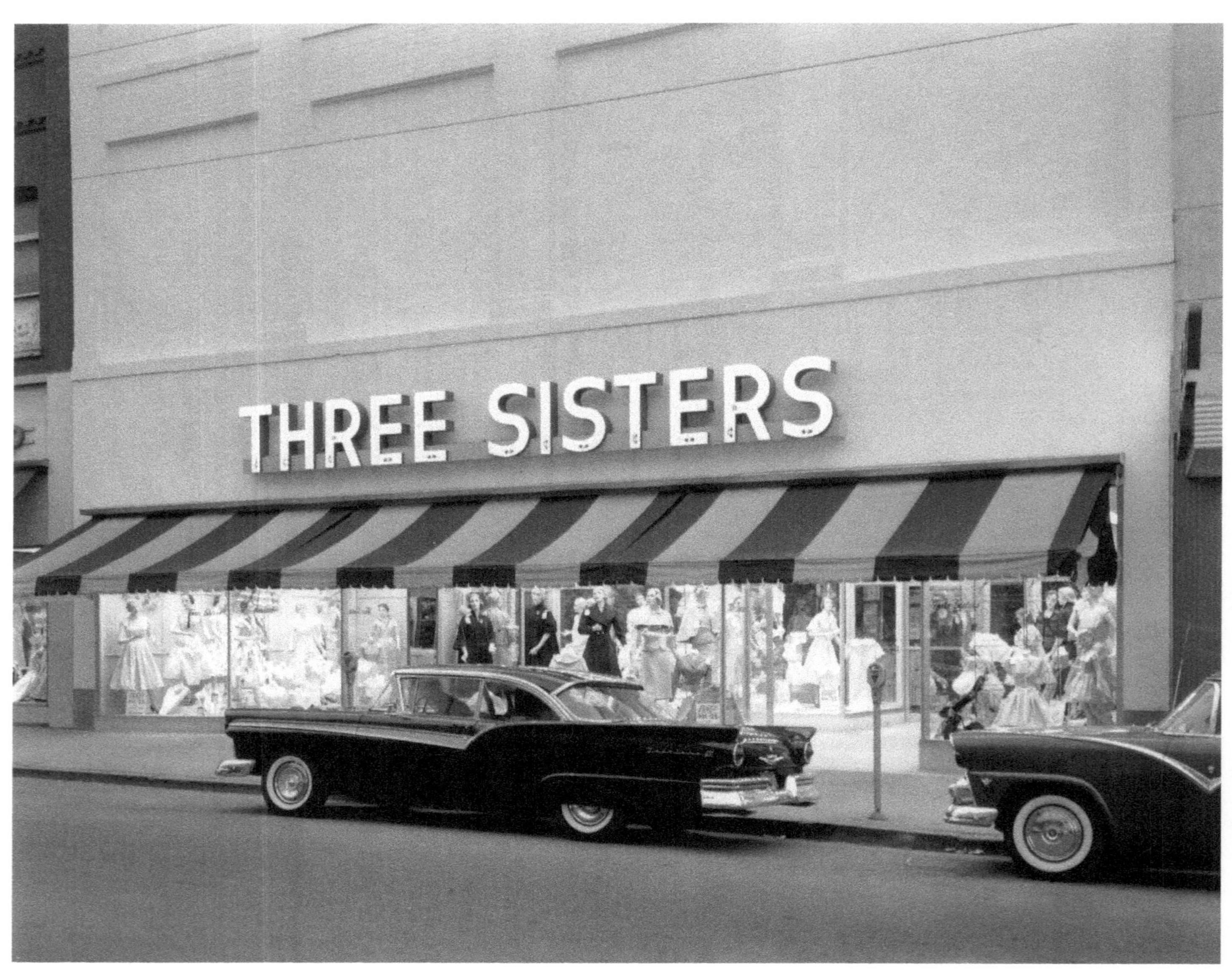


To recover from the downtown blight of the late 1940s, the city council made every effort to lure chain stores, such as this Three Sisters department store on North Liberty Street, to the Winston-Salem area. In this 1957 view, note the parking meters, which provided much-needed revenue.

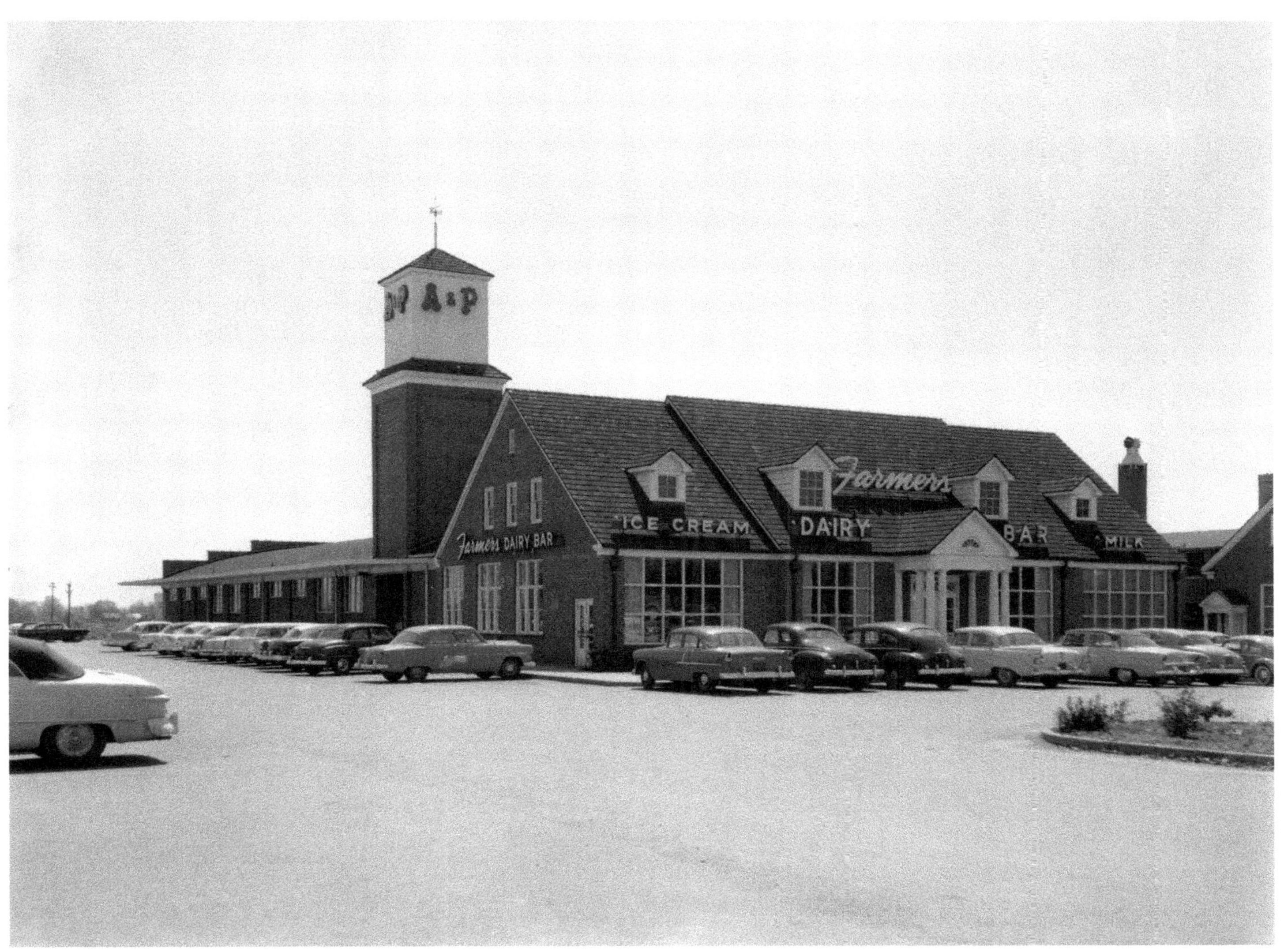


Unfortunately for downtown, merchants discovered that businesses located next to major shopping destinations in the suburbs, such as this new A&P grocery store on Stratford Road, had immense profitability. Farmers Dairy Bar seems to be enjoying great business, despite the fact that this was a chilly January day in 1958.

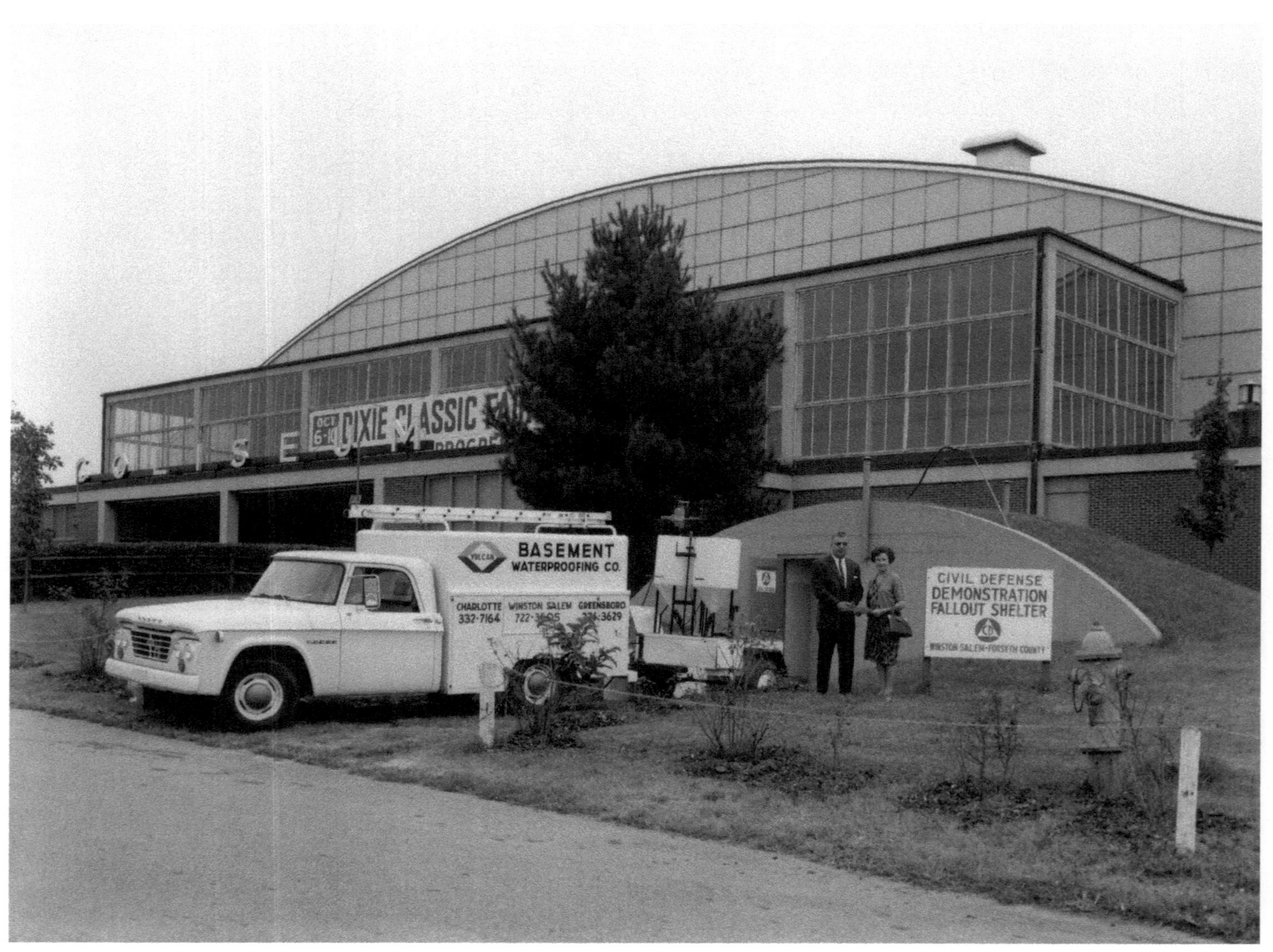


By the late 1950s, the cold war threatened to blaze hot with nuclear war. This Civil Defense Demonstration Fallout Shelter probably caught the eyes of many people attending events at the coliseum.

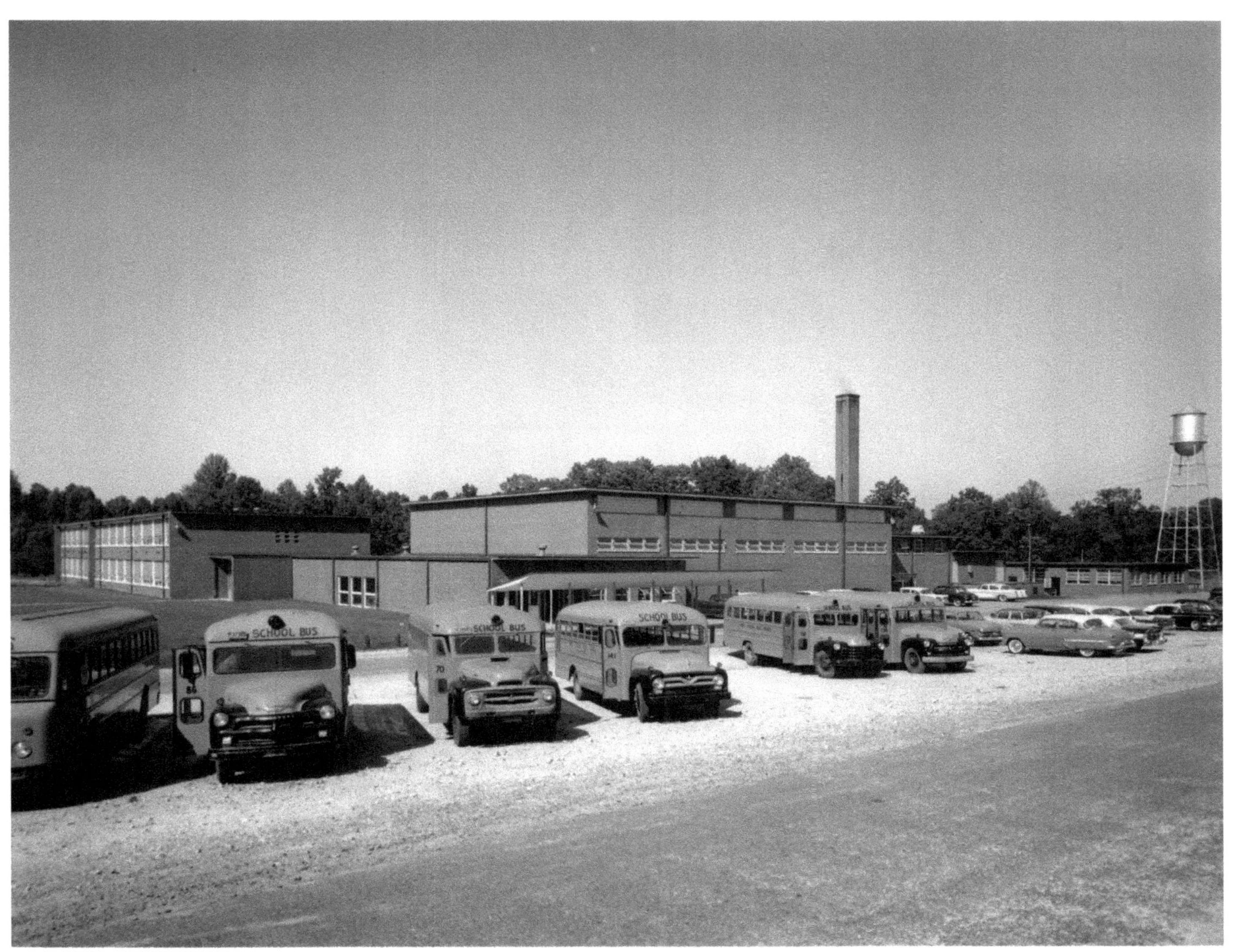


A fleet of modern steel buses transported students to and from Northwest High School in 1958. One year earlier, Gwendolyn Y. Bailey had been the first African American to attend previously all-white R. J. Reynolds High School. It would take fourteen years to completely integrate the school system. The vehicles pictured here may have been involved in the busing efforts that finally completed the process of desegregation.

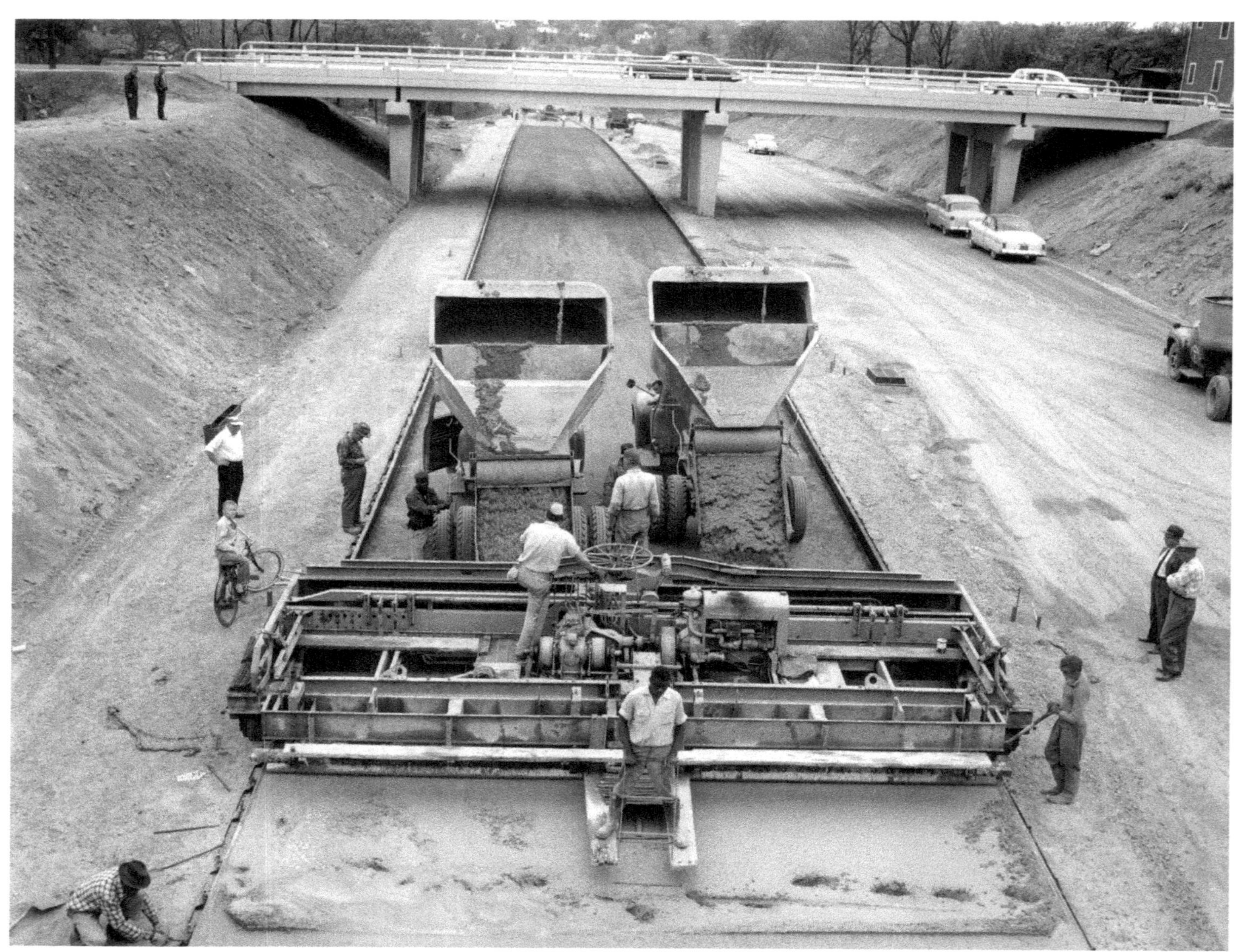

Interstate 40 held threat and promise in the 1950s: threat if it bypassed the city, and promise if it went through the city, thus eliminating downtown traffic congestion and beckoning travelers. Mayor Kurfees and city leaders lobbied for the downtown expressway. They won, and the unfortunate result was the dangerous Hawthorne Curve, a mile of 6 percent grade followed by a vicious 10-degree curve. Here, around 1958, workers grade part of I-40.

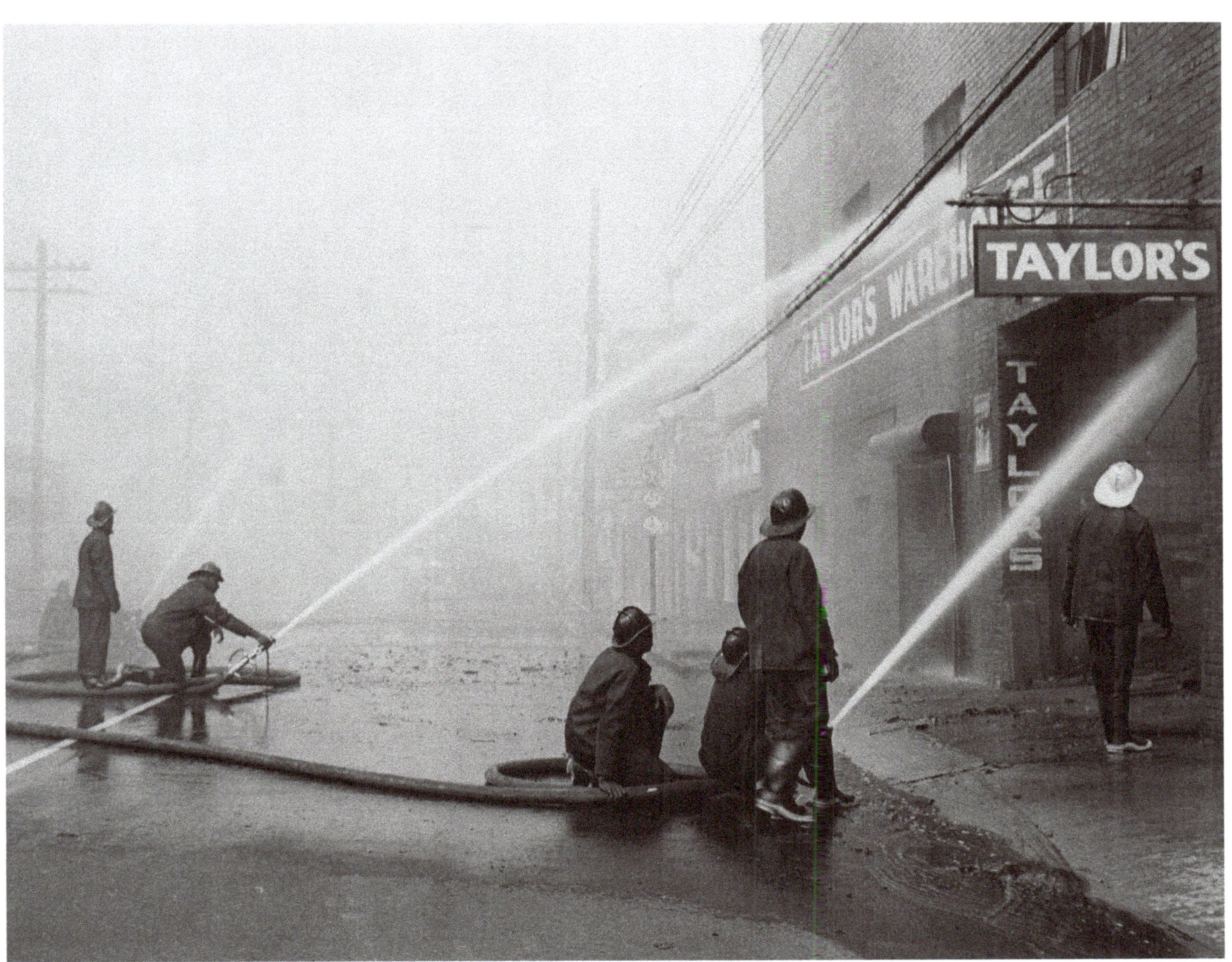


Winston-Salem saw its share of fires through the years, and among the most dangerous were tobacco warehouse fires. Seldom could firefighters save a tobacco warehouse, no matter their training or equipment, and the smell of burning tobacco would waft on the breeze until the flames consumed the structure. Such was the case with the Taylor's Warehouse blaze in 1958.

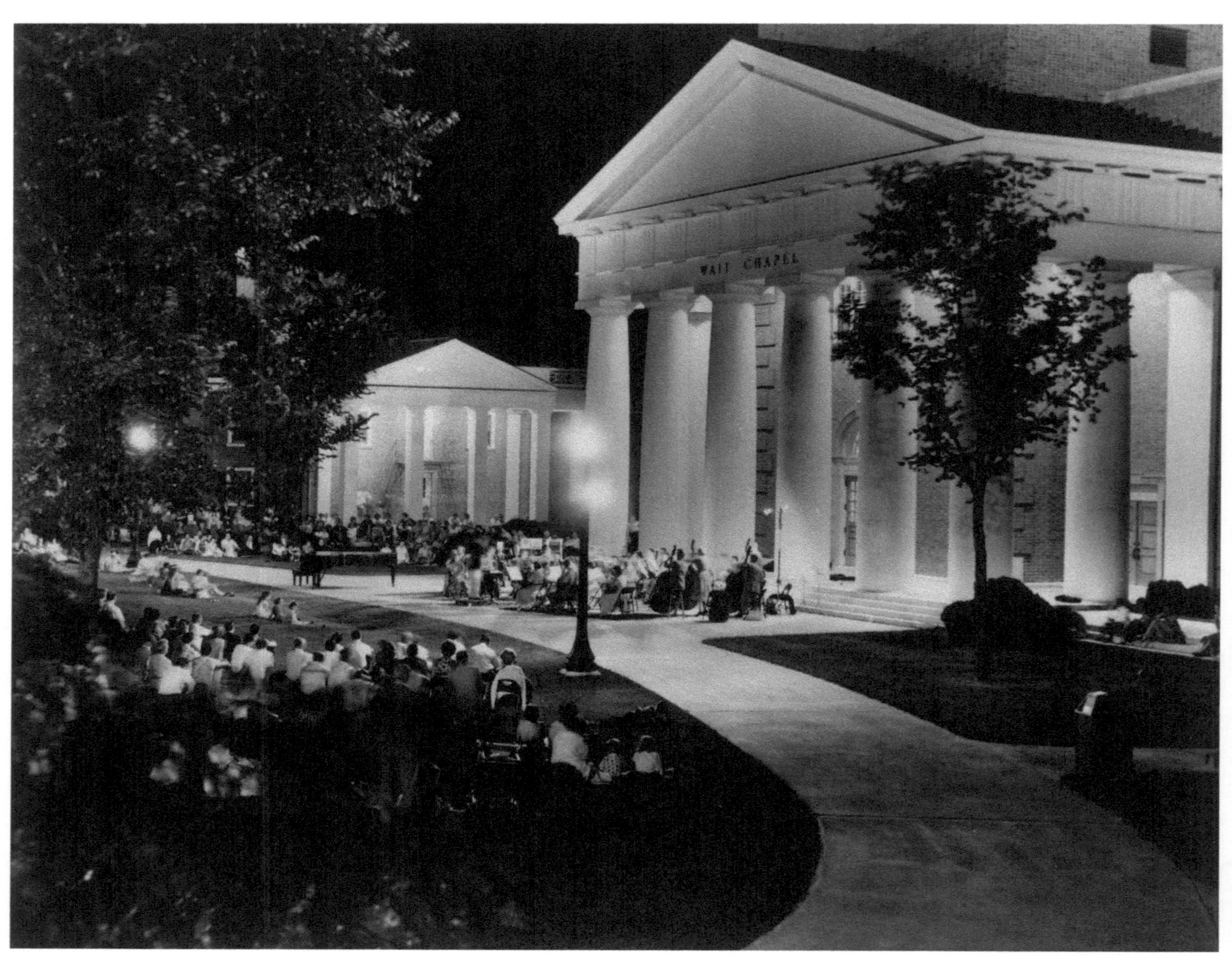


Wait Chapel, on the campus of Wake Forest, glows behind this evening music performance in 1958.

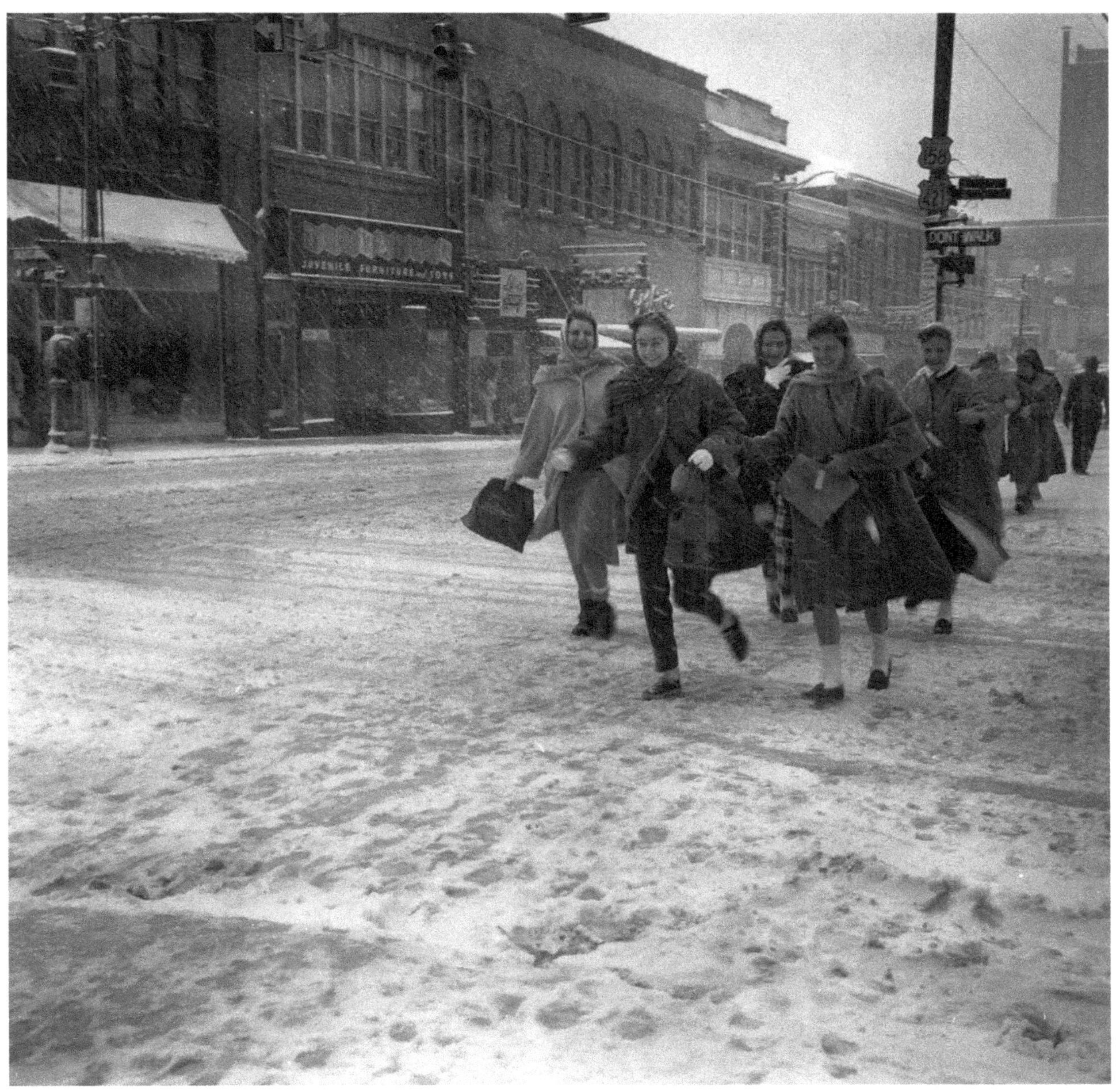


Shoppers rush along a cold, stormy Fourth Street in 1958.

Perhaps cruising, a couple drives by Nelson's Market at the corner of Main and Fourth streets in 1958. A typical activity for young people on Friday and Saturday nights in the late 1950s, cruising gave Winston-Salem's youth a chance to spread their wings, whether they were listening to crooners or that evil rock and roll on the radio.

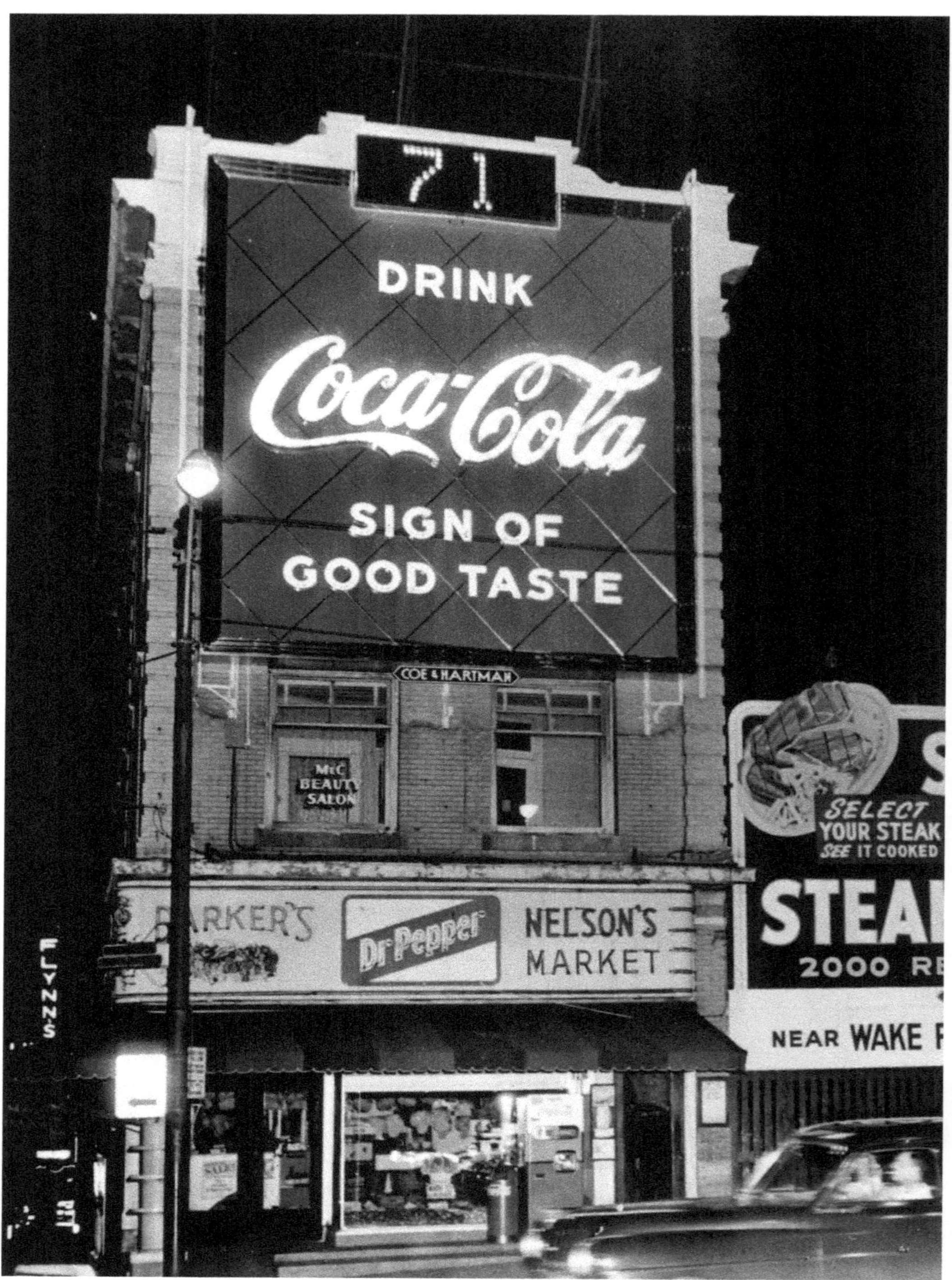

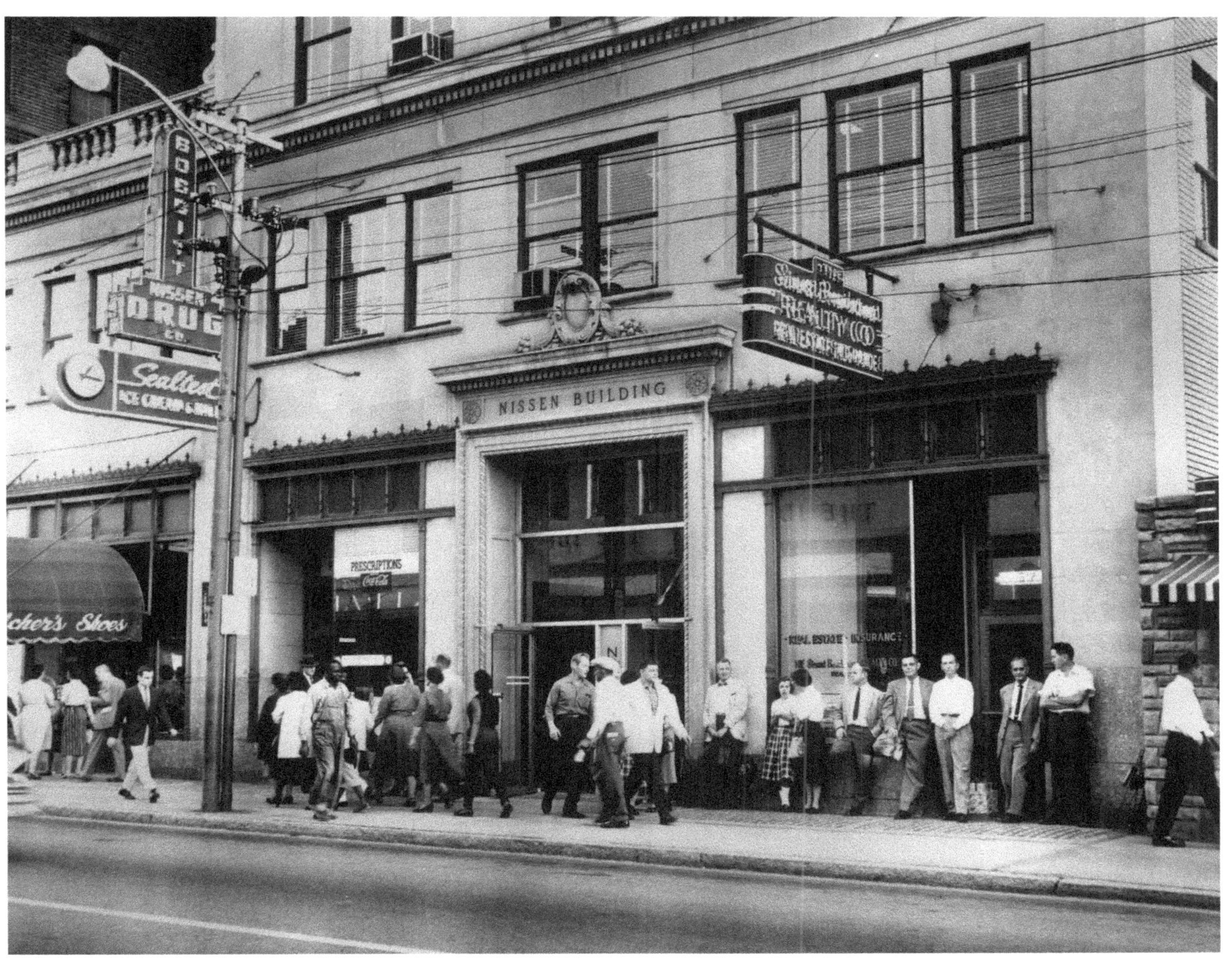


Retail shops filled the lower level of the Nissen Building in 1958. The people standing on the right are probably waiting for a city transit bus.

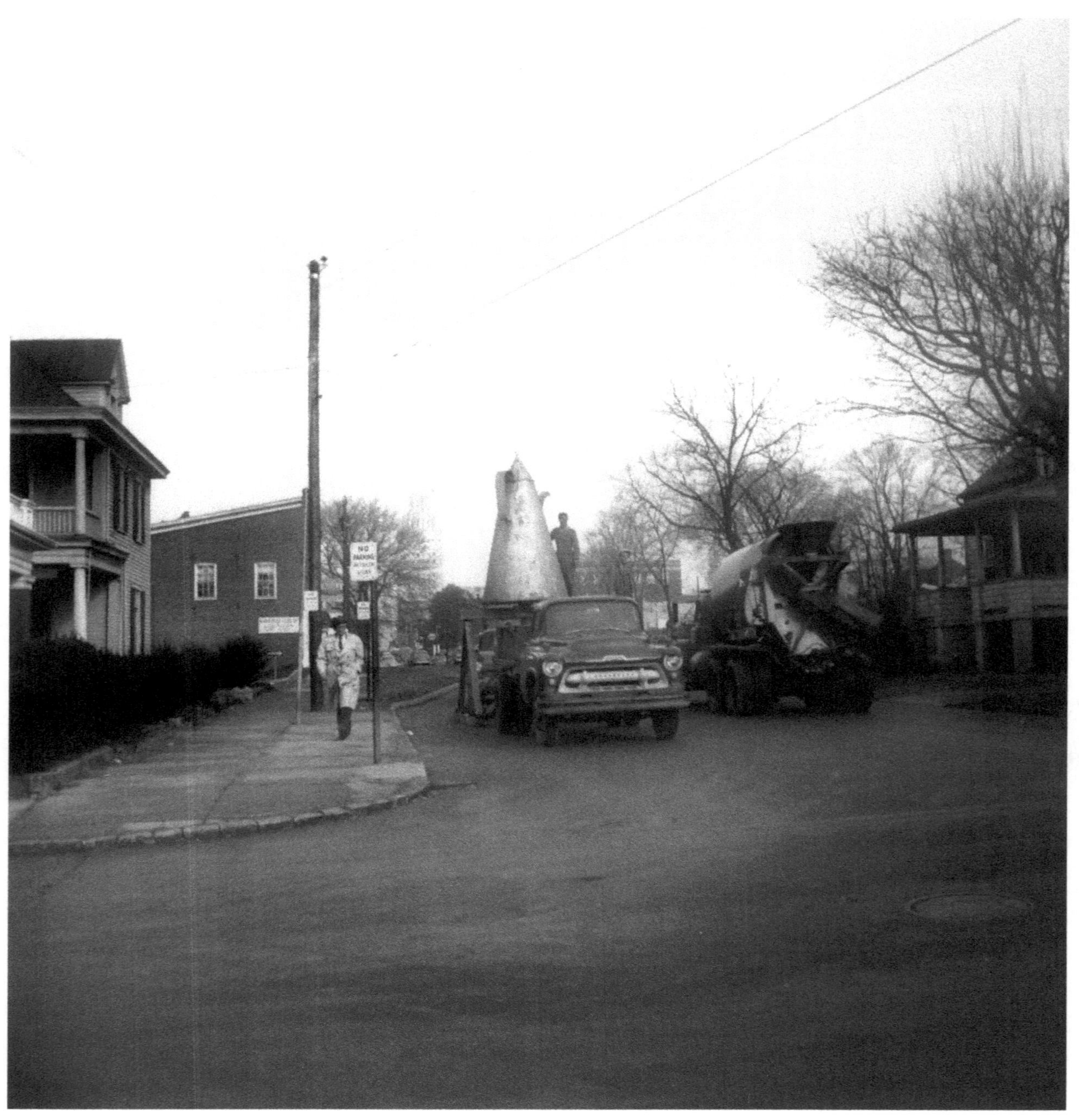

The building of the East-West Expressway threatened the destruction of a city icon: the giant coffee pot that stood in front of the soon-to-be-demolished J. E. Mickey Shop. In 1959, rather than lose such a valued part of its history, the city relocated the coffee pot to its current location on Main Street.

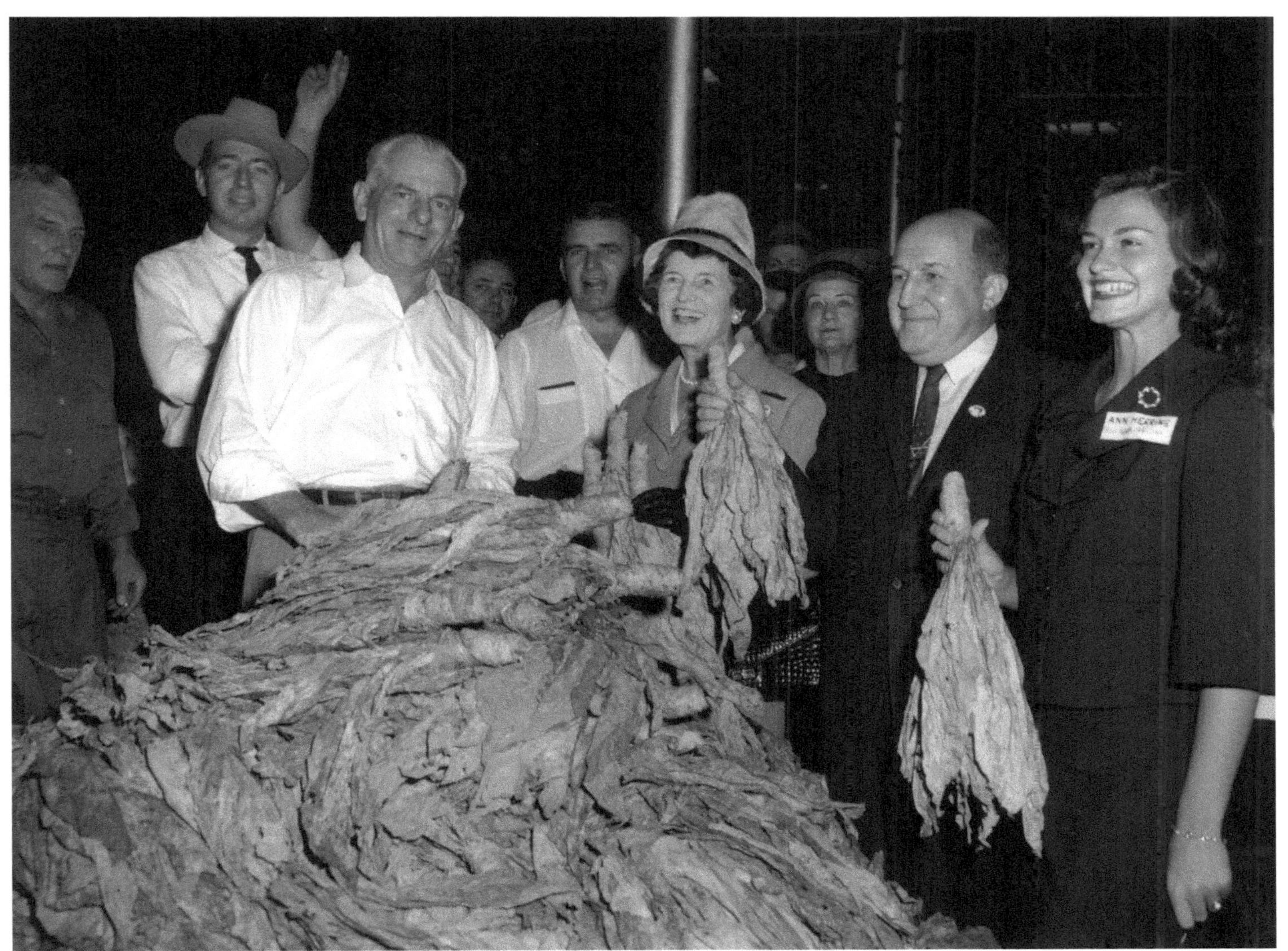


The presidential campaign of 1960 brought much activity to Winston-Salem. In September, Rose Kennedy, at center, stumped for her son John as the tobacco market brought farmers into town. The man to the right of the Kennedy matriarch is Mayor Kurfees, and to the right of him is Miss North Carolina, Ann Herring.

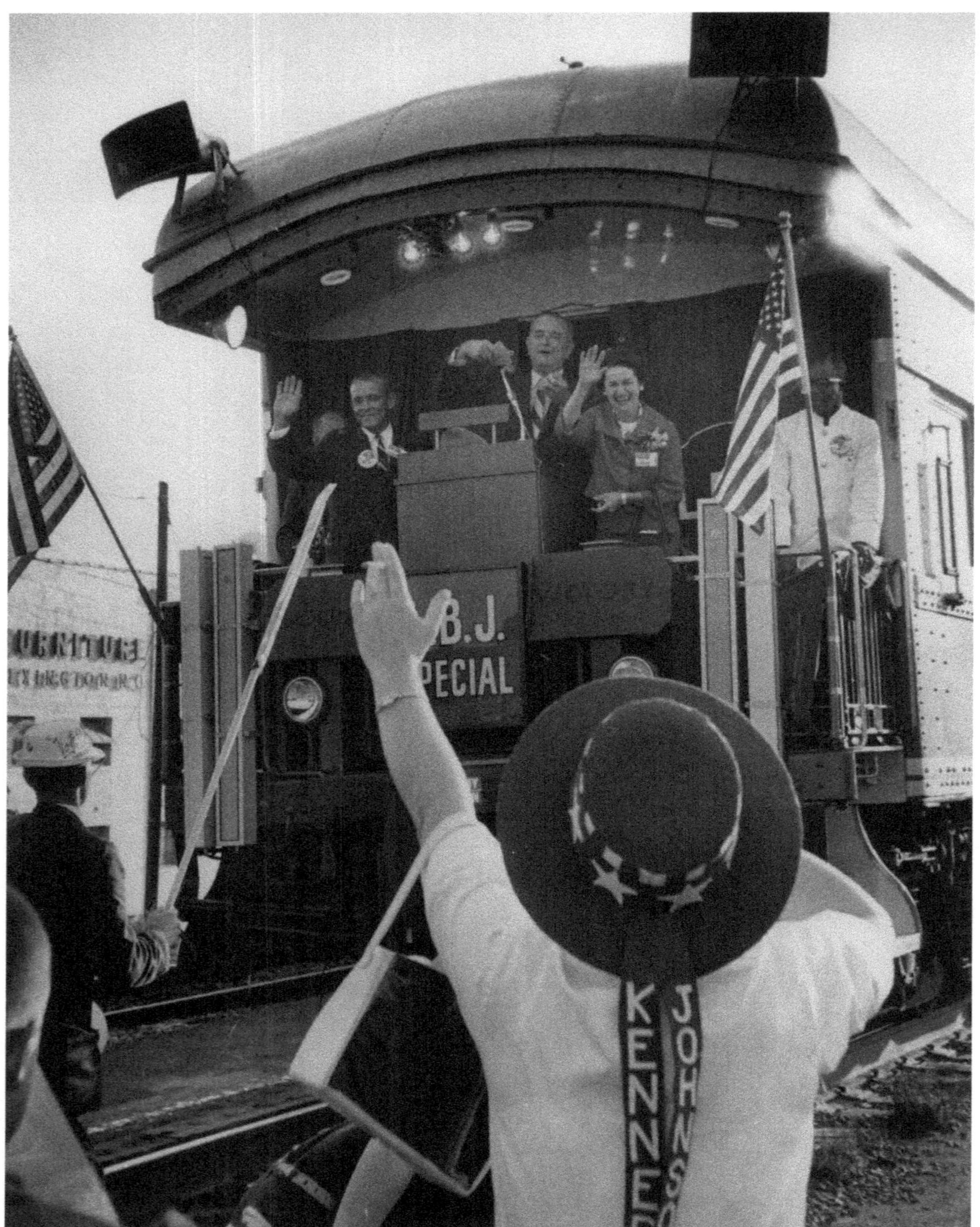


A month after Rose Kennedy's visit, Lyndon and Lady Bird Johnson took the train to Winston-Salem (here they're in Lexington), perhaps finding some of those last-minute votes that would make Johnson vice-president of the United States.

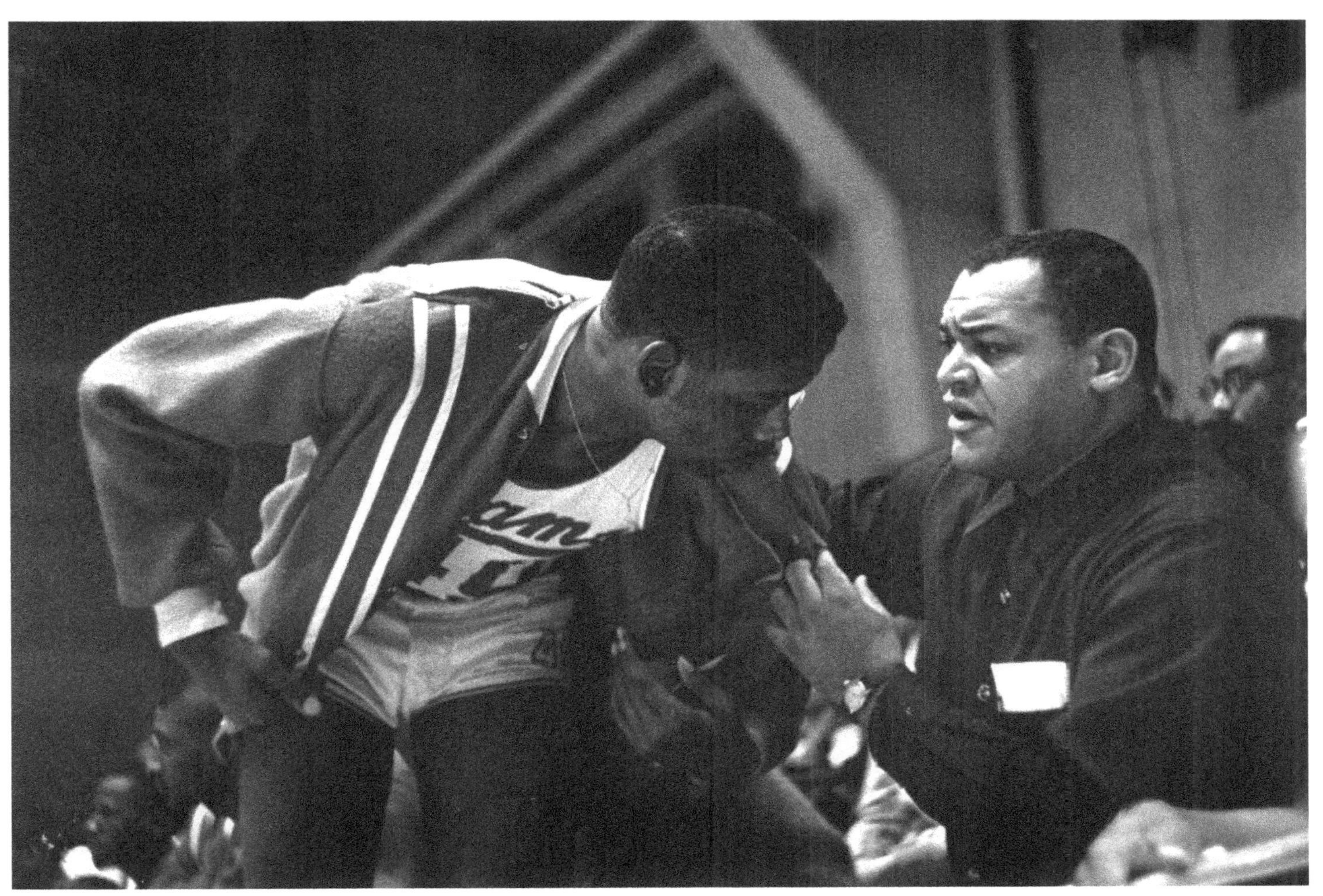

Coach Clarence Gaines, pictured at right in 1961, is a basketball legend. While he was coach at Winston-Salem State, from 1946 until his retirement in 1993, his teams won 828 games and 12 CIAA championships. Coach Gaines ranks fifth on the NCAA's list of basketball coaches with the most wins.

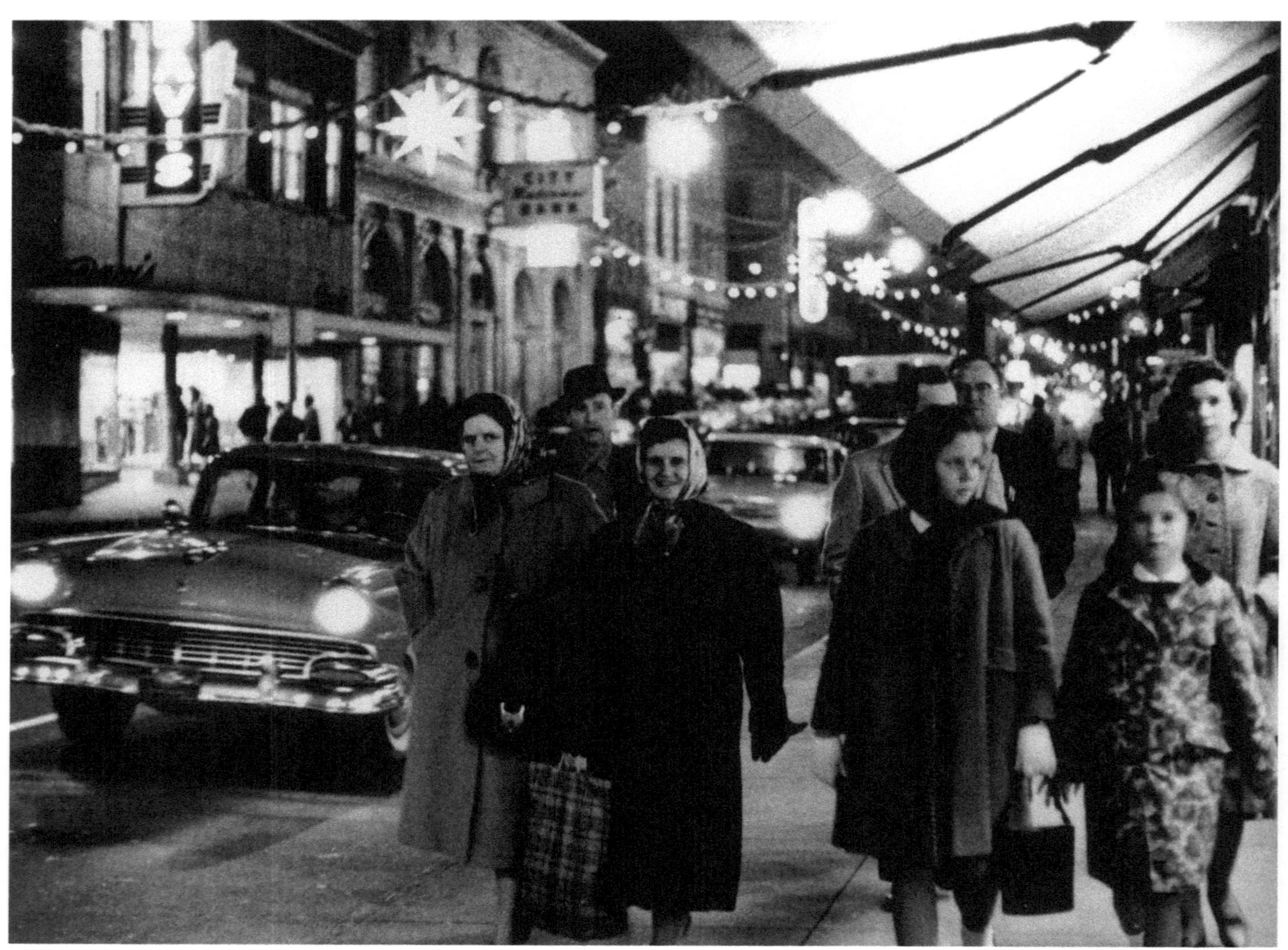

The Cuban missile crisis may have dominated the early autumn of 1962, but with the situation defused, Christmas shoppers throng Fourth Street.

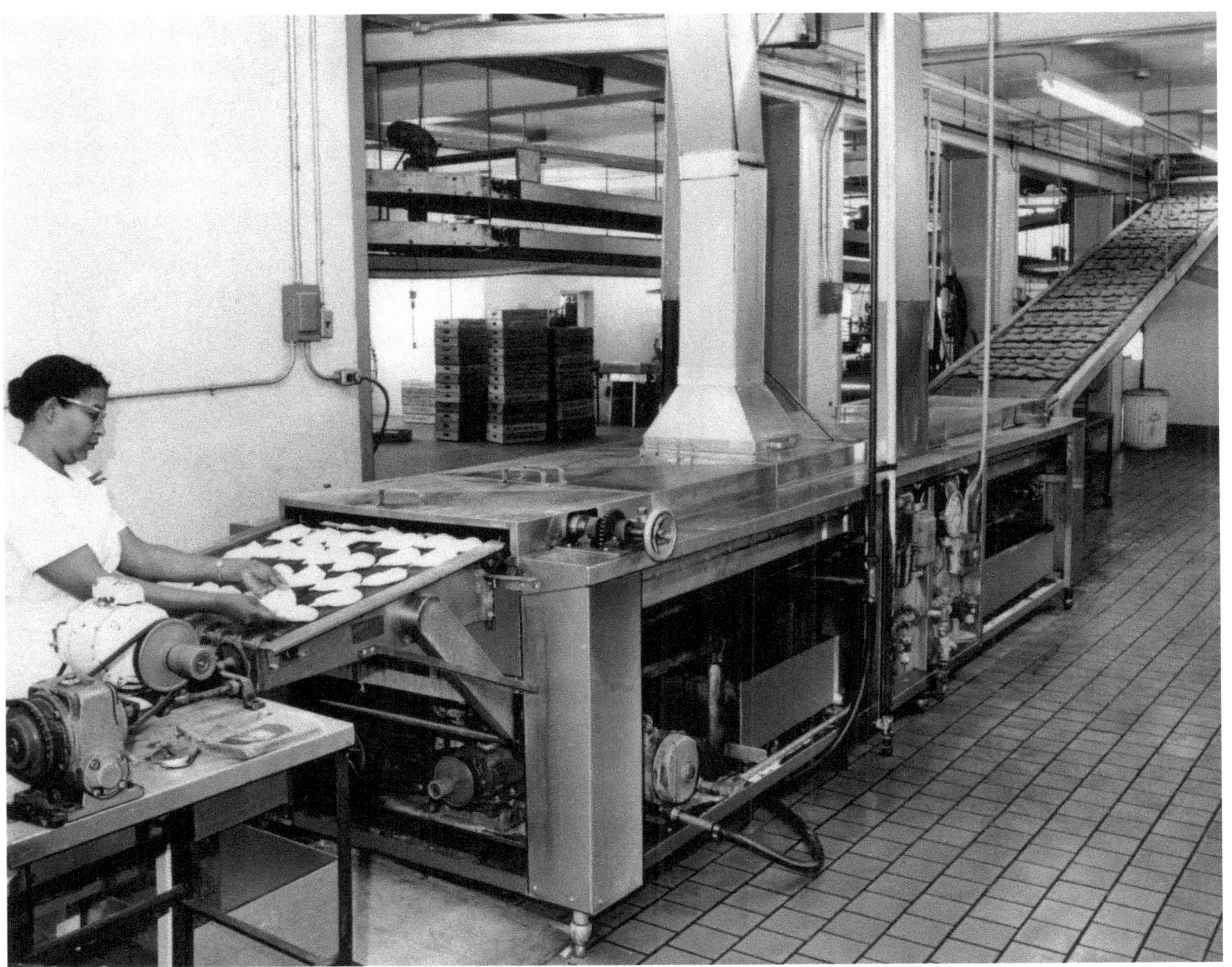

Who needs fried chicken and barbecue when Winston-Salem is the home of a true Southern delicacy: Krispy Kreme doughnuts! Vernon C. Rudolph and partners made the first Krispy Kreme doughnuts in a rented building across from Salem College in 1937. They developed an automatic production line in the 1950s. The lady in this picture is preparing some of the last cut doughnuts in 1961. Beginning the following year, the doughnuts were extruded—and still delicious.

Civic events, such as this parade on West Fourth Street, always brought large, happy crowds to the streets. While the parade car might look 1920s, the Carolina Theatre is featuring Elvis Presley in *Roustabout*, from 1964.

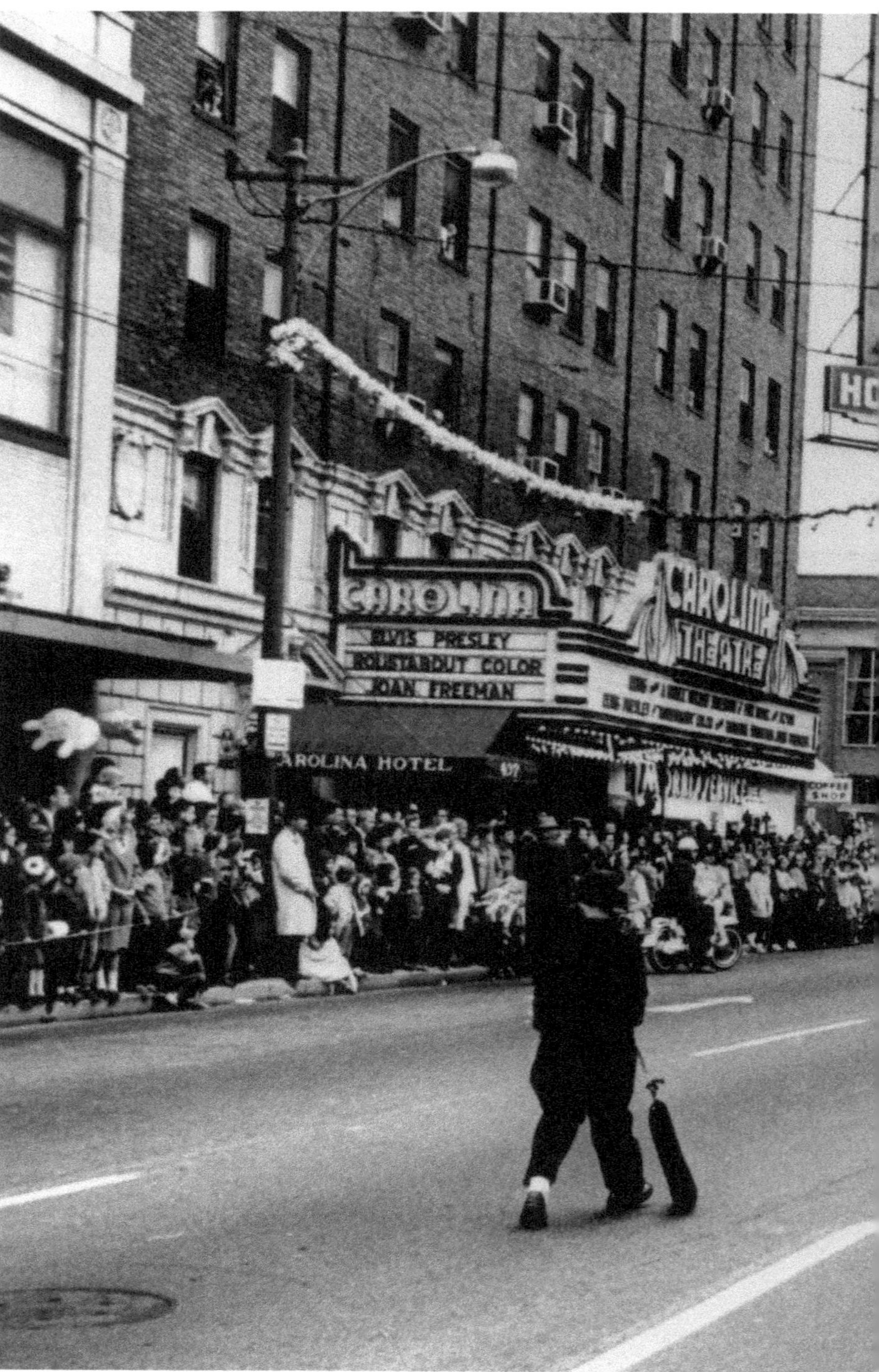

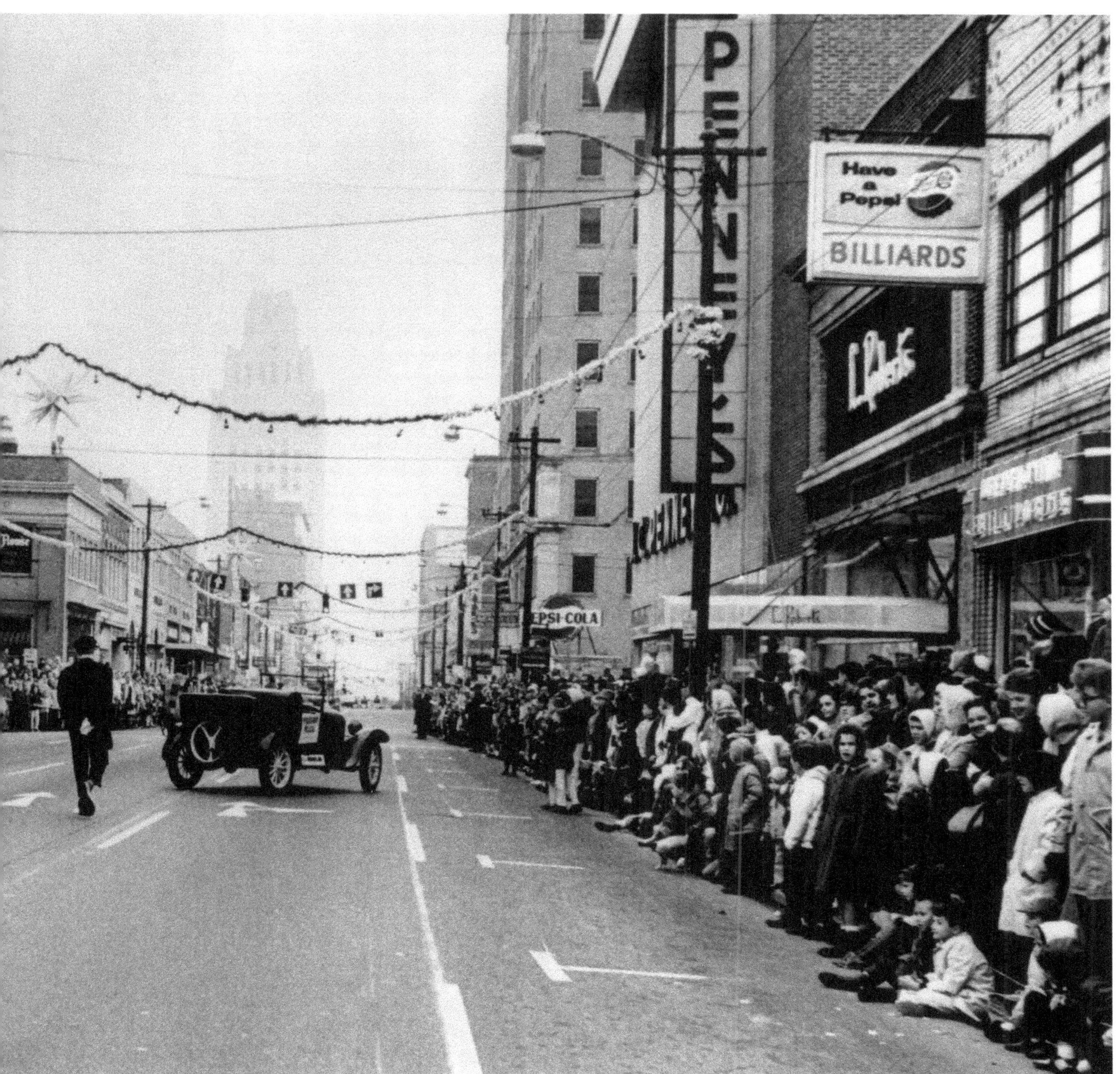
PENNEY'S
Have a Pepsi
BILLIARDS
PEPSI-COLA

Many aging theaters, like the Carolina Theatre, also found use as general-purpose meeting sites and local cultural centers. Here, ladies of Winston-Salem organize for the March of Dimes in 1964. In 1983, a remodeled Carolina Theatre became the Roger L. Stevens Center for performing arts.

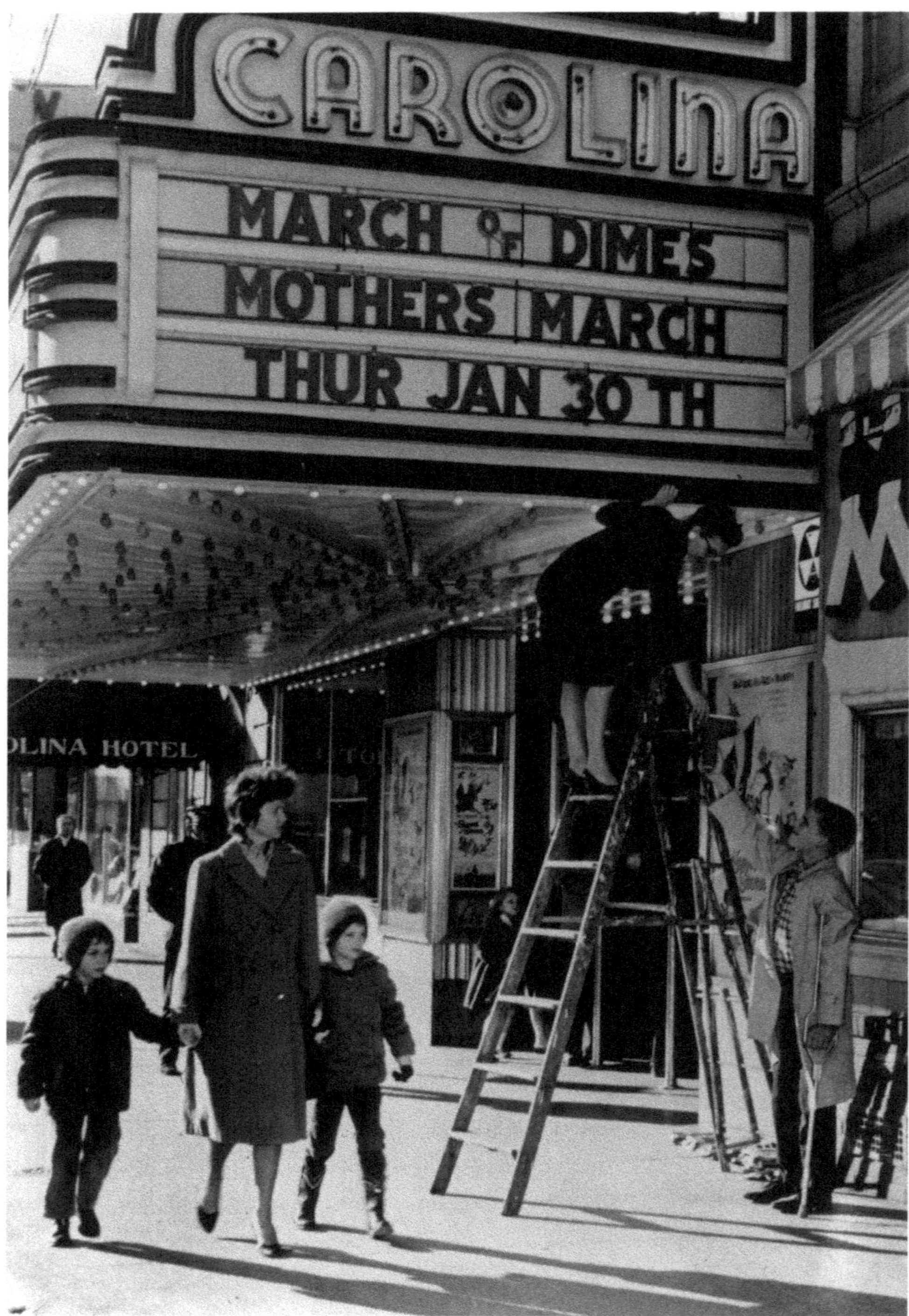

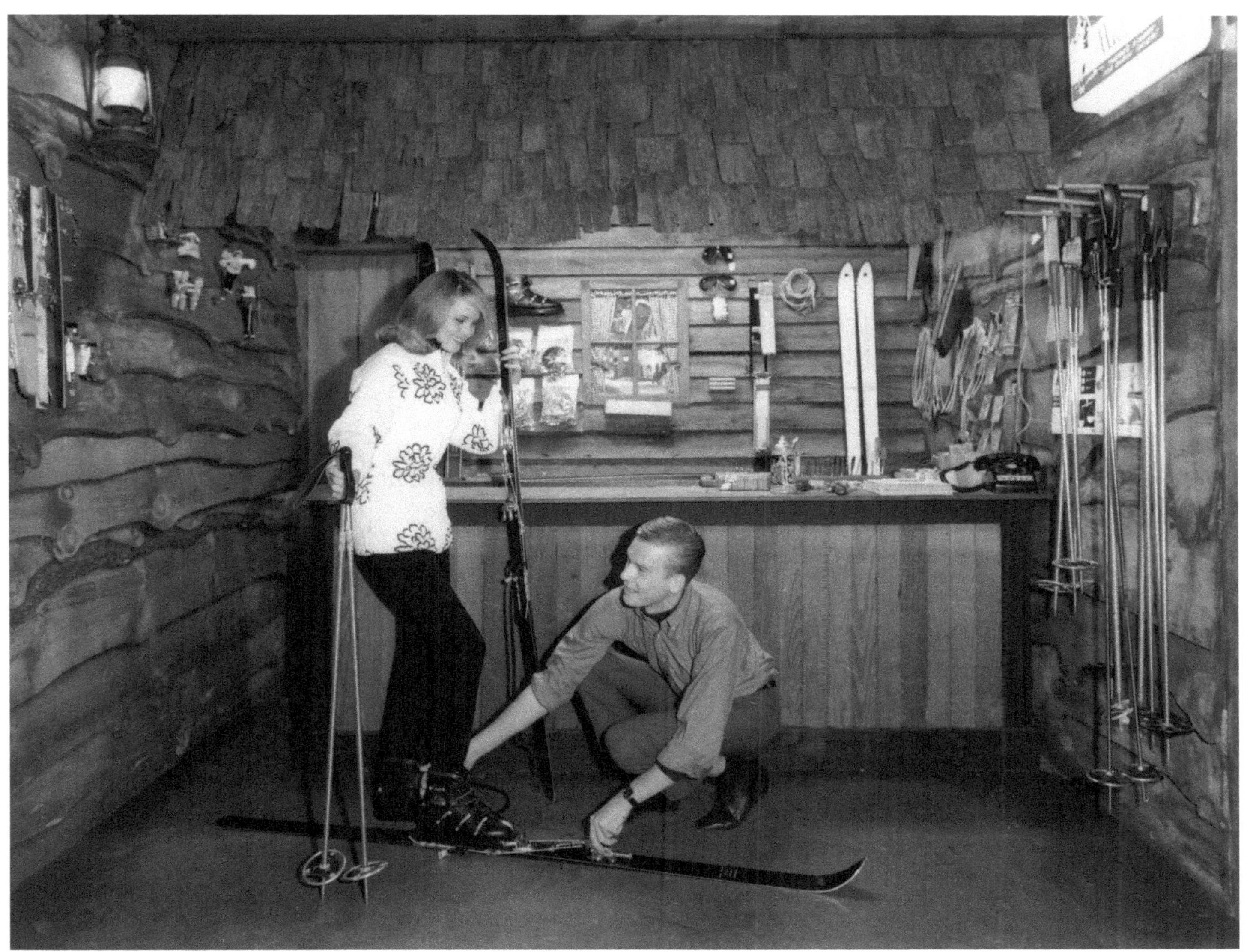

The early 1960s saw many Americans stressing the importance of physical fitness, a legacy of John F. Kennedy's initiatives before his assassination. Skiing was the theme at Sportsman's Supply in October 1964.

The twelve-story Hotel Robert E. Lee towered at the corner of West Fifth and North Cherry streets from 1921 until its demolition in 1972, as it made way for the Winston-Salem Hyatt House. For much of that time, it served as Winston-Salem's premier hotel.

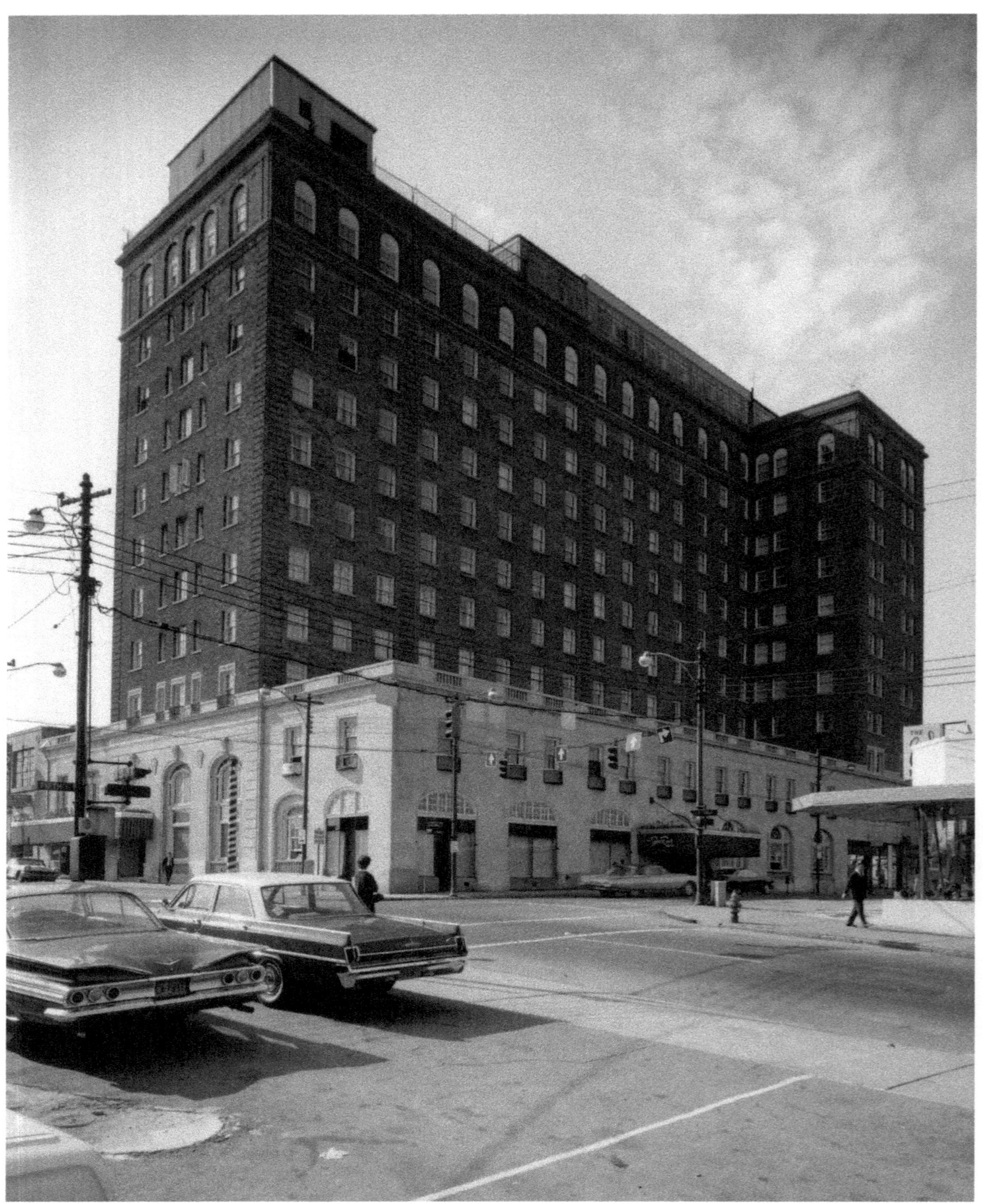

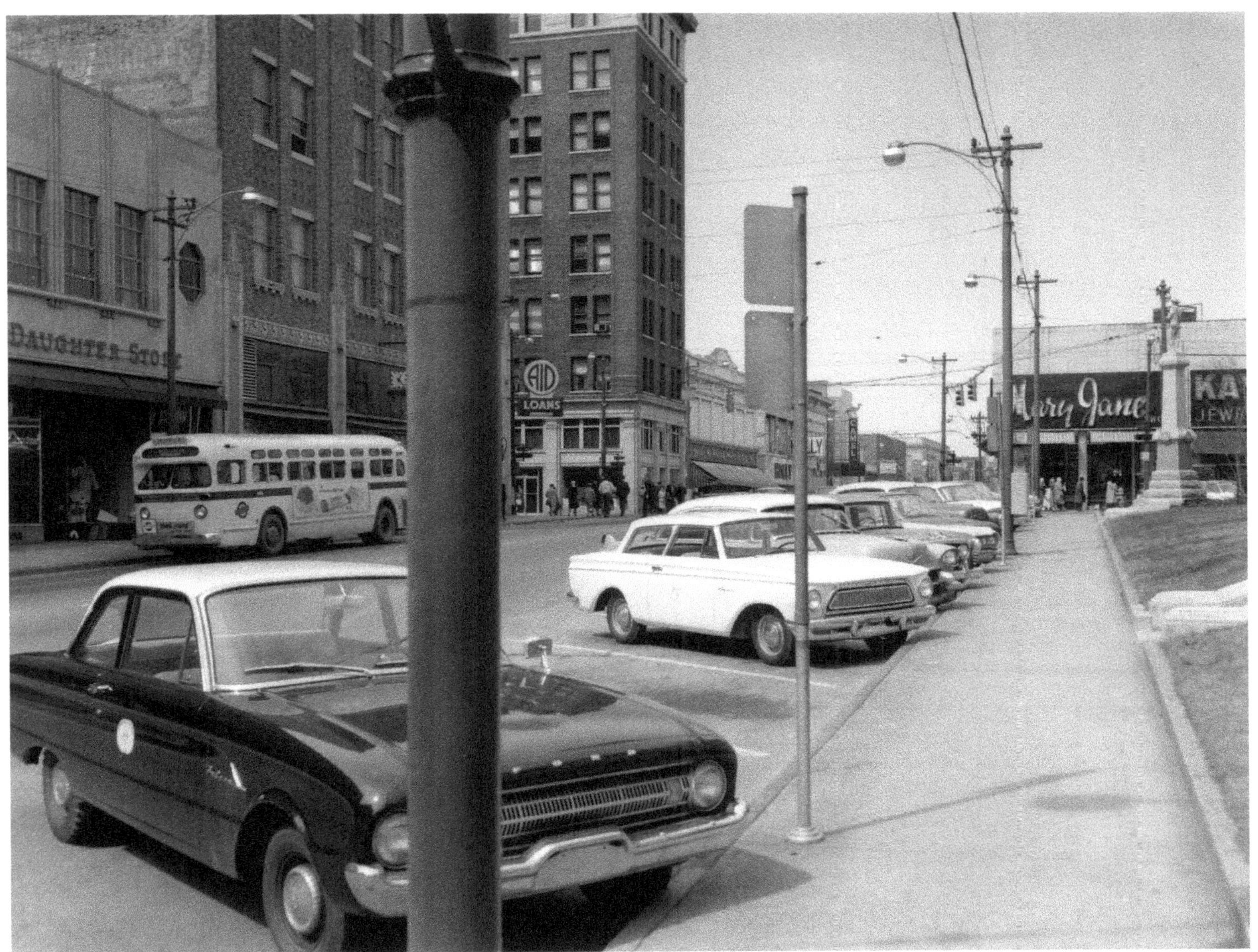


These cars are parked on North Liberty Street, March 1964, with the O'Hanlon Building behind them at center, and the Mothers and Daughters store on the left. Notice that parking meters have disappeared and parking is now on the diagonal. The city transit bus still runs, despite an increasing shift of major shopping establishments away from the downtown area.

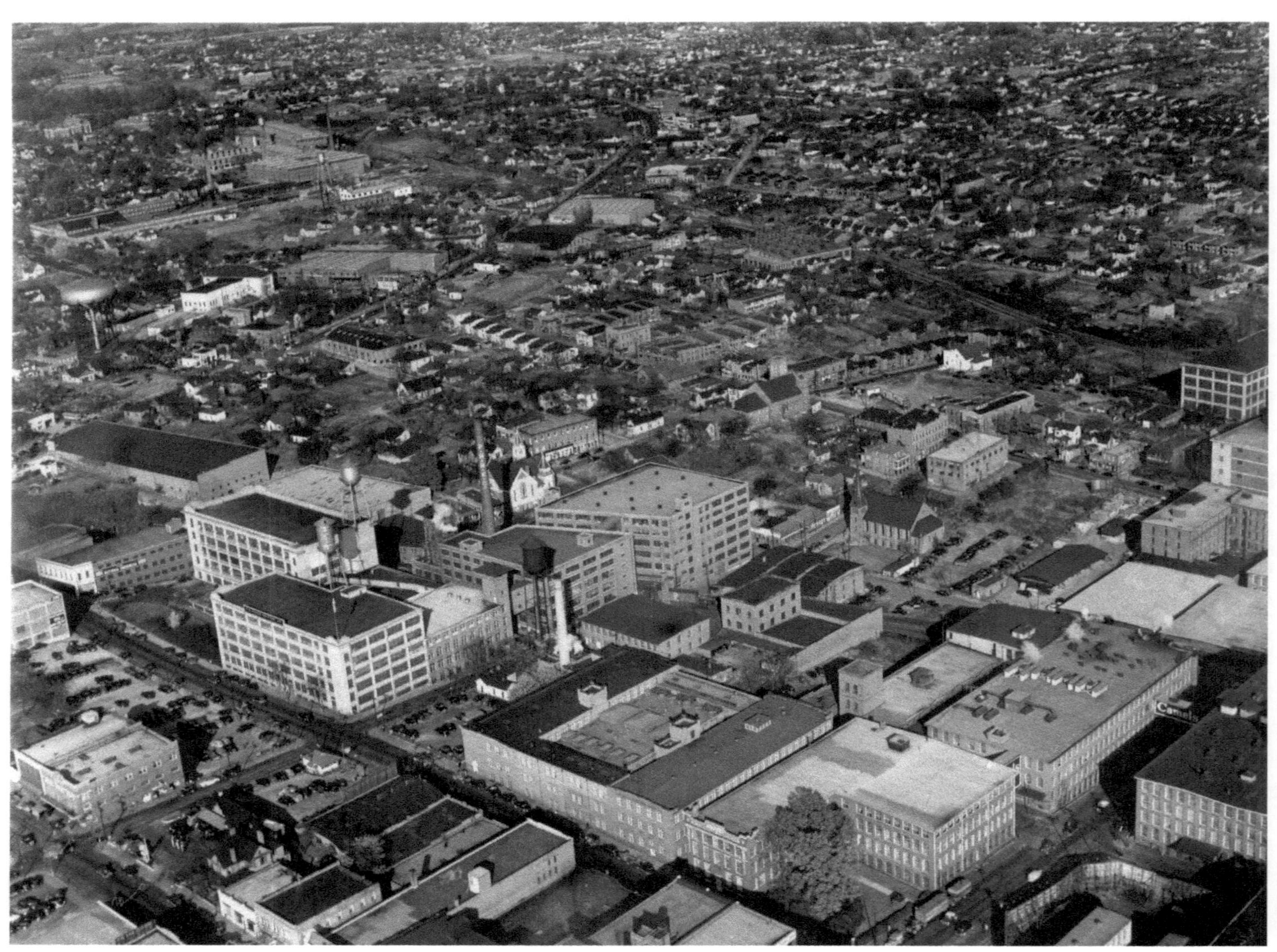

An aerial view, from around 1964, of North Main Street and its intersections with West Fifth and Sixth streets gives some sense of the massiveness of the R. J. Reynolds Tobacco Company facility, which at times employed as much as 20 percent of Winston-Salem's population.

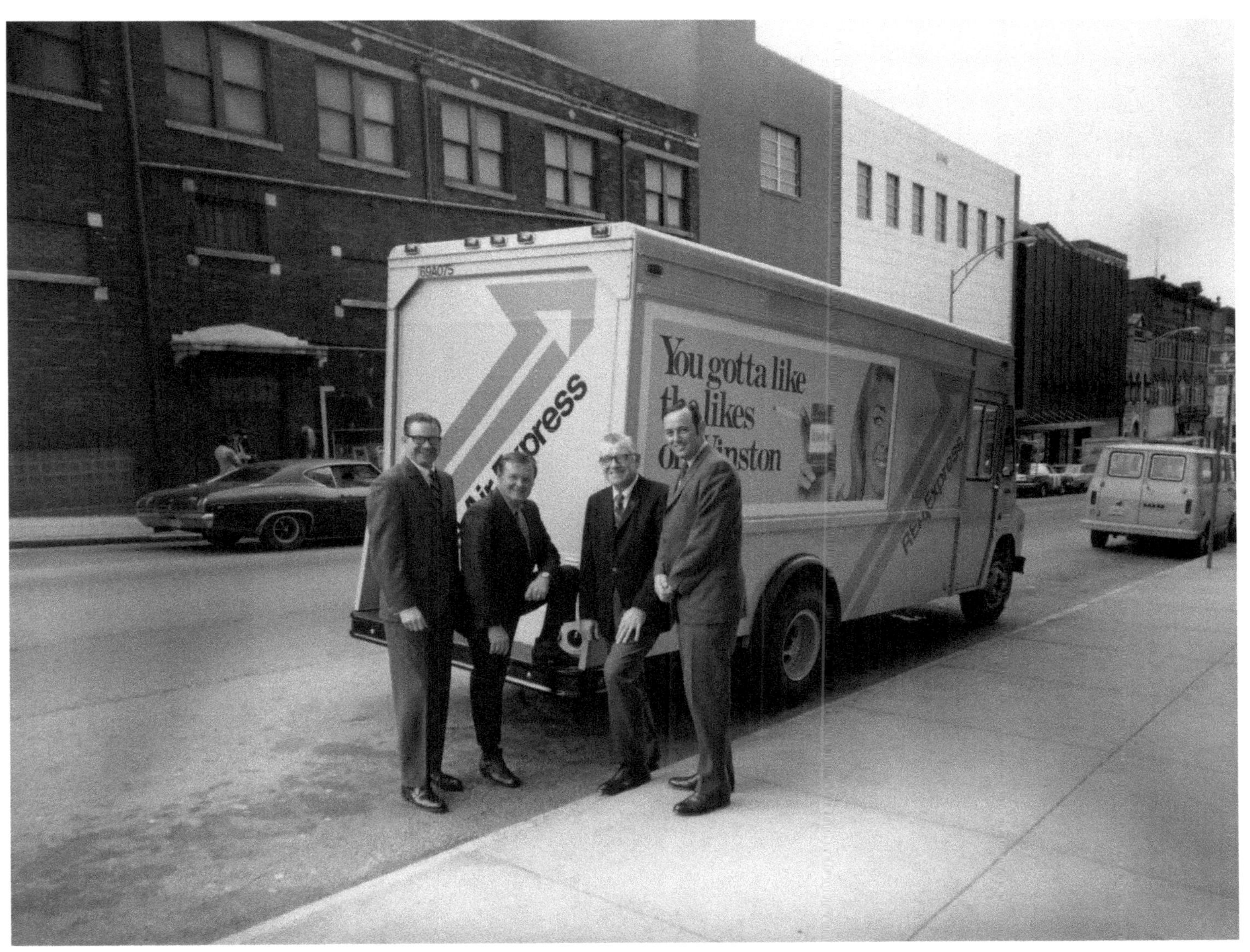


Nothing made freight carriers smile like a contract with R. J. Reynolds Tobacco Company. In this photograph from April 1970, smiling executives stand behind a REA Express truck parked near the Reynolds Tobacco Company entrance on North Main Street.

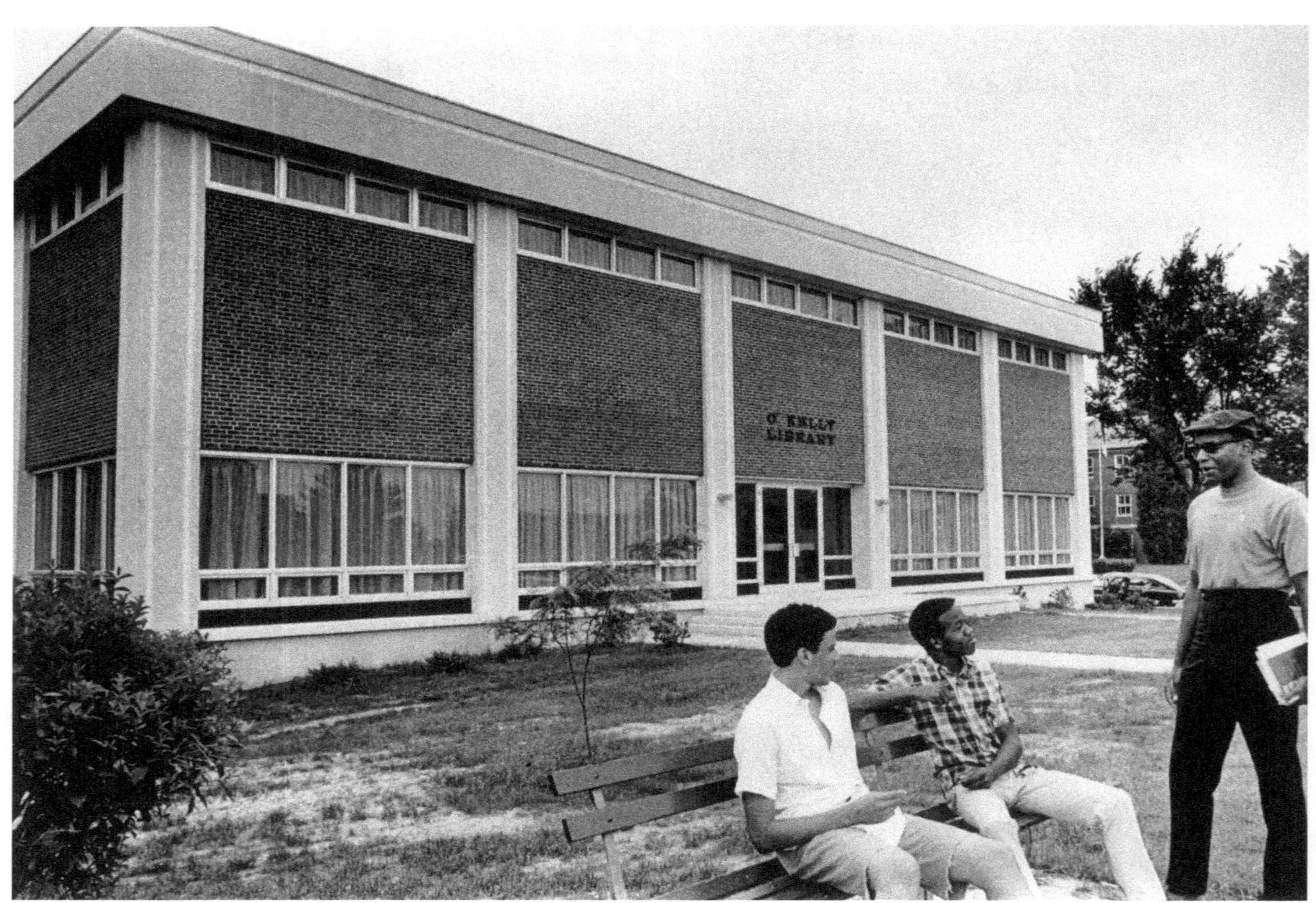

Students enjoy the sun in front of Winston-Salem State University's library in the 1960s. The historically black institution traces its origins to Slater Industrial Academy in 1892, becoming Winston-Salem Teacher's College in 1925, Winston-Salem College in 1961, and a university in 1969. Long a cornerstone of the African American community in Winston-Salem, WSSU now offers quality education regardless of an individual's race.

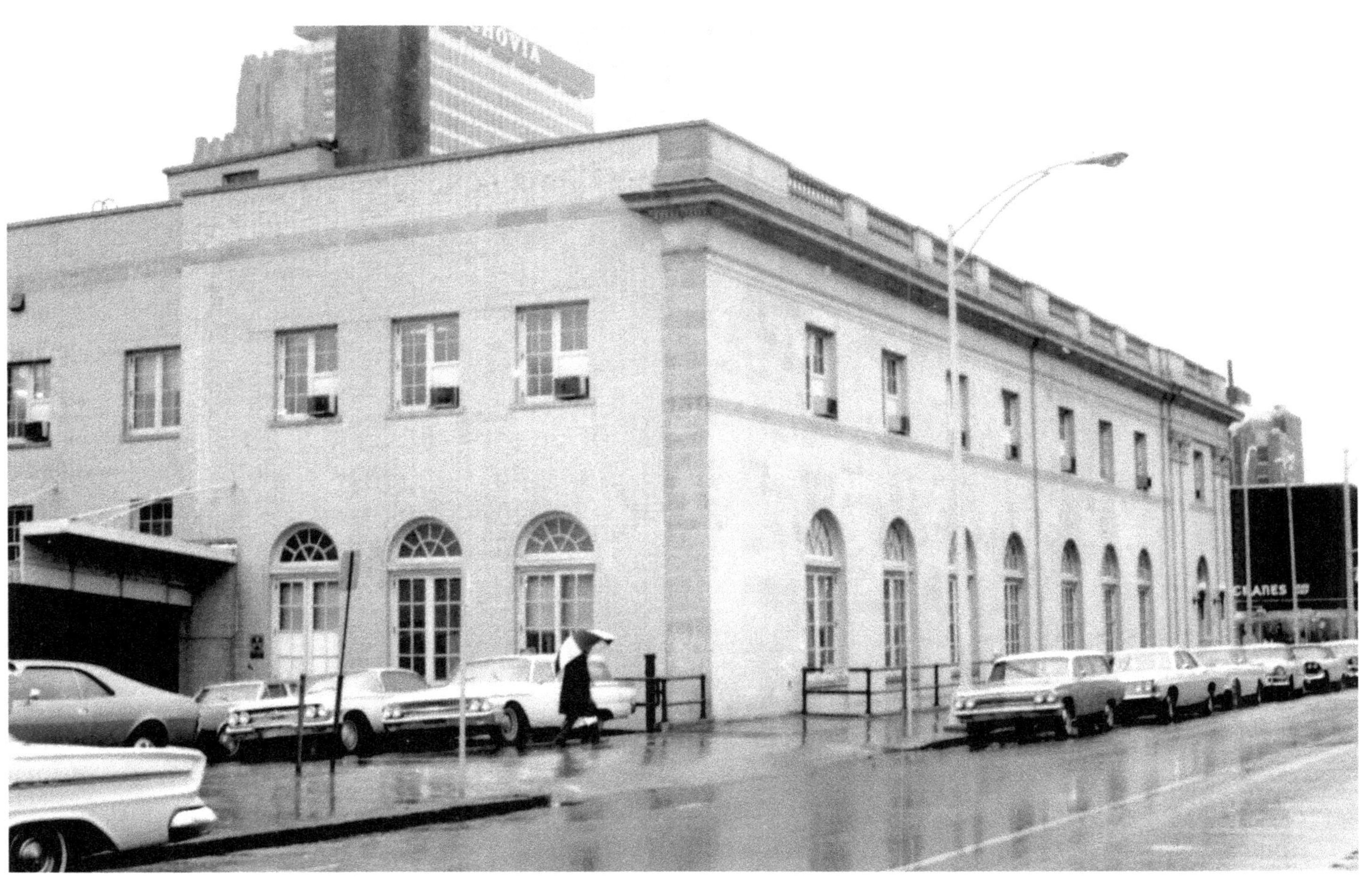

On a rainy day in the late 1960s, the Forsyth County Courthouse seems plain and utilitarian compared to the new Wachovia Building towering behind it.

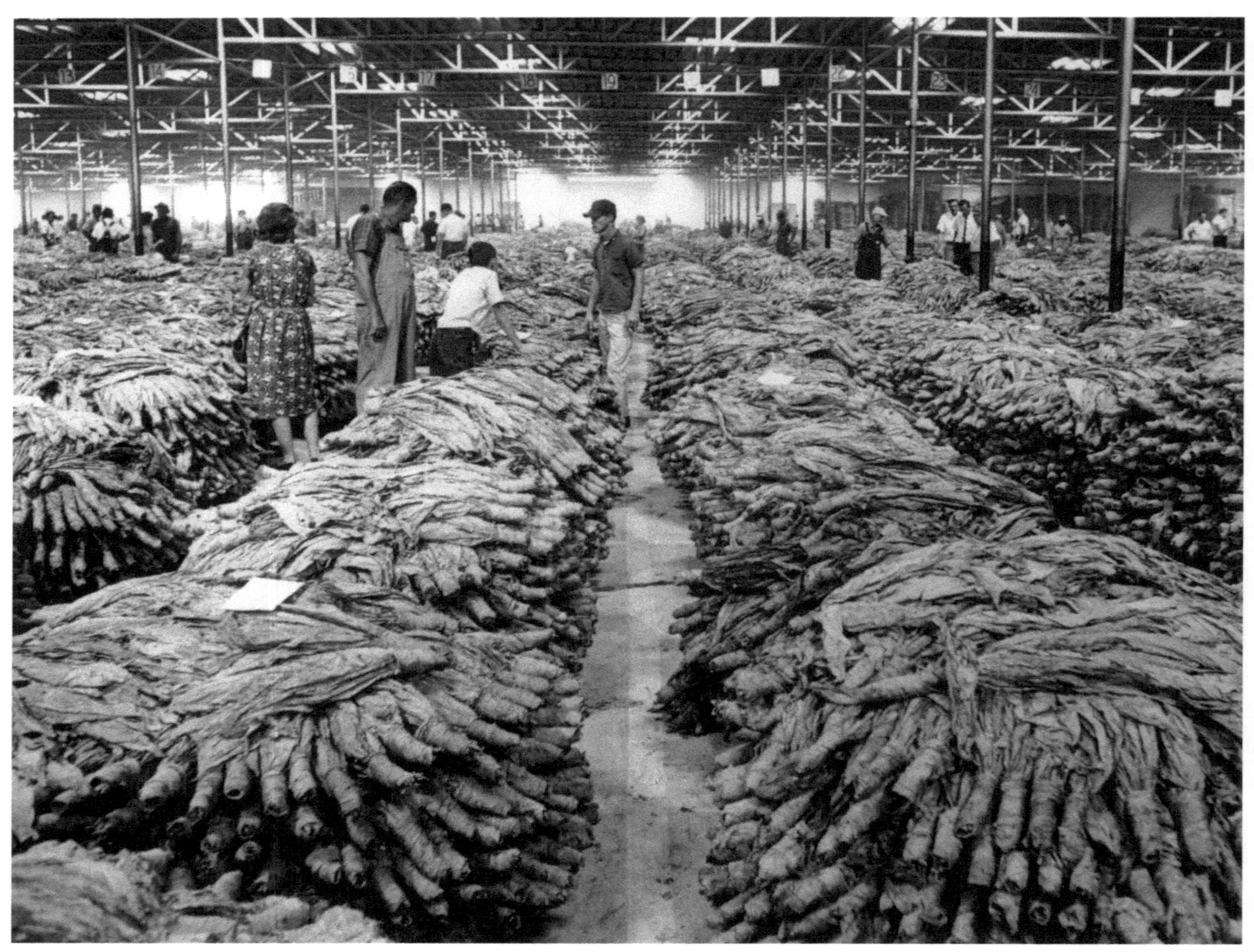

In 1969, auctioneers still chanted and farmers still sweated the results (though little sweat remained after a summer in the fields and barns), despite ever-increasing concerns at the potential dangers of smoking.

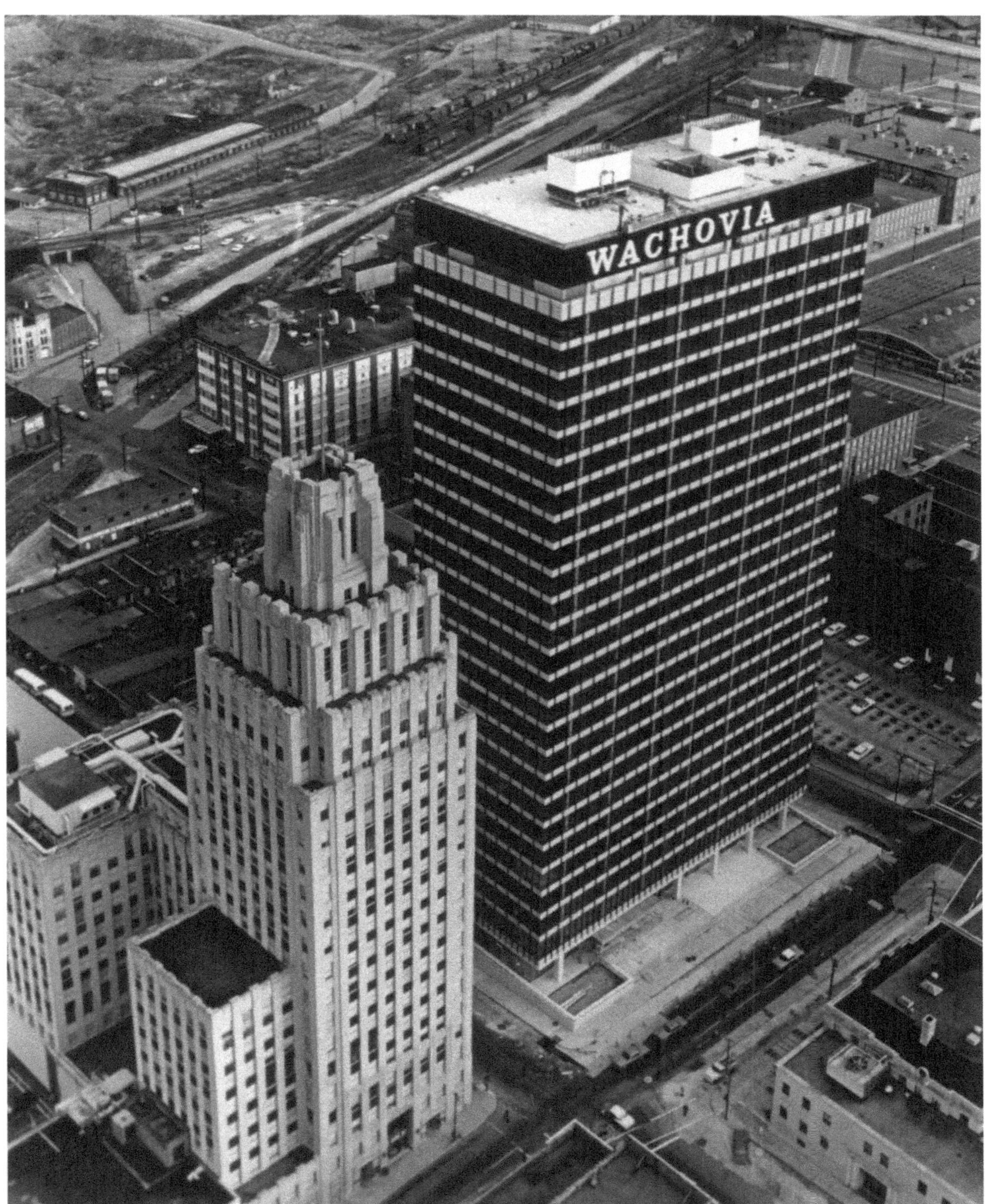


At thirty stories, the Wachovia Building reached even higher than the neighboring Reynolds Building when the Wachovia opened in 1966. It housed the offices of Wachovia Bank and numerous other businesses. Today it is known as the Winston Tower.

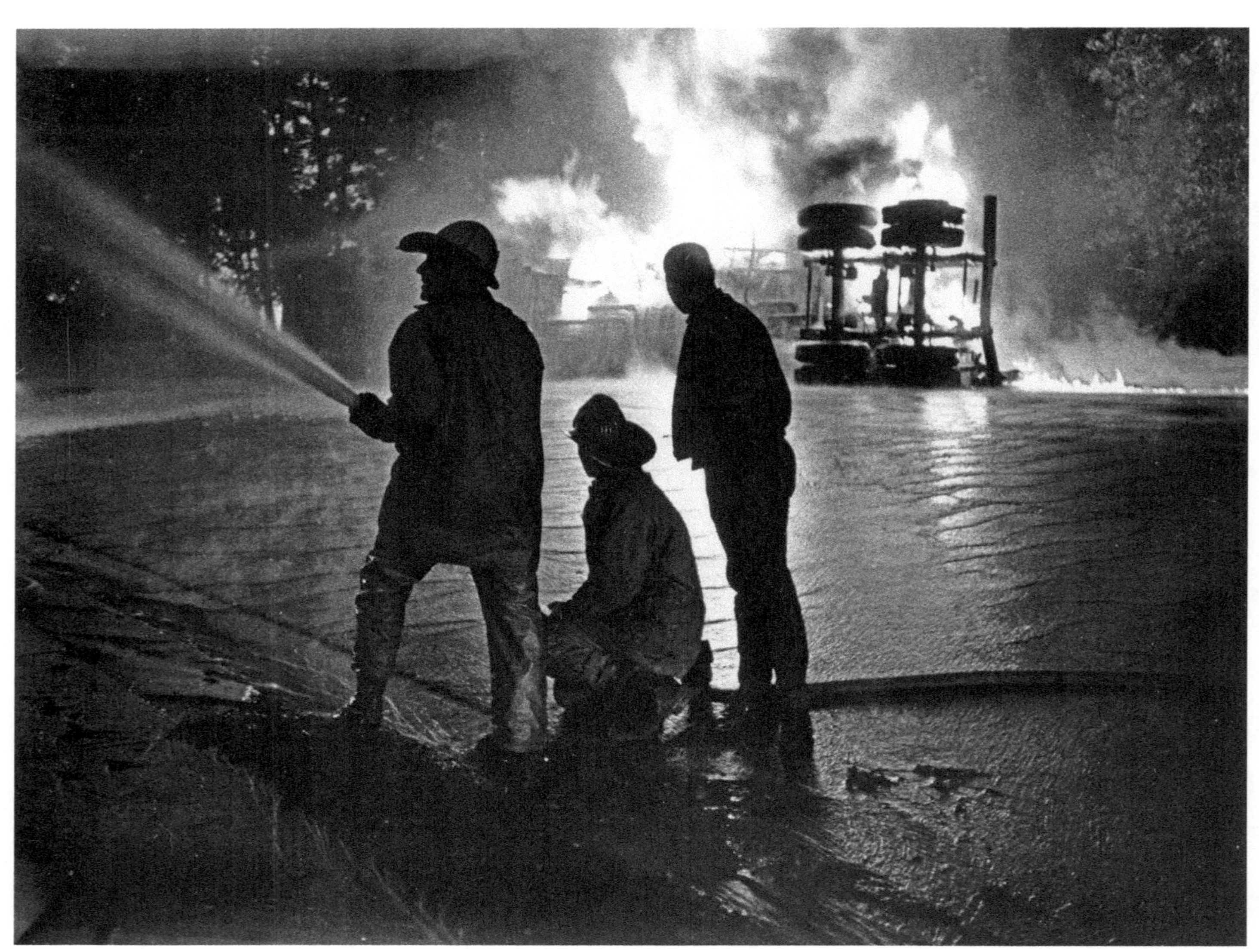

Winston-Salem's firefighters battle a dangerous blaze from an overturned truck in 1969.

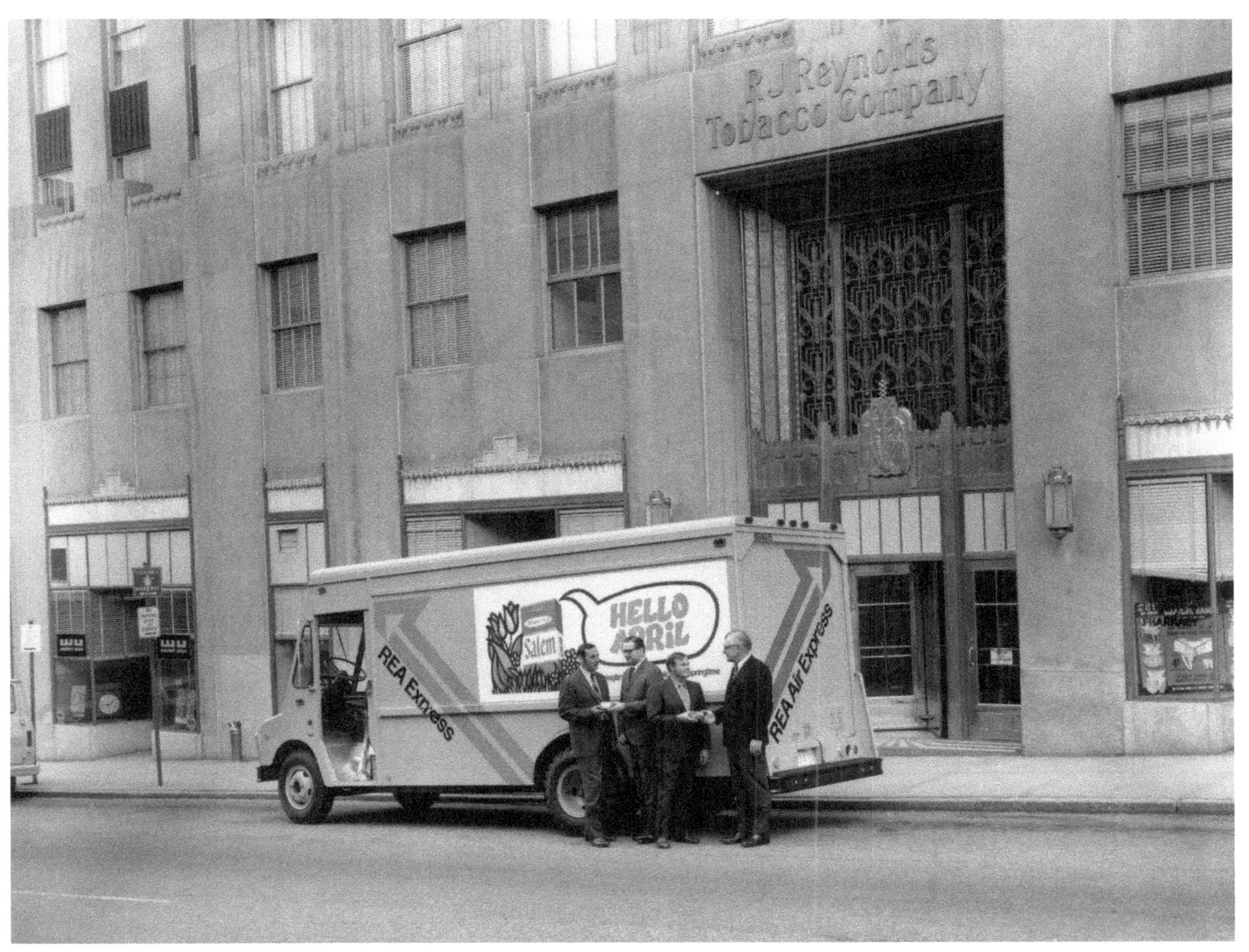


Another view of executives and the REA Express truck reveals the impressive main entrance to R. J. Reynolds Tobacco Company.

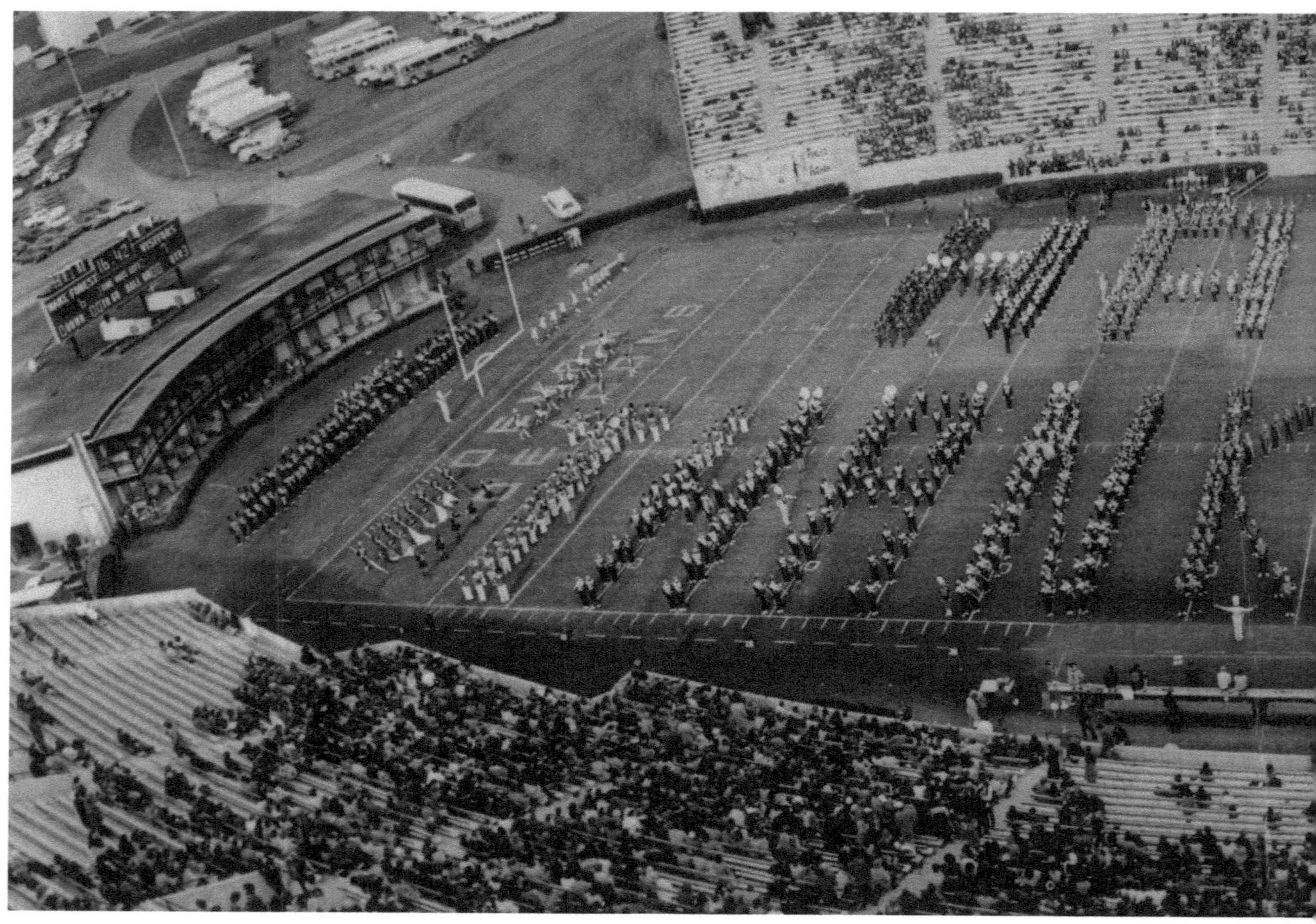

The Wake Forest Demon Deacons dropped another one, this time to Virginia Tech (44-9), on November 25, 1972, at Groves Stadium. To a city built only by the Winston Purse, perhaps losing would be a horrible thing; but a city held together by the Salem Heart knows that there is always next week, next month, and next season.

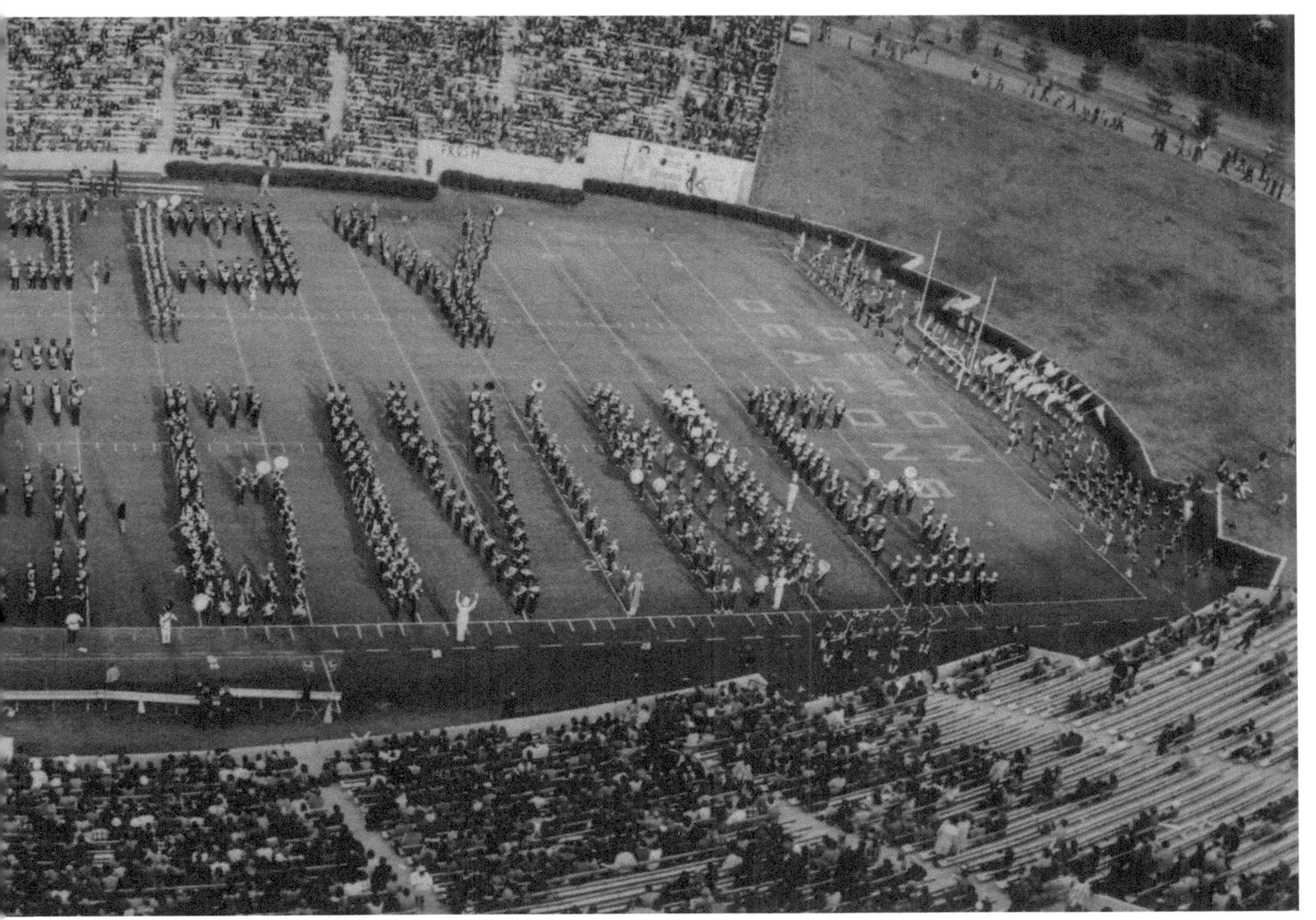
DEACONS

# Notes on the Photographs

These notes, listed by page number, attempt to include all aspects known of the photographs. Each of the photographs is identified by the page number, photograph's title or description, photographer and collection, archive, and call or box number when applicable. Although every attempt was made to collect all available data, in some cases complete data was unavailable due to the age and condition of some of the photographs and records.

**II O'Hanlon Fire**
Courtesy of Forsyth County Public Library Photograph Collection
16173

**VI First Skyscraper**
Courtesy of Forsyth County Public Library Photograph Collection
3982

**X View Across Roofs**
Courtesy of Forsyth County Public Library Photograph Collection
15153

**2 North Liberty Street**
Courtesy of Forsyth County Public Library Photograph Collection
3263

**3 Brown's Warehouse**
Courtesy of Forsyth County Public Library Photograph Collection
3496

**4 Belo House on Main Street**
Courtesy of Forsyth County Public Library Photograph Collection
4225

**5 Star Warehouse on Main Street**
Courtesy of Forsyth County Public Library Photograph Collection
3495

**6 Thomas A. Edison in Salem**
Courtesy of Forsyth County Public Library Photograph Collection
3427

**7 Streetcar in Salem**
Courtesy of Forsyth County Public Library Photograph Collection
3488

**8 Wagons**
Courtesy of the North Carolina State Archives
N.82.11.55

**9 Working Families**
Courtesy of the North Carolina State Archives
N.57.9.63

**10 Joseph Renard Florist and Grocery Store**
Courtesy of Forsyth County Public Library Photograph Collection
5719

**11 Saturday Street Scene**
Courtesy of the North Carolina State Archives
N.62.5.3

**12 Hotel Zinzendorf Under Construction**
Courtesy of Forsyth County Public Library Photograph Collection
3306

**13 Fire at Hotel Zinzendorf**
Courtesy of Forsyth County Public Library Photograph Collection
3308

**14 Winston Police Force**
Courtesy of Forsyth County Public Library Photograph Collection
15157

**15 Forsyth County Courthouse**
Courtesy of the North Carolina State Archives
N.2003.12.13

**16 Women on Liberty Street**
Courtesy of Forsyth County Public Library Photograph Collection
3432

**17 Liberty Street from 4th Street**
Courtesy of Forsyth County Public Library Photograph Collection
3487

**18 Market Stalls at City Hall**
Courtesy of Forsyth County Public Library Photograph Collection
3197

**20 West 4th Street Looking East**
Courtesy of Forsyth County Public Library Photograph Collection
3353

**21** **J. E. Mickey Shop with Coffee Pot in Front**
Courtesy of Forsyth County Public Library Photograph Collection
3252

**22** **Winston's Ladder Truck and Crew**
Courtesy of Forsyth County Public Library Photograph Collection
12426

**23** **Cotton Bales for Fries Cotton Mill in Salem**
Courtesy of Forsyth County Public Library Photograph Collection
15665

**24** **Winston School Parade**
Courtesy of Forsyth County Public Library Photograph Collection
16348

**25** **West 4th Street from Broad Street**
Courtesy of Forsyth County Public Library Photograph Collection
3343

**26** **Forsyth County Courthouse**
Courtesy of Forsyth County Public Library Photograph Collection
3210

**27** **Intersection of West 4th street and Liberty Street**
Courtesy of Forsyth County Public Library Photograph Collection
3377

**28** **Winston-Salem Police Force in Front of the Courthouse**
Courtesy of Forsyth County Public Library Photograph Collection
3262

**30** **Main and 4th Streets**
Courtesy of Forsyth County Public Library Photograph Collection
3265

**31** **North Main Street**
Courtesy of Forsyth County Public Library Photograph Collection
3798

**32** **W. T. Vogler and Sons Jewelry Store**
Courtesy of Forsyth County Public Library Photograph Collection
17414

**34** **Twin-City Concert Band**
Courtesy of Forsyth County Public Library Photograph Collection
12538

**35** **P. H. Hanes Knitting Mills**
Courtesy of the North Carolina State Archives
N.98.6.59

**36** **Salem College**
Courtesy of Forsyth County Public Library Photograph Collection
5686

**37** **Salem College Spring House**
Courtesy of Forsyth County Public Library Photograph Collection
3618

**38** **Reservoir Collapse**
Courtesy of Forsyth County Public Library Photograph Collection
4596

**39** **Reservoir Collapse Onlookers**
Courtesy of Forsyth County Public Library Photograph Collection
16439

**40** **Damage to Railroad After Reservoir Burst**
Courtesy of Forsyth County Public Library Photograph Collection
3471

**41** **Men on Telephone Poles over North Main Street**
Courtesy of Forsyth County Public Library Photograph Collection
12436

**42** **Working in the Fields**
Courtesy of the North Carolina State Archives
PHC42.BX2

**43** **Hege Sporting Goods Store**
Courtesy of Forsyth County Public Library Photograph Collection
12424

**44** **Salem Bandwagon in Parade**
Courtesy of Forsyth County Public Library Photograph Collection
12432

**45** **Salem College Graduation**
Courtesy of Forsyth County Public Library Photograph Collection
3627

**46** **Forsyth County Courthouse**
Courtesy of Forsyth County Public Library Photograph Collection
4254

**47** **Parade Viewing at Main and 3rd Streets**
Courtesy of Forsyth County Public Library Photograph Collection
3344

**48** **Hanes Knitting Interior**
Courtesy of Forsyth County Public Library Photograph Collection
12028

**49** **Winston Automobile Company**
Courtesy of Forsyth County Public Library Photograph Collection
3823

**50 Proctor & Peck Contractors**
Courtesy of Forsyth County Public Library Photograph Collection 3424

**51 4th and Liberty Streets**
Courtesy of Forsyth County Public Library Photograph Collection 3484

**52 Streetcar on Main Street**
Courtesy of Forsyth County Public Library Photograph Collection 3965

**53 Battling the O'Hanlon Fire**
Courtesy of Forsyth County Public Library Photograph Collection 16175

**54 O'Hanlon Building Fire**
Courtesy of Forsyth County Public Library Photograph Collection 16170

**56 Salem Creek Flood**
Courtesy of Forsyth County Public Library Photograph Collection 3337

**57 West End Methodist Episcopal Church**
Courtesy of the North Carolina State Archives N.95.8.25

**58 Slater Industrial Academy**
Courtesy of Forsyth County Public Library Photograph Collection 5736

**59 Working on Streetcar Tracks on Sprague Street**
Courtesy of Forsyth County Public Library Photograph Collection 14505

**60 Movie Theater**
Courtesy of Forsyth County Public Library Photograph Collection 3284

**61 Winston Town Hall**
Courtesy of Forsyth County Public Library Photograph Collection 3194

**62 Picnic**
Courtesy of the North Carolina State Archives N.98.9.22

**64 Hanes Park Skyline**
Courtesy of the North Carolina State Archives N.97.7.8

**65 Vogler Funeral Home**
Courtesy of the North Carolina State Archives N.98.9.26

**66 Construction of Road**
Courtesy of Forsyth County Public Library Photograph Collection 3327

**67 Elks Auditorium Fire**
Courtesy of Forsyth County Public Library Photograph Collection 3389

**68 North Main Street**
Courtesy of Forsyth County Public Library Photograph Collection 16259

**69 Corner of 4th and Main Streets**
Courtesy of Forsyth County Public Library Photograph Collection 16236

**70 Men in Front of the Elmont Theater**
Courtesy of Forsyth County Public Library Photograph Collection 3935

**71 The Smokers Den**
Courtesy of Forsyth County Public Library Photograph Collection 16287

**72 Auto Garage**
Courtesy of Forsyth County Public Library Photograph Collection 3423

**73 North Liberty Street** Courtesy of Forsyth County Public Library Photograph Collection 2537

**74 Aerial View Downtown**
Courtesy of Forsyth County Public Library Photograph Collection 17104

**76 YMCA Building**
Courtesy of Forsyth County Public Library Photograph Collection 13903

**77 West 4th and Cherry Streets**
Courtesy of Forsyth County Public Library Photograph Collection 3972

**78 Salem Brewery and Tan Yard**
Courtesy of Forsyth County Public Library Photograph Collection 3451

**79 Liberty Street at 4th Street**
Courtesy of Forsyth County Public Library Photograph Collection 14984

**80 Hanes Knitting Company**
Courtesy of Forsyth County Public Library Photograph Collection 5910

**81 Pepper Building at 4th and Liberty Streets**
Courtesy of Forsyth County Public Library Photograph Collection 3442

82 **West 5th Street at Liberty Street**
Courtesy of Forsyth County Public Library Photograph Collection
3416

83 **Removing Streetcar Track**
Courtesy of Forsyth County Public Library Photograph Collection
0048

84 **Twin City Club**
Courtesy of Forsyth County Public Library Photograph Collection
3515

85 **West 4th street from Liberty Street**
Courtesy of Forsyth County Public Library Photograph Collection
3975

86 **Motor Sales Company**
Courtesy of the North Carolina State Archives
N.81.3.1

87 **Collapse of Urband Building on Main Street**
Courtesy of Forsyth County Public Library Photograph Collection
3901

88 **Building Collapse Aftermath**
Courtesy of Forsyth County Public Library Photograph Collection
3903

89 **Salem College**
Courtesy of the North Carolina State Archives
N.53.15.166

90 **Charles Lindbergh**
Courtesy of Forsyth County Public Library Photograph Collection
16447

91 **Main Street**
Courtesy of Forsyth County Public Library Photograph Collection
15451

92 **North Main Street**
Courtesy of Forsyth County Public Library Photograph Collection
8544

94 **Liberty and 4th Streets**
Courtesy of Forsyth County Public Library Photograph Collection
12963

95 **Mechanics at Local Airfield**
Courtesy of Forsyth County Public Library Photograph Collection
3800

96 **Corner of West 4th and Main Streets**
Courtesy of Forsyth County Public Library Photograph Collection
15477

97 **Curtiss Condor Airplane**
Courtesy of Forsyth County Public Library Photograph Collection
3679

98 **Salem Tavern**
Library of Congress
HABS NC,34-WINSA,4-4

99 **West 4th Street from Liberty Street**
Courtesy of Forsyth County Public Library Photograph Collection
3983

100 **Salem College**
Library of Congress
HABS NC,34-WINSA,2-3

101 **West 4th Street at Spruce Street**
Courtesy of Forsyth County Public Library Photograph Collection
3977

102 **City Bus**
Courtesy of Forsyth County Public Library Photograph Collection
3845

103 **Salem Boys School**
Library of Congress
HABS NC,34-WINSA,6-10

104 **Transportation Parade**
Courtesy of Forsyth County Public Library Photograph Collection
0626

106 **Lincoln Market**
Library of Congress
LC-USZ62-130482

107 **Antique Business on Main Street**
Library of Congress
HABS NC,34-WINS,14-1

108 **McLean Company Truck**
Courtesy of the North Carolina State Archives
N.80.10.28

109 **Fogle Brothers Lumber Company**
Courtesy of Forsyth County Public Library Photograph Collection
0557

110 **Hotel Zinzendorf on North Main Street**
Courtesy of Forsyth County Public Library Photograph Collection
2532

111 **Diesel Train**
Courtesy of the North Carolina State Archives
N.97.7.179

112 **Selected Dairies Construction**
Courtesy of Forsyth County Public Library Photograph Collection
0534

113 **West 4th Street**
Courtesy of Forsyth County Public Library Photograph Collection
3978

**114 Liberty Street at 4th Street**
Courtesy of Forsyth County Public Library Photograph Collection 0473

**115 Carolina Theatre**
Courtesy of Forsyth County Public Library Photograph Collection 4413

**116 Fire on West 4th Street**
Courtesy of Forsyth County Public Library Photograph Collection 8978

**117 House of the Community Physician**
Library of Congress HABS NC,34-WINSA,5-3

**118 Policemen on Motorcycles**
Courtesy of Forsyth County Public Library Photograph Collection 15084

**119 Sisters House, Salem College**
Library of Congress HABS NC,34-WINSA,8B-2

**120 Nissen Building**
Courtesy of Forsyth County Public Library Photograph Collection 0050

**121 Dedication of Salem Tavern**
Courtesy of Forsyth County Public Library Photograph Collection 16612

**122 Bowman Gray School of Medicine**
Courtesy of Forsyth County Public Library Photograph Collection 0478

**123 Soldiers in Front of the Courthouse**
Courtesy of Forsyth County Public Library Photograph Collection 18588

**124 Winston Mutual Life Insurance Company**
Courtesy of Forsyth County Public Library Photograph Collection 3268

**125 Coffee Pot**
Courtesy of Forsyth County Public Library Photograph Collection 2540

**126 Memorial Coliseum Barometer**
Courtesy of Forsyth County Public Library Photograph Collection 18604

**127 First National Bank Building**
Courtesy of Forsyth County Public Library Photograph Collection 3824

**128 Christmas Parade**
Courtesy of Forsyth County Public Library Photograph Collection 0909

**129 Christmas Parade Marchers**
Courtesy of Forsyth County Public Library Photograph Collection 0911

**130 Smith Reynolds Airport**
Courtesy of Forsyth County Public Library Photograph Collection 2759

**131 Piedmont Airplane**
Courtesy of Forsyth County Public Library Photograph Collection 2538

**132 Piedmont Airlines First Pilot Group**
Courtesy of Forsyth County Public Library Photograph Collection 0961

**133 Dedication of Alumnae Hall at Salem College**
Courtesy of Forsyth County Public Library Photograph Collection 1022

**134 Forsyth County Centennial Parade**
Courtesy of Forsyth County Public Library Photograph Collection 1137

**135 Parade Two-wheeler**
Courtesy of Forsyth County Public Library Photograph Collection 1143

**136 Waiting Outside Davis Department Store**
Courtesy of Forsyth County Public Library Photograph Collection 11806

**138 Car on West 4th Street**
Courtesy of Forsyth County Public Library Photograph Collection 17317

**139 American Legion Members on Steps of City Hall**
Courtesy of Forsyth County Public Library Photograph Collection 9949

**140 East Entrance to Wake Forest Campus**
Courtesy of Forsyth County Public Library Photograph Collection 1593

**141 President Harry Truman**
Courtesy of Forsyth County Public Library Photograph Collection 2051

**142 West 4th and North Main Streets**
Courtesy of Forsyth County Public Library Photograph Collection 9294

**143 Farmers with Tobacco Crop**
Courtesy of Forsyth County Public Library Photograph Collection 1608

**144 Easter Shopping on 4th Street**
Courtesy of Forsyth County Public Library Photograph Collection 1424

**145 Wake Forest Students Visiting Campus**
Courtesy of Forsyth County Public Library Photograph Collection 1726

**146 General Dwight Eisenhower at Podium**
Courtesy of Forsyth County Public Library Photograph Collection 13496

**147 Mamie and General Eisenhower with Mayor Kurfees**
Courtesy of Forsyth County Public Library Photograph Collection 18505

**148 King Brothers Circus**
Courtesy of Forsyth County Public Library Photograph Collection 18375

**149 Band Day at Wake Forest–UNC Football Game**
Courtesy of Forsyth County Public Library Photograph Collection 1899

**150 West 4th Street**
Courtesy of Forsyth County Public Library Photograph Collection 4444

**151 Stringing Tobacco**
Courtesy of Forsyth County Public Library Photograph Collection 8540

**152 Fire Prevention Week Parade**
Courtesy of Forsyth County Public Library Photograph Collection 2090

**153 4th and Marshall Streets**
Courtesy of Forsyth County Public Library Photograph Collection 4464

**154 Wet 4th Street**
Courtesy of Forsyth County Public Library Photograph Collection 4463

**155 Football Practice**
Courtesy of Forsyth County Public Library Photograph Collection 10277

**156 Policeman at Carolina Theatre**
Courtesy of Forsyth County Public Library Photograph Collection 14127

**157 Salem Tavern**
Courtesy of Forsyth County Public Library Photograph Collection 8022

**158 Wake Forest Chapel**
Courtesy of the North Carolina State Archives N.53.13.329

**159 Old Salem**
Courtesy of Forsyth County Public Library Photograph Collection 11108

**160 Wake Forest Entrance Arch**
Courtesy of Forsyth County Public Library Photograph Collection 10333

**161 Wake Forest College Dedication**
Courtesy of Forsyth County Public Library Photograph Collection 2283

**162 Z. Smith Reynolds Library**
Courtesy of the North Carolina State Archives N.53.15.326

**163 Christmas Parade**
Courtesy of Forsyth County Public Library Photograph Collection 11049

**164 Tobacco Hearings in the Courthouse**
Courtesy of Forsyth County Public Library Photograph Collection 10555

**166 1956 Christmas Parade**
Courtesy of Forsyth County Public Library Photograph Collection 14193

**167 Wake Forest vs. Virginia Basketball**
Courtesy of Forsyth County Public Library Photograph Collection 2362

**168 Three Sisters Department Store**
Courtesy of Forsyth County Public Library Photograph Collection FCPL CP.9385A.1

**169 Farmers Dairy Bar**
Courtesy of Forsyth County Public Library Photograph Collection FCPL CP.9421A.2

**170 Civil Defense Demonstration Fallout Shelter**
Courtesy of Forsyth County Public Library Photograph Collection FCPL CP.345931

**171 Northwest High School**
Courtesy of Forsyth County Public Library Photograph Collection
FCPL CP.271B.3

**172 Interstate 40 Construction**
Courtesy of Forsyth County Public Library Photograph Collection
FCPL CP.9444A.1

**173 Taylor's Warehouse Fire**
Courtesy of Forsyth County Public Library Photograph Collection
5013

**174 Wait Chapel**
Courtesy of Forsyth County Public Library Photograph Collection
5027

**175 Stormy 4th Street**
Courtesy of Forsyth County Public Library Photograph Collection
10614

**176 Nelson's Market**
Courtesy of Forsyth County Public Library Photograph Collection
10965

**177 Nissen Building**
Courtesy of Forsyth County Public Library Photograph Collection
11637

**178 Moving the Coffee Pot**
Courtesy of Forsyth County Public Library Photograph Collection
5138

**179 Rose Kennedy, Mayor Kurfees, and Ann Herring, Miss North Carolina, in Tobacco Warehouse**
Courtesy of Forsyth County Public Library Photograph Collection
FCPL CP.1732B.3

**180 Lyndon and Lady Bird Johnson Campaigning in Lexington**
Courtesy of Forsyth County Public Library Photograph Collection
17905

**181 WSSU Coach Clarence Gaines**
Courtesy of Forsyth County Public Library Photograph Collection
8088

**182 Christmas Shoppers**
Courtesy of Forsyth County Public Library Photograph Collection
4471

**183 Krispy Kreme**
Courtesy of Forsyth County Public Library Photograph Collection
FCPL CP.2200B.1

**184 Parade on West 4th Street**
Courtesy of Forsyth County Public Library Photograph Collection
4418

**186 Carolina Theatre Marquee**
Courtesy of Forsyth County Public Library Photograph Collection
6413

**187 Sportsman's Supply**
Courtesy of Forsyth County Public Library Photograph Collection
FCPL CP.3622.1

**188 Hotel Robert E. Lee**
Courtesy of Forsyth County Public Library Photograph Collection
FCPL CP.3589.1

**189 North Liberty Street**
Courtesy of Forsyth County Public Library Photograph Collection
FCPL CP.2906.3

**190 Aerial View, Reynolds Facility**
Courtesy of Forsyth County Public Library Photograph Collection
FCPL CP.1D.1

**191 REA Express Truck**
Courtesy of Forsyth County Public Library Photograph Collection
FCPL CP.10550.2

**192 WSSU Library**
Courtesy of Forsyth County Public Library Photograph Collection
12036

**193 Forsyth County Courthouse**
Courtesy of the North Carolina State Archives
N.70.7.377

**194 Tobacco Warehouse**
Courtesy of Forsyth County Public Library Photograph Collection
18223

**195 Reynolds and Wachovia Buildings**
Courtesy of Forsyth County Public Library Photograph Collection
3241

**196 Truck Fire**
Courtesy of Forsyth County Public Library Photograph Collection
10077

**197 REA Express Truck and Reynolds Building**
Courtesy of Forsyth County Public Library Photograph Collection
FCPL CP.10550.1

**198 Wake Forest at Groves Stadium**
Courtesy of Forsyth County Public Library Photograph Collection
6702

# HISTORIC PHOTOS OF WINSTON-SALEM

In 1766, Moravian settlers, most having migrated to the Crown colony of North Carolina from Pennsylvania, established the town of Salem. Over eight decades, Salem became a key transportation nexus for both east-west and north-south traffic, yet never lost its Moravian trappings. In 1849, North Carolina established Forsyth County and incorporated Winston as its county seat. In the aftermath of the Civil War, this virtually undamaged region of the state began a rapid period of industrial and economic development, spurred by the pungent aroma of Bright Leaf tobacco. Population growth accompanied prosperity; and in 1913, the towns merged into a single municipality: Winston-Salem.

In 2005, Winston-Salem boasted an estimated population of over 200,000, making it the fifth largest city in North Carolina. Its history is as diverse as the two towns from which it arose, one steeped in religious values and the other born from political expediency. This volume captures that diverse history in word and photographic image, a tribute to citizens, past and present, of the fine city of Winston-Salem.

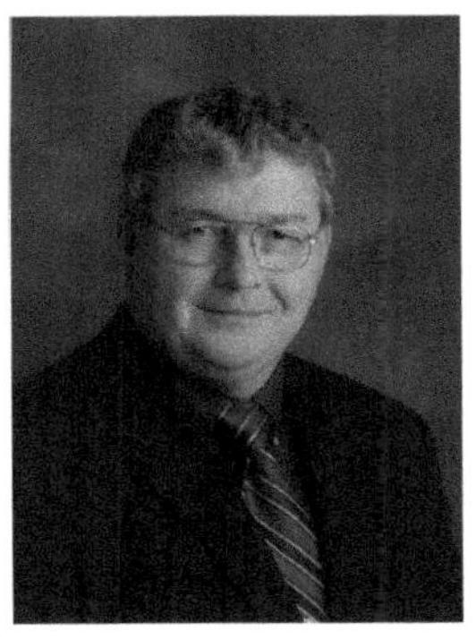

Born and bred a Tar Heel, Wade G. Dudley holds a PhD in history from the University of Alabama, and an MA in maritime history and nautical archaeology from East Carolina University. He teaches North Carolina History, among other courses, at East Carolina University in Greenville, North Carolina. He is the author of the award-winning *Splintering the Wooden Wall: The British Blockade of the United States, 1812–1815* (Naval Institute Press, 2003) and *Drake: For God, Queen, and Plunder* (Potomac Books, 2003), as well as numerous articles, book chapters, and short stories.

Dudley has written *Historic Photos of Wilmington,* also available from Turner Publishing.

WWW.TURNERPUBLISHING.COM

www.ingramcontent.com/pod-product-compliance
Lightning Source LLC
LaVergne TN
LVHW060608110826
845154LV00003B/52

*9781683369974*